PREFACE

 KW-052-046

This collection of articles, entitled *Ukraine in the World*, appears in two parallel editions—as volume 20 of the journal *Harvard Ukrainian Studies*, and as a separate title in the series "Harvard Papers in Ukrainian Studies." It is one product of a comprehensive project conducted by the Ukrainian Research Institute of Harvard University since 1996 to examine the politics and society in newly independent Ukraine. The project has examined a broad spectrum of issues at such fora as conferences and symposia, the Institute's weekly Seminar in Ukrainian Studies, and a variety of scholarly and popular publications. A prominent place in all these programs belongs to issues of Ukraine's foreign policy, external relations, and problems of security. It is to these issues that this volume is devoted.

✳ ✳
✳

In retrospect, it appears paradoxical that at the time when the USSR was in the process of disintegration, and Ukraine was setting out on its untested path of independence, many observers, as well as residents of Ukraine, expected the new state to succeed—albeit after a brief period of transitional pain—first and foremost in the realm of economic development. This was a natural expectation, given the country's wealth in land, natural resources, industrial infrastructure, and its well-educated citizenry. Much more skepticism, and indeed apprehension, reigned with regard to Ukraine's ability to cope with its foreign relations and security problems: with many of its neighbors, Ukraine had a long history of mutual hostility or antipathy; Russia viewed Ukraine's independence as a bitter loss of its own patrimony; and, the presence on Ukrainian soil of a large arsenal of Soviet nuclear weapons raised fears in the international community, particularly in the West, of a new threat to world stability and peace. Moreover, Ukraine appeared particularly ill-equipped to deal with international relations, having virtually no experience in the conduct of foreign policy or trained diplomatic personnel. Ironically, then, it is the economic sphere in which Ukraine has suffered its most bitter failures, while foreign and security policies constitute the country's most signal achievement. Seven years after its proclamation of independence, Ukraine stands as an accepted member and active participant in world diplomacy. Its role in regional and global politics, security and economics still remains to be defined, but it is clear that Ukraine is both an actor and a factor in international relations whose importance cannot be ignored or underestimated. What shape its role ultimately takes will be an ongoing challenge, both for Ukraine's leadership and for the international community.

Ukraine in the World represents a pioneering effort in examining Ukraine's foreign and security relations. Though not a work of synthesis, it offers a comprehensive overview and analysis of its topic in a series of articles by leading experts—scholars, analysts, and practitioners—in their respective fields. The organization of the volume follows a regional pattern: Ukraine's relations are examined first with its neighbors (Russia and the CIS; East Central Europe; and the Black Sea region); with countries of the West (the United States, Canada, and Western Europe); and with the world beyond (the Middle East, Asia, and the Southern Hemisphere). A separate section is devoted to military and security affairs. The broader theoretical and geopolitical context is provided in introductory essays by two eminent specialists and longtime practitioners in foreign policy—Dr. Zbigniew Brzezinski, the former National Security Advisor to the President of the United States, and the Minister of Foreign Affairs of Ukraine, Borys Tarasyuk. The topics covered in this volume by no means exhaust the subject of Ukraine's foreign policy and relations. Ukraine's multilateral relations and participation in international organizations, foreign economic relations, and the creation of a foreign service establishment and the search for policy options in Ukraine are fascinating and important themes. It is to be hoped that the current volume will stimulate research in these fields.

It is inevitable in a collection of this sort that a certain amount of overlap in coverage will occur. This is especially true with regard to Ukraine's denuclearization, so crucial in the country's first years of independence. Thus, in addition to the article devoted specifically to the nuclear weapons question, the issue inevitably arises in discussions off Ukraine's relations with the United States, Russia, and Western Europe, or in connection with broader issues of military policy and regional security. Far from redundant, this seeming overlap, like others, offers the benefit of a variety of viewpoints presented in multiple contexts. Here and throughout, the authors speak in their own voice and from their individual perspective. The views are the authors' own, and do not necessarily reflect the position of the editor or the Ukrainian Research Institute.

I would like to thank, in the first instance, the authors represented in this volume for their intellectual contribution and creative effort, their labors in the revision process to make the volume as up to date as possible, and, not least— their unexampled patience. Of course, this publication was made possible only with the support and assistance of numerous individuals to whom the editor wishes to express his deepest gratitude. At the outset I wish to thank the Director of the Ukrainian Research Institute, Professor Roman Szporluk, under whose aegis this project took shape, as well as the Editorial Board of *Harvard Ukrainian Studies*. Without the extraordinary expertise, dedication, and labors of the Institute's Director of Publications, Robert DeLossa, the volume would scarcely have seen the light of day. Daria Yurchuk, as Editorial Assistant, was responsible for the technical and production aspects of the publication. Dr. James Clem, Executive Director, and Mrs. Patricia Coatsworth, Administrator, gave indispensable support in various phases of the project. Dr. Andrew Sorokowski provided the exemplary translations of the documents presented in the Appendix, and Wei Li translated the article of Professor Jiang Changbin from the Chinese. Ksenya Kiebuzinski provided critical help locating sources and references for several parts of the volume. Larissa D'Avignon made an invaluable contribution in inputting the difficult text. And John DeStefano gave yeoman's service on fronts too varied to enumerate.

This volume has its source in a conference held under the same name in Washington, DC, on 12–14 December 1996, on the occasion of Ukraine's fifth anniversary of independence. The conference was organized in conjunction with the Ukrainian Program of the Institute for European, Russian, and Eurasian Studies of George Washington University, on whose premises it took place. I am grateful for the support and welcoming remarks extended by the University's President, Dr. Joel Trachtenberg. Professor James Millar, the Director of the Institute, served as host on the occasion, and the logistics of the conference were handled with extraordinary efficiency by the Institute's Executive Associate, Suzanne Stephenson. The conference also enjoyed the support of the Embassy of Ukraine, which provided the venue for some events, hosted a reception for the participants, and assisted in the often difficult communications with Kyiv in the preparatory stages. I am most grateful for the unceasing encouragement of Ambassador Yuri Shcherbak in these efforts. Counselor Natalia Zarudna's involvement in every facet of the conference approached the superhuman. Valeriy Kuchynsky and Vasyl Zorya also assumed many burdens to facilitate its success.

The keynote address by Dr. Zbigniew Brzezinski, reproduced in abridged form in this volume, set the high tone for the conference. Its Ukrainian counterpoint was represented by the remarks of then Ambassador to the Countries of Benelux and NATO, and now Foreign Minister of Ukraine, Borys Tarasyuk, also offered in revised form to the readers of the volume. Other high government officials who spoke at the conference included Ambassadors James Collins and Richard Morningstar, as well as Carlos Pascual of the National Security Council on the American side, and Deputy Foreign Minister Anton Buteyko and the military attaché in Washington, Colonel Volodymyr Havrylov, on the Ukrainian side. To all of them go my deep appreciation.

I am grateful also for the assistance in various forms of Professor Peter J. Potichnyj, Dr. Andrew Sorokowski, Trudy Werner, Laura Wayth, and Marianne Hrinda. And the help rendered at the Ukrainian Research Institute by Benjamin Szporluk was incalculable.

Finally, there are no proper words to express the gratitude I feel to two friends and colleagues without whose wise counsel, encouragement and practical support the conference could never have enjoyed its success. These are Dr.

Martha Bohachevsky Chomiak of the National Endowment for the Humanities, and the late Professor Zenovia Sochor Parry of Clark University, to whose memory I dedicate this book.

The conference and the publication of the volume *Ukraine in the World* were made possible through the generous financial support of the Smith Richardson Foundation. Additional funding was provided by the Ukrainian Studies Fund. This support is most gratefully acknowledged.

Lubomyr A. Hajda
Cambridge, Massachusetts

Ukraine in the World

Introduction

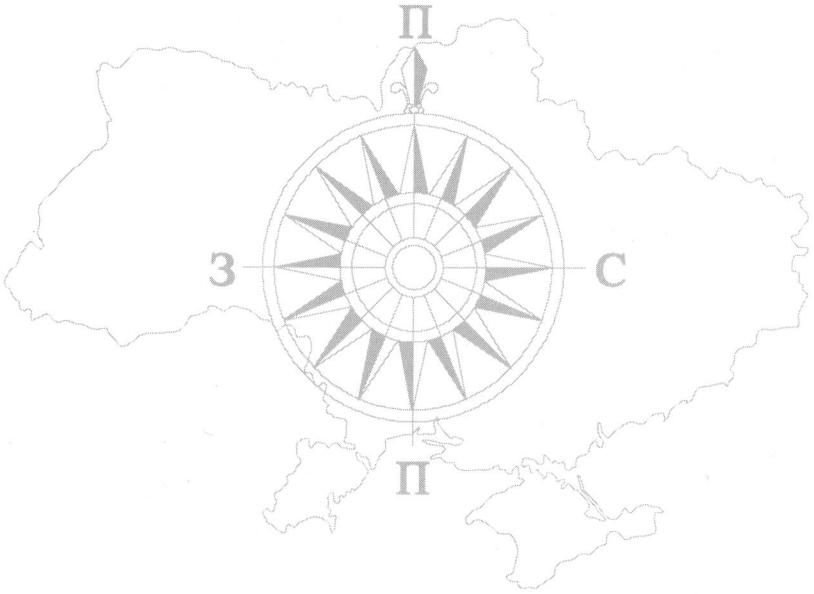

1

Ukraine's Critical Role in the Post-Soviet Space

ZBIGNIEW BRZEZINSKI

It has been five-and-a-half years since the Soviet Union disappeared. Yet what actually happened at the Belavezha meeting in Belarus on 8 December 1991, where an entirely new geopolitical entity was conceived, remains a mystery. The world still does not know the full story of that dramatic night-long session which precipitated, at the overt level, the immediate dissolution of the Soviet empire. That gathering of three key republican leaders, soon to be presidents of their own countries, produced a document providing for the dissolution of the Soviet Union into fifteen separate states. Moreover, it was followed the next day by an equally dramatic confrontation in Moscow between Boris Yeltsin and Mikhail Gorbachev over the fate of the USSR. One of the main issues these two men debated was the role of the Soviet army and whom the army would support under the emerging conditions.

Yeltsin's goals played a critical role in the events unleashed by that mysterious night-long session. We do know that Yeltsin's main interest at this juncture lay not in dissolving the Soviet Union, but in reconfiguring it. He wanted to redefine the elements of the USSR in such a way that Gorbachev would be displaced as president. Yet, even accounting for Yeltsin's personal role, the truly decisive player at the Belavezha meeting was Ukraine. It was Leonid Kravchuk that described the reconfiguration of the Soviet Union, and the resulting Commonwealth of Independent States (CIS), as a "civilized divorce."

It was five years ago, literally in the next two or three weeks from today, that a small team, in fact several small teams, of Ukrainian officers and political leaders undertook something which was quite unprecedented. They traveled to the district commands of the Soviet army and made certain that their hierarchical and communicational links with Moscow were severed, that their loyalty was fully transferred to Kyiv, and that an oath of allegiance was taken by the district commanders or that they were replaced. As a consequence, the Soviet army stationed on Ukrainian soil became, in the course of several weeks, the core of the new Ukrainian national army. And, of course, in the background of all this were the Ukrainian people who had overwhelmingly voted just days earlier for independence and gave impetus to these historically decisive events.

This introduction is a revision and abridgement of a speech delivered by Zbigniew Brzezinski on 12 December 1996 at a conference in Washington, DC, sponsored by the Harvard Ukrainian Research Institute in conjunction with George Washington University and with the support of the Embassy of Ukraine.

Since those historical days, five difficult and painful years have passed. Many Ukrainians have experienced great sacrifice. Not everything has been done in those years that might have been done to bring about the changes sought by the original architects of the new independent state. More might have been done and sooner, for example, about privatization. More also might have been done to revitalize agriculture, which has traditionally been the backbone of the Ukrainian economy. Much more could have been done, also, to stamp out corruption, especially to prevent capital flight out of the country—capital so sorely needed for building new infrastructure and purchasing up-to-date technologies. According to recent Ukrainian Interior Ministry reports, some twenty billion dollars have been smuggled out of Ukraine for deposit in the West. One can only imagine the sum total of damage this has wreaked on the Ukrainian economy and on Ukraine's growth potential.

But having said all that, one fact is also very clear. Ukraine is here to stay and that is a fundamentally important accomplishment. Ukraine is here to stay and that has implications not only for the Ukrainian people. It has global implications in several significant ways. First of all, the fact that Ukraine is here and here to stay transforms the European geopolitical equation. The political landscape of Europe is fundamentally transformed, for Ukraine's existence transforms Russian power by reducing it significantly and thus making it more manageable.

Ukraine's appearance on the map of Europe is comparable in geopolitical significance with the integration of Germany into the emerging European community in the 1990s. This absorption of Germany into Europe removes a predominant power to the West. Ukraine's emergence has a comparable effect in the East, thereby altering the geopolitical configuration of Europe as a whole. This rearrangement is directly pertinent to the future of three countries in particular.

First of all, Ukraine's existence enhances the security of Poland by reducing a traditional dilemma that Poland had always faced, namely that of threatening powers existing simultaneously on its western and eastern frontiers. Ukraine's existence also enhances the security of Romania, which is far more safe today than when it bordered on the Soviet Union or on the Russian Empire. It enhances the security of Turkey and it makes Turkey much more confident in its dealings with its neighbors, and it even shuts off, in effect, a geopolitically significant access by Russia to the Mediterranean region.

Secondly, Ukraine's existence alters the politics of the space formerly occupied by the Soviet Union. Imagine how the CIS would look without an independent Ukraine. It would be simply another empire, with a new name. It would not be imbued, as today, with the refreshing reality of geopolitical pluralism in former Soviet space. Instead it would be dominated by a Russia that still controls Ukraine, which would be, in effect, an imperial entity in a new guise. Ukraine's statehood, moreover, defines the CIS in a fashion that significantly differs from Russia's conceptualization. Indeed, Ukraine's approach to the CIS offers the prospect of enhancing and securing the security of the other newly independent states of the CIS. Its vision of the CIS is of a loosely cooperative community, whereas Moscow's vision is of a tightly and centrally integrated community.

There is a critical political difference between cooperation and integration. Sometimes speakers from Moscow argue that it is improper to criticize Moscow's efforts at integration for they simply mirror what is being done in Europe. What is the difference between the efforts to create the European Union and those to integrate the Commonwealth of Independent States? The European Union is not being constructed within the territory of a previous empire and it is not being constructed on the basis of the previous imperial state's promotion of the integration of its earlier imperial domain. Ukraine's promotion of cooperation and its opposition to integration makes it easier not only for Ukraine but for the other newly independent states to preserve their sovereignty. Indeed, we are seeing increasingly the emergence of a political constellation within the CIS in which the weaker states cluster around Ukraine's position in the debate over the proper demarcation between legitimate cooperation and politically undesirable integration.

Thirdly, Ukraine's occupation of an independent space on the map of Europe helps Russia to transform itself. It compels politically conscious Russians to ask themselves a fundamental question. What is Russia? Where is Russia? Will Russia become, or perhaps is it already, a normal European national state or is it a multinational empire? That debate is raging with great intensity in contemporary Russia and there is no uniformity in the answers. No overwhelming majority exists for one point of view or another, but the fact is that Ukraine's existence confronts Russia with a historically decisive moment of truth. The Russians have to decide what kind of nation or state they want to be in the twenty-first century. An enormous amount depends on the answer they give. So far the answers have been ambiguous. There are some hopeful signs. For one thing, it is quite evident that the Russian people did not want to support Boris Yeltsin's and Defense Minister Pavel Grachev's war in Chechnya. Thus, at the very least they signaled symptoms of imperial fatigue and perhaps even of a more fundamental change in the national mind-set.

That is a hopeful sign, but there are, as we all know, also retrogressive, even dangerous, signals, and these tend to involve, to a significant extent, Russian-Ukrainian relations. Let me state quite categorically that we in the West do not wish Russian-Ukrainian relations to be antagonistic. We are not interested in promoting hostility between these two sovereign states. We think that cooperation between them is desirable and necessary. We would like the relationship to be, to the extent that it can be, like our own relationship with Canada—cooperative, open, but mutually respectful of our national identities and respective sovereignties.

We do not think it should be a relationship of subordination. However, at least some members of the Russian political elite reject the notion of a separate

Ukrainian state, view it essentially as a transitional phenomenon, connected with a transient era of the Russian *smuta*, but consider it as something that will disappear, and perhaps even as a condition that requires some deliberate humiliation and reduction of Ukraine. Here, of course, I have in mind particularly the painful and provocative issue of Crimea.

Sevastopol has now become the focus of demagogy in Moscow, and not only in the Duma. Anyone who watches Russian television every night sees a deliberate provocation. Russian television, as of some recent date, when giving the weather forecast for the major cities of Russia, includes Sevastopol. In Sevastopol itself, the Russian military enjoys de facto status of an occupation army. Its personnel is not subject, in effect, to Ukrainian laws and Ukrainian criminal jurisdiction, which is normal when foreign troops are stationed by mutual agreement on foreign soil.

It is not only in the Duma that we hear demagogic statements. In a recent interview, Igor Tuliev, Minister of CIS Relations in Yeltsin's cabinet, made a number of observations with regard to Sevastopol. He stated that Sevastopol today is experiencing the third great siege in its history. Today, it is being besieged by the Ukrainians. He compliments the people of Sevastopol for having withstood the first two sieges and hopes they will be equally determined in coping with the third. He goes on to warn that in Crimea there are now elements which are supported from the outside, particularly from Turkey, and are engaged in efforts to isolate Crimea from Russia. What is worse, he said, the goal of these isolation tactics is to make it easier for NATO to gain some sort of a foothold. He went on to say that the detachment of Crimea from the Slav world is apparently a NATO objective. Having said this, he pointed out that Ukraine is economically dependent on Russia and he noted that Russia's economic levers should be utilized in dealing with Ukraine. He concluded by saying that it is essential that Sevastopol remain a Russian city within a Russian state because it is needed as a powerful shield for the Slavs against the West. This was a curious statement by a member of a government which was at the same time discussing seriously a charter with NATO.

It is enlightening to review what was actually said in Moscow when Crimea was attached to Ukraine in 1954. As reported by *Pravda* and *Izvestiia* of February 27, 1954, there was a meeting of the USSR Supreme Soviet on February 19, 1954, under the chairmanship of Comrade Voroshilov. Pravda lists the attendees and also mentions that the meeting was attended by the Russian Republic Chairman Tarasov and others, including the chairman of the Sevastopol City Soviet Executive Committee, Comrade Sosnitskii. It goes on to say that Comrade Tarasov, Chairman of the Russian presidium, stated that the Russian people recognize as expedient the transfer of the Crimea Province to the Ukrainian Republic. He also is reported to have said: "Crimean Oblast, as is known, occupies the entire Crimean peninsula and, as it were, is a natural continuation of the southern steppes of Ukraine."

I think it will take time before opinion in Moscow is fully altered. It is, after all, an enormous change for Russia to become accustomed to an independent Ukraine. For Russia, for three hundred years, Ukraine was viewed as part of Russia and hence we have to be patient. It is not an excuse for these attitudes, for they have to be repudiated. It is simply a statement of historical perspective on them. It will take time for them to be altered and we should have no illusions. My own expectation is that the decisive moment in Russia's relationship with Ukraine will come when Ukraine decides on its own relationships, particularly with NATO. That will not happen soon. NATO will be expanding gradually. NATO will start expanding as of next July. We expect the first stage to be completed by the summer of 1999 and I am absolutely convinced that Russia will acquiesce to this expansion of NATO.

Ukraine's future depends on Ukraine becoming in the foreseeable future a de facto Central European state. It is culturally part of the Central European tradition, but it has to become politically and economically a genuine part of Central Europe if it is to survive. This orientation will give Ukraine its own geopolitical identity, one that separates it from its more traditional connection with Eurasia through Russia. Ukraine is already connected with the Central European Initiative. Now, Ukraine must face the fact that Central Europe will be part of NATO. Central Europe will also become part of the European Union someday. If Ukraine is to become a genuine Central European state, these realities will have to be confronted. They will not come to pass probably for another ten or fifteen years, but it will be important for Ukraine to be ready to exercise whatever option it chooses for the sake of its future and well-being. If Russia then acquiesces to whatever Ukraine decides in its relationship with Central Europe, Russia itself would be then defining itself as a European state. That would be a conclusive answer to Russia's basic dilemma—which is: What is Russia? But if Russia opposes or obstructs Ukraine's choices concerning membership in Central Europe, that will be a sign that its imperial vocation is still very much alive. Thus, within a fundamental and historically grounded perspective, defining the future of Ukraine will also be a way of defining the future of Russia.

Until that day comes, Ukraine's geopolitical course is clear. First, Ukraine has to consolidate its geopolitical flanks, which means, in the first instance, engaging in the closest possible cooperation in a variety of economic, political and military activities with Poland, and through Poland with Germany. This route leads to entry into Europe and to obtaining greater European commitment. In addition, it is important for Ukraine to develop good relations and closer links with both Romania and Turkey.

Secondly, it has to stabilize, to the extent possible, its relations with Russia. That means primarily economic cooperation, along the lines of regional cooperation that is emerging internationally, while at the same time defending the concept of the CIS as a cooperative association of states through a web of relationships with other similarly oriented CIS states. I note in particular the development of links between Ukraine and Azerbaijan, and Ukraine and Uzbekistan. These two geopolitically important countries, working together with Ukraine, can help to consolidate the reality of geopolitical pluralism within the space of the former Soviet Union.

Thirdly, Ukraine has to strive to become indirectly, perhaps someday directly, an increasingly integral part of the Euro-Atlantic community. NATO is going to expand and that means that Ukraine's relationship with NATO will also have to deepen and become more extensive. I was pleased that the communiqué issued by the ministerial meeting of the North Atlantic Council, just concluded several days ago, contained the following passage pertaining to Ukraine: "We are committed to the development in coming months, through high-level and other consultations, of a distinctive and effective NATO-Ukraine relationship which could be formalized possibly by the time of the summit next July, building on the document on enhanced NATO-Ukraine relations agreed in September 1995 and taking into account recent Ukrainian proposals." The council also decided to open up a NATO information office in Kyiv, paralleling the one that has been opened in Moscow.

We recently announced the emergence of a strategic partnership between the United States and Ukraine, and it is very important to try to give it as much substance as possible. The American-Ukrainian Advisory Committee, which I chair, last September came up with a series of proposals to make that substance more tangible, and some of them are reflected already in the Brussels communiqué. The U.S. administration itself is increasingly active in pursuing that objective. This has certainly been the goal of those of us who over the last three or four years have toiled for a genuine strategic relationship between the United States and Ukraine, who have insisted that Russia and Ukraine be treated alike. Because of the promise made, because of what has transpired, I think I can end where I started. I can say that Ukraine is here to stay because the Ukrainians want it so and because we also want it so.

2

Ukraine in the World

BORYS TARASYUK

It would be a mistake to say that the foreign policy of Ukraine started the day of the successful nationwide referendum on 1 December 1991 or even the day of the declaration of independence on 24 August 1991. In reality, Ukraine's foreign policy began immediately after the adoption of state sovereignty on 16 July 1990.

A bit less than a month after that declaration, the first bilateral visit of a Ukrainian delegation, led by then Foreign Minister Anatoliy Zlenko, took place, with an official visit to Hungary. Hungary was the first neighboring country that took Ukraine quite seriously and understood perfectly well the major trends developing in Kyiv at the time. This explains why Foreign Minister Géza Jeszenszky of Hungary invited Zlenko to visit Hungary on 27 August. This visit was the first direct bilateral contact between the Ukrainian SSR and a neighboring country. Successful negotiations with President Árpád Göncz of Hungary, Prime Minister József Antall, and Foreign Minister Jeszenszky were followed by the first visit in history of the president of a neighboring country to Ukraine—that of President Göncz in September 1990. Moreover, this was not a visit on the way to or from Moscow (which was quite usual at that time), but a presidential visit from a neighboring country directly to the capital of Ukraine.

Ukraine was eager to extend its first independent contacts to other sovereign states. Among our neighbors, it was not only Hungary which tried to establish a relationship with us at that time. The first visit of the foreign minister of another neighboring country, Poland, by Foreign Minister Krzysztof Skubiszewski, took place in October 1990. The resulting political document, a declaration, was the first of its kind and contained a number of very important provisions. The document with Poland and a similar political document concluded with Hungary during the visit of President Göncz to Kyiv constitute the first written legal documents of Ukraine's foreign policy in the contemporary era. These documents contained all the provisions characteristic of relations between sovereign independent countries, and at that time it was a very courageous step by the capitals of both neighboring countries, taking into account the jealousy and pressure we felt from Moscow.

It was not only our neighbors to the west that were very interested in opening a new page in our relationship—but our biggest neighbor to the east also was keen on developing direct bilateral relations with Ukraine. This explains why the parliamentarians of the Supreme Soviet of the Russian Federation and the Verkhovna Rada of Ukraine—both still parts of the Soviet

Union at the time—took the initiative and prepared a direct bilateral inter-state treaty. The Ukrainian version of the treaty, prepared and endorsed by nationally conscious forces in Ukraine, was completely different from the version the Russians brought with them to Kyiv. It was intensely discussed both in Kyiv and Moscow, and finally signed by the Speaker of the Russian Parliament Boris Yeltsin and the Speaker of the Ukrainian Parliament Leonid Kravchuk in November 1990 in Kyiv. The treaty contained very important provisions concerning the recognition of existing borders and respect for national sovereignty, principles which are still valid and reconfirmed in the most recent Ukrainian-Russian treaty. That first document gave additional legal ground for the UN Security Council to adopt a resolution in 1993 which states that by claiming Sevastopol as a part of Russia, the Russian parliament had violated this bilateral treaty, as well as the objectives and principles of the UN Charter.

The foreign policy of this pre-independence period included other major steps by the Ukrainian side. On the invitation of Bavarian state officials, then Speaker of the Ukrainian Parliament Kravchuk visited Germany and established the first direct contacts with German authorities at the federal level. As a result, in February 1991 there took place the first bilateral contact between President Kravchuk and the president, the vice-chancellor and foreign minister of Germany. This was a very important contact, which in its further development laid the groundwork for an active, viable relationship between Germany and Ukraine, which has lasted up to this day.

One revealing aspect of that visit to Germany worth noting concerns the "language problem." I remember the irony with which the correspondent of Russian (Soviet) television was commenting on this visit to Bonn, saying that the Ukrainians surprised the Germans so much by speaking to them in Ukrainian, which was not understandable to the Germans. This was not the case, however, because the Ukrainian delegation had two first-rate Ukrainian-German interpreters, and in reality there were no problems at all. (This is a vivid example of how some Russians have worked to distort the issues surrounding the use of the Ukrainian language.)

The next step in Ukraine's foreign policy of that pre-independence period was the visit of Speaker of the Ukrainian Verkhovna Rada Kravchuk to Hungary at the end of May 1991. In the course of this visit a record number of ten documents was signed. One of the most important documents was the Declaration on the Realization of Rights of National Minorities, which was the first attempt in Europe to implement the Copenhagen document on national minorities. But it did not comprise simply a compilation of major European principles of respect for national minorities; there were also important provisions concerning the mechanisms for the realization of those principles. As a result, a binational commission was established with representatives of the two governments and respective national minorities, which is still fully functioning—holding meetings twice a year—and overall has proved to be very successful.

The second phase of Ukraine's foreign policy in that period began immediately after the adoption by the Verkhovna Rada of the declaration of independence on 24 August 1991. The immediate reaction of Russia was to question the legitimacy of its borders with Ukraine. This was the first provocative act of Russia, with a hint that the independence declaration could mean the possibility of reconsidering these borders. Certainly, this was one of the powerful reasons for anti-Russian sentiments in Ukraine. These were irresponsible acts by Moscow which instigated anti-Russian sentiments among the Ukrainian population in Ukraine, not to mention the Ukrainian Parliament. As a result, a Russian delegation, led by deputies Anatolii Sobchak and Aleksandr Rutskoi, was sent to Kyiv. This was our first contact with Russia from the position of an independent state, and the Ukrainian parliamentarians tried to mollify the difficulties which had actually originated from Moscow. In addition, the border negotiation process with Russia has been complicated by maritime border issues. Our neighbor is still reluctant to recognize the maritime convention of 1982 which prescribes delineation of borders along the continental shelf.

Another issue of provoked contention was the status of Crimea and the city of Sevastopol. The legal transfer of the peninsula in 1954 was not just a "gift" to Ukraine in celebration of the three hundredth anniversary of its union with Russia, but was done rather for economic considerations: Crimea could not be run by Russia without energy, water, and other resources supplied from the Ukrainian mainland. Regarding Sevastopol, some Russians, led by Moscow Mayor Luzhkov, misled their own legislators in asserting that Sevastopol was never transferred to Ukraine. This is simply untrue—it was transferred along with Crimea. There was always a separate budget line for Sevastopol in the Ukrainian SSR budget, and not in the Russian budget. There is no reference in the Russian constitution to Sevastopol, but in the Ukrainian SSR constitution of 1978 it was mentioned as a city directly under Kyiv's authority. The same is true of the present constitution of independent Ukraine.

Intensive contacts took place between the leaders of the Russian Federation and Ukraine before the December 1991 referendum. The Russians were trying to impose their view that the whole area of "Nova Rossiia" would be a sphere of common interest between Russia and Ukraine. This was a great surprise to us, and certainly it was quite unacceptable to Ukraine—in the corridors there were suggestions to make similar reference to Kuban and other areas in Russia. But fortunately there was enough wisdom on both sides to avoid any references to these issues in bilateral documents.

The development of mutually beneficial, balanced and good neighborly relations with Russia has always been a special aspect of Ukraine's foreign policy. Ties between Kyiv and Moscow should become more pragmatic and constructive. Examples of bilateral partnership cooperation include the co-production of aircraft engines, the implementation of a joint project to manufacture the Antonov-70 airplane—which could become the basis for a future large European aircraft of the 21st century—joint manufacturing of Tupolev-

334 aircraft, tractor equipment, buses, and possibly joint exploration of oil and gas fields in the Black and Azov Seas.

Another problem we had at that time was with our neighbor to the west, Romania. The Romanian parliament made clear-cut territorial claims to parts of Ukraine: Southern Bessarabia and Northern Bukovina as well as Serpent Island. These Ukrainian territories were never a part of Romania—they were taken by Romania by force in 1918. The direct implication of these claims was expressed in the note verbale of the Romanian Embassy in Kyiv to the Foreign Ministry dated 22 April 1993, which declared the treaty on borders between the Soviet Union and Romania of 1961 as one which had ceased to exist. Our numerous proposals to recall this note had no response.

These Ukrainian-Romanian negotiations were going on at a time when Bucharest was vigorously seeking its place as one of the first candidates for NATO membership. Ukraine sometimes heard implied accusations that it was trying to impede these aspirations of its Central European neighbor. Our clear response was that it was not up to Ukraine to decide who would be in the first wave of NATO membership, and that Ukraine never claimed the right of veto for that matter. The only right Ukraine had and openly voiced was to express its concern about the deadlocked bilateral negotiations with Romania in the face of claims to our territories.

The next period is that of the foreign policy of independent Ukraine, starting from 1 December 1991. Our confidence then, and to this day, in Ukraine's irreversibly independent future was most rightfully based on the results of a national referendum and the resolve of Ukraine's president and the government to strengthen and consolidate this independence.

The first neighboring country to officially recognize Ukraine's independence was Poland, on 2 December. The first Western country to do the same was Canada. Nestor Gayovsky was at that time consul general of Canada in Kyiv. He delivered this news late in the evening to Foreign Minister Zlenko, accompanied with a bottle of champagne. Together we celebrated this decision of recognition by the Canadian government.

The foreign policy period right after the 1 December referendum included the first official visit of the prime minister of Hungary József Antall to Ukraine on 5 December. This was the first official bilateral visit of a neighboring leader to independent Ukraine. As a result, a major treaty between Ukraine and Hungary, confirming their common border, was signed, and subsequently the first foreign embassy in Kyiv was opened. With regard to border problems: by December 1996 we had completed the process of legally confirming the borders with four of our six neighbors: Belarus, Poland, Hungary, and Slovakia. At that time the same task was pending in our relations with Romania, Russia and Moldova, the first two refusing for a long time even to negotiate the issue of demarcation and delimitation of our common borders.

Coming back to the first years of our independence, one of the major challenges of Ukraine's foreign policy was to establish not only close bilateral relations with neighboring countries, but also a comprehensive regional framework. In this regard it is important to remember the initiative announced by President Kravchuk in February 1993 in Budapest (which appeared three months before the well-known initiative of Prime Minister Edouard Balladur of France), regarding a pact of stability. It proved that Ukraine was searching for its own way of consolidating regional European stability. One needs to mention here Ukraine's participation from the very beginning in the Black Sea cooperative institutions, and the Central European Initiative, of which we became a member in 1996. We are working to establish a closer relationship with the Central European Free Trade Agreement (CEFTA) with the aim of becoming a full party to this agreement. Ukraine is very active in expanding its cooperation with the Nordic and Baltic countries, gradually becoming a strategic link between the Baltic and Black Sea regions. Being an active mediator in conflicts in some CIS countries, like in the Transdniester region (Moldova), Abkhazia (Georgia), or Nagorno-Karabakh (Azerbaijan), Ukraine is becoming an attractive political center, enjoying the respect of its neighbors. In addition, a wide network of close regional ties is important not only from the political or security point of view, but brings also many economic advantages to Ukraine. Among the most important is diversification of energy sources (and of trade relations as a whole) through negotiating new pipeline routes. Very promising in this respect is the potential for the transport of a significant percentage of oil and gas from the Caspian Sea, across the territory of Ukraine, as a more direct transit route to Europe.

In answer to references about the failure of a Central and East European zone of stability, one should know that this was not because the idea was passed down to the hands of experts from the foreign ministries. The political situation at that time in Central and Eastern Europe dictated that the countries of this region look further west rather than east in trying to receive recognition of their request for membership in NATO and the European Union. My recent acquaintance with the work by Samuel Huntington *The Clash of Civilizations and the Remaking of World Order* was very much disagreeable. In this work, irresponsibly, a new "borderline" is being drawn, leaving Ukraine outside of Europe, ignoring Ukraine's quest for integration into major European and Euro-Atlantic institutions.

Now a few words about the relationship of Ukraine with the CIS. From the very beginning, when the agreement was signed at Belavezha by the three presidents, the people at Ukraine's Foreign Ministry were surprised and struck by the decision of President Kravchuk to sign this agreement because we saw it as a step back from independence. This was the reason why the Ministry made its contribution by assisting the Ukrainian Parliament to prepare reservations to this document, which are still valid and keeping Ukraine at a distance so that it is not "swallowed" by the CIS. We consider the CIS as an instrument of consultation, facilitating the resolution of bilateral issues by the participating countries. To correct a widespread illusion, one should know that Ukraine has never been a full member of the CIS, but one of its founding members which, as lawyers know, makes a big difference. Being a member state would mean that Ukraine would have signed the charter of the CIS, which was never the case. There are at least three levels of engagement in the CIS, and Ukraine's position is a special one. Ukraine does not recognize the CIS as a subject of international law with the right to represent all its member countries. It does not participate in the Tashkent treaty on collective security; it is an associate member of the economic union treaty within the CIS. There are three major groups in the CIS: one concentrated around Russia, one around Ukraine, and the third in between. The first includes those following the reintegrational policy of Russia, namely, our northern neighbor and Tajikistan; the second includes Azerbaijan, Moldova, Uzbekistan, Turkmenistan, and Georgia; the others take various positions depending on the issue at hand. As to Belarus, it is an important neighbor, and its direction matters to Ukraine. Ukraine hopes that the policy of this neighbor-country will someday turn to be more in line with major European integration processes.

The process of European integration, while simultaneously consolidating friendly relations with our immediate neighbors, first of all Russia, has irreversibly become the heart and soul of Ukraine's foreign policy, its main strategic goal and priority. Ukraine has developed dynamic, institutionalized bases and mechanisms of cooperation with the European Union (EU) and NATO. In all aspects of interrelations—political, economic or security— Ukraine is making its solid contribution to a united Europe, especially through establishing good, neighborly relations with surrounding countries and initiating multidimensional regional projects. All this eventually makes Ukraine increasingly welcome to integration processes on the continent, which in its turn makes a favorable impact on internal politics, consolidating consensus among various political forces.

The main issue in Ukrainian-EU relations requires not only the efforts of Ukraine in implementing the Cooperation and Partnership Agreement, but also concrete steps on the part of the European Union to adopt a clear-cut policy towards Ukraine, as the biggest Central and Eastern European nation—for the time being, this is missing. Pursuing full membership in the EU as its long-term strategic goal, Ukraine stands ready for an elaboration at this stage of the European Agreement providing an institutional framework for our associated status.

We absolutely welcome our Romanian, Bulgarian, and other neighbors' prospective admission to the EU—and the sooner the better. We are supportive of one another, and united we form a strong Central and Eastern Europe. At the same time, we could not help but notice, and Ukraine is not alone in this, some possible adverse implications of the future EU enlargement which should be avoided now. We can easily foresee the worsening of the bilateral cooperation in economic, humanitarian and other areas between the new members and their neighboring nations in Central and Eastern Europe that are not included in the first wave of enlargement. Drastic changes in the current trade, customs, and visa regulations on the bilateral level will lead to a worsening of the economic situation in those countries left outside the EU. The gap between the level of involvement of different countries in the European integration process will widen, and it is already resulting in the reemergence of new dividing lines in Europe, and the appearance of new threats to its stability and security.

Ukraine was satisfied with the decision of NATO, declared at the 10 December 1996 Ministerial Meeting, to withhold the deployment of nuclear weapons in new members along our western borders. Ever since, Ukraine has become a close and special partner of NATO, steadily intensifying its political dialogue and practical cooperation. Viewing NATO as an alliance of democratic nations, Ukraine has never opposed its enlargement to the east, considering it instead as an extension of the area of stability, security, and prosperity in Europe. Ultimately, NATO is very likely to evolve into the major pillar of the future security architecture in the Euro-Atlantic area. It is the only truly effective institution capable of coping with new emerging risks and conflicts in post-cold war Europe.

An obvious and widely acknowledged concluding remark is that the stability and security of our region, and of Europe as a whole, to a large extent depends upon the political and economic stability of Ukraine. By supporting and assisting Ukraine, the Western countries—and among them the United States is the undisputed champion—ensure a more stable and prosperous Europe. By helping Ukraine, they invest in the peaceful future of the world. Cooperation with the U.S. has been crucial in consolidating Ukraine as a stable, democratic, viable partner and ally of the United States, strategically located as a bridge, not a buffer, between Central Europe and Russia. And the Euro-Atlantic priority in Ukraine's foreign policy is a strong guarantee of the Ukrainian-American strategic partnership, declared in October 1996.

As we look forward to the celebration of the seventh anniversary of the all-Ukrainian referendum, we can note that Ukraine has achieved a great deal in the past years, having become a respected member of the international community and one of the key players in both regional and global systems of security. Ukraine's integration into Europe may serve as a good example to its neighbors through the promotion of democratic traditions throughout the region. That is the way to secure our rightful place in the world.

Part I

Ukraine's External Relations

3

Ukraine, Russia, and the CIS

ROMAN SOLCHANYK

The past decade has witnessed nothing short of a fundamental transformation in the relationship between Ukraine and Russia. The key factor, of course, was the collapse of the Soviet Union and the emergence of Ukraine and Russia as independent states. At this juncture, the discourse between Ukraine and Russia, which throughout the Soviet period had been focused almost entirely on inter-ethnic (or inter-nationality) questions, was broadened to include international issues, which, moreover, became paramount.[1] Problems of language, culture, and interpretation of historical events were now over-shadowed by problems of state: borders, armies, and nuclear weapons. Neither side, each for its own specific reasons, was especially well prepared for such a dramatic change. Thus, it should not be particularly surprising that Ukrainian-Russian relations in the post-Soviet period have largely been strained, conflictive, and, indeed, unstable. The very fact that it was only in mid-1997, almost six years after the Soviet Union had ceased to exist, that Kyiv and Moscow finally managed to conclude a treaty on "friendship, cooperation, and partnership," which, more-over, has yet to come into force, testifies to the inordinate difficulties of what is perhaps best described as a lengthy and difficult process of "normalization."[2]

Issues, Problems, Perceptions

Most discussions of contemporary Ukrainian-Russian relations have tended to focus on specific issues about which Kyiv and Moscow have divergent opin-ions and viewpoints. Among these, the most prominent and longstanding have been the fate of the Black Sea Fleet and its main base, Sevastopol; the related but larger question of Crimea, specifically whether or not it should rightfully be considered a part of Ukraine; and the role and functions of the Commonwealth of Independent States (CIS). There are a host of other problems and irritants that have exacerbated relations since independence, including sharing out the debts and assets of the former Soviet Union; delimiting and demarcating bor-ders between the two countries; and, more recently, the eastward expansion of NATO and Moscow's renewed concern about the status of the Russian lan-guage in Ukraine. All of these disputes may be said to be quite "normal"—that is, they are easily identifiable and perfectly soluble. Indeed, probably the most difficult and certainly the most emotionally laden issue—the disposition of the Black Sea Fleet—while perhaps not definitively resolved, has been postponed for twenty years by the Ukrainian-Russian agreements concluded on 28 May

1997,[3] which, in turn, paved the way for the signing of the basic bilateral treaty several days later. This is quite an accomplishment, particularly if one recalls that the tension between Kyiv and Moscow over the Black Sea Fleet in early 1992 was such that observers wondered whether the newly formed CIS would promptly fall apart before it managed to get off the ground.

Overall, and in spite of a difficult agenda of unfinished business, the experience of the years since independence has shown that the leaders of Ukraine and Russia are capable of conducting a dialogue, that compromises can be reached, and that seemingly intractable differences can be resolved. At the same time, it is equally clear that there are some fundamental problems in the Ukrainian-Russian relationship that go deeper than disagreements at the negotiating table.

In early 1997, a leading Moscow newspaper published interviews with Ukrainian President Leonid Kuchma and his top national security adviser, Volodymyr Horbulin.[4] The general thrust of both interviews was that relations with Russia were bad and seemed to be getting worse; the leitmotif was that Russia was not taking Ukraine seriously, that its attitude was patronizing and condescending. On the face of it, there is nothing particularly revealing or astonishing in these perceptions. Russia, after all, is having problems of one sort or another with nearly all of the former Soviet republics, including Belarus, with whom it has entered into a "union" of sorts. In this respect, Kazakh President Nursultan Nazarbaev is not alone in his estimate that Moscow's policies in the CIS have had the effect of "not attracting potential allies, but repelling them."[5] Both Kuchma and Horbulin, however, seemed intent to underscore that there was an added dimension to the Ukrainian-Russian relationship, that the problems went beyond the realm of the "normal." Horbulin, for example, said that he was not prepared to offer a rational explanation as to why there were such difficulties, suggesting that a close reading of Freud could provide some insights or that perhaps Dostoevsky might have the answer. But then he added: "I often recall what former U.S. Secretary of State Henry Kissinger told me: 'I never met a single Russian who thought that Ukraine could be independent.'" Kuchma was more forthright, saying that "in Russia they pretend that Ukraine as a sovereign, independent state does not exist." "As I see it," he continued, "in Russia, the stereotype of viewing Ukraine as its constituent part or, at any rate, as the sphere of its prevailing influence has not yet been eliminated." Kuchma returned to the problem a year later, after President Boris Yeltsin's visit to Kyiv and the successful conclusion of the long awaited bilateral treaty. In an interview in *Izvestiia*, the Ukrainian leader, although emphasizing that Ukrainian-Russian relations had vastly improved and that "problems of a political character" were now virtually nonexistent, nonetheless expressed concern about what lay ahead. Specifically, Kuchma called attention to what he termed the "divorce syndrome" in the Ukrainian-Russian relationship, briefly characterizing it as a "complicated political-psychological problem that casts an ominous shadow on the entire complex of Ukrainian-Russian relations."[6]

But why should the Ukrainian-Russian divorce be any different or more complicated than the other divorces that occurred at the end of 1991? Writing several weeks after the collapse of the Soviet Union, Len Karpinskii, then chief editor of *Moskovskie novosti*, framed the problem in stark, almost eschatological terms. Karpinskii argued that one of the redeeming features of the Belovezha accords that created the CIS was that it prevented a complete split between Ukraine and Russia, which, he felt, would have been a "genuine tragedy" for Russian national consciousness. "Millions of Russians," he asserted, "are convinced that without Ukraine not only can there be no great Russia, but there cannot be any kind of Russia at all."[7] This perception emphasizes the degree to which Ukraine is not only and not simply a problem *for Russia*, but, more importantly, that it is also a problem *of Russia*. The defining characteristic of the Ukrainian-Russian "divorce syndrome" is that when Ukraine declared its independence in August 1991 it initiated divorce proceedings not only against the USSR, but also against what many Russians perceived to be "Russia." As Roman Szporluk has pointed out, in imperial Russia Ukrainians (and Belarusians) were viewed as component parts of a greater Russian nation, and what sets them apart from all of the other non-Russians of the former Soviet Union is that many Russians question their very existence.[8] Today, a large segment of the Russian population, and certainly much of Russia's political class as well as its cultural elites, still continues to view Ukraine as an integral part of Russia and Ukrainians as an organic part of the Russian nation. A nationwide poll conducted in Russia in the fall of 1997 by the Center for the Study of Public Opinion showed that 56 percent of respondents felt that Ukrainians and Russians are "one people."[9] The same sentiment was voiced by Yeltsin in an address to his countrymen in November of that year: "It is impossible to tear from our hearts that Ukrainians are our own people. That is our destiny—our common destiny."[10]

Russia's problems in dealing with Ukraine have also been greatly exacerbated by the fact that, with few exceptions, not much of an effort has been made in Russia, either in the mass media or among the intelligentsia, to reexamine and reconsider the historical baggage in the Ukrainian-Russian relationship. A study that focused on the image of Ukraine and Ukrainians in the Russian press after the collapse of the Soviet Union found that, in spite of the fact that the Ukrainian referendum on independence in December 1991 yielded a vote of more than 90 percent in favor, the prevailing trend in the ensuing years was to present a picture of Ukrainian independence in almost conspiratorial terms—that is, as the result of efforts by "nationalist" or "sovereign communist" elites ostensibly working against the genuine will of "the people." The study concluded that, for the most part, "Russian public opinion and the mass media evade serious discussion of the problems that are posed for Russian identity in connection with the formation of an independent Ukraine. A significant spectrum of public opinion continues to view the separation of Ukraine as something artificial and temporary."[11] There are no functioning academic centers or institutes for Ukrainian studies in Russia, and Ukrainian history in the country's leading university is still taught as part of "the general course on the history of the fatherland."[12] As late as 1997, a leading Moscow academic journal could still publish a lengthy two-part article essentially restating the main theses of the Russian classics on "Ukrainian separatism"— namely, that Ukrainian nationalism was largely the invention of a small group of intellectuals headed by the historian Mykhailo Hrushevskyi, who was manipulated by "Polish chauvinists" determined "to set the Little Russians against the Russians and thereby split the Russian Empire from within."[13]

This is not to say that such views hold sway over the entire journalistic and academic community in Russia. In an article entitled "Problems in Relations with Ukraine Remain," the former diplomat and political commentator Aleksandr Bovin, for example, refers to "the emotional background against which practically all of us view relations with Ukraine." He admits that intellectually he understands that Ukraine is independent and that Crimea and Sevastopol are now in a foreign country, but confesses that emotionally he is unable to deal with these realities. "Maybe I'm wrong," says Bovin, "but I have the feeling that a considerable part of the Russian elite simply cannot part with this [divorce] syndrome." But he also offers a solution to the problem:

> Let's think about the situation. Either, or. Either we feel that the separation of Ukraine is an historical misunderstanding, a regrettable, temporary accident, that there is a realistic possibility of changing the course of events or, as a minimum, imposing our will on Kyiv—and then we can and should conduct a brutal, forceful course with respect to Ukraine. Or, after all, we come to the conclusion that, in the foreseeable future, there is no going back, that Ukraine is a truly independent and truly sovereign state that has the "right" to its own policies that correspond to its own interests—and then it follows that we learn how to live with that kind of Ukraine.[14]

Dmitrii Furman, one of a handful of Russian academics specializing in contemporary Ukrainian issues, also focuses on the psychological and the irrational as the core problem in the Ukrainian-Russian relationship: "Grasping the realities, shaking off the nationalist mythology—that is the way to deliverance from the painful Russian and Ukrainian psychological complexes and the psychological tension in Russian-Ukrainian relations."[15] There are representatives of the younger generation of Russian scholars who are interested in Ukrainian history and politics and whose research and publications reflect their awareness of the complexities of the Ukrainian-Russian relationship and offer thoughtful and balanced analyses.[16]

To what extent the Russian political class is moving or is even prepared to move in the same direction is an open question. Yeltsin's apparent conviction that it is "impossible" to sever the special bond between Ukraine and Russia does not inspire a great deal of optimism. Although the Russian President is well-known for his sometimes strange and erratic behavior, Yeltsin's statement on the eve of the Russian-Belarusian "union" that his Ukrainian counterpart "wants to join, but something's hindering him" belies either hopelessly wishful thinking or complete ignorance of Ukrainian realities (or both).[17] Dmitrii Riurikov, Yeltsin's former adviser on foreign policy, is a particularly interesting case of how the "divorce syndrome" affects Russian political behavior. In an interview several years ago, Riurikov briefly noted that there was "something [in Ukrainian-Russian relations] that remains immutable—namely, a psychological layer that we are unable to surmount." He then proceeded, unwittingly, to personify the problem by expressing his irritation at Ukraine's refusal to conduct its relations with Russia on the basis of a "special relationship" and a "special history." Kyiv, he insisted should make a "fraternal grand Slavic gesture" and refrain from constant appeals to its own national laws and international norms as the basis for its policies regarding Russia.[18] In short, Ukraine, as the "younger brother" in this "special relationship," should behave according to its prescribed role. As one moves either to the right or left along the contemporary Russian political spectrum, the prospects for the "normalization" of Ukrainian-Russian relations grows increasingly more questionable. In fact, the right-left delineation in this context is meaningless to the extent that the Russian nationalists and communists share essentially the same views on Ukraine. The convictions of a "traditional nationalist" like Viktor Aksiuchits, who heads the Russian Christian Democratic Movement, appear not to have changed since 1991–1992. In an article in early 1997, Aksiuchits argued that the concept of Slavic unity was valid when applied to Poles or Serbs, but that in the case of the Russians, Ukrainians, and Belarusians it was a ploy intended to cover up the fact that all three constituted a single and indivisible nation. "History," he insisted "does not know either the Ukrainian or Belarussian nations or the "sovereign" states of Ukraine or Belarus."[19] Similarly, Communist Party leader Gennady Zyuganov writes that "Russian civilization" has been torn into three parts:

> In essence, this is a problem of our viability. How it will be solved will determine whether or not our Fatherland will be what it has always been—a unique, distinctive, and self-sufficient civilization. That is precisely why the second strategic task—after the internal consolidation of all healthy political forces—is the task of a new reunification of Ukraine and Belarus with Russia.[20]

Some of Russia's confirmed democrats and proponents of market reforms have also articulated views or policy positions with regard to Ukraine that, at the very least, are quite problematical, and two of the leading contenders to succeed Yeltsin, Moscow Mayor Yurii Luzhkov and former Security Council Secretary Gen. Aleksandr Lebed, have both raised Russian claims to Crimea and Sevastopol.

Before and After Independence

There was a period beginning in May–June 1990, when Yeltsin was elected head of the Russian Supreme Soviet and Russia declared its state sovereignty, during which Ukrainian-Russian relations enjoyed a brief but unprecedented honeymoon. At the time, the major political issue in the Soviet Union was the struggle between the Soviet center, represented by Mikhail Gorbachev as Party leader and USSR president, and the Union republics. It was in the interests of both Russia and Ukraine, the two most important and influential republics, to work together in their efforts to wrest as many prerogatives from the center as possible in the process of asserting their sovereignty. At the time, there was still a Soviet Union and, with few exceptions, no one in Russia gave much thought to what implications the weakening of the Soviet state could have for the legitimacy of the new, democratic, and sovereign Russia and its relations with Ukraine and the other republics.

A concrete example of the "new era" in Ukrainian-Russian relations was the "Declaration of the Principles of Inter-State Relations between Ukraine and the RSFSR Based on the Declarations of State Sovereignty" signed by representatives of the Ukrainian parliamentary opposition group called the People's Council (Narodna Rada) and their Russian counterparts from the Democratic Russia bloc. Noting that the growth of democratic movements in the two republics offered the Ukrainian and Russian peoples "a real chance to open a new page in the history of their relations," the document affirmed: (1) the unconditional recognition of Ukraine and Russia as subjects of international law; (2) the "sovereign equality" of the two republics; (3) the principle of noninterference in each other's internal affairs and renunciation of force in their dealings; (4) the inviolability of existing state borders between the two republics and the renunciation of any and all territorial claims; (5) the safeguarding of the political, economic, ethnic, and cultural rights of the representatives of nations of the RSFSR living in Ukraine and vice versa; and (6) the desirability of mutually beneficial cooperation in various fields on the basis of inter-state treaties and the regulation of disputes in a spirit of harmony.[21] These principles were incorporated into the formal treaty between Ukraine and Russia signed on 19 November 1990, which recognized the territorial integrity of both republics and their existing borders within the USSR. The choice of the Ukrainian capital as the venue for the official ceremonies was not fortuitous. Speaking at a press conference directly after the treaty was signed, Yeltsin pointed out that previous agreements between Ukraine and Russia had been arranged in Moscow on unequal terms and stressed that "we very much wanted to sign this one in Kyiv."[22] The gesture was intended to underline the fundamental change in relations between Ukraine and Russia. Addressing the Ukrainian Supreme Soviet (Verkhovna Rada), the Russian leader announced another fundamental change—a reassessment of Russia's self-image:

I categorically reject the accusation that Russia is now claiming some special role. At the [Supreme Soviet] session, [Nikolai] Ryzhkov said that we allegedly want to shift the center from the center to somewhere in Russia. I categorically reject this accusation. Russia does not aspire to become the center of some sort of new empire. It does not want to have an advantage over other republics. Russia understands better than others the perniciousness of that role, inasmuch as it was Russia that performed precisely that role for a long time. What did it gain from this? Did Russians become freer as a result? Wealthier? Happier? You yourselves know the truth; history has taught us that a people that rules over others cannot be fortunate.[23]

The Supreme Soviets of both republics ratified the document within a matter of days, although some Russian lawmakers questioned the wisdom of adhering to the accord before having sorted out the Crimean question.

In the months that followed, Ukraine and Russia continued to offer the strongest opposition to Gorbachev's plans for a renewed Union. At the same time, it was becoming increasingly clear that the Ukrainian and Russian positions with regard to the center were not identical. Yeltsin, in spite of his personal rivalry with Gorbachev, showed himself to be considerably more flexible and compliant in his dealings with the center than the Ukrainian leadership. Already in September 1990, the Presidium of the Ukrainian Supreme Soviet issued a statement declaring that it would be premature to conclude a new Union treaty before the stabilization of the political and economic situation in Ukraine, the building of a law-based and sovereign state, and the adoption of a new republican constitution.[24] The following month, in response to the demands of student hunger strikers in Kyiv, the Supreme Soviet confirmed the stand taken by its Presidium. The differences between Ukraine and Russia were particularly glaring with regard to the "Nine Plus One Agreement" concluded in April 1991 between Gorbachev and the nine Union republics, including Ukraine, that had participated in the referendum on the preservation of the Soviet Union the previous month. The agreement called for the speedy conclusion of a new Union treaty, recognized the sovereignty of the republics, and conceded the need to broaden their rights significantly. Yeltsin's public comments gave the impression that all major disagreements with the center had been resolved to Russia's satisfaction. Kravchuk, on the other hand, who did not represent Ukraine at the meeting, while praising Gorbachev's concession on the sovereignty issue, nonetheless characterized the document as having "no juridical force."[25] Ukraine's position hardened in June, when the parliament decided not to discuss the new Union treaty until mid-September, arguing that it needed time to determine if the latest draft was in line with its declaration of sovereignty. Russia, on the other hand, approved the new draft in principle in early July; at the end of the month, Yeltsin was quoted as saying that Russia was prepared to sign the document "tomorrow, if you like."[26]

The first serious conflicts between Ukraine and Russia, however, came in the aftermath of Ukraine's declaration of independence on 24 August 1991.

Two days later, Yeltsin's press secretary issued a statement saying that Russia reserved the right to raise border issues with those republics, apart from the three Baltic states, that declared their independence and "discontinue union relations."[27] Later the same day, he explained that the statement applied primarily to Crimea, Donbas, and northern Kazakhstan, all regions with substantial Russian minorities. "If these republics enter the Union with Russia," he explained, "it is not a problem. But if they go, we must take care of the population that lives there and not forget that these lands were settled by Russians. Russia will hardly agree to give away these territories just like that."[28] The situation was further aggravated by remarks made at the time by Anatolii Sobchak and Gavriil Popov, the mayors of St. Petersburg and Moscow, respectively, and two of the most prominent representatives of Yeltsin's team. Popov, in particular, argued that declarations of independence were "illegal"; expressed his full support for Yeltsin's stand on borders; demanded the renegotiation of treaties with secessionist republics; and maintained that, among others, the status of Crimea and Odesa Oblast should be decided by local referendums.[29] The following day, the meeting of the USSR Supreme Soviet was interrupted by the announcement that "an emergency situation" had developed and that a Russian delegation headed by Vice-President Aleksandr Rutskoi was already on its way to Kyiv. As Yeltsin subsequently explained, its purpose was "to tell the Ukrainian people: if you stay in the Union, we will not make territorial claims."[30] The deputies were asked to approve the dispatch of a delegation from the Soviet parliament as well. Both delegations arrived in the Ukrainian capital later that day and were met by a hostile crowd said to be the largest since the student strike of the previous year. After night-long negotiations, with the USSR Supreme Soviet delegation acting as observers, the Ukrainian and Russian sides produced an eight-point communiqué promising joint efforts to avert "the uncontrolled disintegration of the Union state"; recognizing the need for interim inter-state structures for a transitional period with the participation of interested states that were "subjects of the former USSR"; and reaffirming the articles of the 1990 Ukrainian-Russian treaty concerning the territorial integrity of both states and the rights of their citizens.[31] The phrase "former USSR" appears to have been coined at that precise moment.

Ukraine and Russia continued to drift apart in the final months of the Soviet Union's existence. Already at the end of August 1991, Kravchuk maintained that Ukraine could not work on the new Union treaty until after its referendum on independence. By that time, the Ukrainian leader was also insisting that a confederation was the only option for Kyiv. Meanwhile, Gorbachev, Yeltsin, and Nazarbaev reaffirmed their commitment to continue the negotiations in Novo Ogarevo. Several months later, in November, Kravchuk argued that the Novo Ogarevo process no longer existed and that Gorbachev's efforts were a "fraud" in which he would not participate. Relations between Kyiv and Moscow were also becoming increasingly strained. Against the background of growing official concern in Moscow about the rights of Russians and Russian speakers in the non-Russian republics and unspecified pledges of support, Aleksandr Solzhenitsyn, whose moral authority in Russia was then undisputed, issued an appeal in October in connection with the forthcoming Ukrainian referendum on independence in which he argued that the aggregate vote was meaningless. Instead, the results in each oblast should be considered separately to decide the territorial future, as it were, of the given oblast. The thrust of the Nobel laureate's argument was that Ukraine was not a legitimate entity, but rather the product of "false Leninist borders."[32] Very soon thereafter, in the midst of the Ukrainian-Russian debate over the fate of Ukraine's nuclear arsenal, *Moskovskie novosti* printed the sensational news that Russian government officials had discussed the possibility of a nuclear conflict between Russia and Ukraine. Another Moscow newspaper presented a somewhat different version—namely, that Russian leaders had considered a preventive nuclear strike against Ukraine. The story was denied by the Russian defense minister and downplayed by Kravchuk, but then Yeltsin was quoted by Ukraine's first deputy prime minister as having told him that he had indeed discussed the possibility with his generals, but that "it was not technically possible." In Ukraine, the Russian president's explanation had the effect of adding more fuel to the fire. The referendum results appear to have shocked many in Russia. Sobchak, like Gorbachev, tried to argue that the vote for Ukrainian independence should not be construed as a vote against some kind of Union and that, in any case, if Ukraine were to secede Russia would immediately raise territorial claims, referring specifically to the "forced Ukrainianization" of the Russian minority. The St. Petersburg Mayor likened the situation to the conflict between Serbs and Croats in Yugoslavia, with the exception that a nuclear conflict could not be excluded in the Ukrainian-Russian case. Ukraine's plans for a separate army, he warned, posed a "serious threat for all of humanity."[33]

From Kyiv's standpoint, the results of the Ukrainian referendum effectively put an end to any plans for a renewed Union. Yeltsin and the Russian leadership, on the other hand, continued to express their support for some sort of arrangement with the center until the very eve of the Belovezha meeting on 7–8 December. Even as late as 5 December the Russian leader claimed that there was no alternative to a Union treaty. It was only in his address to the Belarusian parliament two days later that Yeltsin, while stressing that Russia always wanted a Union, conceded that the attempt to reconstitute the USSR was a failure.[34] Ukraine and Russia now turned to the difficult process of dismantling the Soviet Union, which brought new tensions to the surface.

After the USSR: The CIS

In some sense, the Belovezha talks can be viewed as the final attempt on Russia's part to preserve the Soviet Union. A full account of what transpired during those two days has yet to be written. According to Kravchuk, the meeting was arranged on Ukraine's initiative already in mid-November 1991. Yeltsin is said to have initially acted as a messenger for Gorbachev, conveying the Soviet president's readiness to entertain wide-ranging concessions on the draft Union treaty as long as Ukraine affixed its signature to the document. In the final analysis, Kravchuk refused to sign the existing draft, make amendments, or propose his own version of the treaty.[35] The result was the agreement between Russia, Ukraine, and Belarus to create the Commonwealth of Independent States. After returning to Kyiv, the Ukrainian leader said that Russia and Belarus would have preferred a closer association, but that Ukraine's position precluded such an arrangement. Yeltsin later admitted that "it was not Russia that seceded from the [Soviet] Union," but that the pressure for independence in most of the republics forced Russia to agree to the CIS.[36]

Against this background, Russia's drive to facilitate greater integration within the CIS, which initially took the form of supporting the establishment of coordinating institutions and supranational bodies within the organization such as the Inter-Parliamentary Assembly and promoting the CIS Charter, are perfectly understandable. In April 1992, the Congress of Russian People's Deputies declared its dissatisfaction with the level of political, economic, and military integration among the CIS member states and called for further efforts along these lines. By the end of the year, Russian lawmakers were suggesting that the parliaments of the former Soviet republics consider forming a confederation or some other form of "drawing together."[37] In Ukraine, on the other hand, Kravchuk was faced with criticism from the parliamentary opposition, which argued that Ukraine's membership in the CIS threatened its independence. The Ukrainian Parliament ratified the agreement forming the CIS on 10 December, but added twelve reservations, including the affirmation of the inviolability of state borders and the right to its own armed forces. Within a week, on the eve of the Alma-Ata (Almaty) meeting that saw eight additional former Soviet republics join the CIS, the parliament adopted a thirteen-point declaration delineating its understanding of the CIS as a loose association of independent states. The move was prompted by what the lawmakers maintained were attempts to form a "new union state" on the basis of the CIS.[38]

From the very start, therefore, it was quite clear that Ukraine and Russia had very different views as to the nature and purpose of the CIS. For Ukraine, the CIS was, in the words of its parliamentary head, Ivan Pliushch, a necessary mechanism for an orderly "divorce process." At about the same time, in February 1992, Kravchuk described it as "a committee to liquidate the old structures."[39] Both Ukrainian leaders essentially saw the CIS as a transitional body, which was reflected in Kyiv's decision to steer clear of the Inter-Parliamentary Assembly and the CIS Charter. As a matter of principle, Ukraine refused to take part in any CIS initiatives aimed at greater integration in the political, military, and security spheres and, accordingly, did not sign the collective security treaty in Tashkent in May 1992. Toward the end of the first year of independence, however, intransigence gave way to a more pragmatic and balanced approach, which can largely be ascribed to the impact of harsh economic realities brought on by Ukraine's devastating dependence on Russian sources of energy and the inability or unwillingness of its leaders to develop a program of market reforms. An important factor was the appointment of Leonid Kuchma, an experienced director of one of Ukraine's largest industrial enterprises, Pivdenmash in Dnipropetrovsk, as prime minister in the fall of 1992. While not proposing shock therapy, Kuchma favored closer economic ties with Russia, maintaining that "anti-Russian actions in politics led to anti-Ukrainian economic consequences."[40] The result was a partial reappraisal of earlier policies with regard to the CIS, at least insofar as the economy was concerned. Accordingly, in April 1993 Ukraine initialed the agreement to form the CIS Consultative Coordination Committee, with the proviso that it would not go beyond its mandate to coordinate economic policies, and at the CIS summit in May Kravchuk signed a joint declaration proposing greater economic integration and a common market for goods and services, while at the same time objecting in principle to the idea of an Economic Union. At the September 1993 summit, which witnessed agreement on the creation of the Economic Union, Ukraine displayed its characteristic wariness by opting for the undefined status of "associate member."

Kuchma's election as president in July 1994 was widely expected to result in a clean break with the previous administration's policies, specifically with regard to Russia and the CIS. The new president had built his electoral campaign around the need for change, promising economic improvement through the restoration of ties with Russia. His slogans, which included official status for the Russian language in Ukraine, fell on fertile ground in the industrial and heavily Russian and Russified eastern and southern regions of the country, which were more visibly affected by the economic crisis and accounted for a larger proportion of the electorate than the central or western regions. At the October 1994 CIS summit, Kuchma signed the agreement establishing the Inter-State Economic Committee, which was envisaged as a body charged with coordinating, executive, and control functions for the Economic Union and represented the first supranational organ to be created within the CIS. But the assumption that Kuchma would be more receptive to political, military, and security integration within the CIS proved unfounded. The new Ukrainian president was quick to point out that Ukraine had not affixed its signature to any documents that conflicted with its constitution or laws, singling out Kyiv's continued rejection of CIS collective security arrangements, and stated forcefully that he did not become president of Ukraine "in order to become a vassal of Russia."[41]

If Ukraine viewed the CIS in terms of divorce, Russia gave every indication that it wanted to strengthen the organization and, indeed, assume its leadership. Very revealing in this regard was a confidential document prepared by Yevgenii Ambartsumov, head of the Russian parliamentary committee on foreign affairs, excerpts from which were leaked in August 1992. The report, which summed up closed hearings on Russia's foreign policy, called for rejection of the Western-oriented course pursued by Russian Foreign Minister Andrei Kozyrev and proposed what was described as a "Russian Monroe Doctrine" for the CIS:

> As the internationally recognized legal successor to the USSR, the Russian Federation's foreign policy must be based on the doctrine that proclaims the entire geopolitical space of the former [Soviet] Union the sphere of its vital interests (along the lines of the USA's "Monroe Doctrine" in Latin America) and to secure from the world community the understanding and recognition of Russia's special interests in this space.[42]

Essentially the same thesis was put forth by Yeltsin in early 1993, when he asked the international community and, specifically, the United Nations, for "special powers as a guarantor of peace and stability" on the territory of the former Soviet Union. By the end of 1993 and in early 1994, it was clear that Russia's policies with regard to the CIS were based on the propositions that it is the dominant player in the post-Soviet space and that the entire territory of the former Soviet Union constitutes a zone of Russia's "historically determined interests" wherein it performs a "special role." This was the substance of Kozyrev's remarks at a January 1994 meeting of Russian diplomats from the CIS countries.[43] At the same time, Yeltsin told Russian lawmakers that the CIS had reached a crucial point in its development that was marked by closer integration and that, in the process, "Russia's mission is to be first among equals."[44] This was a clear departure from the Russian president's earlier renunciation of any claims to a leading role in the CIS. The hardening of Russia's official policy may well have been a response to the December 1993 parliamentary elections, which witnessed a major victory for Vladimir Zhirinovsky's ultra-nationalist Liberal Democratic Party. One of the indications of the shift to the right was the establishment, in addition to the parliamentary committee on foreign affairs, of a separate permanent parliamentary committee on CIS affairs and relations with compatriots, thereby underscoring the perception of the world outside Russia's borders as falling into two categories—the Near Abroad, which encompassed all of the former Soviet republics, and the genuinely foreign countries. The CIS committee was headed by Konstantin Zatulin, who defined Russia's policies toward the CIS as falling within the realm of Russia's domestic affairs and maintained that most of the former Soviet republics had to become Russia's satellites or face extinction. Zatulin's attitude toward Ukraine was vividly reflected in his skepticism about the need to recognize "the historically nonexistent borders of an historically nonexistent state."[45] Other prominent Russian politicians, including representatives of the democratic camp, also voiced their support for various forms of tighter integration. Sergei Shakhrai, a deputy prime minister, announced plans in early 1994 for a new confederation, including unified armed forces and a unified command, confessing that he was motivated by a need for "moral and political compensation" for his role in the destruction of the Soviet Union.[46] Vladimir Shumeiko, head of the upper house of the Russian parliament and chairman of the Inter-Parliamentary Assembly, saw the CIS being transformed into a confederation and "later, maybe, we will even see a federation."[47]

Russia's official policy with regard to the CIS was reflected in plans for development of a long-term CIS integration plan and in the establishment of a slot in the government for a deputy prime minister specifically responsible for CIS affairs. Such documents as the report of the Foreign Intelligence Service, headed at the time by Yevgeny Primakov, entitled "Russia-CIS: Does the West's Position Need Modification?" (September 1994); the Memorandum on "The Basic Directions of the Integrationist Development of the Common-wealth of Independent States" and the accompanying long-term plan proposed by Russia and adopted at the CIS summit in Moscow (October 1994); and the presidentially decreed "Russia's Strategic Course with the States-Participants in the Commonwealth of Independent States" (September 1995) were all geared toward promoting and strengthening integration. The "Strategic Course" spelled out that Russia's "main vital interests in the economic, de-fense, and security areas and in the defense of the rights of Russians" were all to be found on the territory of the CIS, thereby dictating Moscow's priority relations with its member states. The main task was described as "the creation of an economically and politically integrated union of states."[48] In practical terms, by early 1996 Russia expanded its original customs union with Belarus to include Kazakhstan and Kyrgyzstan. At the same time, Russia and Belarus formalized the first of several agreements designed to establish a "union state." Russia's State Duma, the lower house of parliament, went further. In March 1996, it passed two resolutions denouncing and retracting Russia's role in the dissolution of the USSR and the creation of the CIS in December 1991 and, at the same time, it reaffirmed the validity of the Russian vote in the so-called Gorbachev referendum of March 1991 on preserving the Soviet Union.[49] Zatulin's successor as head of the parliamentary CIS committee expressed the sentiments of most of his fellow lawmakers when he explained that his committee's main task was: "To gather together the Great Mother Rus' and, to that end, prepare the necessary legal groundwork."[50]

Ukraine, on the other hand, increasingly moved toward a more balanced foreign policy course between East and West. The Trilateral Statement on denuclearization in January 1994 paved the way for the development of rela-tions with the West, and the following month Ukraine was the first of the CIS countries to sign on to NATO's Partnership for Peace Program. By the spring and summer of 1996, it was clear that Kuchma and his advisers had set a course for Ukraine's "return to Europe." This found its clearest expression in the Ukrainian President's address at a meeting with top foreign affairs officials in July, where he specified that Kyiv's strategic aim was to "integrate" into European and transatlantic organizations while "cooperating" within the framework of the CIS:

I would also like to note that our foreign policy terminology should reflect the principled political line of the state. Along with the strategic choice of adhering to the processes of European integration, Ukraine's firm and consistent line is the line of maximum broadening and deepening of bilateral and multilateral forms of cooperation both within and outside the framework of the CIS while safeguarding the principles of mutual benefit and respect for each other's interests and abiding by the generally recognized norms of international law.[51]

In practice, Kyiv has downplayed the multilateral aspect of its CIS policies and placed primary emphasis on developing and expanding bilateral cooperation with virtually all of the CIS member states.

Ukraine and the Former Republics

Primary consideration has been given to Ukraine's immediate neighbors Belarus and Moldova. The former poses a particular problem because of President Alyaksandr Lukashenka's foreign policy, which is pro-Russian, integrationist, and anti-Western, and his authoritarian and anti-democratic domestic policies. In spite of these constraints, Ukraine has sought to counter the isolation of Belarus, which could have the effect of driving the country further into the arms of Russia, and has worked very closely with Poland to that end. The basic bilateral treaty between the two countries was signed in July 1995, and in May 1997 Kyiv and Minsk signed a state border treaty, the first of its kind in the CIS. Ukraine's interests in Moldova are dictated, above all, by the impact on regional stability of the unresolved dispute over the breakaway Transdniester republic, with its center at Tiraspol where, moreover, Russia's influence remains strong. In addition to Russian peacekeepers, there are still about 3,000 troops of the former 14th Russian Army in the region, and Moscow does not appear to be in a hurry to implement its 1994 agreement with Chişinău on their phased withdrawal. Ukrainians in Moldova overall as well as in the Transdniester region are the largest national minority, a factor that has also been cited by Ukrainian diplomats. During the last few years, Kyiv has played a much more visible role in efforts to mediate the dispute between Chişinău and Tiraspol. In January, 1996, together with the presidents of Russia and Moldova, Kuchma signed a joint declaration that underscored the need for a quick resolution of the Transdniester conflict by defining a special status for the region within Moldova; Ukraine and Russia also assumed the role of guarantors of agreements between the two sides. Both Chişinău and Tiraspol have urged the Ukrainian leadership to send peacekeepers to the region, a proposal that is under consideration in Kyiv, but which would require some form of agreement on Russia's part. In May 1997, Ukraine and Russia added their signatures together with a representative of the Organization for Security and Cooperation in Europe (OSCE) to the Memorandum signed by Moldova and the Transdniester republic on normalization of relations. Further agreements between the four were reached in March 1998. Joint Ukrainian-Moldovan military exercises were held for the first time in June 1998, and plans are underway for a joint peacekeeping battalion similar to the one formed with Poland. Ukraine's relations with Moldova, however, have not been entirely free of problems. In the immediate post-Soviet period, when Moldova's Popular Front still played a prominent role in the country's political life, disputed border claims were a sensitive issue, and it was only in late 1994 that an agreement was signed renouncing mutual border claims. This made it possible to begin talks on delimiting and demarcating the state border, which are nearly completed, and, in turn, facilitated the ratification of the basic bilateral treaty signed in October 1992.

Ukraine's priorities in the Transcaucasus, in addition to political and security issues, have a very clear economic dimension. Specifically, Kyiv has entered into the competition for delivering Caspian oil to international markets by proposing a transit route from Baku in Azerbaijan through Supsa in Georgia and on to a terminal near Odesa. The fact that Georgia and Azerbaijan, together with Moldova and Ukraine, have recently formed the informal grouping frequently referred to as GUAM is an indication not only of the level of cooperation between the four countries, but, as some observers have noted, reveals the degree to which Ukraine has emerged as a respected and influential counterweight to Russia in the CIS. From the standpoints of both Georgia and Azerbaijan, Kyiv's defense of the principle of territorial integrity bolsters their positions with regard to the separatist regimes in Abkhazia and Nagorno-Karabakh, respectively. Tbilisi has a running dispute with Moscow about the role and functions of Russian peacekeepers in Georgia and has asked Kyiv to assume a peacekeeping role. As with Moldova, Ukraine and Georgia are planning a joint peacekeeping battalion that would eventually include Azerbaijan. Among the Central Asian countries, Uzbekistan and Turkmenistan have pursued policies within the context of the CIS that largely overlap with those of Ukraine; the former because of its tough-minded defense of its independence and criticism of Moscow and the latter because of its unswerving principle of neutrality.

The three Baltic states of Estonia, Latvia, and Lithuania are not members of the CIS, and they see themselves to a large extent as already being in Europe as opposed to returning to Europe, which clearly impinges on their foreign policy priorities. Ukraine's relations with Tallinn, Riga, and Vilnius have benefited enormously from Kyiv's policy of supporting the efforts of the Baltic states to join NATO and the European Union.

Needless to say, Ukraine's diplomatic activity in the post-Soviet space is a source of concern for Moscow. In some quarters, Ukraine is perceived as being the driving force behind the emergence of a Tashkent-Baku-Tbilisi-Kyiv axis, whose primary purpose is purported to be the "destruction" of Russia.[52]

The CIS may well be at a turning point in its relatively short history. It is becoming increasingly clear that most of the post-Soviet states, while still tied to Russia in a myriad of ways, have made a great deal of progress in developing a fairly clear sense of purpose and identity. The result has been that they are moving in directions other than Moscow. It has been estimated that by the beginning of 1997 almost 800 multilateral CIS agreements had been signed, but that only somewhat over 200 had been actually implemented.[53] At the October 1997 CIS summit in Chișinău, Yeltsin, who has been reelected to the post of head of the CIS Council of the Heads of States for the last several years, was subjected to harsh criticism for what was described as Russia's inefficient and irrational policies with regard to the CIS. His only supporter was said to be Belarusian President Lukashenka. Russia, it seems, may be drawing the appropriate conclusions. It was agreed that the CIS needed to be reformed. In early 1998, Russian Deputy Prime Minister in charge of CIS affairs Valerii Serov argued that the term "Near Abroad" had to be removed from Moscow's diplomatic parlance because it implied that the independence of the former Soviet republics was a temporary phenomenon and that sooner or later everything would return to the "normal" state of affairs. Serov is reported to have said that it was time to recognize that "a civilized divorce had taken place and that the main thing now was to build our relations on the basis of the realities that are in place."[54] Several months later, in connection with the reorganization of the Russian government, his slot in the Cabinet of Ministers was abolished and matters related to the CIS were transferred to the Ministry of Foreign Affairs. On the face of it, this looks like progress.

Crimea, the Black Sea Fleet, and Sevastopol

The question of Crimea's status, the problem of Sevastopol—concretely, the fact that it was the main base of the Soviet Black Sea Fleet and had a specific administrative status—and the issues, both practical and political, involved in determining the fate of the Black Sea Fleet in the aftermath of the Soviet Union's collapse, have arguably been the most important concrete issues affecting Ukrainian-Russian relations.

The Crimean question is defined by a combination of specific factors that, taken together, have formed one of the most intractable and longstanding problems that confront Ukraine and that impinge directly on the country's stability and on its relations with Russia. First of all, Crimea was formerly part of the Soviet Russian republic. It was transferred to Ukraine in February 1954 by a decree of the Presidium of the USSR Supreme Soviet on the initiative, at least formally, of the Presidium of the Russian Supreme Soviet. Shortly after the collapse of the Soviet Union, reform-minded democrats like Kozyrev argued that the legality of the transfer was highly dubious because the decisions had actually been made by the totalitarian leadership of the discredited Communist Party of the Soviet Union.[55] A second factor is that Crimea is the only administrative region of Ukraine with a majority of ethnic Russians. According to the 1989 census, Russians accounted for 67 percent of the population, while Ukrainians constituted only 25.8 percent; an even larger majority considered Russian to be their native language, including 47.4 percent of the Ukrainians. Today, the proportion of Russians has decreased, largely because of the return of the exiled Crimean Tatars, who numbered 240,000 (9.1 percent of the population) in mid-1996.[56] Third, the Black Sea Fleet is based largely in the Crimean port of Sevastopol, which imparts a military and geostrategic dimension to Russia's policies with regard to the region. But probably the most important factor is simply that most Russians feel that Crimea is Russian territory, that it has little to do with Ukraine, that it should never have been transferred to Ukraine, and that rightfully it should be part of Russia.

Russian claims to Crimea, it will be recalled, were first raised directly in connection with Ukraine's declaration of independence. The first attempt to reverse the 1954 transfer of the peninsula was initiated by Vladimir Lukin, who was then chairman of the Russian parliamentary committee on foreign affairs and foreign economic relations, in January 1992. The committee drafted a resolution "On the Decisions of the Presidium of the USSR Supreme Soviet of 19 February 1954, and the USSR Supreme Soviet of 26 April 1954, Concerning the Removal of Crimea from the RSFSR," which proposed that the lawmakers declare those decisions invalid and void of legal force. At the time, relations between Kyiv and Moscow were severely strained over the Black Sea Fleet and the larger question of the fate of the Soviet military on Ukraine's territory, and the draft resolution was not acted upon so as not to further exacerbate tensions. Not long after, however, a group of nationalist deputies led by Sergei Baburin succeeded in gaining overwhelming approval for a resolution instructing two parliamentary committees to study the constitutionality of the 1954 decisions and suggesting that the Ukrainian parliament conduct a similar review. At the same time, the Russian parliament approved an appeal to its Ukrainian colleagues, urging them to recognize the Black Sea Fleet as an indivisible part of the CIS Strategic Armed Forces. This was done in spite of the fact that the CIS summit in Moscow (16 January) had already agreed that the as yet undetermined part of the Black Sea Fleet that would be transferred to Ukraine did not constitute a strategic force. The degree to which the Russian parliamentarians saw the Crimean and Black Sea Fleet issues as intertwined became apparent from the leaked excerpts of a letter from Lukin to Ruslan Khasbulatov, the parliamentary speaker, recommending, among other things, that Crimea be used as a bargaining chip in the Black Sea Fleet dispute. Lukin argued that after parliament invalidated the 1954 decisions on Crimea, the Ukrainian leadership would be confronted with a dilemma: either it agreed to the transfer of the Black Sea Fleet and its bases to Russia, or Crimea's status would be called into question. The letter also referred to the "special relationship" between Russia and Ukraine, which, Lukin argued, Ukraine wanted to sever by orienting itself toward the West.

In the spring of 1992, Yeltsin sent Rutskoi to Crimea and the breakaway Transdniester republic, where the Vice-President openly claimed that Crimea was part of Russia. Asked if he was aware of military equipment being transferred from Crimea to Russia, Rutskoi responded sarcastically: "Why should we transfer anything from Russia to Russia?"[57] His remarks caused a stir in Ukraine and coincided with a warning from Yeltsin that any attempt on Ukraine's part to change the status of the Black Sea Fleet unilaterally would result in its being placed under Russian jurisdiction and subsequently transferred to the CIS strategic forces. Kravchuk, in the meantime, signed a decree on 5 April 1992 on measures to create Ukraine's armed forces, which presupposed a navy based on the Black Sea Fleet. This prompted Yeltsin to issue his own decree making good his earlier warning. The war of decrees was suspended at the end of April as part of an agreement reached in Odesa that committed both sides to a moratorium on unilateral actions and provided for a working group to prepare a treaty on the Black Sea Fleet. At the same time, nationalist Russian lawmakers attempted to place the Crimean question and the Black Sea Fleet issue on the agenda of the Sixth Congress of Russian People's Deputies. The following month, on 21 May, a closed session of the Russian parliament adopted a resolution declaring the 1954 decisions on Crimea "without the force of law" and urged that the Crimean problem be resolved through Russian-Ukrainian negotiations, with Crimea's participation, and on the basis of "the will of its population." It was against this background that Baburin was quoted as telling the Ukrainian ambassador in Moscow: "Either Ukraine reunites with Russia, or there will be war."[58]

The first Kravchuk-Yeltsin summit in Dagomys in June 1992 did not produce a solution to the problem of the Black Sea Fleet, stipulating only that discussions should continue on the formation of Ukrainian and Russian naval forces on the basis of the Black Sea Fleet. The two leaders met again in Yalta in August and decided that the Black Sea Fleet would be divided after 1995. In the interim, it was removed from CIS subordination and placed under the direct command of both presidents. The June 1993 summit in Moscow resolved that the "practical formation" of the Russian and Ukrainian navies was to begin in September and that the fleet was to be divided evenly in accordance with further agreements. The Massandra summit in September 1993 ended in confusion, with the two sides backing conflicting interpretations of what had transpired. The controversy focused on whether or not the Ukrainian side had actually agreed to surrender its half of the Black Sea Fleet and its infrastructure in return for the cancellation of all or part of Ukraine's debts to Russia. The first more or less concrete agreement was reached in Moscow in April 1994, stipulating that the Russian and Ukrainian fleets would be based separately and that Ukraine would receive 15–20 percent of the warships and was followed by a more detailed agreement in Sochi in June 1995.[59] None of these documents, it should be pointed out, were ratified by either side.

Having "disposed" of the Crimean question, at the end of 1992 the Russian Congress of People's Deputies turned its attention to the status of Sevastopol. Acting on the basis of a little-known decree adopted in October 1948 by the Presidium of the Russian Supreme Soviet that gave the city a separate adminis- trative and economic republican status, the lawmakers argued that because Sevastopol was not, strictly speaking, a part of Crimea it, therefore, was never actually transferred to Ukraine. Accordingly, in July 1993, the Russian parlia- ment passed a resolution, without a single dissenting vote, affirming Sevastopol's "Russian federal status," providing for its financing from the Russian budget, and calling for negotiations with Ukraine on the city's status as the main base of the single Black Sea Fleet. Dmytro Pavlychko, then chairman of Ukraine's parliamentary committee on foreign affairs, qualified the move as tantamount to a declaration of war; Yeltsin and the Russian Ministry of Foreign Affairs denounced the resolution. For the first time in the Ukrainian-Russian dispute, the international community, including the United Nations, publicly criticized Russia for violating internationally accepted norms and agreements.

The new bicameral Russian parliament elected at the end of 1993 was considerably more moderate than its predecessor, although it, too, reacted to developments in Ukraine. In connection with Crimea's decision in May 1994 to, in effect, renew its claim to independence by restoring its earlier constitu- tion, the State Duma adopted an appeal to the Ukrainian parliament cautioning against any forceful moves in the conflict between Simferopol and Kyiv, but at the same time praising the Ukrainian leadership's handling of the situation and promising to promote a constructive compromise. Later in the year, however, prompted by the Ukrainian parliament's revocation of a host of Crimean laws judged to be in violation of the Ukrainian constitution, Russian lawmakers approved a declaration saying that, although they recognized the reality of Crimea being part of Ukraine, they were concerned by Kyiv's actions and suggested that these could jeopardize the ongoing negotiations on the Black Sea Fleet and the signing and ratification of the basic Russian-Ukrainian treaty. Russia's position on Crimea was seriously weakened by its campaign in Chechnya, although this did not prevent Luzhkov from declaring Sevastopol a district of Moscow while on a visit to the city. The Ukrainian leadership took advantage of Russia's predicament in the spring of 1995 by abolishing Crimea's constitution and its presidency and temporarily subordinating the Crimean government to the central government. Representatives of the Russian government were cautious in their reactions, stating that Crimea was an inter- nal Ukrainian matter. The State Duma, however, did issue a statement express- ing its concern about the impact of these developments on Russian-Ukrainian relations, referring specifically again to the Black Sea Fleet talks and the negotiations on restructuring the Ukrainian debt. Less than a month later, however, Yeltsin, in his first response to Kyiv's actions, insisted that the treaty with Ukraine could not be signed until Russia was assured that the rights of the Crimeans were being respected; later, he added that the unresolved problem of the Black Seat Fleet also precluded his visit to Kyiv. At about the same time, Kozyrev made the sensational statement, without referring specifically to Crimea, that in some cases the use of direct military force might be necessary to protect Russia's compatriots abroad.[60] In the aftermath of a meeting between Yeltsin and Ukraine's acting Prime Minister Yevhen Marchuk in mid-April, it became clear that the Black Sea Fleet was the main obstacle to the signing of the basic treaty. Russia's point of departure was that all of Sevastopol should serve as the base for the Black Sea Fleet, which meant, in effect, that Ukraine would have to yield jurisdiction over the city to Russia. The Ukrainian leadership refused to yield on this point as a matter of principle. The Russian parliament, in the meantime, continued to play an obstructionist role. In October and December 1996, it passed several resolutions and statements that called into question the division of the Black Sea Fleet, the status of Sevastopol, and, indeed, Crimea as a whole. By this time, however, it appears that Moscow's concern about Kyiv's Western orientation—specifically, its courting of NATO, overshadowed all other issues.

Conclusion

The status of Crimea and Sevastopol have been primary concerns for Russia's elected representatives, who accurately reflect the mood of their electors.[61] For someone like Luzhkov, whom many observers consider to be the favorite to succeed Yeltsin, Sevastopol, in particular, has become something in the nature of a preoccupation. After one of his frequent visits there in early 1998, the Moscow Mayor articulated his position in a very straightforward manner: "Relations between Russia and Ukraine will not be clear until a question of principle, the status of the eternally Russian lands Crimea and Sevastopol, is solved."[62] In the final analysis, however, neither Crimea nor Sevastopol could stand in the way of concluding the basic treaty between Ukraine and Russia, which is the required initial step paving the way for the "normalization" of relations. In some sense, Russia had little choice but to acquiesce. Its hands were tied by commitments to respect Ukraine's territorial integrity in international agreements such as the Trilateral Statement (January 1994) and the Budapest agreements of the OSCE (December 1994). More important, however, was the realization that Ukraine's "European choice" posed the danger of completely "losing" Ukraine unless concessions were made. In February 1995, the treaty was finally initialed after Moscow dropped its insistence on a clause providing for dual citizenship and a compromise was reached on a clear formulation of what constitutes the inviolability of borders. This left the Black Sea Fleet as the only serious outstanding issue. Eventually, in early 1997, Russia abandoned its previous policy of linking an agreement on the Black Sea Fleet to the treaty, which paved the way for the long awaited state visit by the Russian president to the Ukrainian capital and the ceremonial signing. In February 1998, Kuchma made his first state visit to Russia and signed a wide-ranging and long-term program of economic cooperation. But problems still remain. Most important, the State Duma has given no indication that it is prepared to ratify the treaty. On the contrary, it has demonstrated that it is ready to exploit non-issues such as the alleged linguistic discrimination of Russians and Russian-speakers in Ukraine as a pretext for rejecting the document. The first concrete steps have been taken on delimiting and demarcating the state border between the two countries, which eventually should result in a formal treaty, although it is clear that the Russian side prefers so-called transparent borders and would like to formalize the concept of CIS "external borders." Specialists on both sides have decided that further negotiations are apparently necessary in order to implement the base-line agreements on the Black Sea Fleet. The discussions on the debts and assets of the former Soviet Union seem to be going nowhere. In the meantime, no one is quite sure how Ukrainian-Russian relations will develop in the post-Yeltsin era.

NOTES

1.   Admittedly, something approximating international relations between Soviet republics had already made its appearance during the late *perestroika* period. Specifically, in November 1990, Leonid Kravchuk and Boris Yeltsin, at the time heads of their respective parliaments, signed a treaty in Kyiv that had all the accoutrements of an inter-state document, with each side "recognizing the other as sovereign states." For the text, see *Radians'ka Ukraina* 21 November 1990, and below, Appendix A, pages 319–29.

2.   The treaty was signed in Kyiv on 31 May 1997 and ratified by the Ukrainian parliament by an overwhelming majority on 14 January 1998. As of July 1998, the Russian parliament had not ratified the document. For the text of the treaty, see *Uriadovyi kur'ier* 3 June 1997.

3.   For the texts of the three agreements and the protocol signed by the then Prime Ministers Viktor Chernomyrdin and Pavlo Lazarenko, see *Vestnik voennoi informatsii* 10 (October 1997): 15–18; 11 (November 1997): 9–10; and 1 (January 1998): 17–19. For an analysis, see James Sherr, "Russia-Ukraine *Rapprochement*?: The Black Sea Fleet Accords," *Survival* 39(3) Autumn 1997: 33–50.

4.   *Nezavisimaia gazeta* 20 February 1997 and 5 February 1997, respectively.

5.   *Nezavisimaia gazeta* 16 January 1997.

6.   *Izvestiia* 24 February 1998.

7.   *Moskovskie novosti* 22 December 1991.

8.   Roman Szporluk, "Belarus, Ukraine and the Russian Question: A Comment," *Post-Soviet Affairs* 9(4) October–December 1993: 366.

9.   Interfax, 27 October 1997. This figure has remained fairly stable. In June 1993, a poll conducted among Russia's urban population yielded a 63 percent affirmative response to the same question. See *Novoe vremia* 37 (September 1993): 6.

10.   For the text, see *Krasnaia zvezda* 22 November 1997.

11.   A. I. Miller, "Obraz Ukrainy i ukraintsev v rossiiskoi presse posle raspada SSSR," *Politicheskie issledovaniia* 1996 (2): 135.

12.   *Kievskie vedomosti* 28 May 1997. This problem is discussed in some detail by Roman Szporluk, "Reflections on Ukraine after 1994: The Dilemmas of Nationhood," *The Harriman Review* 7(7–9) March–May 1994: 5–6.

13.   S. M. Samuilov, "O nekotorykh amerikanskikh stereotipakh v otnoshenii Ukrainy," *SShA—ekonomika, politika, ideologiia* 1997 (3): 89. See also the rejoinder by A. Garan' [O. Haran'], "O 'rasizme' Grushevskogo i

ukrainskom natsionalizme kak 'pol'skoi intrige,'" *SShA—ekonomika, politika, ideologiia* 1998 (1): 125–27. Readers interested in a representative sample of Russian interpretations of "Ukrainian separatism" are referred to the recently published *Ukrainskii separatizm v Rossii. Ideologiia natsional'nogo raskola. Sbornik* (Moscow, 1998).

14. *Izvestiia* 5 March 1998.

15. See his introductory chapter "Russkie i ukraintsy: trudnye otnosheniia brat'ev," in Dmitrii Furman, ed. and comp., *Ukraina i Rossiia: obshchestva i gosudarstva* (Moscow, 1997), 16.

16. I have in mind, specifically, the scholarly and publicistic works of Aleksei Miller and Arkadii Moshes. Miller is a specialist on 19th and early 20th century Ukraine. He contributed to the Furman volume cited above ("Rossiia i Ukraina v XIX–nachale XX v.: nepredopredelennaia istoriia," 71–87) and edited, together with V. F. Reprintsev and B. N. Floria, and contributed to a collection of articles on Ukrainian-Russian relations entitled *Rossiia–Ukraina: istoriia vzaimootneshenii* (Moscow, 1997). Moshes specializes in contemporary Ukrainian affairs. See, among others, his *Vnutripoliticheskoe razvitie i vneshniaia politika Ukrainy v 1991–1995 gg.* (Moscow, 1996) [=Doklady Instituta Evropy, Rossiiskaia Akademiia Nauk, 27].

17. Quoted in the *Financial Times* 27 March 1996.

18. *Kievskie vedomosti* 28 April 1995.

19. *Nezavisimaia gazeta* 27 February 1997.

20. Gennadii Ziuganov, *Geografiia pobedy. Osnovy rossiiskoi geopolitiki* (Moscow, 1997), 248–49.

21. For the text, see *Literaturna Ukraina* 6 September 1990.

22. *Vechirnii Kyiv* 21 November 1990.

23. *Molod' Ukrainy* 2 December 1990.

24. For the text, see *Radians'ka Ukraina* 28 September 1990.

25. *Komsomol'skoe znamia* 6 May 1991.

26. *Los Angeles Times* 31 July 1991.

27. For the text, see *Rossiiskaia gazeta* 27 September 1991.

28. Reuters, 27 August 1991.

29. Central Soviet Television, 27 August 1991.

30. TASS, 29 August 1991.

31. For the text, see *Molod' Ukrainy* 30 August 1991.

32. *Russkaia mysl'* (Paris) 11 October 1991. A year earlier, *Komsomol'skaia pravda* and *Literaturnaia gazeta* published Solzhenitsyn's well-known

brochure "Kak nam obustroit' Rossiiu?" in which he proposed that a new "Russia" called the Russian Union be formed on the basis of the Russian, Ukrainian, and the Belarusian republics as well as a part of Kazakhstan.

33. *Le Figaro* 4 December 1991, and AFP, 9 January 1992.

34. For a detailed discussion, see Roman Solchanyk, "Russia, Ukraine, and the Imperial Legacy," *Post-Soviet Affairs* 9(4) October–December 1993: 353–54. For an excellent treatment of Yeltsin's position on the preservation of the Soviet Union, see Marc Zlotnik, "Yeltsin and Gorbachev: The Politics of Confrontation," in Mark Kramer, ed., *The Collapse of the Soviet Union* (forthcoming).

35. See the interviews with Kravchuk in *Paris Match* 26 December 1991; Russian Television, 11 February 1992; *Sobesednik* 15 April 1992; and Leonid Kravchuk, *Ostanni dni imperii . . . pershi roky nadii* (Kyiv, 1994), 11–37.

36. See Yeltsin's address to the Sixth Congress of Russian People's Deputies in *Rossiiskaia gazeta* 23 April 1992.

37. ITAR-TASS, 14 December 1992.

38. For the texts, see *Holos Ukrainy* 14 December 1991 and 21 December 1991, respectively.

39. *Nezavisimaia gazeta* 12 February 1992, and AFP, 20 February 1992.

40. *Uriadovyi kur'ier* 16 October 1992.

41. *Nezavisimaia gazeta* 28 October 1994.

42. *Izvestiia* (Moscow evening ed.) 7 August 1992.

43. *Diplomaticheskii vestnik* 3–4 (February 1994): 28–30.

44. *Rossiiskaia gazeta* 12 January 1994.

45. *Nezavisimaia gazeta* 24 March 1995.

46. *Moskovskie novosti* 3–10 April 1994.

47. ITAR-TASS, 9 June 1994.

48. For the text, see *Diplomaticheskii vestnik* 10 (October 1995): 3–6.

49. For the texts, see *Sobranie zakonodatel'stva Rossiiskoi Federatsii* 13 (25 March 1996): 3153–3154.

50. *Delovoi mir* 6 February 1997.

51. *Uriadovyi kur'ier* 18 July 1996.

52. See the report entitled "SNG: Nachalo ili konets istorii?" authored by Konstantin Zatulin and Andranik Migranian in *Nezavisimaia gazeta*, 26 March 1997.

53. *Novoe vremia* 3 (26 January 1997): 4.

54. *Izvestiia*, 22 January 1998. See also *The Economist* 31 January 1998: 53.

55. TASS, 23 January 1992, and *Rossiiskaia gazeta* 24 January 1992.

56. S. M. Chervonnaia, "Vozvrashchenie i integratsiia krymskikh tatar v Krymu: 1990-e gody," in V. A. Tishkov, ed., *Vynuzhdennye migranty: integratsiia i vozvrashchenie* (Moscow, 1997), 148. For somewhat different figures, see Jane I. Dawson, "Ethnicity, Ideology and Geopolitics in Crimea," *Communist and Post-Communist Studies* 30(4) December 1997: 429.

57. Quoted in *Nezavisimaia gazeta* 7 April 1992.

58. *Izvestiia* (Moscow evening. ed.) 26 May 1992.

59. These agreements are conveniently reprinted in S. P. Kudriashov, S. O. Odarych, Iu. M. Orobets', and M. V. Tomenko, *Karta Sevastopolia: triumf prezydentiv, trahediia Ukrainy* (Kyiv, 1997). For a detailed discussion of the Black Sea Fleet question, see Nikolai Savchenko, *Anatomiia neobiavlennoi voiny* (Kyiv, 1997).

60. *The Washington Post* 19 April 1995, and the *Los Angeles Times* 21 April 1995.

61. A nationwide survey in December 1996 showed that 70 percent of respondents felt that Sevastopol should be a part of Russia. See *NG-Stsenarii* 10 April 1997.

62. Quoted in *Trud* 24 February 1998.

4

Ukraine and East Central Europe

STEPHEN R. BURANT

In the aftermath of the failed coup attempt in Moscow in late August 1991, Ukrainian leaders, who for more than a year had been attempting to loosen the reins of Moscow over their republic, firmly set out on a course to achieve independence. In contrast to the Baltic republics, whose independence during the interwar period had given them a distinct status within the Soviet Union in the eyes of the West, Ukraine—because it was perceived to have been under the sway of the Russians (and only the Russians) for centuries—had not established itself as a nation meriting independence. Moreover, many Western opinion-makers and policymakers even questioned whether Ukrainians were a people distinct from the Russians. Thus, Kyiv had both to convince other governments to recognize Ukraine's independence and to persuade them that Ukrainians were a nation separate from the Russians.

Central European states—Poland, Czechoslovakia, Hungary, and Romania—were essential to Ukrainian efforts to achieve these two goals. They had all undergone anti-communist revolutions and themselves were all seeking to "rejoin Europe," a euphemism for integration into trans-Atlantic and West European institutions. Like Ukraine, the Central European states were trying to leave Moscow's orbit. The Central Europeans recognized that an independent Ukraine was a *sine qua non* for their own independence from Moscow—with Ukrainian statehood, Russian borders were now several hundred kilometers farther east, except for Kaliningrad Oblast.

As a result of the post-World War II settlement, Ukraine had gained significant territory from Poland, Czechoslovakia, and Romania. In addition, there were ethnic Ukrainian minorities in Poland and Romania, as well as ethnic Polish, Hungarian, and Romanian minorities in Ukraine. An independent Ukraine thus needed to secure the recognition of its borders by these former Soviet satellites and to ensure adequate treatment for ethnic Ukrainian minorities in those neighboring states where they lived. Toward these objectives, Kyiv needed to assuage concerns in the Central European states regarding their own ethnic minorities in Ukraine. Moreover, to the extent that Ukraine could normalize relations with its western neighbors, it could demonstrate to the West that it deserved aid and integration into European institutions. Similarly, the Central European states needed to normalize relations with Ukraine as evidence that they would not "import" into NATO or West European organizations conflicts over borders or ethnic minorities. Normalized relations between Ukraine and its Central European neighbors also would preclude efforts by

Moscow to exploit any differences to Ukraine's detriment—and to the detriment of the Central European states. Most important, for both Ukraine and the Central European states, normalizing relations with each other was a means to reduce uncertainty—that is, insecurity—at a time when the postwar European order was undergoing a profound transformation.

It is the purpose of this chapter to examine these issues in detail. The study begins with a discussion of efforts by the Kravchuk and Kuchma administrations to establish a Central European identity for Ukraine through membership in Central European groups and organizations. President Leonid Kravchuk put much emphasis on this effort; he largely failed. President Leonid Kuchma, initially perceived as more pro-Russian than his predecessor, has achieved far more success in this respect. From these general considerations, the study turns to an examination of the four sets of bilateral relations between Ukraine and its Central European neighbors.

The Issue of Identity

The identities of individuals or groups are established by the entities to which they belong and, some analysts argue, by the entities to which they aspire to belong.[1] The Kravchuk administration, to establish an identity for the Ukrainian nation distinct from Russia in the eyes of the West and its own people and to gain political support from Central European countries, claimed a Central European identity for Ukraine.

Ukrainian elites perceived in the early 1990s, and continue to perceive today, that Russians cannot imagine Ukraine existing apart from Russia. The Russian stance has spawned a series of disagreements between Russia and Ukraine, including territorial claims against Ukraine by prominent Russian leaders and the Russian parliament and disputes over the Black Sea Fleet and its infrastructure in Sevastopol. In view of these conflicts, Ukraine until early 1994 was unwilling to hand over to Russia its nuclear weapons. Failure to do so, however, meant that the West, already skeptical of Ukrainian efforts to secure a lasting independence from Russia, was reluctant to offer Ukraine political and economic aid to bolster its statehood against Russian threats. Moreover, Ukraine, though a participant in the Commonwealth of Independent States (CIS), doubted the effectiveness of that organization in obtaining a "civilized divorce" of former Soviet republics from Moscow and tended to see it as a vehicle for re-establishing Russian domination over the post-Soviet space.

Central Europe appeared to represent a way out of Ukraine's isolation. In 1990 Foreign Minister of the Ukrainian SSR, Anatoliy Zlenko, averred that:

> a common history existing a thousand years and a deep cultural, linguistic, and ideological closeness have linked us with neighboring Poland. The western regions of Ukraine and the eastern provinces of Poland . . . are similar in makeup of population and economy . . . Our border with Czechoslovakia,

Hungary, and Romania is shorter than that with Poland. But there are also
. . . ethnic . . . influences, economic ties, trade, mixed marriages, the common
Danube waters . . . .[2]

Here Zlenko claims a historical, economic, and cultural relationship between
Ukraine and Central European nations, with the implication that Russian domination cut off Ukraine from this affiliation. In line with such claims Kyiv
sought to enter the Visegrád triangle.

The triangle emerged at the 15 February 1991 summit in Visegrád, Hungary, of Hungarian Prime Minister József Antall, Polish President Lech
Wałęsa, and Czechoslovak President Václav Havel. These leaders resolved to
coordinate their efforts at creating liberal democracies, market economies, and
civil societies. They also wished to share experiences in preparing for membership in the European Community and NATO and to try to resist Soviet, and
later Russian, efforts to keep their countries under Moscow's wing.

Bronisław Geremek, then chairman of the Polish Sejm's foreign affairs
commission, asserted in December 1991 that Mykhailo Horyn, at the time a
vice-chairman of the mass national-democratic organization Rukh and a Ukrainian parliament deputy, had told him that "Ukraine is very interested in joining
the triangle Warsaw-Prague-Budapest."[3] At a conference in Warsaw in February 1992, attended by prominent Ukrainian policymakers, as well as their
Polish counterparts, the Ukrainians pushed hard for Visegrád membership.[4]
President Kravchuk, concerned about Moscow's reaction, in early 1992 hesi-
tated to express outright Ukraine's desire for membership in the triangle.
Nonetheless, during his summit in Warsaw with Wałęsa in May 1992, he
pointed out that a "quadrilateral is a more complete geometrical figure than a
triangle and provides more possibilities."[5]

Ukraine was obviously unsuccessful in gaining acceptance into the Visegrád
group. Wałęsa was sympathetic to Ukrainian concerns, though other Polish
officials, notably then Foreign Minister Krzysztof Skubiszewski, were less so.
Antall and Havel opposed Ukraine's membership.[6] The ostensible reasons
were the need to maintain group cohesion and the lag between Poland, Czechoslovakia, and Hungary, on the one hand, and Ukraine, on the other, in implementing political and economic reforms. But several other considerations
doubtless made the Visegrád leaders loath to embrace Ukraine. First, these
countries had gone to great lengths to establish a Central European identity for
themselves, and arguments such as Zlenko's failed to convince them; they
believed that admitting a former Soviet republic would have impeded their
efforts to forge this identity. Second, inclusion of Ukraine would have drawn
Russian wrath. Third, these countries in large measure were taking cues from
the West on foreign and security policy; they could not count on Western
backing for such a step.

Ukraine's lack of success in gaining Visegrád membership was a policy
failure for Kravchuk. A similar failure was Ukraine's inability to garner support for the creation of a "security and stability zone" in East-Central Europe in

1993. Kravchuk first proposed this idea in late February in Budapest after meetings with Antall and President Árpád Göncz.[7] The Ukrainians, believing that all states lying between Russia and NATO faced similar security problems and that the West would do nothing in the near term to resolve them, proposed that Austria, Poland, Ukraine, Belarus, the Czech Republic, Slovakia, Hungary, Romania, Moldova, Bulgaria, and the Baltic states combine to ensure their own security. The goals of the effort were quite modest: all states would agree to respect each other's sovereignty and territorial integrity, renounce territorial claims and the use of force against each other, cooperate in preventing conflicts, promote disarmament and weapons controls, and develop border cooperation.[8] Though the stated objective was to enhance the security of the member states, the creation of a group of such states having Ukraine as a member would have strengthened Ukraine's claims to be a Central European state, not a "Eurasian" one linked to Russia and the CIS. It was this very possibility that led the Russians and the West, which saw the zone as an effort at isolating Russia, to criticize the concept, though the Ukrainians advertised the zone as a "bridge" between Russia and Western Europe.

Among the prospective members, Hungary alone expressed support for the concept.[9] Owing to Poland's weight in the region, its backing was crucial, and the Ukrainians lobbied the Poles hard in the run-up to the second Wałęsa-Kravchuk summit, which took place in May 1993 in Kyiv. Though Wałęsa had earlier raised the possibility of creating a "NATO-B" among Central and East European states—a proposal of which the Ukrainians reminded the Poles—Warsaw was not interested because it had already decided to pursue NATO membership. In addition, the United States and NATO apparently persuaded Wałęsa to try to dissuade Kravchuk from pursuing the security zone idea.[10] Neither Wałęsa nor Kravchuk mentioned it publicly; the summit's communiqué noted the "Kravchuk initiative" would be entrusted "to responsible officials in the foreign ministries," effectively killing the idea.[11]

During the Kravchuk administration, Ukraine's lone success in achieving membership in a group of Central European states came with the formation of the Eastern Carpathian Euroregion (ECE). The Council of Europe has registered more than thirty Euroregions, which are meant to encourage open borders between states that have been enemies in the past and involve projects in trade, transportation, and culture undertaken by border districts of neighboring countries. On 14 February 1993, in Debrecen, Hungary, the foreign ministers of Hungary, Ukraine, Poland, and Slovakia signed an agreement to set up the ECE, composed of several Hungarian and Slovak jurisdictions, Ukraine's Transcarpathia oblast, and two provinces (województwa) in Poland.[12] For Ukraine, the undertaking assumed an importance that outweighed the rather modest nature of the project: Zlenko in Debrecen said that owing to the formation of the ECE, Ukraine was beginning the process of integrating into Europe.[13]

By the time the electoral campaign for the Ukrainian presidency began in 1994, Kravchuk had little to show for his efforts to develop a Central European identity for his country. Kuchma, who won the office in July 1994, stemmed from eastern Ukraine, which is more culturally, economically, and politically oriented toward Russia than the central and western regions. He refrained from calling Ukraine a Central European country, advocating instead a reinvigoration of economic ties with the CIS in general and with Russia in particular. More important, he spoke throughout the campaign of Ukraine's cultural and historical ties to Russia. In his inaugural address Kuchma outlined his conception of Ukraine's place in the so-called Eurasian sphere:

> Historically, Ukraine is part of the Eurasian cultural and economic space. Ukraine's vitally important national interests are concentrated on this territory of the former Soviet Union . . . . We are also linked with those countries— former republics of the Soviet Union—by traditional scientific, cultural, informational, and even family ties. Ukraine's self-isolation and its voluntary refusal to campaign vigorously for its own interests in the Eurasian space was a serious political mistake . . . I am convinced that Ukraine can assume the role of one of the leaders of Eurasian economic integration and establish civilized, mutually favorable relations between interested parties.[14]

This vision was diametrically opposed to that of western Ukrainians, who viewed Kuchma as oriented toward a "fraternal union with Russia."[15] Central European policymakers doubtless also had such fears. However, Kuchma's pro-Russian orientation did not last long. First, in October 1994 Kuchma announced a comprehensive reform program to accelerate marketization, stabilize Ukraine's financial and monetary systems, and integrate Ukraine into the world economy. Such a policy necessitated a change of focus: Kuchma made clear that Ukraine would continue to pursue ties with Russia and the CIS, but not at the expense of ties with the United States and Western Europe, in which Kyiv placed great hopes for assistance to facilitate these reforms. Second, because Kravchuk in January 1994 had signed the Trilateral Statement, according to which Ukraine agreed to ratify the Nuclear Non-Proliferation Treaty as a non-nuclear state, the West was far more willing to render such aid. Third, Kuchma and his team, like Kravchuk and his advisers, quickly found that Russian leaders had not shed their imperial mentality and were not willing to treat Ukraine as an equal partner.

In 1994–1995 Kuchma visited all G-7 states except one.[16] In early 1995, according to the foreign economic relations ministry's Draft Guidelines for International Activities of Ukraine, cooperation with the CIS countries and the Baltic states was the first priority, followed by relations with the European Union (EU). The third priority was Canada, the United States, and Japan. Central Europe was in fourth place, along with China, the Persian Gulf countries, and the newly industrialized countries of Asia.[17] For their part, the Central European countries, poor by Western standards and undergoing their ɔnomic transformation, had no resources to assist Ukraine's transition ᴛᴏ ᴛʜᴇ ᴍarket and little interest in Ukrainian goods.

But by pursuing ties with West European countries and the United States, Ukrainian leaders assuaged concerns of Central European policymakers that they might reorient Ukraine toward the CIS and Russia. In addition, Kuchma made clear Ukraine's desire eventually to enter the EU and, in September 1995, Ukraine gained membership in the Council of Europe, firmly putting Ukraine on a course of European integration.[18] This goal, and the steps Ukraine was taking to achieve it, created the possibility of collaboration between Ukraine and the Central European states, which had consistently pursued such a policy themselves since 1990.

Central European leaders responded by approving Ukrainian membership in the Central European Initiative (CEI) in September 1995. Ukraine had sought membership in the *Hexagonale*, a predecessor of the CEI, in 1992 and gained associate membership in the CEI in 1994. The group undertakes projects in transportation, energy, and science and technology; one of its objectives is to prepare non-EU members for participation in that organization, a mission from which Ukraine should benefit considerably.[19]

In October 1995, then Prime Minister Yevhen Marchuk, in Warsaw for a CEI meeting, acknowledged Ukraine's traditional Central European ties when he said "Ukraine and Poland are neighbors sharing a common history."[20] In early 1996 Kuchma began doing so as well; in a speech in Geneva on 28 March, Kuchma said that

> as a significant part of Central and Eastern Europe, Ukraine regards the deepening of European integration as one of its foreign policy priorities, wishing as it does to occupy a worthy place in its geopolitical environment and promote democratization and Europeanization .... Ukraine's strategy lies in approaching common European structures in two parallel ways, directly and through membership in Central European institutions.[21]

Kuchma, who by mid-1996 was regularly referring to Ukraine as a Central European country, had come to use the same arguments in support of this claim that Zlenko had used six years earlier.[22]

The effort to focus on relations with Central Europe, and thereby secure an identity for Ukraine as a Central European country, met with another success in June 1996 as Kuchma participated in the fourth informal meeting of Central European presidents, which took place that year in Łańcut, Poland. President Aleksander Kwaśniewski, taking advantage of the prerogative accorded the sponsor to invite a new participant, turned to Kuchma, over the objections of some of the other presidents, notably Havel.[23] Though the session was only informal, it was an important symbolic step for the Ukrainian leadership. Kuchma, who was delighted to be at "such an authoritative forum of countries," expressed particular gratitude to Kwaśniewski for "pulling Ukraine into Europe."[24]

Several factors account for the invitation. Central European countries—especially Poland and Hungary, but also Germany—had come to recognize that Ukraine would play a key role in the evolving European security system. Moreover, Ukraine's participation was a signal that Kyiv—by virtue of its efforts at economic and political reform, as well as its policies toward ethnic minorities—ought to be considered down the road for EU membership. (By contrast, then President Ion Iliescu of Romania, whose government pursued restrictive policies toward its ethnic minorities and made claims against Ukrainian territory, did not participate.) Finally, Kuchma's presence signaled to the Russians that the Central Europeans would try to assist Ukraine in "rejoining Europe."

Less successful have been Ukrainian efforts to gain membership in the Central European Free Trade Agreement (CEFTA)—composed of Poland, the Czech Republic, Slovakia, Hungary, Slovenia, and Romania—which emerged from the Visegrád group. CEFTA has brought down trade barriers among its members but is an organization that may not last, in view of the likelihood that most of its participants will join the EU in the next decade. Ukraine's chances of entering this organization anytime soon are virtually nil: requirements include membership in the World Trade Organization (WTO), which Ukraine as of mid-1998 had yet to join; associate membership in the EU (Ukraine in 1994 signed a partnership and cooperation agreement with the EU, which is not so far-reaching); and bilateral free trade agreements with all CEFTA members. The larger problem is that economic reforms in Ukraine still lag far behind those of the CEFTA states; thus, most members have not placed a high priority on Ukraine's accession to this group, though they support it in principle.

Ukraine and Poland

Poles and Ukrainians share a history that is doubtless as complex as the history of Ukrainian-Russian relations. The extension of Polish domination over parts of Ukrainian territory dates to the mid-fourteenth century. By the time of the formation of the Polish-Lithuanian Commonwealth in 1569, virtually all Ukrainian lands were under direct Polish rule, which lasted in the western regions to the partitions of Poland in the late eighteenth century. Social, economic, and religious differences proved intractable, and led to numerous uprisings by the peasantry and Cossacks, especially the Khmelnytskyi insurrection in 1648, that have colored mutual perceptions of Poles and Ukrainians to this day.

In the 19th and early 20th centuries, Polish and Ukrainian interests, both in the Russian Empire and especially in Austrian Galicia under the Habsburg Monarchy, were irreconcilable: Polish nationalists dreamed of reconstituting Poland within the boundaries the Commonwealth had in 1772, before the first partition. Ukrainian nationalists, active mainly in Austrian Galicia, condemned the impact of the centuries-long Polish rule on Ukrainian lands and identified with popular rebellions against the Poles.

After World War I, Poland gained dominion over what is today western Ukraine (the oblasts of Lviv, Volhynia, Rivne, Ternopil, and Ivano-Frankivsk); more than five million Ukrainians lived in the Polish Second Republic. Ukrainian society exhibited a basic hostility to the Polish state; the regime, in turn, attempted to Polonize Ukrainian lands. During 1941–1945, the Polish Home Army and the Ukrainian Insurgent Army fought for control over western Ukraine; tens of thousands of civilians on both sides died in the fighting, though the Poles suffered more casualties than the Ukrainians.[25] In 1947 Polish military forces forcibly resettled 150,000–250,000 Ukrainians from southeastern Poland to the western and northern parts of the country, in what is known as "Operation Vistula" (*Akcja Wisła*).

Soviet and Polish communist propaganda exploited this historical legacy to ensure that the populations of both Poland and Ukraine looked to Moscow for protection from each other. According to Teodoziy Starak, Ukraine's envoy to Poland in the immediate post-independence period, Ukrainian schoolchildren read how "Ukraine was always on the verge of destruction and the Poles were always just about to eat us up, were it not for the goodness of Moscow, which saved us."[26] In Poland, official propaganda depicted Ukrainians as bandits and murderers.[27] In view of this propaganda, which only reinforced preexisting negative stereotypes, it is not surprising that a 1992 public opinion poll showed that Poles regarded Ukraine least favorably among a group of countries, rating it even below Russia.[28]

In the 1960s and 1970s, however, Polish émigrés were rethinking Poland's relationship to the Ukrainians, as well as to the Lithuanians and Belarusians. Articles in the Paris-based journal *Kultura* advocated reconciliation between Poland and its eastern neighbors and urged renunciation of any effort to regain Lviv, Vilnius, or the Belarusian lands Poland had held during the interwar period. *Kultura* strongly influenced the Polish opposition in the late 1970s and 1980s.

Some of the very people who wrote on this topic in the underground journals (for example, Jacek Kuron, Adam Michnik, Antoni Macierewicz, and Grzegorz Kostrzewa-Zorbas) entered positions of power and influence in the Polish government and Sejm after Solidarity took over from the communists in 1989. The Solidarity government—drawing on the ideas of *Kultura*; taking advantage of the sovereignty declarations by the RSFSR, the Ukrainian SSR, and the Belarusian SSR in mid-1990; and looking toward the possible collapse of the Soviet Union—in 1990 implemented the so-called two-track policy in relations with Moscow and the Soviet republics. In testimony before the Polish Senate, Foreign Minister Krzysztof Skubiszewski said Poland would try to achieve relations with the republics corresponding to their degree of independence from the center, adding that in some respects these ties would resemble relations between independent states. In mid-October 1990 Skubiszewski met with officials from the Soviet government, as well as with those from the RSFSR, Ukraine, and Belarus, signing declarations of friendship and cooperation with the RSFSR and the Ukrainian SSR.[29] In the Polish-Ukrainian declaration, Warsaw promised to facilitate Ukraine's participation in all-European processes and organizations and called for negotiations on the exchange of diplomatic, consular, and trade officials. The declaration also contained a reference to the "ethnic and cultural kinship of the Polish and Ukrainian peoples" and expressed hope that the "positive heritage of their long relationship" would enhance current ties. The document put Moscow on notice that Ukraine no longer oriented itself solely to the all-Union government or to Russia and, in effect, constituted a repudiation of more than forty years of Soviet and Polish communist propaganda about the relationship of Poles and Ukrainians to each other.[30]

In view of the declaration, and of the sympathies Solidarity evoked among Ukrainian national-democrats, Ukrainian officials placed enormous hopes in Poland. After the failed coup attempt in Moscow, Yuri Shcherbak, a leading democratic activist, told *Gazeta Wyborcza* that how Poland conducted its relations with Ukraine would influence relations between Ukraine and other states. Ivan Drach, then chairman of Rukh, told *Tygodnik Powszechny* that Ukraine's "road to Europe . . . really does lead through Poland." Government representatives shared these sentiments; Ukraine's envoy to Poland, Teodoziy Starak, for example, in early 1992 said "Poland has special significance for us."[31]

Shortly after Ukraine's independence declaration on 24 August 1991, Zlenko traveled to Warsaw seeking the establishment of diplomatic relations. Poland—fearing Moscow's reaction as well as the reactions of Western governments, which were not keen to see the Soviet Union collapse—was unwilling to take that step. According to the German analyst Karl Hartmann, the Ukrainian delegation thus was not fully satisfied with the visit.[32] Nonetheless, Ukraine received more political support from Poland than from any other country at the time, with the possible exception of Hungary. The two sides signed an agreement on cooperation between their two foreign ministries and a consular convention (according to which the Polish consulate in Kyiv would be accredited to the Ukrainian government, not to the Soviet government). The joint communiqué obligated both sides to establish diplomatic relations in the near future.[33] The tacit understanding was that such relations would be established soon after Ukraine's referendum on independence, slated for 1 December 1991, in which majority support for independence was expected. Poland was the first state to recognize Ukraine's independence, doing so on 2 December 1991.

But differences over Ukrainian policy quickly emerged within the Polish government, showing the limits of Warsaw's support for Kyiv. In January 1992, then Ukrainian Defense Minister Kostiantyn Morozov looked to Poland for cooperation in the military sphere. He assured the Poles that Ukraine would hand over all its nuclear weapons to Russia; the Poles, in return, affirmed that Ukraine did not constitute a threat to Poland. The sides envisaged joint weapons production, Polish training of Ukrainian soldiers, and supplies of spare parts to each other's armed forces. However, the Polish foreign ministry resisted these understandings, believing more attention needed to be paid to Russia's views: Russian troops were still on Polish soil and Poland was dependent on Russia for energy and raw materials supplies. Moreover, Poland had to take account of the views of the West, particularly the United States, which remained wary of independent Ukraine.

Events surrounding the Wałęsa-Kravchuk summit in May 1992 also demonstrated that Polish officials sought to put some distance between their country and its eastern neighbor. According to Hartmann, Kravchuk came to Warsaw seeking something approaching an alliance with Poland, including relations of a military nature.[34] On the first day of his visit, he said that Ukraine's relations with Poland were closer than with any other state and that "strong ties to Poland weaken the dependence of Ukraine on Russia." The next day, Kravchuk, doubtless disabused of any notions of an alliance by Polish officials, drew back, saying "we treat all European states equally." Right after Kravchuk's visit, Wałęsa traveled to Moscow for a summit with President Boris Yeltsin, showing that Warsaw was pursuing a policy of "equal distance" between Moscow and Kyiv.[35]

Nonetheless, "equal distance" suggested that Poland gave Ukraine a higher priority relative to Russia than any Central European or Western state—again, with the possible exception of Hungary; all Western countries favored Russia. During the Wałęsa-Kravchuk summit, the two leaders signed a basic treaty that, inter alia, affirmed the inviolability of borders; called for political, cultural, economic, and scientific cooperation; and outlined policies and rights regarding the ethnic Ukrainian minority in Poland and the ethnic Polish one in Ukraine.[36] The treaty itself was a significant step in Ukraine's efforts to enhance its international standing: it demonstrated that Ukraine could come to terms with a nation with which it had serious ethnic and territorial conflicts in the past, showed that Kyiv sought to integrate into Europe, and gave Moscow notice that it would not be able to exploit any Ukrainian-Polish differences to the detriment of Ukraine's sovereignty.

The mid-January 1993 visit of then Prime Minister Hanna Suchocka to Kyiv indicated the extent to which the Ukrainians looked to Warsaw as a counterweight to the Russians, notwithstanding Warsaw's policy of "equal distance." Indeed, Kyiv had few other options, in view of the lack of support from the West. At the time, some Polish observers suggested the visit was unsuccessful because Suchocka did not meet with Kravchuk, who was in Israel, and because she was advised not to go to Lviv, in view of anti-Polish sentiments there.[37] However, during their meeting then Prime Minister Kuchma referred to Poland as Ukraine's economic partner number one, despite the fact that Ukraine conducted 80 percent of its trade with Russia. Moreover, Suchocka publicly stated that Poland was interested in the internal stabilization of the CIS, with the affirmation of Ukraine's independence.[38] The visit's timing overrode any considerations of the importance of a Kravchuk-Suchocka meeting: it took place on the eve of a CIS summit at which members were to sign a Commonwealth charter. The visit was thus yet another signal to Moscow that Kyiv would pursue an independent course—and that Warsaw would offer it at least some political support along the way.

Thereafter, relations stagnated for more than two years, notwithstanding the May 1993 Kravchuk-Wałęsa summit. For example, in mid-1993, while Moscow and Kyiv were engaged in sensitive talks on raising prices for the transit of Russian gas and oil via pipelines than run through Ukraine, Poland and Russia initialed an accord to build a gas pipeline from Russia through Belarus and Poland to Germany. Kuchma called the move "an anti-Ukrainian act"—it deprived Ukraine of considerable leverage over Russia because the gas pipeline that runs through Ukraine is the only one that supplies Russian gas to Europe.[39]

Another blow came in early 1994, with the trial of Ukrainian Security Service Major Anatoliy Lysenko, whom the Poles had arrested the previous August on espionage charges. Lysenko, together with his family, had entered Poland seeking advice on an operation for his son; he used a regular passport, not a diplomatic one, and did not inform his superiors of his plans. He was charged with recruiting a Polish citizen (a smuggler) for espionage purposes, but the nature of his "undercover" activities appeared to consist of asking a Polish citizen a few questions about the Przemyśl area and helping the smuggler bypass customs.[40] At most, such an episode merited Lysenko's quiet expulsion; the trial made it a bilateral issue. The Polish government has never offered a convincing explanation for its actions. Warsaw may have used the arrest to signal Moscow that it would not draw too close to Kyiv. Or, the arrest may have stemmed from a Russian provocation to drive a wedge between Kyiv and Warsaw. If so, it was successful: then Ambassador to Poland Hennadiy Udovenko in late February 1994 said Ukrainian-Polish relations "are still developing . . . . The Polish side is currently oriented toward Russia and does not want to annoy Moscow."[41]

The stagnation in fact stemmed from political and economic factors. Some Polish observers cite as a turning point the assumption of power by a leftist coalition composed of the Democratic Left Alliance (SLD) and the Polish Peasant Party (PSL) in November 1993.[42] There is some truth to this argument. Then Foreign Minister Andrzej Olechowski enunciated a major initiative on Poland's eastern policy in February 1994. The proposal involved strengthening people-to-people contacts between Poland and its eastern neighbors and implementing programs to assist these countries to build democratic institutions and market economies.[43] However, Olechowski, like the defense and interior ministers, was a Wałęsa appointee; the coalition, especially the PSL, did not want Olechowski to gain credit for an initiative that might have benefited Polish farmers. Moreover, then Prime Minister Waldemar Pawlak (PSL) thought he saw in Russia a market for Polish agricultural products and thus did not want to alienate the Russians by pursuing ties with Ukraine. Similarly, business interests linked to the SLD did not want relations with Ukraine to jeopardize their economic links with Russian entities and thus may have lobbied against close relations with Ukraine.[44]

But the downturn in relations actually preceded the left's assumption of power: it was during Suchocka's tenure that the Poles turned down Kravchuk's stability zone proposal, the Polish-Russian gas pipeline accord was initialed, and Lysenko was arrested. The foreign policy establishment (including Wałęsa and his advisers) beginning in mid-1993 became so focused on NATO accession that it all but neglected Poland's eastern neighbors. In addition, Poland's NATO aspirations made it even more dependent on Western favor and thus more vulnerable to Western pressure, a vulnerability the West exploited in getting the Poles to resist Kravchuk's project. Along similar lines, Warsaw was not only solicitous of Moscow for economic reasons, but also because of the NATO enlargement issue: the Polish government, cognizant of Russian opposition to expansion, was reluctant to antagonize Moscow even more by intensifying its relationship with Kyiv. Finally, as noted above, Kuchma campaigned for the presidency in 1994 on what appeared to be a pro-Russian platform. Following his election, Warsaw had an excuse to put the Polish-Ukrainian relationship on hold until it could assess the impact of Kuchma's victory on bilateral ties.

By early 1995 it had become clear to Warsaw that Kuchma was not willing to return Ukraine to the Russian orbit. Polish policymakers had also come to understand that Poland's security depended as much on insulating Ukraine against Russia's efforts to reestablish its hegemony over it as on gaining NATO and EU membership. Subordinating Ukrainian security policy to Moscow would have reproduced the threat from Russia that Poland had faced for centuries and might have prompted second thoughts about enlargement among some NATO members. In addition, the West had begun to pursue a more favorable policy toward Ukraine after the signature of the Trilateral Statement and Kuchma's announcement of an economic reform program in October 1994, as well as in view of rising concerns about Russian intentions toward the Soviet successor states.

But in Poland domestic politics again intervened to preclude initiatives toward Kyiv: in late 1994 and early 1995 Wałęsa was engineering Pawlak's ouster. A government headed by Józef Oleksy (SLD) assumed power in February 1995; Pawlak thus was no longer around to block initiatives on eastern policy. In mid-1995 Warsaw began a series of small steps toward Kyiv to help strengthen Ukraine's international standing. Poland pushed hard for Ukraine's membership in the Council of Europe, which it achieved in September, months before Russia. It was also largely owing to Poland's efforts that Ukraine became a full member of the CEI.

Bilaterally, the relationship picked up a momentum that as of mid-1998 had yet to exhaust itself. The two sides in autumn 1995 decided to form a joint peacekeeping battalion; it is scheduled to be ready for deployment in late 1998 or early 1999. The two defense ministers in October 1995 resolved to hold meetings every six months in an effort to deepen military cooperation on a range of issues.

In the economic sphere, then Deputy Prime Minister Grzegorz Kołodko in February 1996 offered ECU20 million in government credit guarantees to finance Ukrainian-Polish economic undertakings in Ukraine; Poland previously had not taken such an initiative with any other government. Trade turnover in 1997 amounted to $1.62 billion, compared with $1.4 billion the year before. As of mid-1998, more than 600 Polish-Ukrainian joint ventures were active in Ukraine. The overwhelming majority were small trading enterprises; but Polish "Bizon" combine harvesters are being manufactured in Kovel.[45] In March 1997, the two sides concluded a memorandum on liberalizing free trade; the Ukrainians want a free trade agreement, which will assist them in entering CEFTA, but such an accord must await Ukraine's accession to the WTO.

Some three weeks after Kuchma participated in the Łańcut meeting in June 1996, he and Kwaśniewski held a summit in Warsaw. Kuchma extolled Polish support for Ukraine's Council of Europe and CEI memberships; the two leaders also concluded an agreement on visa-free travel, making Ukraine the first CIS state with which Poland signed such an accord. The only negative aspect of the summit was the Polish side's reluctance to renounce the possible stationing of nuclear weapons in Poland once it became a NATO member. Kwaśniewski did much to rectify that problem when he stated some months later that he did not see the need for placing such weapons on Polish soil.[46] In fact, NATO has made it clear that it will not station nuclear weapons in the new member states.

One sign of the burgeoning relationship was the joint statement in November 1996 of Kwaśniewski, Kuchma, and Lithuanian President Algirdas Brazauskas on the deteriorating political situation in Belarus. The declaration, a Polish initiative, expressed concern over Belarusian President Aliaksandr Lukashenka's efforts to establish a dictatorship in Belarus and called upon Belarusian leaders to observe internationally recognized political norms and civic rights. The statement was a signal to Moscow that these three governments themselves had interests in a country that Russia deems to fall solely within its sphere of influence—and that these interests did not necessarily coincide with Moscow's. It was also a first step in forging a political axis among the three countries, which share the strategic and political objectives of EU membership and close relations with NATO, if not integration into the alliance.

In a similar vein, on 27 May 1997 Kuchma and Kwaśniewski participated, together with the presidents of the Baltic states, in a summit in Tallinn devoted to regional security. The session took place on the same day that Russia and NATO signed the so-called Founding Act, which created the NATO-Russian

Permanent Joint Council for consultations on security issues. Some Central European and Baltic officials feared the Act might provide a basis for decisions on European security without the participation of NATO aspirants and Ukraine. The Tallinn summit's communiqué clearly stated the interests of its participants on this matter: "security is indivisible and every country has a right to decide for itself what methods to use to ensure its security."[47] This language constituted a rebuff to Russian President Yeltsin, who has underscored Russia's firm opposition to NATO membership for any former Soviet republic. Moreover, balance of power factors were at play in the Tallinn session: the Belarusian and Russian leaderships a week earlier had concluded another in a series of agreements on integrating their two countries. More specifically, for Kuchma it was a chance to distance his country further from the CIS in favor of collaboration with countries that share his goal of integration with Western institutions but that are not likely to attain it in the near term (with the exception of Poland).

Though Ukrainian officials, academics, and policy analysts have expressed fears that after Poland becomes a NATO member, Warsaw will turn its back on Ukraine,[48] these kinds of initiatives suggest that such a policy change is unlikely. Too many political ties now bind Poland and Ukraine, the United States seeks to use such ties to promote democratic and market reforms in Ukraine, and Poland itself wishes to avoid the role of a front-line state in NATO and is thus pushing for the intensification of political and military ties between the alliance and Kyiv—utilizing toward this end the Charter on a Distinctive Partnership signed by President Kuchma and leaders on 9 July 1997.

By contrast, Poland's prospective membership in the EU will hinder the overall relationship. The EU wants Poland to enforce visa requirements for citizens of the Newly Independent States, a stipulation called for by the Schengen Accord. In talks with EU officials, Warsaw has maintained that such a condition would obstruct economic intercourse between Poland and Ukraine as well as daily contacts between average Ukrainians and Poles. EU officials are pursuing a hard line on this issue; Warsaw will make every effort to postpone implementation of these regulations until Poland actually enters the EU, which will probably not occur until 2002 at the earliest (some Union officials want them implemented by the end of 1998), and have promised Ukrainian officials that they will devise a visa regime that meets EU criteria while also permitting ease of access to Poland for Ukrainians.

Bilateral ties have intensified owing to certain shared strategic and political objectives. But a necessary, though not sufficient, condition for the growing relationship has been the fact that those ethnic minority problems that do exist have not become politicized at the national level. There are about 219,000 ethnic Poles in Ukraine and 350,000–700,000 ethnic Ukrainians in Poland.[49] Both populations are dispersed—ethnic Ukrainians in Poland because of Operation Vistula. The ethnic Polish population in Ukraine has been fairly quiescent, except for objecting to the transformation of former Roman Catholic churches into Greek Catholic ones throughout the 1990s. The Polish government has done little for this minority; in view of the troubled history of Ukrainian-Polish relations it has not wanted to antagonize Ukrainian nationalists.[50]

Ethnic Ukrainians, led by the Union of Ukrainians in Poland, want the government and the legislature to address the moral and legal consequences of Operation Vistula: winning condemnation of it by the Sejm (the Senate condemned the operation in August 1990) and annulling the decrees from the 1947–1958 period that nationalized the property of ethnic Ukrainian organizations and private citizens. The Union also seeks the bestowal of rights of combatants to people imprisoned at the Jaworzno concentration camp in the 1940s. In the Przemyśl area, ethnic Ukrainians have been subject to harassment by a small minority of Poles. The latter have succeeded in preventing the planned restitution of the fomer Greek Catholic cathedral of St. John (after World War II, the Roman Catholic church of St. Teresa) to the Ukrainians, and even forestalled a meeting of Pope John Paul II with Ukrainian faithful there earlier; the subsequent architectural modifications to the church (the dismantling of its cupola in 1997) furthur exacerbated local ethnic tensions.

To address the anti-Ukrainian attitudes that still exist in Poland and, to a lesser extent, the anti-Polish sentiments that are present in western Ukraine, Presidents Kuchma and Kwaśniewski, during the latter's May 1997 state visit to Ukraine, signed a "Joint Declaration by the Presidents of Poland and Ukraine on Agreement and Reconciliation."[51] The declaration is not a legal document, but it sets a moral tone for both societies through its appeal to Ukrainians and Poles to acknowledge that members of each nation acted wrongfully toward each other in the past, and that prior wrongs suffered at the expense of the other nation were no justification for retribution.

The document was negotiated over a period of many months, doubtless because the sides had to consider the political impact of acknowledging culpability for actions that large segments of each nation continue to consider morally justified. The declaration condemns, inter alia, Warsaw's anti-Ukrainian policies in the interwar period, Stalinist persecutions of ethnic Poles in Ukraine in the 1930s, and the massacres of Poles in Volhynia in 1942–43. It also acknowledges Operation Vistula as a "separate dramatic page in the history of our relations . . . which dealt a blow to the Ukrainian community in Poland." In the months following the declaration, the two presidents have taken further steps at reconciling their two nations, most notably through their attendance at a ceremony unveiling a monument to the victims of the Jaworzno camp in late May 1998.

Ukraine and Slovakia

Ukrainian-Slovak relations present a stark contrast to Ukrainian-Polish relations: both Slovaks and Ukrainians for centuries were "subject peoples" who did not have the interaction with each other that each had with elites of nations that dominated them (Poles, Russians, and Austrians in the case of the Ukrainians; Hungarians in the case of the Slovaks). In the 1990s relations between Ukraine and Slovakia have been correct, but not intense. However, the pro-Russian sentiments among members of Prime Minister Vladimír Mečiar's coalition in Slovakia doubtless have been worrisome to Ukrainian policymakers.

Even before Slovakia became independent on 1 January 1993, relations between Ukraine and Czechoslovakia were not particularly close. According to Olga Alexandrova, as long as the USSR existed Prague manifested a certain reserve toward the republics—Prague feared that Ukraine's independence could spur Slovakia to move in that direction.[52]

Ukraine recognized Slovakia on 1 January 1993; the two governments reached agreement on a basic treaty about six months later. Slovakia supported Ukraine's admission into the Council of Europe and the CEI; Bratislava also backs Ukraine's membership in CEFTA, possibly because most of the other CEFTA members will join the EU before Slovakia and therefore may abandon CEFTA eventually. Ukraine's membership, together with that of, say, Lithuania and Bulgaria, thus could be a way to keep CEFTA going.

There is no indication that Slovak policymakers see an independent Ukraine as essential to their country's security or that Ukrainian policymakers view Slovakia as a partner for Ukraine on its road to Europe. To be sure, Western countries have expressed reservations concerning the Mečiar coalition's allegiance to democratic principles; such reservations precluded Slovakia's membership in the first tranche of new NATO members and an invitation from the EU to begin accession negotiations in 1998. Therefore, Slovakia is not the best partner for Ukraine in this respect. As important, Slovak politicians often express pro-Russian sentiments. Ján Slota, chairman of the Slovak National Party (a member of Mečiar's coalition), has condemned NATO's expansion plans and its attempts to advance to "the Russian border."[53] In March 1995, during a meeting with Russia's Prime Minister Viktor Chernomyrdin, Mečiar stated that "Slovakia never had, does not have, and never will have any disagreements with Russia."[54] No other leader in the region could make that claim. In return for getting a cold shoulder from NATO and the EU, Mečiar and his coalition allies have looked to Russia for support or at least have tried to let the West know that Slovakia has another option; for example, Bratislava has cultivated military and intelligence ties to Moscow. Slovakia, moreover, is almost completely dependent on Russia for its energy supplies and thus is vulnerable to Russian pressure in this respect.

From Kyiv's perspective, Slovak links with Moscow threaten to weaken Ukraine's geopolitical position. Its northern neighbor, Belarus, is for all practical purposes a Russian vassal. Though Slovakia will in no case play such a role, any orientation on Bratislava's part toward Moscow would give the Russians further leverage over Kyiv. In recognition of this prospect, Warsaw, Prague, and Budapest continue firmly to support Bratislava's integration into NATO, both to undercut the "Slavophile" faction in Slovakia and to prevent the exploitation of Slovakia's predicament by Russia.

There is one sore point in the Ukrainian-Slovak relationship—perceived backing on Slovakia's part for the existence of a Carpatho-Ruthenian minority, which also inhabits Ukraine's Transcarpathia Oblast (whose territory had belonged to Hungary until 1918, was joined to interwar Czechoslovakia, and in 1945 was ceded to the Ukrainian SSR) and which Kyiv does not recognize as a nationality separate from the Ukrainians.[55] According to the 1991 census in Czechoslovakia, some 17,000 people claimed Carpatho-Ruthenian nationality and some 14,000 claimed to be ethnic Ukrainians.[56] In Ukraine estimates of the number of people who may identify themselves as Carpatho-Ruthenians range from 30,000 to 600,000, though the latter figure seems to include people considering themselves Carpatho-Ruthenian/Ukrainians.[57]

The Society of Transcarpathian Ruthenians emerged in February 1990, seeking autonomy for Transcarpathia, if not outright independence. This group, working with the Hungarian Cultural Association of Transcarpathia, managed to place on oblast ballots for the 1 December 1991, all-Ukrainian independence referendum a question concerning autonomy for Transcarpathia; in the oblast referendum some 78 percent of the voters supported autonomy.[58]

Three weeks after the referendum the Society of Transcarpathian Ruthenians sent a letter to then Czechoslovak Federal Assembly Chairman Alexander Dubček requesting annulment of the 1945 treaty ceding the region to the USSR. The group contended that the treaty was, inter alia, an obstacle to the Carpatho-Ruthenians' right to recognition as a nation, to their right to national self-determination, and to the creation of an independent state called the "Carpathian Republic." Czechoslovak authorities ignored the appeal, but representatives of the Civic Democratic Union-Public Against Violence, at the time the second strongest party in Slovakia's coalition government, in January 1992 said the 1945 cession of "Subcarpathian Rus" had been illegal and that the Czechoslovak government should acknowledge the desires of the oblast's inhabitants in developing a policy on the issue.[59] On 15 May 1993, Carpatho-Ruthenian activists in Bratislava proclaimed "Subcarpathian Rus" an independent member of the CIS and created a provisional government.[60]

Bratislava has supported the codification of the Carpatho-Ruthenian language and backed the creation of the Carpatho-Ruthenian Language and Cultural Institute in Prešov in January 1993.[61] The Ukrainian Foreign Ministry, in a statement on Ukrainian-Slovak relations, has noted that "in practice Slovakia pursues a policy of eroding the ethno-cultural unity [of its ethnic Ukrainian minority] by means of drawing an artificial contrast between Ukrainians and Rusyns" (Carpatho-Ruthenians).[62] The Slovaks retort that they cannot prevent the expression of this identity by people who wish to cultivate it.

Ukraine and Hungary

Hungary's connections with Ukraine rival Poland's in length of time, though they extended over a much smaller territory—the present-day Transcarpathia Oblast. This region was part of the Kingdom of Hungary from the eleventh century until ceded to Czechoslovakia by the Treaty of Trianon in 1920. One imprint of this long association was the presence of a strong Hungarian minority in the region. Another, the result of Magyarization policies pursued most vigorously in the half-century before World War I, was the slow development of national consciousness among the local population and the split in national orientation among Magyarophiles, Russophiles (oriented toward the Russian Empire), Ukrainophiles, and supporters of a local Carpatho-Ruthenian identity. These tendencies, indeed, continued under interwar Czechoslovakia and the brief Hungarian re-occupation during World War II, by which time, however, the Ukrainian movement was in the ascendant. This history formed the background for the development of Hungarian-Ukrainian relations as the Soviet Union approached its collapse.

In his 22 May 1990 speech presenting his government's program to parliament, Prime Minister József Antall noted that because one-third of all ethnic Magyars live outside Hungary, good relations with Hungary's neighbors were essential, as was the securing of minority rights for ethnic Hungarians in these countries.[63] Equally important, Antall and his coalition entered power determined to extricate Hungary from the Soviet sphere of influence and pursue Western integration.[64] Antall took advantage of Hungary's relative smallness (compared with, say, Poland) and geopolitical position (it did not border Germany and was not necessary to the supply of Soviet troops in eastern Germany) to announce his country's intention to withdraw from the Warsaw Pact in June 1990. Weakening the Soviet center would advance the goal of freeing Hungary from Soviet hegemony. Thus from its inception the Antall government was sympathetic to Ukrainian aspirations for autonomy within the USSR and then for independence. Successive Hungarian governments also have well understood that Hungary's integration into trans-Atlantic and West European structures depended on normalized relations with its neighbors.

Relations between Hungary and the Ukrainian SSR were established even before those between the latter and Poland. In September 1990 President Árpád Göncz became the first head of state to visit Kyiv after the republic's sovereignty declaration (he also visited Transcarpathia). The communiqué underscored Ukraine's desire to participate in all-European processes and Hungary's willingness to facilitate such efforts; the two sides also agreed to establish economic relations independent of Moscow as well as direct military contacts.[65]

In May 1991 Kravchuk, then chairman of Ukraine's Supreme Soviet (Verkhovna Rada), reciprocated Göncz's visit with a trip to Hungary. The two sides signed several agreements, including a consular convention and a Declaration on Basic Principles of Cooperation. The most important agreement was one on ethnic minorities, according to which both governments were to respect their citizens' right to decide to which national group they belong; to ensure preservation of minorities' cultural, ethnic, linguistic, and religious identities; and to establish a joint committee on national minorities.[66] In the wake of the visit, Ivan Drach, then chairman of Rukh, said "Hungary, together with Poland, is the hope of Ukraine."[67] For Hungary, Ukraine had assumed particular significance because, in contrast to Slovakia, Romania, and Yugoslavia, it pursued relatively liberal policies toward its ethnic Hungarian minority. The minorities agreement ensured that Hungary was not isolated in the region on this issue.

Events in the wake of Ukraine's independence referendum on 1 December 1991, underscored Kyiv's importance to Budapest. Two days after the balloting Hungary became the first state to establish diplomatic relations with Ukraine. Three days later, the two governments concluded a basic treaty; that this happened so quickly after the referendum suggests it had been negotiated earlier and was ready for signature upon completion of the polling.

The Hungarian parliament ratified the treaty on 16 May 1993; controversy, however, marked the run-up to the vote. Deputies from Antall's own center-right Hungarian Democratic Forum criticized the accord because it contained a clause on the mutual renunciation of territorial claims. These deputies did not advocate Hungarian efforts to reacquire parts of Transcarpathia, where ethnic Hungarians in Ukraine predominate; they were concerned that the agreement with Ukraine would set a precedent for treaty negotiations with Slovakia and Romania because it appeared to exclude even peaceful border changes, which the Helsinki accords allow. The Hungarian right had harbored hopes that the "injustices" of the 1920 Trianon treaty, according to which Hungary lost significant territory to Romania, Czechoslovakia, and Yugoslavia, and of the 1947 Treaty of Paris, which confirmed Hungary's postwar borders, might be rectified. The government tried to argue that the treaty with Ukraine did not set a precedent for other sets of negotiations because Ukraine was not a sovereign state in 1947, when the Paris treaty defined Hungary's borders; that rejection of the treaty would tarnish Hungary's image in the world; and that the clauses of the accord dealing with ethnic minorities went far toward guaranteeing collective minority rights, something the Romanians and Slovaks have rejected and the Hungarians have strenuously supported.[68]

In Hungary there has been a consensus on Ukraine's importance to the country's security. According to a message from Antall to Hungarian ambassadors in mid-1993, "it is obvious that our relations with Ukraine among our immediate neighbors have special significance. It is in our fundamental interest to help, accept, and support Ukraine as a major power in Europe, not only as a buffer state, but also as a counterbalancing force."[69] Hungary, then governed by the Antall coalition, was the only country to offer support for Kravchuk's proposal for a security and stability zone in East-Central Europe. Similarly, the platform of the Hungarian Socialist Party, which won the mid-1994 parliamentary elections, averred that the "preservation of Ukraine's sovereignty and economic independence, and the development of Hungarian-Ukrainian relations, directly affect Hungary's security."[70]

As with the Ukrainian-Polish relationship, Hungary's NATO membership will not hinder ties with Ukraine. However, Hungary's EU accession will affect this relationship in ways similar to the impact of Poland's membership in the Union on Warsaw's ties with Kyiv: Hungarian officials warned Foreign Minister Borys Tarasyuk during his late April 1998 visit to Budapest that all new EU members must unconditionally observe the strictures of the Schengen Accord.[71]

Despite Hungarian officials' favorable sentiments toward Ukraine, bilateral relations have not achieved the intensity of Ukrainian-Polish ties. One factor is disparity in population: Hungary is about one-fifth the size of Ukraine, making it difficult for the two states to build an equal partnership. Second, Hungarians did not play the intense historical role in Ukraine that Poles did. Though such roles are often the cause of resentment, they can also incline nations to see a larger responsibility to help their neighbors—Austria's role in Central Europe is another example of this phenomenon. Third, Hungary's foreign policy seems to have all it can handle. The country borders the conflict zone in former Yugoslavia and Budapest did not sign a basic treaty with Bratislava until early 1995 or one with Bucharest until September 1996. Even so, problems with ethnic Hungarian minorities in Slovakia and Romania remain.

Politicians across Hungary's political spectrum have extolled Ukraine's policies toward its ethnic Hungarian minority as a model for the region. This minority numbers about 163,000 people, of whom 156,000 live in Transcarpathia.[72] They reside in a relatively compact territory in the oblast: two-thirds are residents of Berehovo Raion, and there are sizable ethnic Hungarian minorities in Uzhhorod (16.6 percent), Mukachiv (20.2 percent), and Vynohradiv (29 percent).[73]

The ethnic Hungarians began to organize in 1989, forming the Hungarian Cultural Association of Transcarpathia. It supported autonomy for the oblast as well as creation of a Hungarian national autonomous district in Berehovo, which 81 percent of its residents backed in a referendum that took place together with the all-Ukrainian referendum on independence and the oblast referendum on autonomy.[74]

In fact, ethnic Hungarians have enjoyed substantial latitude to cultivate their national traditions. The number of unilingual Hungarian-language schools has been rising since 1989, after a two-decades-long decline. In December 1992, the chief presidential representative in the oblast issued regulations requiring that street and office signs be posted in minority languages and that government employees know the language of any ethnic group that is locally in the majority.[75] Hungary itself has provided considerable aid to the Magyar minority, and Kyiv has not objected to such efforts.[76]

Nonetheless, there have been complaints. For example, Kyiv has not created a Hungarian national autonomous district in Berehovo. Moreover, though ethnic Hungarians are well-represented, and even overrepresented, in legislative bodies in the oblast and its elements, this is not the case for public administration, in which proportions are reportedly low even in Berehovo.[77] However, these problems are minor compared with the circumstances of ethnic Hungarian minorities in Romania, Slovakia, and Yugoslavia.

The only problem involving the ethnic Hungarian minority in Ukraine that became a bilateral issue concerned ethnic Hungarian efforts in summer 1996 to commemorate the 1,100th anniversary of the Magyars' entry into the Carpathian basin. The Democratic Union of Hungarians in Ukraine (formerly the Hungarian Cultural Association of Transcarpathia) wanted to erect a monument at the Vereshetskyi pass, one of the routes that the Magyars may have taken into what is today Hungary. The Union thought it had permission from oblast officials to build the monument, but Ukrainian nationalists subsequently pressed the authorities to halt the construction, arguing that the desire to erect the structure represented territorial revisionism on the part of the ethnic Hungarians. Hungary's then Foreign Minister László Kovács termed the episode "regrettable," but it did not affect bilateral relations for long: President Göncz, visiting Ukraine in November 1996, termed the situation of the ethnic Hungarian minority there "perfect in political terms."[78]

Ukraine and Romania

Romania is the lone country in East-Central Europe with which Ukraine has had serious political conflicts. Territorial and ethnic minority issues lay at the root of these problems. Specifically, Romania has been loath to recognize Ukrainian sovereignty over two regions considered part of its national patrimony—northern Bukovina and southern Bessarabia.

The province of Bukovina—historically connected with Galicia, for centuries under Ottoman Turkish rule, and from 1774 through World War I a part of the Habsburg Monarchy—has long been bi-national in population, with Ukrainians predominating in the north and Romanians in the south. A degree of equilibrium was achieved under Austrian rule, but Romanian sovereignty over the area in the interwar period was marked by harsh discrimination against Ukrainians. The northern part of the province was annexed to Soviet Ukraine in 1939, and again after World War II, as Chernivsti Oblast. It contains a sizable Romanian population, while southern Bukovina, which remained within the borders of Romania, has a smaller Ukrainian minority.

Bessarabia is a region that was historically a part of the principality of Moldavia, under tsarist Russian rule from 1809 through the Revolution, and incorporated into interwar Romania. Its southern part is especially diverse in ethnic composition, with no group in the majority, but with a Ukrainian plurality, followed by Romanians (Moldovans), Bulgarians, Gagauz, Russians, and others. After World War II, most of Bessarabia (with the addition of a sliver of Ukrainian territory in the Transdniester area) was constituted as the Moldavian SSR, but southern Bessarabia was attached to the Ukrainian SSR, first as the separate oblast of Izmail, and after 1954 as part of Odesa Oblast.

Until mid-1997 Ukraine and Romania had failed to reach agreement on a basic treaty. The Romanians sought to regain parts of northern Bukovina and southern Bessarabia lost in the settlement ending World War II; moreover, the Romanians advocated negotiations over the status of Serpent Island in the Black Sea. The Romanian government, legislators, and media also registered serious complaints over Ukraine's policy toward its ethnic Romanian minority.

This nationalistic stance presented a conundrum because it ran counter to Bucharest's strenuous efforts to be included in the first tranche of new NATO members (other obstacles included Romania's retarded political and economic reforms and, until September 1996, the lack of a basic treaty with Hungary). The alliance had long made clear that no state asserting territorial claims against its neighbors or engaged in ethnic disputes with them would be considered for membership. A basic treaty with Ukraine entailing, inter alià, Romania's recognition of Ukraine's territorial inviolability thus constituted a necessary, though not a sufficient, condition for Romanian success in entering NATO. Presidents Kuchma and Emil Constantinescu finally signed the accord on 2 June 1997, some five weeks before NATO's Madrid summit, which formally extended invitations to new members.

Romania's position on Ukraine's territorial integrity ran counter to Bucharest's interests for other reasons as well. Romanian policymakers understood that an independent Ukraine enhanced Romania's security because it meant a reduction in the potential Russian menace to their country. Thus, the questioning of Ukraine's territorial integrity threatened to weaken its eastern neighbor, which in turn could have been exploited by Russia to Romania's detriment. Moreover, Bucharest, especially in 1992–1993, looked to Ukraine as an ally in resolving the issue of Transdniester separatism in Moldova.

Under Nicolae Ceaușescu, the communist regime managed to establish for Romania a semi-independent status within the Soviet bloc; to do so it cultivated Romanian nationalism as a foundation on which to rest regime legitimacy. Ceaușescu's successors, led by President Ion Iliescu and the political apparatus grouped around him, in turn drew on the dictator's legacy to legitimate their own standing. This legacy, according to Vladimir Tismaneanu, involved, inter alia, exaltation of the nationally homogeneous community and an exploitation of *völkisch* themes and mythologies.[79] The desire to regain territory that had been part of Romania during the interwar period accords with such sentiments.

On 24 June 1991, the Romanian parliament passed a "Declaration on the Molotov-Ribbentrop Pact and Its Consequences for Our Country" that denounced the Soviet assumption of control over Bessarabia and northern Bukovina as "odious," "brutal," and a "patent act of imperialist annexation." The resolution described northern Bukovina and Bessarabia as "sacred Romanian lands" and declared the "occupation of these age-old Romanian territories" to have been "null and void from the very beginning" from the perspective of international law.[80] The government's statements on the subject were less vehement; nonetheless, then Foreign Minister Adrian Nastase declared Romania had never recognized Soviet "rights" to the territories or consented to any territorial cession, but had simply withdrawn under the threat of superior force.[81]

The Ukrainians responded quickly: a parliamentary statement held that the Romanian parliament's declaration "in effect raised territorial claims against Ukraine"; termed northern Bukovina and southern Bessarabia "ancient Ukrainian lands" that Ukraine had "helped to liberate from foreign rule"; contended that the border resulted from the postwar settlement, not the Molotov-Ribbentrop Pact; and noted the Romanian declaration violated the letter and spirit of the Helsinki accords.[82]

The Romanian parliament upped the ante in November 1991, declaring it would not recognize the results of Ukraine's independence referendum in those "Romanian territories forcibly included as part of the USSR"; the government issued a similar statement. Kyiv responded by canceling a planned visit by Foreign Minister Zlenko to Bucharest.[83]

Romania has claimed additional territory as well. At a December 1995 press conference, an adviser to then Foreign Minister Teodor Melescănu said Romania would demand a review of the 1948 protocol that made Serpent Island, located in the Black Sea some 27 miles from the mouth of the Danube, a part of the USSR. Control of the island gives Ukraine the right to exploit a 200-mile exclusive economic zone around it; the continental shelf may contain oil and gas deposits. Bucharest maintained that Serpent Island is simply a rock and thus that Ukrainian territorial waters, the continental shelf, and the economic zone around it should run from mainland Ukraine, not from Serpent Island. Were the island to be declared a rock, a part of the continental shelf would be available to Romania for exploitation.

The conflict over territory held up agreement on a basic treaty. The Romanians sought inclusion in the accord of a condemnation of the Molotov-Ribbentrop Pact, something to which Kyiv would not agree. Had the Ukrainians done so, the onus would have been placed on them to redress the injustice by negotiating the transfer of the territory in question. The Romanians maintained that although they wanted to regain formerly Romanian territory, they would not resort to the use of force. Romanian officials believed, rightly, that the Helsinki accords do not preclude peaceful border changes; not surprisingly, Bucharest was reluctant to include in the treaty a clearly worded statement on the inviolability of existing borders.

No state would agree to cede part of its territory to another. In fact, Romanians always reacted vehemently to any suggestion by Hungarian officials that borders between Romania and Hungary be redrawn. The Romanians, however, never singled out Ukraine in this respect: Romania still has not signed basic treaties with Moldova or Russia because, among other reasons, neither will agree to include a condemnation of the Molotov-Ribbentrop Pact in these accords.

Related to the border issue were tensions over ethnic minorities, particularly the ethnic Romanian minority in Ukraine. There are about 135,000 ethnic Romanians and 325,000 ethnic Moldovans in Ukraine; some 100,000 ethnic Romanians and 85,000 ethnic Moldovans live in Chernivtsi and 145,000 ethnic Moldovans live in Odesa Oblast (Bucharest does not recognize a separate Moldovan nationality).[84] The number of ethnic Romanians was much higher in these lands in the interwar period, but Soviet authorities exiled large numbers of ethnic Romanians to labor camps or to distant regions of the USSR. Romanians also believe that Soviet census figures consistently understated the population of ethnic Romanians in Ukraine.

Articles in the Romanian press, citing Romanian officials, frequently alleged that ethnic Romanians in Ukraine were subject to denationalization and "flagrant discrimination."[85] Presumably such statements were meant to legitimate Bucharest's efforts to regain formerly Romanian lands. After all, only Romania could be expected to ensure Romanian cultural continuity in these territories. However, neither Poland nor Hungary has raised concerns about the treatment of their co-nationals in Ukraine; why Kyiv would pursue a discriminatory policy against the ethnic Romanian minority alone was unclear. Such statements also ignored the fact that the Soviet government, not contemporary Ukraine, was responsible for discrimination against, and forced resettlement of, ethnic Romanians in the 1940s and 1950s. Finally, it was unclear what Romania would have expected of the hundreds of thousands of Ukrainians who live in formerly Romanian territories; Romanian authorities doubtless considered their residence there illegitimate.

Kyiv argued that northern Bukovina and southern Bessarabia are Ukrainian territory not because of the Molotov-Ribbentrop Pact, but because the 1947 Paris treaty, which the Ukrainian SSR signed, affirmed the postwar borders. Furthermore, in 1948 Romania and the Soviet Union signed a document according to which Serpent Island became Soviet territory. The Helsinki accords, in turn, confirmed these boundaries.

The Ukrainian position on the bilateral treaty was that if the Romanians insisted on a condemnation of the Molotov-Ribbentrop pact, the accord also had to contain a condemnation of Romania's seizure of Ukrainian lands in 1918 and of the Hitler-Antonescu agreement on the occupation of Ukraine. Kyiv, however, preferred to avoid the issue completely.

The ice finally broke in mid-1997. In late 1996, following the victory of Emil Constantinescu in Romania's presidential elections, a new government assumed power in Bucharest that was less beholden to nationalist forces than its predecessor. The new government at first pursued the previous government's line on the issues dividing the two sides. But this government also faced the prospect of being excluded from the first tranche of new NATO members owing to the lack of a basic treaty with Ukraine. The government feared the domestic political repercussions of being left out—justifiably so in view of the fact that more than 80 percent of the populace supported their country's membership in the alliance. Ukrainian negotiators were able to exploit Romania's desire for an agreement before NATO's Madrid summit to get Bucharest to accept Kyiv's position on most of the contentious points. Other areas of disagreement were left to subsequent negotiations.

The treaty does not condemn the Molotov-Ribbentrop Pact; rather, the preamble holds "as unjust the acts of totalitarian and military-dictatorial regimes that have in the past had a negative effect on relations between the Ukrainian and Romanian peoples . . . ."[86] Such language implicitly condemns the pact but does not entail the corollary that territorial changes must be made to remedy its consequences. Such language also implicitly condemns the Hitler-Antonescu condominium vis-à-vis Ukraine.

Both Article I and Article II oblige the two states to respect each other's territorial integrity; Romania thus agreed to acknowledge Serpent Island as Ukrainian territory. This issue, however, was subject to a separate convention to be negotiated, according to which Ukraine agreed not to deploy offensive military weapons there; the two sides also agreed to hold talks on the delimitation of the continental shelf and both states' exclusive economic zones in the Black Sea, and to take this issue to the International Court of Justice if no agreement could be reached two years after the start of such negotiations, provided a treaty on the state border between Ukraine and Romania comes into effect. Both treaties were under negotiation as of mid-1998.

Article XIII requires the two states to apply internationally recognized rights of individuals belonging to national minorities, naming those rights outlined in various documents of the Council of Europe, the Organization of Security and Cooperation in Europe, and the UN General Assembly. In addition, the treaty seeks to enhance contacts between national minorities and their mother country by calling for the establishment of Euroregions in the areas of the upper Prut and the lower Danube rivers.

Conclusion of the treaty seems to have had a cathartic effect on Bucharest's approach to Kyiv, though it failed to gain Romania a first-tranche invitation to NATO.[87] The accord allowed other aspects of the relationship mentioned above to take center stage: the shared strategic goals of Kyiv and Bucharest. One month after the treaty signing, Kuchma, Constantinescu, and Moldovan President Petru Lucinschi met in Izmail, Ukraine, where they signed a trilateral statement on cooperation and a trilateral protocol involving the creation of the Lower Danube Euroregion and a free economic zone in the area of Reni (Ukraine), Galaţa (Romania), and Giurgiuleşti (Moldova). From Kyiv's perspective, such cooperation adds another vector to its foreign policy and promises Romanian help in assisting it (and Moldova) in distancing themselves from the CIS. For Bucharest, it was a chance to show the West that it could play the role of regional leader.

Conclusion

Ukraine has succeeded in entering Central European groups, and thus staking a claim to a Central European identity, precisely because it has achieved such good relations with Poland and Hungary. Poland, in particular, helped Ukraine gain CEI membership and secured Kuchma's participation in the Łańcut summit. As additional CEI members enter the EU, Ukraine can only benefit further from membership in this group. CEFTA accession seems to depend on Ukraine alone: other members would agree to it if Ukraine were able to achieve more in the way of economic reform and if Ukraine were to become a member of the WTO.

Elites in Poland, Hungary, and Romania look to Ukraine as essential to their countries' security. Publics, especially in Poland, seem less convinced, which points to a significant weakness in this relationship: the lack of an effective public diplomacy on the part of Poland toward Ukraine and on the part of Ukraine toward Poland. For example, though the Poles and Ukrainians have long talked about establishing a Polish information and cultural center in Kyiv and a Ukrainian one in Warsaw, as of mid-1998 they had not done so. The costs would be minimal, but the payoff considerable—laying the groundwork for overcoming the distrust the average Pole still feels for Ukrainians.

Slovakia could pose a problem for Ukraine if instability ensues there as a result of Prime Minister Mečiar's slide toward authoritarianism or if Mečiar turns further toward Russia in response to being shunned by the West. The opposition, however, is by no means as pro-Russian as members of the Mečiar coalition.

Certain nationalist groups in Romania continue to castigate the government's "sell-out" to Ukraine and the latter's treatment of its ethnic Romanian minority, but the issue has not hurt the government among the general populace, even though Romania's NATO membership has been deferred. President Kuchma's support for Romania's alliance accession has doubtless taken some of the wind out of the nationalists' sails. The incipient cooperation among regions of Odesa Oblast and neighboring areas of Romania and Moldova also looks promising because the governments went into the endeavor with concrete projects already sketched out. If the projects under discussion come to fruition, they will promote interaction between Romanians on both sides of the border, thereby further undercutting Romanian nationalists' efforts to make an issue out of Kyiv's treatment of their co-nationals in Ukraine.

Ukraine's relationship with its western neighbors must be counted among the most successful aspects of its foreign policy. The Ukrainian-Polish relationship and, perhaps, the Ukrainian-Romanian relationship show that peoples in the region are capable of overcoming past territorial conflicts; the Ukrainian-Hungarian relationship shows that governments in East Central Europe are capable of pursuing an enlightened policy toward ethnic minorities. In a part of Europe that in this century has been ridden with territorial and ethnic strife, these are no small accomplishments.

NOTES

The views expressed herein are the author's alone and do not necessarily represent those of the Department of State or the U.S. government. I would like to thank Roxane Sismanidis for her help on this project.

1. Melvin Croan, "Lands In-between: The Politics of Cultural Identity in Contemporary Eastern Europe," *East European Politics and Societies* 3 (2) Spring 1989: 178–79; Iver B. Neumann, "Russia as Central Europe's Constituting Other," *East European Politics and Societies* 7, 2 Spring 1993: 349–69.

2. Anatoliy Zlenko, "The Ukraine, the UN, and World Diplomacy," *International Affairs* December 1990: 5. Actually, Ukraine's border with Romania is longer than that with Poland.

3. "Warszawa, Praga, Budapeszt, Kijów?" *Rzeczpospolita* 21–22 December 1991.

4. "Konferencja polsko-ukraińska nt. "Droga Ukrainy do Europy'," *Sprawy Międzynarodowe* 1992 (4-6): 149–70, esp. 151; Edward Krzemień, "Ukraina na czwartego," *Gazeta Wyborcza* 14 February 1992.

5. J.K., "Czworobok zamiast trójkąt," *Życie Warszawy* 20 May 1992; "Ukraina chce być neutralna," *Gazeta Wyborcza* 20 May 1992.

6. "Three Visegrád Leaders Discuss Ties," *Új Magyarország* 14 March 1992, in Foreign Broadcast Information Service, *Daily Report: East Europe* (hereafter, FBIS-EEU) 25 March 1992: 2–3.

7. Roman Solchanyk, "Ukraine's Search for Security," *RFE/RL Research Report* 21 May 1993: 5.

8. "Wzmocnienie regionalnej stabilizacji i bezpieczeństwa w Europie Środkowo-Wschodniej," *Gazeta Wyborcza* 24 May 1993; "Vklad v budivnytstvo bezpeky dlia vsikh," *Holos Ukrainy* 10 July 1993.

9. Solchanyk, "Ukraine's Search for Security," 5.

10. Andrzej Łomanowski, "Wałęsa, Krawczuk, i zaniechana strefa," *Gazeta Wyborcza* 26 May 1993.

11. Andrzej Łomanowski, "Cisza nad NATO-bis," *Gazeta Wyborcza* 25 May 1993. In April 1996, Kuchma advocated a return to the idea of a political and economic association of Central and East European states. No one has taken him up on this concept. See "Kuchma Addresses Europe Assembly on Issues," Interfax, 23 April 1996, in Foreign Broadcast Information Service, *Daily Report: Central Eurasia* (hereafter, FBIS-SOV), 24 April 1996: 62.

12. Z.L., "Cztery do jednego," *Rzeczpospolita* 11 February 1993; "Wszystkie góry są nasze," *Gazeta Wyborcza* 12 February 1993;

Anatolii Hryhor'iv, "Karpats'kyi Ievrorehion—Shcho tse take?" *Holos Ukrainy* 17 February 1993.

13. Mirosław Czech, "Polska i Ukraina—działanie i rozmowy," *Kultura* April 1993: 88. Subsequently, the oblasts of Lviv, Chernivtsi, and Ivano-Frankivsk joined the ECE. The Mečiar government in Slovakia, seeing the ECE as an effort by Hungary to spread Hungarian influence in the area, later forced the Slovak jurisdictions to leave. The Bug Euroregion, composed of Volhynia Oblast and four Polish provinces emerged in late 1994. See "Volyn' i Pol'shcha—vzaiemnovyhidne spivrobitnytstvo," *Holos Ukrainy* 30 December 1994.

14. "Leonid Kuchma sklav prysiahu na virnist' ukrains'komu narodovi," *Holos Ukrainy* 21 July 1994.

15. "Poky shcho maiemo rozhevi nadii. A chas pokazhe istynu," *Vysokyi zamok* 21 July 1994.

16. "Ukraina i svit. Iak vony spivisnuiut? Interv'iu ministra zakordonnykh sprav Hennadiia Udovenka," *Holos Ukrainy* 27 December 1995.

17. "Foreign Economic Policy Guidelines Detailed," Infobank, 16 March 1995, in FBIS-SOV, 16 March 1995: 36.

18. On Kuchma's desire to join the EU, see, for example, "Kuchma: Aim to Join European Union Next," UNIAN, 26 September 1995, in FBIS-SOV, 27 September 1995: 75.

19. CEI members, in addition to Ukraine, include the Czech Republic, Slovakia, Hungary, Austria, Poland, Italy, Croatia, Slovenia, Bosnia-Herzegovina, Belarus, Albania, Bulgaria, and Romania; the last four achieved membership at the same time as Ukraine.

20. "Nadrabianie straconego czasu. Rozmowa z Jewhenem Marczukiem, premierem Ukrainy," *Rzeczpospolita* 9 October 1995.

21. "Ukraina i Ievropa. Z vystupu Prezydenta Ukrainy Leonida Kuchmy u zhenevs'komu mizhnarodnomu tsentri konferentsii 21 bereznia 1996," *Uriadovyi kur'ier* 28 March 1996.

22. For Kuchma's references to Ukraine as a Central European country, see "Nova arkhitektura bezpeky v Ievropi nemozhlyva bez Ukrainy. Vystup Prezydenta Ukrainy L.D. Kuchmy na Asamblei ZES 4 chervnia 1996 roku," *Uriadovyi Kur'ier*, 8 June 1996; and Foreign Broadcast Information Service, "Ukrainian President on NATO, Nuclear Disarmament," *Lidové Noviny*, 20 November 1996. In this last article Kuchma stated that "Ukraine is in Central Europe and a part of it used to belong to the Austro-Hungarian Empire, as did the territories of the Czech lands, Moravia, and Slovakia."

23. "Czech Commentator Views Polish-Ukrainian Relations," *Lidové Noviny*, 28 June 1996, in FBIS-EEU 18 July 1996: 46.

24. Mykola Makhnichuk, "My ne hosti u Ievropi," *Uriadovyi kur'ier* 11 June 1996; "Polish President Summarizes Summit," PAP, 8 June 1996, in FBIS-EEU 10 June 1996: 2–3. Kuchma did not participate in the 1997 gathering in Slovenia but took part in the 1998 meeting in Levoča, Slovakia.

25. See Ryszard Torzecki, *Polacy i Ukraińcy* (Warsaw, 1993).

26. "Envoy Assesses Polish-Ukrainian Relations," *Za vil'nu Ukrainu* 10 October 1992, in Foreign Broadcast Information Service, *Central Eurasia* 18 November 1992: 96.

27. Roman Solchanyk, "Ukraine and Poland: An Interview with Adam Michnik," *Report on the USSR* 5 January 1990: 20.

28. "Francja dobra, Ukraina zła," *Gazeta Wyborcza* 10 July 1992.

29. The attempt to sign such a declaration with Minsk ended in a fiasco because officials still beholden to the center dominated the Belorussian SSR.

30. The declaration was published in *Rzeczpospolita* 13 November 1990.

31. Edward Krzemień, "To, co uczyni Polska, będzie sygnałem dla innych," *Gazeta Wyborcza* 9 September 1991; "'Nasza droga wiedzie przez Polskę.' Z Iwanem Draczem, przewodniczącym ukraińskiego 'Ruchu,' rozmawiają Wojciech Pięciak i Andrzej Romanowski," *Tygodnik Powszechny* 13 October 1991; "Polska ma dla nas szczególne znaczenie.' Fragmenty wypowiedzi Ambasadora Ukrainy w Warszawie, Teodozjusza Staraka," *Kultura* January 1992: 122–24.

32. Karl Hartmann, "Polens Ostpolitik und die Ukraine," *Osteuropa* October 1995: 949–50.

33. Edward Krzemień, "Polska-Ukraina," *Gazeta Wyborcza* 9 September 1991; "Zapowiedź wymiany ambasadorów," *Życie Warszawy* 9 September 1991.

34. Hartmann, 954.

35. Wojciech Pięciak, "Z Ukrainą Lachów dola . . .'," *Polityka* 31 May 1992; Hartmann, 954–55.

36. "Traktat między Rzecząpospolitą Polską a Ukrainą o dobrym sąsiedztwie, przyjaznych stosunkach i współpracy," 18 May 1992. Courtesy of the Embassy of the Republic of Poland, Washington, DC.

37. See Piotr Kościński, "Nie będzie spotkania z prezydentem," *Rzeczpospolita* 12 January 1993.

38. Grzegorz Górny, "Gorące przyjęcie bez Krawczuka," *Życie Warszawy* 13 January 1993; Witold Pawłowski, "Lady szok," *Polityka* 23 January 1993.

39. Sławomir Popowski and Maja Narbutt, "Antyukraiński gazociąg," *Rzeczpospolita* 1 September 1993; Ilya Prizel, "Warsaw's Ostpolitik: A New Encounter with Positivism," in *Polish Foreign Policy Reconsidered*, eds. Ilya Prizel and Andrew Michta (Houndmills, Basingstoke, Hampshire, UK, 1995), 116.

40. Volodymyr Chikalin, "Sprava Maiora Lysenka," *Vechirnii Kyiv*, 12 February 1994; Jerzy Jackowicz and Andrzej Łomanowski, "Wpadka szpieg z Ukrainy," *Gazeta Wyborcza*, 18 January 1994.

41. "Posol Ukrainy v Respublike Pol'sha Gennadii Udovenko: ". . . platim Rossii za arendu ogromnye valiutnye sredstva'," *Kievskie vedomosti* 24 February 1994.

42. "Partnerstwo dla postoju. Z Aleksandrem Smolarem, politologiem, członkiem Rady Krajowej Unii Wolności, rozmawiają Edward Krzemień i Rafał Zakrzewski," *Gazeta Wyborcza* 28–29 January 1995; Antoni Z. Kamiński, "Dlaczego Polska nie ma polityki wschodniej," *Rzeczpospolita* 8 March 1995; Wojciech Zajączkowski, "Spór o Moskwę," *Rzeczpospolita* 16 May 1995; and Kazimierz Orłoś, "Dlaczego boję się Rosji?" *Tygodnik Powszechny* 2 July 1995.

43. "Pragniemy ociepłenia stosunków z Rosją," *Rzeczpospolita* 18 February 1994.

44. Agnieszka Magdziak-Miszewska and Sławomir Popowski, "Umiejętność być sobą," *Rzeczpospolita* 7 March 1996.

45. Jędrzej Bielecki, "Żelazne problemy," *Rzeczpospolita* 29 February 1996; "Handel idzie w górę," *Nowa Europa* 4 February 1997; Anton Kriukov, "Sbrosit' staruiu kozhu!" *Zerkalo nedeli* 19–25 October 1996; Vasyl' Iurychko, "Ukraina–Pol'shcha: vzaiemovyhidna spivpratsia," *Uriadovyi kur'ier* 20 March 1997; Sambor Kwas, "Polski kredyt dla Ukrainy," *Prawo i Gospodarka* 12 May 1998; and "Prezydenty zustrilysia v Zheshuvi," *Uriadovyi kur'ier* 26 May 1998.

46. Foreign Broadcast Information Service, "Polish President Speaks on NATO Expansion," Lecture Delivered by Polish President Aleksander Kwaśniewski at the Royal Institute of International Affairs, Chatham House, London, 24 October 1996.

47. Foreign Broadcast Information Service, "Baltics, Poland, Ukraine Sign Joint Communiqué in Tallinn," Radio Tallinn Network, 27 May 1997.

48. See Andrzej Kaczyński, "W duchu prawdomównej przyjaźni," *Rzeczpospolita* 1 July 1997; "Pol'shcha z vlasnoi initsiatyvy vid Ukrainy ne vidvernet'sia," *Holos Ukrainy* 25 July 1997; Witold Rodkiewicz, "Jubileusz paryskiej 'Kultury' w Kijowie," *Kultura* October 1997: 104–105.

49. Stephen Rapawy, "Ukraine and the Border Issues," (Washington, DC, May 1993), 36; David McQuaid, "The Growing Assertiveness of Minorities," *Report on Eastern Europe* 13 December 1991 21.

50. Nikolay Iwanow, "Die Polen in der Ukraine," *Osteuropa* (February 1996), 164–73.

51. The declaration was published in *Rzeczpospolita*, 22 May 1997.

52. Olga Alexandrova, "Von einer Sowjetrepublik zu einem europäischen Staat: Anfänge der Aussenpolitik der Ukraine," *Berichte des Bundesinstituts für ostwissenschaftliche und internationale Studien* 14 (1992): 29–30.

53. "Commentary Sees Decline in NATO 'Euphoria'," *Hospodarské Noviny* 5 October 1995, in FBIS-EEU 10 October 1995: 20.

54. Andrzej Niewiadowski, "Niebezpieczeństwo nacjonalizmu," *Rzeczpospolita* 17 September 1996.

55. For one interpretation of the emergence of the Carpatho-Ruthenian national identity, see Paul Robert Magocsi, *The Shaping of a National Identity: Subcarpathian Rus' 1848–1948* (Cambridge, MA, 1978).

56. Rapawy, 16.

57. "Zakarpacie pragnie autonomii," *Biuletyn Ukraiński* No. 12 (Warsaw, 1994), 16.

58. Roman Solchanyk, "The Politics of State Building: Centre-Periphery Relations in Post-Soviet Ukraine," *Europe-Asia Studies* 46(1) 1994: 62.

59. Alfred A. Reisch, "Transcarpathia and Its Neighbors," *RFE/RL Research Report* 14 February 1992: 46.

60. Ibid., 45; "Zakarpacie pragnie autonomii," 15.

61. Niewiadowski, "Niebezpieczeństwo nacjonalizmu"; Paul Robert Magocsi, "The Birth of a New Nation, or the Return of an Old Problem? The Rusyns of East Central Europe," *Canadian Slavonic Papers* 34(3) (September 1992), 219.

62. Anatolii Martsynovs'kyi, "Chomu v Slovachchyni rozdilena ukrains'ka obshchyna?" *Holos Ukrainy* 6 March 1996.

63. Alfred A. Reisch, "Hungarian Foreign Policy and the Magyar Minorities: New Foreign Policy Priorities," *Nationalities Papers* 24(3) September 1996: 447.

64. In some respects, Antall was pursuing goals that the last communist government (headed by Miklos Németh) had felt free to pursue. See Joseph C. Kun, *Hungarian Foreign Policy: The Experience of a New Democracy* (Washington, DC, 1993), 50–51.

65. Kun, *Hungarian Foreign Policy*, 104; Alexandrova, "Von einer Sowjetrepublik zu einem europäischen Staat," 22–23; Zlenko, 5.

66. Istvan Madi, "Carpatho-Ukraine," in *Contested Territory: Border Disputes at the Edge of the Former Soviet Union*, ed. Tuomas Forsberg (Brookfield, VT, 1995), 138–40; Alfred A. Reisch, "Agreements Signed with Ukraine to Upgrade Bilateral Relations," *Report on Eastern Europe*, 21 June 1991, 14.

67. Cited in Reisch, "Agreements Signed with Ukraine to Upgrade Bilateral Relations," 16.

68. According to Article 17, "In full harmony with the Paris Charter on the new Europe and other relevant CSCE documents, the two sides express their conviction that the friendly relations between their peoples, as well as peace, stability, and democracy, demand the mutual protection of the ethnic, cultural, language, and religious identities of the national minorities, and every condition must be created to guarantee this protection." Cited in "Jeszenszky Interviewed on Basic Treaty with Ukraine," *Új Magyarország* 6 May 1993, in FBIS-EEU 10 May 1993: 18.

69. "Antall Sends Letter to Ambassadors Meeting," *Új Magyarország*: 21 July 1993, in FBIS-EEU 22 July 1993: 21.

70. "MSzP's Foreign, Security Policy," *Kihívások és válaszok: 1994–1998*, in FBIS-EEU (Supplement) 8 February 1995: 51.

71. Stepan Vash, "Vizit v znak priznatel'nosti. No s namekom," *Zerkalo nedeli* 7–15 May 1998.

72. Rapawy, 36 and 39.

73. Paul Robert Magocsi, "The Hungarians in Transcarpathia (Subcarpathian Rus')," *Nationalities Papers* 24(3) September 1996: 525.

74. Ibid., 531–32.

75. Susan Stewart, "Ukraine and Policy toward Its Ethnic Minorities," *RFE/RL Research Report* 16 September 1993: 61.

76. Reisch, "Hungarian Foreign Policy and the Magyar Minorities," 449.

77. "Ethnic Hungarians at Ukraine Minority Conference," *Kárpáti Igaz Szó*, 7 February 1995, in FBIS-SOV, 9 March 1995: 36.

78. "Kovács: Anti-Hungarian Campaign in Ukraine 'Regrettable,'" MTV Television Network, 10 August 1996, in FBIS-EEU 12 August 1996: 16–17; "Arpad Gentz: 'Vsegda, kogda Vengriia zabyvala posmotret' s Zapada na Vostok, ona popadala v bedu,'" *Kievskie vedomosti* 12 November 1996.

79. Vladimir Tismaneanu, "The Quasi-Revolution and its Discontents: Emerging Political Pluralism in Post-Ceauşescu Romania," *East European Politics and Societies* 7(2) Spring 1993: 309–310.

80. Vladimir Socor, "Annexation of Bessarabia and Northern Bukovina Condemned by Romania," *Report on the USSR* 19 July 1991: 24.

81. Ibid.

82. Ibid., 25–26.

83. Solchanyk, "The Politics of State Building," 63.

84. Rapawy, 36–38.

85. Iuliia Mostovaia, "Iz bol'shoi rumynskoi tuchi malen'kii antiukrainskii dozhd'. No, vozmozhno, s bol'shimi posledstviiami," *Kievskie vedomosti* 26 January 1994.

86. "Dohovir pro vidnosyny dobrususidstva i spivrobitnytstva mizh Ukrainoiu ta Rumuniieiu," *Uriadovyi kur'ier* 5 June 1997.

87. The Romanian chamber of deputies ratified the treaty on 17 June 1997, and the Senate on 7 July; the Ukrainian parliament approved the accord on 17 July 1997.

5

Ukraine, Turkey, and the Black Sea Region

DUYGU BAZOGLU SEZER

Ukrainian-Turkish relations today are a by-product of the disintegration of the Soviet Union. An understanding of the regional context is therefore essential to a study of Ukrainian-Turkish relations.

The Black Sea has become one of the most dynamic, new regions in the world in the post-Soviet era. This is a vast region stretching from the Balkans in the west to the Caspian Sea in the east, that is home to almost a dozen countries, big and small. Because the region sits at the eastern and southeastern-most fringes of Europe on the one hand, and the western and southern borders of Russia on the other, the character of the dominant relationships and issues in the region will inevitably have important implications for European security.

For the last two centuries the Black Sea region lacked an autonomous personality: it was basically a Russian (and later Soviet) domain. The emergence of Ukraine in 1991 as an independent state on the northern shores of the Black Sea is the key development that has overturned the centuries-old order. Today there are three major actors in the region: Russia, Ukraine, and Turkey. In other words, the retrenchment of Russian/Soviet power has by default contributed to the emergence of Ukraine and Turkey as regional powers, introducing a nascent three-power trilateral relationship. Given this new configuration of power, Black Sea politics today is closely affected by the nature and issues of two sets of diadic relationships: Ukrainian-Russian and Turkish-Russian. It is too early still to view budding Ukrainian-Turkish relations as a defining force.

This survey examines the evolving Ukrainian-Turkish relationship against the background of the shifts in the geopolitical configuration in the Black Sea region brought about by the disintegration of the Soviet Union. Because Ukrainian-Turkish bilateral relations have been energized only in the aftermath of the breakup of the USSR it will be important to see, first, how the Black Sea region is being reshaped in terms of major new forces, influences, and issues in the wake of the retreat of Russian/Soviet power. It is primarily against this context, in particular Russia's redefined regional role, that Ukrainian-Turkish relations possess significance from the perspective of international politics and European security.

The Black Sea: A New Playing Field for New Public and Private Actors

Broadly speaking, the following developments have ushered in an entirely new geopolitical environment in the Black Sea region: the end of Russian hegemony and the concomitant progression toward a pluralist regional system; increasing openness to the West; the eruption of local conflicts; the potential emergence of the Black Sea region as a major trading hub; and timid steps toward regional institution-building.

Taken together, these developments have galvanized a complex web of forces for discord and cooperation, but the former have so far prevailed. In other words, the process of adjustment to the post-Soviet status quo has bred powerful conflicts and tensions. More significantly, from the perspective of Black Sea politics Moscow's relations with Ukraine and Turkey have come under new strains and stresses. Generally speaking, Russia has reacted to the post-Soviet developments in the Black Sea region in a spirit of frustration, as they cumulatively have represented part of Russia's global retreat. In contrast, Ukraine and Turkey have welcomed the general outlines of the new order, as they are perceived to be serving each country's national interests. Implicitly, if not explicitly, Ukraine and Turkey have displayed identical positions toward many of the controversial issues in which Russia has been involved, or possibly been the driving force, as shall be seen in the discussion of Ukrainian-Turkish bilateral relations below.

From Hegemony to Pluralism

The most profound change in the Black Sea region has come about by the collapse of the *ancien régime*, leading to a thorough reconfiguration of the "correlation of forces" of the last several centuries. The fundamental element of that order had been Russian-Soviet hegemony and dominance over the entire stretch of the area, except on the southern shores of the Black Sea, controlled by Turkey since the conquest of Constantinople in 1453.

Russia's advance to and eventual control over the Black Sea had represented the culmination of a long and persistent drive by Muscovy since the mid-sixteenth century to establish itself in the lands occupied earlier by the Golden Horde in Eastern Europe. The Russian conquests of the Khanates of Kazan in 1552 and Astrakhan in 1554 at the lower Volga basin first opened the way for Russian advances into the eastern domains of their former Mongol-Tatar masters.[1] In its gradual push southward Russia made its biggest gains when Bohdan Khmelnytskyi, the leader of the Cossack insurrection against Poland, turned for support to Muscovy—an act that eventually brought Ukraine under Russian rule after 1654. The final victory in the "opening" of the Black Sea to Russia came in 1774 with the Treaty of Küçük Kaynarca, which ended the dominance maintained by the Ottoman Empire in the area since 1487 when the Khanate of Crimea entered Turkish protection.[2] The Russian navy, built at the Baltic shipyards by Catherine II to force entry into the Black Sea from the Mediterranean, defeated the Ottoman navy at the battle of Çeşme on the Aegean. The Treaty of Küçük Kaynarca thus marks, among other things, the beginning of the rise of Russia as the dominant naval power in the Black Sea. By its terms Crimea was made independent—only to be annexed by Russia later, in 1783.

Ukraine's decision in 1991 to choose independence and opt out of the Soviet Union has been the defining event that has reversed the direction of this history. Russia suffered an enormous political-territorial retreat in Eastern Europe, including 2,782 kilometers of coastline in the northern Black Sea. This also included Crimea, one of the most important strategic spots in the world. The loss of this massive territory, with a huge advanced military industrial complex on it,[3] and the loss of the corresponding Black Sea coastline have threatened Russia's position as a European as well as a Mediterranean power.

The declaration of independence by Georgia on the eastern Black Sea contributed to Russia's loss of control over further territory and coastline with strategic importance to the security and defense of the Caucasus. This loss has largely remained theoretical, however, as Moscow has regained effective political influence and military presence in the war-torn southern Caucasus through its role as the ultimate mediator and "peacekeeper" or, in some views, instigator in most of the conflicts in the former Soviet space.

These losses cumulatively have reduced Russia's position in the Black Sea region to that of a medium power by regional and global power calculations—with the qualification, of course, that it continues to be one of the world's two nuclear superpowers.

Opening to the West

From Bulgaria to Ukraine, Georgia, and Azerbaijan, the countries around the Black Sea are redefining their international identities and affiliations in the direction of the West. Bulgaria and Romania have explicitly proclaimed their desire for political, economic and military integration with the West. At the Madrid NATO Summit in June 1997, Romania barely missed an invitation to join the Atlantic Alliance along with Poland, Hungary, and the Czech Republic. Ukraine has declared neutrality in its world orientation but with a decidedly pro-Western, pro-integrationist thrust.

In contrast, Russia's westward turn is qualified. Caught for years now between Euro-Atlanticist and Eurasianist sentiments, and in a debate over the true Russian identity that has nurtured those sentiments, Russia's assessments and calculations concerning the aim and nature of its relations with the West are ambivalent at best.

Georgia and Armenia are the only states in the region who have retained a significant role for Russia in their security policies, the former because of Russia's role in Abkhazia and the latter because it views Moscow as its ultimate protector against external threats. The nature of the relationship between Moscow and the two small states in the south was one of dependence by two weak and troubled client states on a powerful patron. Georgia has lately signaled serious second thoughts, however, about the effectiveness of Russia as a security provider. Since 1997, President Edvard Shevardnadze has been increasingly more critical of Russia's peacekeeping/peacemaking role in secessionist Abkhazia, threatening to evict Russia from four military bases it has operated unless it ensures the country's territorial integrity.[4] Incidentally, Ukraine has been one among several CIS countries in the region which have offered to help with peacekeeping in the Abkhaz-Georgian conflict.

Georgia's evolving independence from Moscow has had implications on another level, too. It has enlarged an informal grouping of countries within the Commonwealth of Independent States (CIS) which are opposed to deep integration under the roof of the CIS. This group now includes Georgia, Ukraine, Azerbaijan, and Moldova and is known by the acronym GUAM.

In the military arena, NATO's Partnership for Peace (PfP) program has effectively extended the political-military influence of the West across the Black Sea and its hinterland.[5] During the Soviet era, the entire Black Sea region formed the territory of the Warsaw Pact except in the south, where Turkey stood as the single NATO ally. Today, all former Warsaw Pact members and the Newly Independent States (NIS) have joined the PfP and signed individual partnership programs. Joint ground and naval exercises have been held among NATO and PfP partners, with Moscow largely viewing NATO's new role in the Black Sea with skepticism.[6] In 1996, Russia refrained from taking part in the Cooperative Partner '96 exercises held in Romania on 22–28 July and the Black Sea Partnership '96 exercises held off the coast of Turkey on 9–14 September.[7] The Russian Foreign Ministry lodged a strong protest with NATO against Sea Breeze '97 naval exercises conducted on 22–29 August 1997 in Odesa and the Donuzlav peninsula in Crimea.[8] In the end, NATO had to soften the initial scenario in which a hypothetical ethnic uprising against the government in Kyiv was aided by a foreign power!

Proliferation of Local Conflicts

The Black Sea region ranks first among the regions of the post-Soviet space in the number of local conflicts that have turned into armed fighting. Secessionist armed conflicts in Moldova, Georgia, Azerbaijan, and Chechnya have generated, separately through cross-fertilization, a chain of destabilizing turbulences across the entire Caspian, Caucasus, and Black Sea axis.

The prospects for the future of regional stability look bleak despite the apparent lull in all the conflicts in the last few years. On the positive side, normalization in Russian-Ukrainian relations began with the signing of the long-delayed state treaty in May 1997. The agreement on the division of the Black Sea Fleet further contributed to the normalization. Cease-fire agreements have held between Tbilisi and Abkhaz and Ossetian secessionists, and between

Baku and the Armenian secessionists in Nagorno-Karabakh. Russia and the Ichkerian Republic of Chechnya signed a peace treaty in summer 1997.

On the negative side, negotiated settlement has evaded all conflicts. Mutual mistrust and hardened positions have been sustained. Talks on the future status of the so-called Transdniester republic in Moldova has dragged on for years. Levon Ter-Petrosyan, former president of Armenia, lost his office in elections in February 1998 to a hard-liner, Robert Kocharian, because he was receptive to an Organization for Security and Cooperation in Europe (OSCE)-sponsored plan on Nagorno-Karabakh which was conciliatory. Russian-Chechen relations continue to be gravely troubled. These and the dormant secessionism in Crimea are powerful reminders that the post-Soviet regional status quo is yet to attain peace, stability and permanence.

The negative reverberations of the secessionist conflicts have gone beyond national boundaries to affect, among others, Russia's relations with Ukraine and Turkey. Despite the current tranquility over the Crimean question at the official level, the ability of nationalists in Crimea and Russia in the long-term to destabilize Ukrainian-Russian relations cannot be ignored. On the eastern flank of the Black Sea, the conflicts in the Caucasus have cast dark clouds on Russian-Turkish relations. The longer these negative dynamics fester in the region, the less likely it seems that initiatives such as the Black Sea Economic Cooperation (BSEC) project will acquire real substance and swift results.

The Black Sea as a Trading Hub

The Black Sea region has emerged as a major potential venue for the movement of goods, more specifically fossil fuels, from Central Asia and Azerbaijan to the west. As these resource-rich but land-locked former Soviet republics have opened up to the world, they have discovered that they depend on transit through neighboring countries in order for their goods to reach world markets. The Black Sea region thus is one of the most attractive venues for the transport of Caspian Sea oil.

The sudden transformation of the region into a potential major trading hub between Central Asia and Azerbaijan on the one hand and Europe on the other has injected a new element of rivalry into regional relations. The race has been over the main pipeline to be built to transport Caspian Sea oil to Europe. The Russian-Turkish competition to get the main pipeline to pass through their respective territories has been the most aggressive one in this multi-player regional power game.[9] Bulgaria and Georgia, since 1995, and Romania and Ukraine, more recently, have joined the bandwagon to claim a stake in the prospective wealth expected to flow from Caspian Sea oil. The visit by President Emil Constantinescu of Romania to Azerbaijan and Georgia in July 1998, to lobby for a Baku-Supsa-Constanța pipeline is one example of the intense diplomatic activity by Black Sea littoral countries in order to get a big slice of the energy pie.[10] In its part, Ukraine has been lobbying for a pipeline from

Supsa to Iuzhne (on the Adzhailiikskyi Estuary, northeast of Odesa) presumably to take the oil to central and northern Europe.[11]

The prospect of exporting millions of tons of Caspian Sea oil through the Black Sea has also raised concern about the possible negative environmental impact of such trade. This concern was most acutely felt in Turkey, which fears that the expected manifold increase in the tanker traffic through the Turkish Straits would pose grave environmental and security hazards to Istanbul, a city of over ten million inhabitants.[12] Accordingly, in summer 1994 Turkey began to impose stricter controls on the traffic of merchant shipping. On the other hand, the Montreux Convention of 1936, which defines the international regime of the Straits, mandates the freedom of navigation for merchant vessels. Russia, the principal user of the Turkish Straits, views the Turkish move as a hostile act designed to undercut Russia's regional influence as the principal exporter of Caspian Sea oil from the Black Sea port of Novorossiisk. The Turkish reluctance to see the Straits be put in jeopardy by super tankers carrying Caspian Sea oil offered Bulgaria, Ukraine, and Rumania the opportunity to exploit their geographical location for the passage of pipelines to Europe.

Steps Towards Regional Institution-Building

The Black Sea Economic Cooperation (BSEC) project, which was agreed upon in June 1992 by eleven states (Albania, Armenia, Azerbaijan, Bulgaria, Greece, Georgia, Moldova, Romania, Russia, Turkey, and Ukraine) in response to a Turkish initiative, represents the only all-inclusive effort to promote regional cooperation.

Foreseeing some of the radical changes, and the attendant problems, in store for Europe in general and for the Black Sea region in particular, Turkey's President Turgut Ozal in 1990–91 came up with this vision of Black Sea cooperation for long-term prosperity and peace in a volatile region. If realized, BSEC would serve, in particular, as a vehicle for the promotion of private-sector cooperation in such non-political areas as trade, communications, transportation and the environment. The short-term goal of the Turkish architects of this arrangement was to create a regional outlet for the goods and services of the economies in transition. In the long term, they hoped that habits of cooperation that would be acquired along the way in these limited areas would spill over into political relations.[13]

The BSEC initiative has eventually attained a highly developed institutional structure.[14] At the summit meeting in Yalta on 5–6 June 1998, leaders signed a charter formally establishing BSEC as a regional organization. However, its record of success as an engine of regional cooperation has remained marginal primarily because of the constraints imposed: a) by the ongoing political and military tensions among many of the participating states; and, b) by the structural weaknesses of the economies of the NIS and the former socialist countries in the Balkans participating in the project. Aware of the gloomy future that awaits the region in the event that business would be conducted as usual, ten presidents and Russian Prime Minister Sergei Kiriyenko ended the Yalta summit with a unanimous warning that war threatened the troubled region's prosperity.[15]

The environment is one of the few areas where the political will to develop a coordinated intergovernmental approach seems to have become the strongest. The Black Sea is known as the world's largest anoxic water mass.[16] The degradation of its ecosystem and the unsustainable use of its natural resources are explained by a variety of factors such as high pollution loads from the rivers it receives and inadequate development and management policies of the coastal countries. The Danube River introduces over half of the nutrient input into the Black Sea.

In April 1992, the six littoral states adopted the Convention on the Protection of the Black Sea Against Pollution, known as the Bucharest Convention, which came into force in spring 1994. In April 1993, they adopted the Odesa Declaration to encourage a common policy framework and to determine policy priorities in order to promote the rehabilitation, protection and preservation of the seriously deteriorated marine environment within specific environmental goals and time-frames. The environment ministers met in Istanbul on 30–31 October 1996 to adopt the Strategic Action Plan for the Rehabilitation and Protection of the Black Sea.

Clearly, the will to attack the common environmental problems in the Black Sea seems to be gaining momentum. The European Union, the United Nations and the World Bank have, with their various projects, encouraged the littorals to be more caring towards the Black Sea. Yet, intergovernmental cooperation and coordination still remain an extremely limited, though by no means not an insignificant process. The adoption of the Strategic Action Plan, followed later by the adoption of national action plans, are the most promising signs of future progress. Otherwise the occasionally heard polemical question of "who pollutes the most?" could result in the irreversible ecological death of the Black Sea.

Is a New Black Sea Being Born?

The Black Sea region is thus being transformed into the playing field of multiple actors and forces from within and without the region. New and old actors, influences and issues have been reacting and interacting to ultimately "open" the Black Sea once again, but in contrast to 1774, this time in a reverse process in which Russia has been forced to yield to the entry of new local, regional and international private and public actors into what was a former Russian/Soviet domain.

Will Russia Accept the New Status Quo?

It is too early, however, to conclude that Russia has conceded the loss of strategic control in the Black Sea. Even if the independence of Ukraine seems irreversible, Ukraine's territorial integrity remains vulnerable to pressures from Russia and the Russian diaspora in Ukraine. Eastern Ukraine and Crimea remain a bone of contention for Russian nationalists even though Moscow's official line respects Ukraine's borders. It is significant that for years Russia had used the Black Sea Fleet dispute to stall the conclusion of a treaty of friendship which would endorse the current Russian-Ukrainian borders: the treaty was finally signed in 1997, but has yet to be ratified by the Russian Parliament (Duma). The following statement, made in spring 1998 by Gennady Zyuganov, the leader of the Communist Party of the Russian Federation, is indicative of the mood at least among the nationalists and communists concerning the future of Ukraine: "The Sevastopol issue cannot be resolved separately from the issue of the union of the three Slavic states (Russia, Ukraine and Belarus)."[17]

Russia's love affair with Crimea in general and its ports at Sevastopol in particular, and the Russian military's insistence on maintaining a strong presence in Georgia are the most meaningful indications of the consensus among the Russian political class to retain a position of strength in the Black Sea. Russia's strategic interests in the Black Sea have two interrelated but geographically disparate focal points: Crimea and the Caucasus. Russia would need to anchor its navy in Sevastopol in order to recapture at least part of its maritime dominance. "A powerful Black Sea fleet in the Crimea would serve as an instrument to keep Kyiv under political pressure, to encourage centrifugal trends in Crimea, and to give Russia a lever over the strategic calculations of Turkey, Bulgaria, Romania and Moldova."[18]

In addition, a powerful Russian fleet in the Black Sea would serve as an instrument of control in the Caucasus, both south and north. President Yeltsin elaborated this thinking during a visit to Krasnodar Krai on the Black Sea in mid-April 1996, about the time of his unrealized visit to Kyiv, with the following:

> "Russia will not be Russia without the Black Sea . . . This is not only a matter of history, not only national feelings and prestige. Russia needs to have a fleet in the Black Sea in order to protect reliably its Black Sea lands and the Northern Caucasus."[19]

In a pronouncement issued on 9 September 1996, the Russian Security Council underscored the strategic complementarity between the Black Sea and the Caucasus. According to the Security Council, the purpose of the Black Sea Fleet was, "the protection of the legitimate interests of Russia in the Caspian-Black Sea region."[20]

In short, therefore, the post-Soviet order is one of fluidity and uncertainty in the Black Sea region, marked by deeper tensions. The fundamental reason is the Russian inability yet to fully come to terms with the loss of empire.

Ukrainian-Turkish Relations

As was stated earlier, Ukrainian-Turkish relations are a post-Soviet phenomenon. This is true, of course, for the modern times. However, if one turns the pages of history to the sixteenth and seventeenth centuries, one comes across prolonged encounters between Ottoman Turks and Ukrainians due to the former's imperial extension deep into eastern Europe and the northern Black Sea littoral. Often hostile, these relations included periods of political and military cooperation. Hetman Khmelnytskyi, for example, concluded a short-lived alliance with the Ottoman Empire in 1648, as did Hetman Petro Doroshenko in 1669.[21] As President Leonid Kuchma recognized in one of his speeches during his official visit to Turkey on 26–27 November 1996, the Ottoman Turks at various times and in various ways lent support to the idea of an independent Ukraine. In fact, the Ottoman Empire refused to recognize the union of 1654 with Moscow until about a century later when its power in the northern Black Sea was receding.[22] There is a modern episode of Turkish support for moves for Ukrainian independence as well. In 1918, Turkey was in the forefront of the countries who swiftly extended diplomatic recognition to the short-lived Ukrainian National Republic.

Broadly speaking, Ukrainian-Turkish relations in the post-Soviet era have gone through two phases. The first phase was one of high optimism on both sides in the early years of independence. The second phase has been one of cautious, controlled relations on the part of Kyiv, as the West moved to extend strong support to Ukrainian independence. The first phase roughly coincides with the tenure of President Leonid Kravchuk, the second—with that of his successor, Leonid Kuchma.

President Kravchuk's Search for a Regional Partner

The period between 1991 and 1994 was marked by numerous signs both in Kyiv and Ankara of a mutual desire to cultivate extensive, multidimensional relations of friendship and cooperation—and that at as quick a pace as feasible.

The basic rationale behind this mutual attraction was geopolitical: the wish to reinforce the post-Soviet order in the Black Sea through bilateral and regional cooperation. However, it would be inadequate to maintain that it was merely the weight of the prevailing geopolitical circumstances that pulled the two sides together. President Kravchuk's deeper interest in and understanding of modern Turkey contributed to his ability to evaluate it in a more positive way than would be the case among other former Communist leaders whose view of Turkey were shaped purely by the seventy-year old anti-Turkish Soviet indoctrination.[23] President Kravchuk became a strong supporter of the idea that Turkey was in a position to play a positive role of leadership in the region.[24]

The external influences that mobilized Kyiv's interest in Turkey as a potential regional partner were powerful in the early years of independence. Even though Ukrainian independence was formally recognized by Russia with the Belavezha agreements of 8 December 1991, many in the Russian political elite contested the legitimacy of Ukrainian statehood. This debate was focused above all else on Crimea, with Russian nationalists and the Crimean Russians appealing to regional sentiments and challenging Ukrainian sovereignty over the peninsula.

Second, the West was initially cool to Ukraine. The fundamental element in the Western, and more specifically the American, approach to newly independent Ukraine was the severe concern over nuclear weapons proliferation by inheritance. The longer President Kravchuk's Ukraine delayed denuclearization, the greater the frustration felt in the United States, and Russia, with Kyiv. It was only after President Kravchuk signed the Trilateral Statement at the Moscow summit on 14 January 1994, pledging Ukraine to a non-nuclear-weapons status by June 1996, that an entirely new page in the West's attitude began to unfold. The victory of Zhirinovsky's ultra-nationalist Liberal Democratic Party and the communists at the national elections to the State Duma in December 1993 had already made a dent in the West's evaluation of Ukraine. The West literally offered to become Kyiv's protector politically and economically—and was accepted as such—only after these developments.

In other words, friendship and cooperation with Turkey, one of the three most powerful neighbors in the Black Sea region, emerged as a convenient geopolitical alternative to Ukraine's almost total isolation in the early years of independence. From the Turkish perspective, relations with Ukraine also seemed to address an important geopolitical concern: the desire for the preservation of the post-Soviet status quo in the Black Sea region. The independence of Ukraine was essential to the fulfillment of this goal. Hence the decision of Turkey to extend unequivocal support to Kyiv in its post-1991 struggle with Moscow for full sovereignty and independence.

This fundamental thinking in the Turkish approach to the post-Soviet order in Eurasia has been the motive force behind Turkey's active diplomatic initiatives with the NIS and the former Warsaw Pact countries in East and Central Europe. While Turkey's interest in the Turkic states of Central Asia has been widely publicized, however, this aspect of its new diplomacy has received little, if any, attention. Diplomatic contacts have intensified with the Baltics, Poland, Romania, and Moldova through exchanges of high-level exchanges of official visits and the signing of numerous economic and cultural cooperation agreements. Most recently, for example, President Suleyman Demirel of Turkey paid an official visit to Moldova on 25–26 July 1998.

Against the background of the mutual awareness by Ukraine and Turkey of the complementarity of their geopolitical interests—and the sense of urgency galvanized not only by the tensions surrounding Ukrainian-Russian relations but by the civil wars in Georgia, Azerbaijan, and Moldova—Ukraine under President Kravchuk and Turkey engaged in a highly active bilateral diplomacy, reinforced by regional initiatives.

President Kravchuk's visit to Ankara on 3–4 May 1992, became the first official visit to Turkey by a Ukrainian head of state.[25] The treaty of friendship and cooperation signed during this visit constitutes the fundamental political and legal instrument in which the parties affirm their mutual respect for each other's independence and territorial integrity. Politically, this pledge translates into Turkish support for Ukraine in its quest for full independence from Russia and sovereignty over Crimea. President Suleyman Demirel of Turkey paid an official visit to Ukraine on 30 May–1 June 1994. The highlights of the visit were the exchange of the instruments of ratification of the treaty of friendship signed in 1992, and President Demirel's promise of Turkish assistance in the repatriation of Crimean Tatars to their homeland by constructing 1,000 homes.

Numerous projects for economic, commercial and defense cooperation were taken up in this period, some of which found their way into agreements. In January 1994, an oil pipeline agreement was signed, envisaging the transport of Middle Eastern oil through Turkey to Odesa. The project has been resisted by the authorities in Odesa, on environmental grounds. Meanwhile, the so-called "luggage trade" flourished, as returning Ukrainian visitors to Istanbul flooded the Ukrainian markets with inexpensive Turkish consumer goods—which incidentally, became a convenient form of trade between Turkey, a haven for such goods, and the neighboring CIS states.

On regional and international security issues as well, including the controversial issue of Russian versus multinational peacekeeping in the Southern Caucasus, Ankara and Kyiv took similar positions. Turkey viewed as legitimate Ukraine's demands for security guarantees as a precondition for giving up the Soviet-era nuclear weapons on its soil. On its part, Kyiv largely kept a low profile on Turkish moves to bring new regulations to commercial traffic in the Straits for the protection of the environment and the security of Istanbul—a position that has hardened under the Kuchma regime.

The Turkish initiative on BSEC tabled in 1991 offered a new opportunity to President Kravchuk to press for regional cooperation. He and President Edvard Shevardnadze of Georgia became the most outspoken proponents of regionalism in its broadest sense. At the founding conference held in Istanbul on 25 July 1992, they advocated that the new initiative take on a security dimension as well. For both leaders, Turkey seemed to be well-placed to take on the leadership role—a position not shared by Russia, Greece, and Bulgaria.

As was already intimated, the initial euphoria and momentum in Ukrainian-Turkish relations has dissipated since late 1994 for one basic reason: the West has embraced Ukraine. With this newfound reassurance and prestige Kyiv no longer felt the urgency in seeking regional partners and allies in its struggle with Moscow to maintain its preferred world outlook. It is possible that President Kravchuk, with his keener sense of the power of regional relationships, might have pursued a more nuanced course. After two years of inertia between 1994 and 1996, however, relations have been revitalized by presidential diplomacy. Ukraine's diplomatic activism since 1996 in the Black Sea region, Israel, and Turkey suggest that Ukraine is reconsidering the value of regional relationships to supplant its westward turn.

President Kuchma: From Balance and Caution to Self-Confidence

President Kuchma paid an official visit to Turkey on 26–27 November 1996. Originally scheduled to take place in early July, the visit was postponed due to the Russian presidential elections. He arrived in Ankara at the end of an official visit to Israel.

President Kuchma's policy toward Turkey appears to have evolved within the framework of two overriding though somewhat contradictory, foreign policy considerations: first, the need to normalize relations with Russia; and second, the need to expand and diversify the bases of international support for Ukrainian independence.

The first element had been apparent as far back as 1994, during the presidential elections, when Kuchma campaigned for a pro-Russian foreign policy. Ukrainian-Russian relations have indeed moved in the direction of normalization since 1994—even if the real momentum had started with President Kravchuk's pledge to give up nuclear weapons. The Russian-Ukrainian treaty of friendship and cooperation, finally signed in May 1997 after much foot-dragging by Moscow, is the most obvious evidence of the rapprochement under way between the two countries.

The policy of seeking normalized relations with Russia called for correct behavior not only in Kyiv's relations with Moscow, but also with third parties, too, such as Turkey, for Russia was clearly restive about Turkey's presumed aggressive ambitions in the post-Soviet Black Sea. Thus, Russia accused Turkey of plotting to fill the "vacuum of power" created in the Black Sea and the Southern Caucasus by the breakup of the Soviet Union. These messages apparently were not lost on the Ukrainian leader. Unlike President Kravchuk, who did not refrain from an open confrontation with Moscow in the most difficult years of independence, President Kuchma did not seem willing to risk Moscow's anger by overtly playing up the importance of Turkey as a friend and a potential ally of Ukraine.

The second element in President Kuchma's thinking—the need to expand and diversify the bases of international support for Ukrainian independence—appears to have evolved as a clear foreign policy objective largely after he assumed office. The most outstanding policy outcome of this consideration has been Kyiv's increasingly more determined turn to the West. President Kuchma and high-ranking officials have since 1995 defined "integration with the West" as the country's strategic goal, while placing relations with the East merely in the category of "cooperation."[26]

In this grand balancing act by Ukraine between the West and the East, relatively low-key, controlled, though still friendly, relations with Turkey should prove to be a valuable source of strength for Ukrainian diplomacy, not only in regional affairs but in European affairs as well. The advantages to Kyiv of reviving the momentum in Ukrainian-Turkish relations came to the fore in the Joint Communiqué issued at the end of President Kuchma's visit to Turkey. Behind the routine calls for friendship and respect for the principles of international law on matters of the independence, sovereignty and territorial integrity of states, there was a blunt reminder that Ukraine and Turkey

> expressed their concern at attempts by certain political circles to return to a former state structure in the region of the former Soviet Union in defiance of the historic choice of the concerned peoples to set up their own independent and sovereign states. The President of the Republic of Turkey stressed in the same perspective the prime importance Turkey attaches to Ukraine's independence and territorial integrity as well as to the success of its on-going political and economic reforms as one of the key elements of stability and security in Europe.[27]

The visit of President Kuchma breathed new life into initiatives to increase the volume of bilateral trade; to accelerate scientific, technological and cultural exchanges; and to invigorate the slackening momentum to strengthen regional cooperation. Ten new agreements in these fields were signed during the president's visit. The Joint Communiqué called for the enhancement of efforts to protection the environment of the Black Sea. The "Agreement on the Prevention of Double Taxation" and the "Agreement on the Reciprocal Encouragement and Protection of Investments" were designed to stimulate greater interest in the private sector to undertake joint projects in each other's countries.

The year 1998 witnessed intensification of diplomatic contacts between the two countries. On 12–13 February 1998, Turkish Prime Minister Mesut Yilmaz, and on 21–23 May, President Suleyman Demirel paid official visits to Kyiv. Both leaders also made a point of visiting Simferopol and Bakhchesarai on the final day of their visit.

The Joint Communiqué signed by Demirel and Kuchma expressed, among other things, the hope that mutual relations would reach a level of "constructive partnership"; that the two countries would examine the possibility of concluding a free trade agreement; that they were ready to further develop dialogue and collaboration on energy with particular emphasis on oil and natural gas transportation, oil refining and electric power; and that they agreed to deepen their dialogue on defense matters and to continue their cooperation in the military field at the bilateral level as well as within the framework of the successfully developing relations between NATO and Ukraine.

A total of eight agreements and protocols were signed to promote cooperation in health and medical sciences, education (several hundred Turkish students are studying at Ukrainian universities where tuition is low and admission requirements less demanding), environmental protection, finance, consular relations and arms industry. The agreement on arms production is classified.[28]

Armaments trade and perhaps co-production seem to be among the most promising areas of potential cooperation in the military field. Ukraine is hoping to sell 1,000 T-84 tanks Turkey in a deal estimated to be worth around 2 billion dollars. It faces strong competition from Russia and others also keenly interested in taking part in this and future tenders by Turkey for the modernization of the Turkish Armed Forces. The military agreement signed in May has raised eyebrows in Moscow, as this comment in Moscow-based *Segodnia* indicates: "The recent visit to Kyiv by Turkish President Suleiman Demirel . . . shows that Ukraine is ready to make friends with a NATO member against Russia . . . Moscow should give special attention to Demirel's emphasis on the need for 'multilateral cooperation with Ukraine within NATO's framework;' . . . Local observers interpreted this remark as a response to the intended delivery of Russian S-300 anti-aircraft missiles to Greece [and Cyprus—DS]. This is quite consonant with Kyiv's foreign policy conception—'to make friends against Russia.'"[29]

Trade continues to be the most advanced aspect of Turkish-Ukrainian relations. The volume of official trade in 1997 stood at $1.2 billion. The balance heavily tilts in favor of Ukraine as Ukrainian exports of machinery and steel products make up roughly four-fifths of this trade. According to figures provided by the State Customs Service of Ukraine for the first six months of 1998, Turkey comes third in Ukraine's foreign trade after Russia and China. The volume of trade for that period stood at $361.3 million. The unofficial shuttle trade, which in 1997 stood around $1 billion, is where Turkey is at an advantage. That trade, however, might be on a downward trend.

The regional competition over prospective pipelines for the transportation of the Caspian Sea basin fossil fuels has introduced a new element of tension into Turkish-Ukrainian relations. However, kept low-key, it has been better managed than the open Turkish-Russian struggle on the same issue. The May summit in Kyiv gave President Kuchma the opportunity to reiterate the importance that his country attached to obtaining alternative sources of oil supplies and its resolve to work to secure participation in the transport of Caspian oil. While it was announced that the two presidents reached agreement on Ukraine's participation in talks on Caspian oil, President Demirel sounded a word of caution: "But it is important to remember the owners of oil are not Ukraine or Turkey."[30] It seems clear that Turkey views the Ukrainian alternative not as a viable one because of the strategic (reliance on the Soviet-era Druzhba pipeline) and commercial challenges (the need for bigger investments for new pipelines in Ukraine as opposed to the Baku-Çeyhan pipeline) that it appears to entail.

Crimea

Clearly Crimea is potentially the most critical topic in Ukrainian-Turkish relations, because of the special ties between Turks and Crimean Tatars for centuries.[31] It is an issue that has the potential to unite or divide the two countries. However, to all appearances it seems to have had a unifying impact so far—unifying because Turkey has chosen to support Ukrainian claims of sovereignty over Crimea, by implication rejecting Russian claims to it either on historical or legal grounds, or both.

The original Kravchuk-Demirel commitment to mutual respect for each other's territorial integrity, reiterated at successive meetings, has served as a solid, stabilizing factor in the relations. Equally importantly, Turkey has repeatedly stated that it views the Crimean Tatars as a bridge between the two countries. In May 1998, President Demirel deliberately underlined this once again, adding that: "Our relations with the Crimea are part of our relations with Ukraine." In other words, Ankara has no political or territorial ambitions in Crimea. It feels that Turkey's national interests are best served under the present status quo. Obviously, some within the Crimean Tatar diaspora in Turkey might be expected to take exception to the official position.

Kyiv seems to welcome Turkish interest in the Crimean Tatars as a source of funding for the resettlement of the returning Tatars. The Joint Communiqué of May 1998 refers to Ukraine's "deep satisfaction with Turkey's increasing contribution in the resettlement of the Crimean Tatars in their ancestral lands, within the framework of the recently launched 1000-unit housing project." Turkey several years ago had undertaken to finance the construction of these houses as an act of humanitarian assistance. The financing of 140 houses have already been completed. Turkey further promised to extend Eximbank credits to projects in Crimea that would create jobs for the unemployed Tatar population.[32]

It is not only Kyiv which welcomes Turkish credits and investments in Crimea. The Crimean Prime Minister Arkadiy Demydenko who visited Turkey in March 1996, also expressed hope for the speedy realization of this project.[33] Crimean officials and businessmen who greeted Demirel in Simferopol repeatedly invited Turkish participation in the development of Crimean economy. There is quite an active Turkish business community in Crimea.[34]

The visit of President Demirel, and Prime Minister Yilmaz before him, to Bakhchesarai was the occasion of much emotion among Crimean Tatars. Mustafa Cemilev, head of the Crimean Tatar *Mejlis* and deputy in the Ukrainian parliament, said Demirel's visit was of historic importance because it was the first visit by a Turkish head of state to Crimea since the peninsula was attached to Russia.

It is important to note in this connection that an estimated five-million strong Crimean Tatar diaspora lives in Turkey. Volga-Tatars and Bashkirs are estimated to number around two million. Another eight-to-ten million Turks claim Caucasian ethnic origin. In other words, Turkey is the land of a large diaspora from the former Russian/Soviet empire who emigrated to Turkey in the peak years of Russian expansion and Russian/Soviet repression.[35] Each one of these groups are represented in the cross-section of the Turkish society and have powerful lobbies. The demographic composition of Turkey's population makes Russia especially uncomfortable, as it serves as a reminder of the potential links between its own ethnic Turkic and the Caucasian populations and their cousins in Turkey. It is partly from this larger perspective that Moscow follows with discomfort the Turkish interest in the welfare of the Crimean Tatars. In a sense, therefore, Crimean Tatars sit at the center of the Ukrainian-Russian-Turkish trilateral relationship.

Needless to say, the Crimean Tatars take their own independent positions not only on issues of local significance but on more fundamental issues such as the territorial integrity of Ukraine. From the first day of Ukrainian independence, they have been staunchly in favor of the preservation of the territorial integrity of Ukraine. The *Mejlis* refuted nationalist claims by Russia's State Duma to Sevastopol, arguing that such a position amounted to claims on the territorial integrity of Ukraine, and urging President Kuchma to implement Article 17 of the constitution, which bans deployment of foreign military bases on Ukrainian territory.[36]

As for the prospects for peace and stability in Crimea, they appear gloomy from several angles. The economy is depressed. Political relations with Kyiv are not optimal. Nor are ethnic relations among the peninsula's three dominant nationalities. The situation of the Crimean Tatars is especially unsatisfactory both economically and politically. The unemployment rate is extremely high. The Turkish offer of help in providing funds for housing and investments will definitely fall short of alleviating their problems. Crimean Tatar leaders voice their frustration with what they say is Kyiv's 'open neglect' of their problems, especially that of citizenship involving nearly 120,000 of the returnees.[37] Over the last several years international and regional organizations have tried to draw the attention of the international community by reporting on the depressive local circumstances but no improvement has been obtained. In 1996 the United Nations and OSCE observers reported that more than half of the 250,000 Tatars who returned survived in such abysmal conditions that violence could erupt easily.[38]

Crimean Tatars feel frustrated because despite personal pledges, President Kuchma seems unable to offer solutions to critical issues that would affect the Tatar community's long term political, social, and economic well-being as a viable element of a multi-ethnic society. The truth of the matter is that the difficulty in acquiring Ukrainian citizenship by the repatriates and socio-economic deprivation, together, help create a deprived underclass.

President Kuchma is perceived as a leader who has failed to carry though his promises. Writing in summer 1998 on the occasion of Kuchma's vacation in Crimea, the Tatar press reminded its readers that a year ago the president had asked *Mejlis* Deputy Chairman Refat Chubarov to draw up suggestions on how to facilitate the procedures for obtaining citizenship. While visiting some Tatar villages, he had pledged two million hrivnas from the national budget to help revitalize the local economy. Chubarov submitted his report but nothing has come out of it or of the promised funds until summer 1998.[39]

The lack of improvement in the economic and political conditions of Crimean Tatars bring to mind a fundamental question, of course: How seriously is Kyiv committed to the cause of the healthy repatriation of Crimean Tatars in their ancestral homeland?

Conclusion

Ukrainian-Turkish relations are still evolving. The experience of the last seven years leads us to conclude that the direction of bilateral relations between the two neighboring countries across the Black Sea have been, and will continue to be, closely influenced by Ukraine's relations with Russia and the West.

For a variety of reasons—historical, cultural and economic—the two countries are only just beginning to discover each other as potential partners, but the process of that discovery is beset by several disadvantages. The fundamental disadvantage is what has brought them together in the first place: fear of the revival of the Russian Empire—even though the rationale and intensity of their shared apprehensions vary significantly between the two. On the other hand, neither country is capable of offering credible reassurance against such an eventuality. Operating under this essential constraint, Ukrainian-Turkish bilateral relations were bound to suffer in the event that either one of the two countries felt that an alternative and stronger source of protection could be cultivated somewhere else. This is exactly what has happened in the case of Ukraine which has come to look to the West in its search for security against Russia. For Ukraine, bilateral relations with Turkey and within the regional framework of the BSEC can only be supplementary to its developing fundamental relationship with the West.

One should also remember that the fear of Islamic fundamentalism and radicalism in the 1990s in Christian countries located on the frontier of the Christian and Islamic civilizations would need to be taken into account when considering the future prospects of Ukrainian-Turkish relations. A predominantly Moslem country, modern Turkey's secular political system has been a source of reassurance to its neighbors as a buffer against Islamic radicalism. Yet, the domestic balance within Turkey itself has been changing, with the Islamist Welfare Party[40] having gained sufficient electoral power to preside over a coalition government for about a year in 1996–97. The record of the Welfare Party on foreign policy was definitely not one that strived to export Islamic fundamentalism to Muslim minorities in the neighboring countries like Greece, Bulgaria, Ukraine, and Moldova.

Whether they are inching or galloping, the generally positive nature of Ukrainian-Turkish relations is an important factor of peace and stability in the Black Sea region and in Europe. Ukrainian Prime Minister Valeriy Pustovoitenko reflected a keen awareness of this positive force for regional stability when he said on the occasion of President Demirel's visit to Kyiv in May 1998, that "the development and deepening of Ukrainian-Turkish relations was the most important factor for safeguarding regional stability and creation of a new architecture of European security."[41]

It seems highly likely that enhanced NATO-Ukrainian relations since mid-1997 has contributed to a new awareness in Kyiv that cooperation with Turkey, the only NATO ally in the Black Sea basin, can only be a positive contribution to Ukraine's westward foreign policy.

NOTES

1. Halil Inalcik, "Struggle for East-European Empire, 1440–1700: The Crimean Khanate, Ottomans and the Rise of the Russian Empire," *The Turkish Yearbook of International Relations*, 21 (1982–1991), 1–17. This recent article is a useful guide to the history of prolonged Turkish presence in northern Black Sea between 1473–1774. For Ukrainian perspectives on the same topic and the Russian, Polish, and Turkish rivalry in the region, see, Danylo Husar Struk, ed., *Encyclopedia of Ukraine*, vol. 5 (Toronto, 1993), 319–21.

2. Alexander Halenko, an Ottomanist at the Academy of Sciences of Ukraine, challenges the traditional view that the Black Sea had been "closed" by the Ottomans before its "opening" by the Russian Empire in 1774. See Halenko, "Was the Black Sea 'closed' before its opening by the Russians?" from the abstract of the paper presented at the conference of "The Ottomans and the Sea" organized by the Skilliter Centre for Ottoman Studies, Newnham College, Cambridge, UK, 29–30 March 1996, 2.

3. Ustina Markus, "An Ailing Military Industrial Complex" *Transition* 2(4) 23 February 1996: 52.

4. "Russia Awaits Official Georgian Stance on Peacekeepers," Foreign Broadcast Information Service (henceforth, FBIS) FBIS-SOV-98-220, 8 August 1998.

5. In May 1997, NATO Foreign Ministers met in Sintra, Portugal, and decided, among other things, to enhance the PfP program. The primary objective of the heightened importance attached to the PfP by NATO member countries was to involve partners more deeply in planning and carrying out PfP exercises. See, Sergio Blanzino (Deputy Secretary General of NATO), "A Year after Sintra: Achieving Cooperative Security through the EPAC and PfP," *NATO Review* 46(3) Autumn 1998: 4.

6. Some Russian analysts argue that these activities represent the intention of NATO to shift its southern flank from the eastern Mediterranean to the Black Sea, see, Nicolai A. Kusnetzky, "Geopolitical Aspects of Russian Politics in the Black Sea Region," in Nicolai A. Kovalsky, ed., *Russia: The Mediterranean and the Black Sea Region* (Moscow, 1997), 205.

7. "Russia Eyes Naval Exercise," *Monitor* 2(143) 23 July 1996 [Jamestown Foundation, brdcast@jamestown.org].

8. For protestations in the Russian press against PfP exercises in the Black Sea, see, "Which Way is Sea Breeze Blowing?"*Current Digest of the Post-Soviet Press* (henceforth, CDPSP) 49(17) 28 May 1997: 19.

9. For Russian views on the competition on the oil pipelines, see, "Compromise Struck on Caspian Oil Pipeline Routes," *CDPSP* 47(41) 8 Novem-

ber 1995: 8; for Turkish views, see, Temel Iskit, "Turkey: A New Actor in the Field of Energy," *Perceptions* (a quarterly journal of the Turkish Foreign Ministry) 1(1) March–May 1996: 58–82.

10. "Georgia Romania July 2, 1998," TURKISTAN-Newsletter (BUSI-NESS) 98(107-07-1998) 6 July 1998 [kryopak@WORLDNET. ATT.NET].

11. For Ukrainian views on the advantages of using Ukrainian territory for the transport of Caspian Sea oil, see, State Committee of Oil, Gas and Oil Refining Industry of Ukraine, *Eurasian Oil Transport Corridor: Caspian Oil to European Markets through Ukraine, Project Presentation*, (Kyiv, January 1998).

12. Turkish official statistics show that in 1994, a total of 19,630 merchant vessels passed through the Straits. With 5,114 vessels, Russia was the biggest user of the Straits followed by Ukraine, Malta, Syria and Greece. See, Republique de Turquie, Ministere des Affaires Etrangres, *Rapport Annuel Sur Le Mouvement Des Navires À Travers Les Detroits Turcs, 1994, 58-ème année* (Ankara, 1995), 46–48. According to Turkish press reports, the Turkish Foreign Ministry believes that there has been a 500 percent increase in the total number of vessels transiting the Turkish Straits, from 9,144 in 1960, to 46,914 in 1995. "Moskova Ankara'ya karsi sertlelsiyor," (Moscow hardens toward Ankara) *Posta*, 31 Temmuz (July) 1997. For Russian views on the Turkish position, see, "We Cannot Consider It Lawful," *CDPSP* 46(13) 27 April 1994: 26.

13. The historical record shows that Turkey was the original source of inspiration and the singular force that pushed forth the idea of a Black Sea cooperation scheme among regional countries in the wake of the end of the Cold War. This point is important not simply to get the historical record right but also as a clue to those who wish to understand the true founding ideas behind the project. Today, when the BSEC has been recognized as a positive sub-regional organization, there are some attempts, at least at the intellectual level, at redefining and/or ill-defining the original purposes of the project. Needless to say, these efforts would fail the test of historical evidence. For the original concepts that went into the creation of the BSEC, see, Duygu Bazoglu Sezer, "Black Sea Economic Cooperation Project: Anarchy, the Demise of Bipolarity, and the Turkish Call on the Regional Players to Cooperate rather than Defect," United Nations Institute for Disarmament Research, *Conference on European Security in the 1990s: Problems of South-East Europe*, Conference Proceedings (Geneva, 1992), 153–63.

14. For general information see, BSEC Permanent International Secretariat, *The BSEC: The Present and the Future* (Istanbul, 1994), and *Black Sea Economic Cooperation: Handbook of Documents* (Istanbul, 1995).

15. Pavel Polityuk, "Ukraine: Black Sea States Say War Clouds Region's Prospects," Reuters, 5 June 1998.

16. The information in this paragraph has been obtained at the Global Environment Facility/Black Sea Environmental Programme, sponsored by the World Bank, Dolmabahçe Sarayi, Istanbul, November 1996.

17. *BBC Summary of World Broadcasts (BBC/SWB)* 25 March 1998: B/16.

18. "Struggle for the Heart of Europe," *The Fortnight in Review* (1)9 [Jamestown Foundation brdcast@jamestwon.org].

19. "Russia: Yeltsin: Black Sea Fleet Part of 'Strategic Security," FBIS-SOV-96-075: 11.

20. "Russia: Security Council to Take Control of Black Sea Fleet Issue," FBIS-SOV-96-175, 9 September 1996: 11.

21. Inalcik, 7; Volodymyr Kubijovyč, ed., *Encyclopedia of Ukraine,* vol. 2 (Toronto, 1988), 170. See also, A. Zhukovsky, "Turkey," in Danylo Husar Struk, ed., *Encyclopedia of Ukraine*, vol. 5 (Toronto, 1993), 319–21. In interviews with the author in August 1996, some Ukrainian intellectuals have argued that Khymelnytsky should have joined the Ottoman Empire, for that would have meant that Ukrainian independence would have come much sooner, in the pattern of the Balkan peoples.

22. Inalcik, 12–13.

23. There is an unwritten theory among Turkish and Ukrainian scholars which argues that the systematic anti-Turkish Soviet indoctrination in Ukraine was designed to inhibit the interest of Ukrainian scholars in conducting research on the history of Ukrainian-Turkish relations in order to uncover portions of their history.

24. Interview with former President Leonid Kravchuk, Kyiv, 20 August 1996.

25. For an excellent survey of Ukrainian-Turkish relations during the Kravchuk era, see, Oles M. Smolansky, "Ukrainian-Turkish Relations," *The Ukrainian Quarterly* 51(1) Spring 1995: 5–34, from which I have benefited greatly.

26. "Ukraine: Kuchma Stresses Stability in Relations with Russia," FBIS-SOV-96-137, 16 July 1996: 44; "Ukraine: Kuchma Seeks Further Integration Into Europe," FBIS-SOV-96-110, 6 June 1996: 44. For statements by members of the establishment, see, Oleksandr Moroz, "The Path to Europe," *Politics and the Times* (a quarterly journal of the Foreign Ministry of Ukraine, in English) 1 (October–December 1995): 6–9; Volodymyr Horbulin, "Ukraine's Place in Today's Europe," *Politics and the Times* 1 (October–December 1995): 10–15; Henadiy Udovenko, "An

Open, Predictable and Pragmatic Foreign Policy," *Politics and the Times* 1 (October–December 1995): 16–24.

27. *Turkish-Ukrainian Joint Communiqué,* Turkish Ministry of Foreign Affairs, Ankara, 27 November 1996, 3.

28. Chris Bird, "Tanks, Oil To Dominate Turkish Leaders's Ukraine Trip," Reuter's News Service 20 May 1998; Pavel Polityuk, "Ukrainian, Turkish Leaders Mull Oil Transport," Reuters, 21 May 1998; Alexander Yegorov, "Russia: Tank War Between Russia and Ukraine," *Kommersant* 29/05/1998 [retrieved from Reuters News Agency].

29. Viktor Yadukha, Viktor Lugovik, "Ukraine: Kiev is Ready to Make Friends with Turkey, Against Russia," *Segodnia* 26 May 1998 [retrieved from Reuters News Service].

30. Mikhail Melnik, "Ukraine: Kuchma Says Ukraine Wants to Take Part in Caspian Oil Project," Itar-Tass World Service, 22 May 1998 [retrieved from Reuters News Service].

31. Clearly the revival of interest in ethnic kin living as minorities in other countries has been a universal phenomenon in the post-Cold War and post-Soviet era. This has been equally true for Turkey, especially with regard to the more isolated Turkic communities in the former Soviet Union like the Gagauz Turks in Moldova. Since 1991 Turkey has not only cultivated cultural relations with the 200,000-strong Gagauz community but actively encouraged them in the early years of independence to reach an accommodation with Chişinaŭ on the understanding that Moldova would not integrate with Romania.

32. For a recent study on "deported peoples" in the former Soviet Union, see the article by Vladimir I. Mukomel and Emil A. Pain in Vitaly Naumkin, ed., *State, Religion and Society in Central Asia: A Post-Soviet Critique* (Reading, 1993), 144–61.

33. "Ukraine: Crimea: OSCE Mission Not Needed," FBIS-SOV-96-100, 22 May 1996: 45.

34   The author was a member in the delegation that accompanied President Demirel to Ukraine.

35. For a brief treatment of the exodus of Tatars and Caucasians to Turkey to escape Russian repression, see, Paul B. Henze, *Turkey: Toward the Twenty-First Century* (Santa Monica, CA, 1992), 29.

36. "Crimea and the Black Sea Fleet," *OMRI Daily Digest* 2(210) October 30, 1996 [omripub@omri.cz].

37. "Ukraine: Tatar Leaders Voice Resentment at Kyiv's 'Open Neglect,'" FBIS-SOV-96-130, 5 July 1996: 48.

38. James Rupert, "Tatars Return to an Inhospitable Home in Crimea," *International Herald Tribune* 11 January 1996: 2; Matthew Brzezinski, "For Tatars, Coming Home to Crimea Brings Yet More Dislocation," *The Wall Street Journal* 14 August 1996: l.

39. *Avdet* 5 August 1998, in *Digest of Crimena Press,* in *Turkistan Newsletter, Crimea Bulletin/Kirim Bulteni* 98-2(141-26) August 1998.

40. The Welfare Party was banned by the courts in early 1998 on charges of having violated the constitution.

41. "Ukraine: Pustovoytenko Meets Turkish President Demirel," *BBC/SWB/ FORMER USSR,* 25 May 98 [retrieved from Reuters News Service].

6

U.S.-Ukrainian Relations: Past, Present, and Future

SHERMAN GARNETT

Relations between the United States and Ukraine, formally established in January 1992, a month after Ukraine's referendum on independence, have developed rapidly since the two sides resolved their deadlock over nuclear disarmament. Kyiv is now a frequent stop for senior American officials. The U.S. and Ukraine have formed a bilateral commission headed by the Ukrainian President Leonid Kuchma and the United States Vice-President Al Gore to tackle outstanding foreign policy, security, and economic issues. Ukraine has become a leading recipient of U.S. foreign assistance. In October 1996, the two nations declared their relationship a "strategic partnership."

Yet the course of U.S.-Ukrainian relations has not always run smoothly. Nuclear issues dominated the first two years and crowded other questions off the agenda. The nuclear period of the relationship still casts a long shadow over relations. Both sides praise what the bilateral relationship has become, though these relations are likely to be tested in the near future by Ukraine's internal stagnation and the negative influence it exerts on the development of broad-based political and economic ties.

To weather future problems, Washington and Kyiv have developed a special relationship across a broad range of issues; the question is whether that relationship will continue to move forward or stumble on the obstacles that remain. These obstacles include Ukraine's unfinished work of internal consolidation, the abnormal state of Ukrainian-Russian relations, Europe's continued indifference to Ukraine, and a persistent split within the United States over the extent of its long-term national interests in Ukraine. Even under the best of circumstances, these obstacles will be a real constraint on how far and how fast these relations will develop.

Though initial Ukrainian overtures for better relations in the early 1990s were spurned by a reluctant United States worried about Ukrainian fragility or nuclear ambitions, Kyiv has always understood the need to cultivate political, moral, and material support for its independence in Washington and other major European capitals. U.S. and Western European support substantially improves Kyiv's chances for overcoming its two major strategic challenges, consolidating a secure and prosperous state, and normalizing its relations with Russia.

The real question is whether the United States is similarly committed to Ukraine. This essay will concentrate on U.S. policy toward Ukraine, beginning with the nuclear question. It will then turn to enduring obstacles in the way of strong, post-nuclear bilateral ties. Finally, it will examine bilateral and regional policies that will best ensure that U.S. national interests are protected and the bilateral relationship endures.

The Absence of Building Blocks

Before examining the development of bilateral U.S.-Ukrainian ties, it is useful to remember how little foundation had been laid for them. There was no Ukrainian state until 1992. U.S. officials, with the exception of then Secretary of Defense Dick Cheney, largely looked at the Ukrainian declaration of sovereignty and subsequent moves to separate Ukraine from the USSR with shock and horror. And even Cheney's approach was that of someone prudently preparing for the end of the old order, not someone fervently wishing for the new. President Bush delivered his warning against "suicidal nationalism" in Kyiv, not three weeks before the events that led to the fall of the Soviet Union.[1]

The United States has a large and active Ukrainian-American community. Its members approached both the legislative and executive branch at this time with advice and insight. However, as subsequent events demonstrated, they were not as close to the emerging Ukrainian political leadership as their Baltic-American counterparts. No senior posts in the new Ukrainian state went to members of the diaspora community, as happened in Estonia. The United States had little expertise on Ukraine, but Ukrainian-Americans could not by themselves fill this gap. They were naturally asked to fill important diplomatic or analytical jobs dealing with Ukraine, but their views were frequently—and unfairly—discounted by policymakers as biased.

With the nuclear issue dominating the beginning of U.S.-Ukrainian relations, it is not surprising that the community of strategic and arms control analysts and practitioners provided another important perspective on Ukraine and U.S.-Ukrainian relations. Yet this group knew a great deal about nuclear weapons and little about Ukraine. By and large this group expected Ukraine to try to keep its weapons and tended to see many Ukrainian political and defense steps solely through the prism of nuclear policy. As a result, the U.S. government often looked at the nuclear problem as a matter that should and could be separated from nation-building and the formation of relations between these new states. In retrospect it is clear that neither Ukraine nor Russia treated the nuclear question as an autonomous issue, but rather as part of a whole package of issues from debt relief to the division of the Black Sea Fleet that defined Russian-Ukrainian relations.[2]

It is only as the U.S. government's own capabilities to understand Ukraine grew and important outside experts and prominent statesman added their voices to the Ukrainian-American community, that U.S. policy began to become more balanced and subtle. Starting at the Pentagon but including all key government agencies, groups of analysts and policymakers appeared who dealt exclusively with Ukraine. By 1993, a small group of such people was in place. On the outside, Zbigniew Brzezinski created an American-Ukrainian Advisory Committee, bringing prominent Americans together with their Ukrainian counterparts. This group issued a series of recommendations that urged U.S. policy to supplement its focus on nuclear disarmament with an appreciation of the strategic importance of an independent and stable Ukraine.

The Ukrainian side was also hampered by its lack of expertise on the specific issues that complicated the U.S.-Ukrainian relationship. History will record the contributions to the consolidation of Ukrainian independence by a small but talented group of Ukrainian officials, often with experience in the Soviet Ukrainian diplomatic service. However, outside the upper reaches of the president's staff, Foreign Ministry and Ministry of Defense, positions were filled by the inexperienced and sometimes by the unimaginative.

Different methods of policy-making and implementation in Washington and Kyiv exacerbated the basic problems faced by both countries. Washington expected that the Ukrainian government could operate with the same level of decentralization as the U.S. The United States had literally hundreds of experts and mid-level policy officials at work on nuclear and security issues. Once senior leadership made the fundamental decisions, relatively junior officials could negotiate and even take decisions for the U.S. on carefully delimited technical aspects of the issue. No such system existed on the Ukrainian side. With Ukraine, no progress could be made on even highly technical issues without the intervention of a small group of very senior officials, including the prime minister, the foreign and deputy foreign ministers, and senior advisors to the president. The 1994 Trilateral agreement was at several crucial junctures literally the work of the three presidents themselves. The U.S. side was continually frustrated by the lack of decentralization on the Ukrainian side on what it considered "technical matters." For the Ukrainians, however, there were no technical matters that were not somehow connected to strategic decisions about Ukrainian security policy and even the consolidation of the Ukrainian state.

The Opening Phase: Lessons of Nuclear Disarmament

In many respects, U.S. policy toward Ukraine is riding on the momentum created by nuclear disarmament. The most impressive fruits of strategic partnership have been in the security field, often negotiated with the alumni of the nuclear negotiations. In 1996–1997, Ukraine voiced strong support for NATO enlargement. The U.S., in turn, spearheaded efforts within NATO to establish a special NATO-Ukrainian partnership, spelled out in a special charter adopted at the mid-1997 Madrid Summit. In 1998, Ukraine agreed to pull out of a Russian-led deal to provide nuclear technology to Iran, at substantial cost to the Kharkiv region. These and other positive steps in the U.S.-Ukrainian security relationship are a direct result of the success of the nuclear talks.

The last Soviet warhead left Ukraine in mid-1996. Though many factors, including Ukraine's own domestic politics, contributed to the success of this effort, what separates this issue from others is the role played by the United States. U.S. engagement made a profound difference. Given resource constraints and other serious problems between Kyiv and Moscow, it is likely that Russian-Ukrainian bilateral talks on this issue would not have reached a resolution. Even if other factors in Ukraine and Russia could be counted upon to prevent the nuclear issue from escalating to a confrontation, a delay in the momentum on Ukrainian disarmament could well have cast a pall over successful efforts in 1995 to extend the Nuclear Non-Proliferation Treaty (NPT) indefinitely. It certainly would have greatly added to uncertainty in the region and would have further constrained Ukraine's search for external assistance for its 1994 economic reform package. Though Ukraine's relations with the International Monetary Fund (IMF) have often been rocky, there would be no such relations at all without the nuclear success.

Indeed, there was no way to develop a more positive U.S. and Western approach to Ukraine and Ukrainian independence except by handling the nuclear question just as it was. Many critics, including this author, believed that the final and successful U.S. policy approach—mixing incentives for expanded political relations and economic reform with continued firmness on nuclear disarmament—should have been tried from the very beginning, not after nearly two years of misunderstanding and mutual recriminations. However, even if a broad-based policy were tried from the beginning, the nuclear issue would have still been at the center and serious U.S.-Ukrainian political and economic relations could not have developed normally without its resolution.

The nuclear question unfolded in three distinct phases. The first can be described as a stage of declarations and romanticism on the Ukrainian side and great anxiety on the part of the West. It lasted until mid-1992. Ukrainian intentions during the first period are well represented by the 1990 resolution, adopted by Ukraine's Supreme Soviet (Verkhovna Rada; referred to as "Parliament" after independence), affirming the country's status as a neutral and non-nuclear power. In Kyiv, there were great expectations of global support, both moral and material. Western leaders, on the other hand, feared the impending collapse of the USSR; they trusted Soviet President Gorbachev more than the promises of a still uncertain legislative body. In private, they feared—and exaggerated—what President Bush expressed publicly during his August 1991 visit to Kyiv on the very eve of Ukrainian independence—namely, the dangers of the above-mentioned "suicidal nationalism." Formal U.S. recognition of Ukrainian independence, when it came in late December 1991, was conditioned on fulfillment of Ukraine's pledge to become a non-nuclear state.

The second phase began with the signing of the Lisbon Protocol in spring 1992 and ended with the U.S.-Ukrainian-Russian Trilateral agreement in January 1994. For the West, the Lisbon Protocol settled the status of nuclear weapons on the territories of Ukraine, Belarus, and Kazakhstan. The Soviet successor states became part of the START treaty by committing to its early ratification and accession to the Nuclear Non-Proliferation Treaty as non-nuclear weapon states "in the shortest possible time."

Yet what appeared to the United States to be the end was for Ukraine only the beginning. The Ukrainian leadership was coming face to face with the realities of statehood. Internally, economic hardship and regional tensions seemed to challenge the very notion of Ukraine's survival. The relationship with Russia was hitting its first real hurdles, with tensions surfacing in spring 1992 over possession of the Black Sea Fleet and other issues. Further, the Ukrainian leadership was slowly coming to understand the massive costs associated with fulfilling its nuclear commitments. Thus, for Ukraine, the hard part of negotiations began *after* the Lisbon Protocol.

Needless to say, Ukraine's wavering, after signing the Lisbon Protocol, was viewed in the United States as a lack of good faith. In fairness, there were other factors—in particular Ukraine's lack of experience in judging what it required and what it should get for its agreement to the Lisbon Protocol. The $150 million in aid linked to Ukrainian agreement was in fact hardly adequate for starting, let alone sustaining, the costs of dismantling and transferring the nuclear warheads and the safe elimination of the silos and delivery systems left behind. And while it is primarily Ukraine's own responsibility to reform its economy and stabilize its political system, with Western aid playing a subordinate role, the nuclear issue was not of Ukraine's making, and its resolution was not of major concern to Ukraine alone. U.S. assistance was not only money well spent; it was vital to supporting a process of disarmament that accorded with vital national interests. This crucial middle phase lasted from mid-1992 until the conclusion of the Trilateral agreement in January 1994.

The third phase was one of implementation of Ukraine's nuclear commitments and the broadening of U.S.-Ukrainian ties. It began with the Trilateral Statement in January 1994 and came to an end in June 1996 with the removal of Ukraine's last nuclear weapons. During this phase, Ukraine formally acceded to the NPT as a non-nuclear weapon state and received a set of security assurances from the NPT Depository States. Though work continues on silos and delivery systems, the period after June 1996 can be genuinely characterized as a post-nuclear one, in which the shape of the relationship will be determined by a broad set of political, economic, and security—not nuclear—issues.

During this intense two-and-a-half-year period, U.S.-Ukrainian relations several times appeared on the verge of collapse. Yet at crucial moments, U.S., Ukrainian, and Russian negotiators found the right mixture of compromise. All three sides wanted a deal. The U.S. side added a crucial element of funding, both in direct support to disarmament and through the U.S. purchase of highly enriched uranium from Russia (which gave the latter a fiscal basis to compensate the Ukrainians as they demanded). In addition to the overview below, the details of this story are told elsewhere in this volume.[3]

The nuclear negotiations, however, created basic personal and institutional links between the U.S. and Ukraine. It cemented these links by an important success, one that paid dividends at the NPT Review Conference in 1996 and elsewhere. It allowed those who saw Ukraine only as a potential nuclear renegade to appreciate its strategic importance, the positive influence a stable and independent Ukraine would have on the entire neighborhood and the positive steps the fledgling Ukrainian state had taken in establishing its legitimacy in the eyes of a regionally and ethnically diverse population.

It was during the second phase that the United States confronted the starkest options for dealing with Ukraine and decided upon a course that led to broadening political, economic, and security ties with Ukraine. How the United States arrived at that cause is best understood by examining three key policy crossroads of the period: (1) the spring 1993 U.S. policy review; (2) the response to the Ukrainian Parliament's conditional ratification of START I in November 1993; and (3) the conclusion of the Trilateral agreement itself in January 1994.

The Spring 1993 U.S. Policy Review

Already in late 1992, it was clear to Washington policymakers that the Lisbon Protocol could not be implemented without U.S. engagement. The Bush administration attempted to broaden its approaches to Ukraine in late 1992. There was a single, high-level Ukrainian visit to Washington by Deputy Foreign Minister Borys Tarasyuk, but a broad strategic dialogue did not develop, given President Bush's defeat in November. The transition to a new administration and its early concentrated focus on supporting Russian reform left Ukraine on the back burner until early spring of 1993.

The Ukrainian government, prodded by critics in the Parliament and the desire to secure political and economic support from the West, moved away from its earlier stress upon dismantling the weapons in favor of receiving specific economic assistance and security guarantees. From at least fall 1992 on, the Ukrainians stated explicitly that getting from commitments in principle to the actual dismantling and withdrawal of nuclear warheads would require real negotiation. At a November 1992 press conference, President Kravchuk said that Ukraine should have "appropriate compensation" for nuclear disarmament and, in addition, "certain guarantees" for its security. He repeated this message frequently in late 1992 and early 1993.

Nevertheless, Washington expected the Ukrainian Parliament to address at least the ratification of START I in January 1993. Under the Lisbon Protocol, President Kravchuk had committed Ukraine to ratification of START I and accession to the Nuclear Non-Proliferation Treaty as a non-nuclear weapon state *in the shortest possible time,* but January came and went. On 10 February 1993, the speaker of the Parliament stated that START ratification was not a priority.[4] On 18 February, the Parliament formally postponed consideration altogether. In April, 162 deputies signed an open letter "on Ukraine's nuclear status." The letter underscored Ukraine's status as a successor to the USSR and "as a nuclear power." It confirmed Ukraine's "right of ownership of the nuclear weapons on its territory" and underscored the importance of compensation and of "state independence, national security, and territorial integrity."[5]

The Russian side, recognizing the drift in Ukrainian domestic opinion, advocated redoubled efforts and diplomatic pressure to bring about Ukrainian compliance. Moscow press reports regularly warned of possible safety issues as Ukraine took over administrative control of nuclear and other military sites. The best example of the Russian approach occurred later in the year, at the September 1993 Russian-Ukrainian summit meeting at Massandra, in Crimea. At this meeting, Russian leaders exerted considerable pressure on President Kravchuk to agree to a comprehensive deal on the Black Sea Fleet, nuclear disarmament, and debt relief. There is evidence that senior Ukrainian officials agreed to such a package in advance.[6]

The centerpiece of this Russian package was a swap of at least partial debt forgiveness for Ukraine's share of the Black Sea Fleet. But the Russians overplayed their hand. They misjudged their capacity to impose a comprehensive deal and Kravchuk's power to accept and enforce it. The results of the Massandra summit split the Ukrainian government so severely that any hope for the agreement quickly unraveled. Prime Minister Kuchma, one of those who favored the swap of the Ukrainian share of the Black Sea Fleet for debt relief, resigned in early September 1993. An open split developed between Kravchuk and Defense Minister Kostiantyn Morozov, who resigned in October 1993 because he favored Ukrainian insistence on complete Russian withdrawal from Crimea as the *sine qua non* of a deal on the Black Sea Fleet.

In the aftermath of Massandra, the Russian side saw that Ukrainian weakness was not simply something to be exploited; it was also a danger to regional stability and to the Russian-Ukrainian relationship as a whole. With this increasing Russian concern about Ukrainian stability came a growing if reluctant appreciation that progress in nuclear talks required the financial and other incentives that could only be provided by the United States—in a trilateral framework. Massandra convinced the Ukrainian side, particularly President Kravchuk, that Ukraine's internal weakness was seriously affecting the stability of the government. Indeed, Kravchuk listed the Massandra summit as one of the two major problems he faced during 1993: "Russia then [at Massandra] saw how hard the [summer 1993 miners'] strikes were hitting Ukraine and that it was brought to its knees by internal problems. On top of that there was external pressure, and people were taking advantage of our weakness."[7]

President Kravchuk understood that there would be no sustained financial aid or security ties without resolution of the nuclear question. A bilateral negotiation with Russia would result in pressure that Ukraine could not control. There is little doubt that Kravchuk's experience at Massandra—where he was confronted by intense Russian pressure and deep division within his own government on the Black Sea Fleet issue—played a key role in his decision to

accelerate negotiations with the United States and to seek a trilateral framework for resolving the nuclear issue.

The need for trilateral negotiations or for an expanded agenda was not at
first prevalent in the U.S. government. In fact, the prevailing U.S. mood in
early 1993 was a mixture of anxiety over long-range Ukrainian nuclear intentions and anger about Ukraine's failure to fulfill its obligations. Though no
formal linkage existed between nuclear disarmament and economic assistance,
Washington could not sustain even modest assistance while Ukrainian nuclear
intentions were uncertain.

Yet faced with the lack of progress, in early 1993, the U.S. government
began to review its Ukrainian policy. No one in the U.S. government questioned the basic nuclear elements of the policy and no serious player—in fact,
no player at all—advocated tolerance for a Ukrainian nuclear deterrent.[8] The
nuclear elements of the policy remained: to continue to press Ukraine to fulfill
its obligations and to provide financial assistance for this purpose. Differences
of view did emerge, however, over whether the key to Ukrainian compliance
was to expand U.S. policy of engagement or to tighten the screw still further.
The review ended with a decision to engage Ukraine in a broad discussion of
improved economic, political, and security ties, implementation of which
would be linked to the resolution of the nuclear issue. In May 1993, then U.S.
Ambassador-at-Large Strobe Talbott visited Kyiv to discuss a "turning of the
page" in U.S.-Ukrainian relations. Discussions between Ukraine and the
United States focused not simply on outstanding nuclear matters but also on
economic assistance, expanded military and defense ties, and a renewed political relationship between the United States and Ukraine. In essence, the U.S.
side sought to sketch the kind of relationship that could arise once the nuclear
problems were removed. This initial visit did not reverse months of mutual
suspicion, but it did begin a process that brought senior levels of both governments together in an atmosphere of give-and-take on the full set of issues.

Ambassador Talbott's visit was quickly followed, in early June, by Secretary of Defense Les Aspin's visit to Kyiv. Aspin came directly from a meeting
with Russian Minister of Defense Pavel Grachev, in which the two sides
discussed U.S. proposals for early dismantling of nuclear systems in Ukraine.
These proposals included arrangements for international monitoring designed
to meet Kyiv's concerns about the dismantling, transfer, and final dispensation
of the warheads. Ukrainian Minister of Defense Morozov visited Washington
in July, promising cooperation on the dismantlement of nuclear weapons.
Regular diplomatic consultations and correspondence continued, including discussions on economic, political-military matters, and defense relations in October. By the time of Secretary of State Warren Christopher's visit to Kyiv in
October 1993, the U.S.-Ukrainian dialogue had been restored. A genuine trilateral negotiating process had also emerged, bringing together Ambassador
Talbott and Deputy Foreign Ministers Georgii Mamedov and Borys Tarasyuk
for regular discussions.

The Conditional Ratification of START I

In November 1993 the Parliament conditionally ratified START I.[9] The resolution laid out a number of conditions and demands. Some appeared to define the conditions for a nuclear deal; others, particularly the unilateral amendment of the Lisbon Protocol, seemed to be trying to scuttle the trilateral talks. Kravchuk and other senior officials quickly reassured the United States, Russia, and the world that this action was not the final word on the matter. However, it would be wrong to see the parliamentary vote solely as an act of defiance. The links between the senior levels of the Kravchuk government and of the Parliament ensured that, whatever the Parliament as a whole had originally intended, the November ratification became a basis for the January 1994 Trilateral agreement. Indeed, according to some of the key players, the resolution itself was drafted in the President's office and sent to the Parliament, where it was approved with little modification.[10]

For the West, the resolution presented real problems. Neither the United States nor Russia could consider it a legally acceptable ratification of START I. The resolution declared that Ukraine was not bound by Article Five of the Lisbon Protocol—which committed Ukraine to become a party to the NPT as a non-nuclear weapons state "in the shortest possible time." It reasserted Ukraine's claim to ownership of the weapons and set forth a series of conditions that would have to be met before its ratification would be legally binding on Ukraine.

The dilemma in Washington was clear. Should this text be read as shutting the door or opening it? A case could be made that the Parliament had finally gone too far, overturning the Lisbon Protocol and seeking the right to retain under START a significant portion of the nuclear warheads on Ukraine's territory. However, the text also contained specific conditions that could be read as a formal negotiating proposal on security assurances, compensation, and other key issues. In several places, the text made plain that these conditions were not final or gave the President of Ukraine latitude to negotiate further. Even in point six of the resolution, which claimed that Ukraine was bound by START to eliminate only a portion of the weapons on its territory, there was language stating that this formulation "did not preclude the possibility of the elimination of additional delivery vehicles and warheads according to procedures that may be determined by Ukraine." Points five and eleven explicitly asked the President of Ukraine to negotiate with other parties. Finally, point twelve asked the President to approve a schedule and exercise control over the elimination of the nuclear systems to be dismantled. These points were important in Washington's assessment of the resolution.

Washington could never accept the Parliament's explicit rejection of Article Five of the Lisbon Protocol as a permanent statement of Ukraine's obligations, but it could explore the basis of an interim deal that would lead to a reconsideration of this statement. In essence, Washington acknowledged that START and the NPT had been temporarily de-linked and that an interim agreement might be required for that linkage to be restored. It is clear from subsequent negotiations and the conclusion of the Trilateral agreement that Washington in the end chose to interpret the Parliament's action as at least something that could be overcome and perhaps an opening of the door. Eight weeks later, the Trilateral Statement was signed, with the Parliament rescinding its November resolution and ratifying START without conditions in February 1994.[11]

The Trilateral Agreement

By the end of 1993, the new U.S. policy toward Ukraine and continued bilateral and trilateral negotiations had put in place the basic foundation for agreement. In Ukraine, the growing sense of crisis, brought on by economic and political demands of striking miners in June and the Massandra Summit in September, made the need to resolve the nuclear issue more pressing. Washington began to see in Ukraine's actions an opportunity to move forward. The announcement on 20 December 1993 that Ukraine would deactivate twenty SS-24s was seen in Washington as a clear signal that President Kravchuk and his government were going to find a way to complete negotiations and deal with the Parliament. Indeed, without some prior understanding with at least the senior parliamentary leadership, Kravchuk would not have risked taking such a step with regard to the SS-24s. Moscow was also interested in a deal that would preserve the basic framework of Massandra and begin the process of nuclear disarmament in Ukraine. The Russians understood that the United States brought energy and financial resources to the arrangement and that U.S. presence ensured that progress on the nuclear question would not be reversed by some future bilateral issue, as had happened in the aftermath of Massandra. The Russians were also sure that, on the nuclear question, U.S. and Russian interests coincided. The Russian side trusted the U.S. side, even when tactical differences emerged, to advance the common agenda of achieving a non-nuclear Ukraine.

On 14 January 1994, Presidents Clinton, Kravchuk, and Yeltsin signed the Trilateral Statement in Moscow. This agreement explicitly linked Ukraine's nuclear disarmament to its broader economic and security conditions, although opinion in Ukraine was divided over whether the agreement went far enough. The significance of the Trilateral agreement is that it provides a multilateral framework within which to address nuclear and other issues. It legitimizes U.S. interest in issues that would ordinarily remain bilateral matters between Moscow and Kyiv.

The nuclear portions of the agreement committed Ukraine to the "elimination of all nuclear weapons, including strategic offensive arms, located on its territory in accordance with the relevant agreements and during the seven year period as provided by the START I Treaty . . . " Ukraine agreed in particular that "all nuclear warheads will be transferred . . . to Russia" and that "all SS-

24s on the territory of Ukraine will be deactivated within ten months by having their warheads removed." Within the same time period, "at least 200 nuclear warheads from RS-18 (SS-19) and RS-22 (SS-24) missiles will be transferred from Ukraine to Russia for dismantling." Ukraine was guaranteed compensation for the highly enriched uranium, beginning with 100 tons of low enriched uranium underwritten by a U.S. advance payment of $60 million.[12] These provisions reaffirmed Ukraine's commitment to complete nuclear disarmament over the period of START implementation by transferring nuclear warheads to Russia. President Kravchuk also agreed to maintain pressure on the Parliament to accede to the NPT as a non-nuclear state, which it did in October 1994. The sides agreed on concrete interim steps for early deactivation of all SS-24s, a good-faith beginning on the transfer of warheads to Russia, and Russian compensation to Ukraine for the value of the nuclear materials. Unlike previous agreements, the Trilateral agreement provides performance standards against which Ukrainian (and Russian) behavior can be judged.

Three additional elements distinguish the Trilateral agreement from previous Russian-Ukrainian agreements or even the Lisbon Protocol. First, both in principle and in practice, the agreement established a truly trilateral framework in which to address future issues. U.S. involvement brought needed financial resources and technical expertise, but also important experience in seeing agreements implemented. Previous Russian-Ukrainian negotiations had at best reached agreements in principle, only to founder in the technical follow-up. The U.S. presence added a force for balance in a situation that could easily be derailed if it remained bilateral.

Second, the agreement provided for security assurances that were formally extended to Ukraine by the United States, Russia, and the United Kingdom once Ukraine acceded to the NPT as a non-nuclear-weapon state. These assurances fell far short of the kinds of guarantees that Ukrainian negotiators and parliamentary leaders regularly demanded. Yet they provided the strongest language to date on the recognition of existing borders to which Russia has ever agreed—and paved the way for the recognition of borders embodied in the comprehensive Ukrainian-Russian treaty of 1997. These assurances, based on existing language in CSCE documents and the NPT, provided basic pledges that the powers will refrain from the threat or use of force against Ukraine; that they will not employ measures of economic coercion; and that they will not use nuclear weapons against Ukraine. These assurances are political, not legally binding. For Ukraine, they probably represented the best deal obtainable.

Finally, the Statement committed the United States to further technical and financial aid. President Clinton promised "to expand assistance" beyond the minimum of the $175 million already envisaged. President Kravchuk's visit to Washington in March 1994 led to an agreement to double economic assistance to $350 million.

The Trilateral Statement was only the first step toward a final resolution of the nuclear question in Ukraine. Subsequent efforts to implement this agree-

ment, both on the political side (NPT accession, the formal exchange of security assurances) and on the technical side (the actual dismantling and transfer)
have brought the sides to the end of the transfer process. The roots of this
success undoubtedly lie in the spring 1993 shift in U.S. policy, which, while it
continued to adhere to a strict insistence on Ukrainian nuclear disarmament,
began to engage Ukrainian concerns more broadly. At each subsequent point,
the U.S. government retained confidence in this strategy.

Post-Nuclear Trends and Enduring Obstacles

It is difficult to overestimate the legacy of the nuclear period in U.S.-Ukrainian
relations. The resolution of the nuclear question created a pattern of U.S.
engagement and cooperation with Ukraine. Once the Trilateral Statement was
signed, political ties between the two countries rapidly expanded. President
Kravchuk visited Washington in February 1994. U.S. programs of technical
assistance began in earnest. The election of Leonid Kuchma as president in the
summer of 1994 and his economic reform program announced in October
added further momentum to the relationship. Ukraine became soon thereafter
the third largest recipient of U.S. foreign assistance. It received the regular
attention of U.S. Secretary of State Warren Christopher and Secretary of Defense William Perry. The latter especially made frequent visits to Kyiv. In May
1995, President Clinton himself visited Kyiv. In September 1996, the U.S. and
Ukraine agreed to create a binational commission, chaired by Vice-President
Al Gore and President Kuchma respectively. This commission consists of four
committees dealing with foreign policy, security trade and investment and
other economic issues.

During Foreign Minister's Hennadiy Udovenko's visit to Washington in
October 1996, the two sides described their relationship as a "strategic partnership." The United States was the driving force behind the language in the
December 1996 NATO Ministerial communiqué stating the alliance's support
for Ukrainian political and economic reform and acknowledging that "the
maintenance of Ukraine's independence, territorial integrity and sovereignty is
a crucial factor for stability and security in Europe."[13] U.S.-Ukrainian cooperation laid out the basic principles incorporated in the NATO-Ukraine Charter the
following year. Ukraine has also joined the Missile Technology Control Regime, broadly expanded defense and military contacts with the U.S., NATO
and other Western countries, taken an active role in IFOR and SFOR missions
in Bosnia and generally been a good friend of the U.S.

However, political and economic stagnation within Ukraine threatens the
momentum generated by accomplishments in the security field. The bilateral
relationship, however close it has been in some fields and between key individuals in both governments, simply cannot expand if Ukraine is economically
and politically stagnant. Despite real progress to date in Ukraine's effort to
develop a "European choice" for the future, its size, location and the need to

continue the work of internal reforms and consolidation make it an awkward fit in the new Europe. Ukraine will remain an awkward fit for at least a decade or more.

Ukraine is not wholly a country of the Commonwealth of Independent States, nor does it wish to be, yet it is unable to make a credible near term claim on Europe's core institutions. Its stability is crucial to the region as a whole and to key European powers and institutions, yet these powers and institutions have few ready-made solutions to offer Ukraine. Many in Europe still see Ukraine as an alien country on the periphery, not a serious candidate for the European Union. The future of U.S.-Ukrainian relations depends on managing four enduring obstacles that are directly related to Ukraine's unique position in the new Europe, its internal stagnation and its still undefined position in the minds of American and European diplomats

The first obstacle is Ukraine's internal political and economic situation. There is no longer a question of whether Ukraine will survive as a state. The internal Ukrainian consensus on independence is strong and there are no realistic alternatives to statehood. The real question is what kind of state will Ukraine become. The broad alternatives can be stated starkly as a choice between gradually becoming a part of Europe or remaining relegated to Europe's periphery. A European Ukraine requires bold choices and actions that have so far eluded the Ukrainian political leadership. A peripheral Ukraine comes by default: the leadership need only follow the political rules of the game already deeply ingrained in the country.

Despite the 1994 reforms and occasional bursts of progress, Ukraine has much work ahead of it to create stable state structures and a thriving market. The diversity of its regional, political and economic interests makes it unlike Poland or the Baltic states, where there is no question of the basic Western orientation of these countries. In Ukraine, there remain deep divisions among regions and ethnic groups over the market and the way the state should run. Civil society is weak, leaving major political matters in the hands of a narrow circle of regional and central elites. Economic reform is progressing, albeit slowly. Thus the gap between Ukraine and the rest of Europe is wide and could get wider before it starts to close.

These internal problems will continue to shape Ukraine's ability to change within and to respond to the outside world. Its political stability will also continue to rest on a narrow foundation as well. The positive trends in U.S. policy toward Ukraine have yet to account for these internal trends. That policy must be formulated to survive the shocks and setbacks that could emerge, as well as support reforming tendencies within Ukraine that at present have only shallow roots within the Ukrainian government and society.

The second obstacle is the state of Ukrainian-Russian relations. Ties between Moscow and Kyiv have been more pragmatic and constructive than many analysts initially imagined they could be. In particular, at the highest levels of both governments, there is a willingness to diffuse tension, forge agreement or delay action to keep relations on track. In May 1997, the two presidents finally signed long-delayed agreements on friendship and the disposition of the Black Sea Fleet. The relationship also weathered Russia's 1996 imposition of quotas and import duties on Ukrainian vodka, sugar and other products.

Yet Ukrainian-Russian ties are still far from normal. Basic issues from territorial recognition to the presence of Russian forces remain under perpetual negotiation. Key issues include the implementation of the Black Sea Fleet agreement, provisions of which will keep Russian naval forces in Crimea for two decades. Ukraine remains heavily dependent on Russian energy and, despite a debt restructuring in 1995, owes Russia billions of dollars

Underlying these unresolved questions is a more basic difference about the relationship itself. Kyiv and Moscow have very different views of the future of their relationship. Russia seeks in the future to establish what one Yeltsin advisor called "a fraternal Slavic compromise," an integrated relationship far closer than normal state-to-state ties.[14] Russia does not want to thwart a broad-based integration of this sort by a settlement of outstanding issues that would normalize the relationship and thus freeze it. Ukraine wants an unambiguous state-to-state relationship. But Ukraine is too weak and internally divided to impose such a relationship on Russia. As both sides come face to face with their fundamental differences, there is a danger of drift in the relationship.

Given the potential for future instability in Crimea or for disagreements between Ukraine and Russia, this drift is dangerous. Russian-Ukrainian relations need to be placed on a normal, treaty-based foundation. A crisis in Crimea would have tragic consequences under any circumstance, but would be much more serious if the legal status of Russian forces there, or even of Sevastopol itself, were unresolved in Russian minds. Such a turn in Russian policy is unlikely in the Yeltsin era, but that era is coming to a close. The United States and its NATO allies have an enormous stake in seeing Ukraine and Russia normalize their relations, but the have done little to date to suggest to either party that they have anything at stake at all. In the next decade, Ukrainian-Russian difficulties will almost certainly intrude upon U.S.-Ukrainian ties. Kyiv will certainly turn to Washington for support, as surely as Moscow will try to keep Washington out of such matters. Future Ukrainian-Russian difficulties will almost certainly force the U.S. either to back up its words of support with concrete actions or reveal them as empty phrases.

The third obstacle is that key European states and institutions have yet to acknowledge Ukraine's strategic significance or to fashion policies which are commensurate with that significance. In Western Europe, Germany has made the most serious efforts. It almost every respect, it is Ukraine's best friend among the states of the European Union. The Ukrainian-German summit in Kyiv in September 1996 produced half a dozen trade agreements, including German backing for the modernization of the Odesa airport. Germany also agreed to lead the effort within the European Union for the negotiation of a

Ukrainian-EU free trade agreement, though little has been accomplished in the nearly two years since. There is an EU-Ukrainian cooperation agreement, negotiated in 1994, but it is only slowly making its way through the various European parliaments. Europe has yet to respond positively to Ukraine's long-term ambitions to enter Europe or even to recognize Ukraine's immediate strategic importance. There is still a virtual neglect of Ukraine in the chancelleries of Europe.

In European minds, Chornobyl still occupies the first place among European-Ukrainian bilateral issues. Ukraine's internal problems and historic ties to Russia and the former Soviet space are taken as justification of this neglect, even as Ukraine's impact on European stability and prosperity increases. With Russia responding negatively to NATO expansion, there is a good chance that Europe's wariness toward Ukraine will grow.

Why is Europe's lack of a Ukrainian policy an obstacle to U.S.-Ukrainian relations? Simply put, the positive momentum in U.S.-Ukrainian ties cannot survive without allied support. As with other important economic, political and security issues, U.S. support for Ukraine must become part of the overall Western agenda. Crucial economic and political supports for sustaining this momentum require European resources and leadership. European opinion is especially crucial in the normalization of Ukrainian-Russian relations. While U.S. efforts are frequently seen in Moscow against the backdrop of a larger tradition of geopolitical rivalry, French, British, and German concerns could not be so easily dismissed.

But the final obstacle is the instability of the current U.S. policy consensus on Ukraine. Despite appearances to the contrary, internal divisions have persisted within and outside the U.S. government over Ukrainian policy. The most important division is between those who see the emerging security environment of Eastern and Central Europe justifying a continued and even expanded policy toward Ukraine, and those who doubt whether any U.S. vital interests are involved at all in a post-nuclear Ukraine. This division is unlikely to surface in the fair weather that U.S.-Ukrainian relations currently enjoy, but it cannot help but emerge when ties with Ukraine demand hard choices or resource commitments.

Those who want to limit U.S. exposure in Ukraine are helped by the lack of U.S. investment and trade. Some U.S. companies, once interested in the Ukrainian market, have pulled out. Others have complained of the corruption and chaos that prevent normal business to flourish. In the Cold War, of course, the United States sustained a number of important relations solely on geopolitical and strategic considerations. However, Ukraine's strategic value alone will not carry the relationship, or at least not provide the kind of cooperation and interaction both sides want.

Some will say that this assessment is far too negative. The positive trend lines U.S.-Ukrainian relations are clear, they will argue, and irreversible. Yet such an argument is persuasive only if U.S. policy clearly rests on a broad-based recognition of the new regional dynamics of Eastern and Central Europe and Ukraine's pivotal role there. By this standard, U.S. policy is not yet firmly anchored. Moreover, a wise policy would privately and publicly admit the obstacles that remain. U.S. policy deserves high marks in some areas, but no better than an "incomplete" in others. The U.S. has made great efforts to communicate its support and advice to the Ukrainian leadership on key matters of economic reform. It has maintained a strong defense dialogue, though this dialogue has avoided the hardest issues of Ukrainian defense reform. There is little evidence that U.S. policy makers and analysts understand the ups and downs of Ukrainian politics. Washington praises Ukrainian constitutional reform, but has apparently not noticed how little impact the 1996 constitution has on the day-to-day disposition of power and influence in Kyiv. The U.S. has barely begun to grapple with the European neglect of Ukraine; and it has lost ground, compared to 1993–1994, in ensuring that its views are heard in both Moscow and Kyiv on the need to ensure a full normalization of Russian-Ukrainian relations. It is thus far too early to say whether U.S.-Ukrainian ties are on a secure and enduring footing.

Fashioning a Post-Nuclear Ukrainian Policy

U.S. domestic priorities and resource constraints hardly encourage a radical expansion of foreign commitments, yet the United States and NATO could not remain aloof in the event of a major crisis of Ukrainian statehood or of Russian-Ukrainian relations. Ukraine is too close to a vulnerable Central Europe to assume that a crisis there could be contained. U.S. and Western interests in Ukrainian stability will only grow as Poland enters NATO. The most commonly heard alternative to Western engagement in a future crisis is to leave the situation to Russia. Yet even if this were a desirable policy option, Russia is currently too weak to assume such a role, and Ukraine is internally too diverse to submit to it. Russian attempts to intervene directly in Ukrainian politics would escalate a crisis, not control it. If the United States chooses to limit its exposure in Ukraine because it perceives it has already dealt with its primary concern (i.e., nuclear weapons), it will face the paradox of not wanting to overextend itself when the costs are low, but an almost inevitable requirement to take part in a crisis when the costs are high.

Ukraine will continue to be a crucial factor in Russia's self-definition as a major power. The United States and its NATO allies have a stake in seeing Russia and Ukraine develop strong bilateral ties on a normal state-to-state foundation. It does not want to see, scattered on the edge of expanded Western security and economic communities, the preconditions for major inter-state conflict. It has an interest in the resolution of outstanding Russian-Ukrainian differences, the settlement of the Black Sea Fleet issue, and the emergence of a stable Crimea as an integral part of the Ukrainian state. Getting the Ukrainian-Russian relationship right is an essential part of the U.S. policy of supporting political and economic reform within Russia, for continued internal progress in Russia depends upon a stable external environment and Russia's reconciliation with this new environment.

Ukraine's unique problems compel U.S. and Western policymakers to think about the countries between NATO and Russia. These countries hold the key to whether Western plans for NATO and for cooperation with Russia are compatible. What is needed now is a post-nuclear policy that will enhance security and internal cohesion for Ukraine and the region as a whole.

The first element of such a policy should be a *coherent definition of U.S. and Western interests in Ukraine and the surrounding regions of Eastern and Central Europe.* The United States must understand what is at stake in Ukraine, particularly in the event of its internal failure or external friction with Russia. From this perspective, a whole host of issues not captured by—and potentially complicated by—NATO expansion or Russian policy demand attention, including CIS integration, regional conflicts, and the basic building blocks of independence and prosperity for the states of this region. The implementation of a sophisticated *regional* policy requires understanding of events in places such as Kyiv, Warsaw, and Minsk. Strained U.S. and Western resources and domestic preoccupations would seem to urge against a sophisticated, multilateral approach to the region. Yet it is precisely these resource constraints, together with the U.S. policy successes of the past five years with relatively small resources, that make small investments in the region attractive. In many cases, U.S. and Western engagement provide the strongest impetus for economic and political reform measures which are weakly supported in Ukraine.

A second element of a new policy toward Ukraine should be to *preserve and expand existing mechanisms for cooperation, leverage, and influence.* These mechanisms grew out of the nuclear period of relations, but their utility extends far beyond nuclear issues. In the long run, the trilateral negotiating framework is as important as the Trilateral Statement itself. It is an additional security assurance given to Ukraine that—while it falls short of an absolute guarantee from the United States—promises U.S. engagement (and that of the West in general) in a broad range of questions crucial to Ukraine and Russian-Ukrainian relations. This structure is unlikely to survive the end of the nuclear disarmament process without continued U.S. investment of diplomatic time and energy as well as funds.

The need for this kind of investment is by no means self-evident in Washington, and it is actively resisted in Moscow. When the Ukrainian ambassador to Washington paid his respects to the departing Russian ambassador in early 1994, he suggested that both men drink a toast to the recently concluded Trilateral agreement as a model for resolving future issues. The Russian ambassador responded that the trilateral approach was fine for nuclear issues, where U.S. and Russian interests coincided, but that such a mechanism was not in Russia's interest in other Russian-Ukrainian issues, where U.S. and Ukrainian interests are more likely to overlap.[15] Many Russian political leaders share this view.

Formal trilateralism, particularly at the senior levels, has almost disappeared since early 1994. The high-level group led by Deputy Secretary of State Talbott and Deputy Ministers Mamedov and Tarasyuk has been disbanded. Foreign ministers and heads of state have not met trilaterally since early 1994—not even at the Budapest Meeting in December 1994, where the last step in the nuclear disarmament process was carried out with the formal offering of security assurances to Ukraine by Russia, the United States, and the United Kingdom. In January 1996, the three defense ministers did meet in Ukraine; they were there to blow up an SS-19 missile silo. They met again in June to celebrate the completion of warhead transfers, but little effort was made to turn the agenda toward post-nuclear questions.[16]

The drift away from trilateralism by definition removes many Ukrainian-Russian issues of importance from the immediate and easy reach of U.S. and Western policy. If Ukrainian-Russian relations were to experience moments of tension or even crisis, U.S. influence would be easier to exert if mechanisms of consultation did not have to be created anew in a difficult context. Particularly as NATO expansion decisions are made, the re-establishment of strategic dialogue at the deputy foreign minister level is crucial. The defense ministers should also hold regular trilateral discussions. A trilateral perspective needs to permeate the bilateral meetings of the parties, particularly the rare but important meetings between heads of state. Perhaps the U.S.-Russian agenda is already overburdened with problems, but it is important that Ukraine and Russia be aware of U.S. and Western interest in the normalization of their relations.

A third element of a new U.S. approach to Ukraine *should focus on Western Europe and Japan.* The United States must encourage its allies to deepen ties with Ukraine. Ukraine's slow economic reform remains a sticking point with Europe: the overabundance of Ukrainian steel, chemicals, and agricultural products makes long-term EU-Ukrainian economic cooperation difficult. Following the early failed pattern of U.S. nuclear policy, the Western European countries have individually—and collectively through the European Union—taken a one-sided view of Ukraine's problems and importance by linking normal ties to the closure of Chornobyl. Japan has provided—reluctantly—only nuclear-related aid. The United States should push both Western Europe and Japan to support the kind of incentives and assistance package that has been put together in mid-1998 for Russia. Ukraine's needs are far more modest that the $20 billion plus set aside for Russia by the IMF, World Bank, governments and private banks, yet the impact of a serious package linked to serious Ukrainian reform efforts would be enormous.

A fourth element of a new approach should be *to preserve the basic support for military stability already present in the region.* The low levels of conventional forces, the reduced strategic nuclear presence, and the absence of battlefield deployments of tactical nuclear weapons create favorable military conditions in the region—certainly the most favorable in several generations. These conditions are the result of the swift political changes that have taken place since the 1980s, reinforced by a set of arms control treaties that only partially regulate these forces. NATO expansion, deepening CIS military integration, and unilateral defense decisions by states of the region could reverse the momentum toward a stable military balance at lower force levels. Decisions in all three of these key policy areas must be informed by a common interest in preserving and stabilizing the current military situation in the region.

The fifth element should be a *clear policy on CIS integration*. It is not enough for U.S. policy to state that integration in the former USSR should be voluntary. Nor is it a constructive response to look upon all integration as merely the resurrection of Russian imperialism. Some of the weakest states of the former Soviet Union are likely to see their future survival very closely tied to cooperation with Russia. The basic principles that the United States should adopt are close to those guiding current Ukrainian policy on integration. Integration must not undermine state sovereignty or have adverse security consequences for the region as a whole. It must be open to the outside world.

A sixth needed feature of a new approach relates to *broader questions of Europe's security institutions*. NATO is and will remain the dominant element of any future European security structure. The OSCE is not a counterweight to NATO in Europe. The U.S. and its allies have to make NATO-Ukrainian and NATO-Russian institutions work.

Finally, *the U.S. has to tell the truth to its strategic partner*. It cannot force the Ukrainian leadership to act against its immediate political interests, particularly as rivals emerge to President Kuchma in the 1999 presidential elections. It cannot impose economic reforms on an unwilling country. Yet the U.S. must be a strong stimulus for these reforms by reminding Ukraine of the choice it faces and the consequences of failing to act. It must also sketch out—as it did so successfully to a Ukraine unsure of whether it should proceed with nuclear disarmament—the support Kyiv can count on if it recognizes the seriousness of the situation and makes the hard reform decisions needed for the country to move forward.

Conclusion

Ukraine presents the United States with the special challenge of more clearly defining its role in the new Eastern and Central Europe. For the United States, the question remains how best to protect its overarching security interests—in nuclear issues, in the moderation and transformation of Russian power, in Ukrainian independence, and in regional stability. This essay has argued that these interests can best be protected by a new engagement in Ukraine and the region as a whole. Such a new engagement would neither cede Ukraine to some mythical Russian geopolitical space, nor force the United States to play the role of constant counterbalance to Russia. Neither role is consistent with U.S. interests or capabilities.

A policy of engagement in Ukraine requires a definition of U.S. interests not chained to Cold War thinking about spheres of interest. It requires that the United States work toward an outcome in which Russian power is moderated both by its internal transformation and by the success of its neighbors, which are neither sources of instability in their own right nor the pawns of other great powers. Russia has had little experience with this kind of neighbor. It is not impossible, but it is unlikely that Russia and Ukraine or its other neighbors will be able to work out this kind of relationship on their own. There clearly is a role for the United States and its allies in encouraging the emergence of a genuinely *regional* system, but it requires that the United States understand the power it has to shape a new order in the region—in particular its interests in and influence over the stability of Ukraine and of Ukrainian-Russian relations.

With the passing of the Cold War and the emergence of crises in regions unknown to most Americans, the temptation is strong to narrow U.S. policy focus and limit U.S. commitments. The experience of successful work on the nuclear issue strongly counters this temptation. U.S. and Western power and influence will remain an instrument of consequence to the future stability of Ukraine and Central and Eastern Europe as a whole. Learning how to use that instrument in a new security environment is the challenge facing the post–Cold War generation of Western and American statesmen.

NOTES

1. "Remarks by the President in Address to the Supreme Soviet of the Ukrainian Soviet Socialist Republic," The White House, Office of the Press Secretary, 1 August 1991.

2. See, for example, the list of "Ten Difficult Barriers Dividing the Presidents of Ukraine and Russia," *Izvestiia* 15 January 1993. The problem of nuclear weapons is listed fourth.

3. See Nadia Schadlow, "The Denuclearization of Ukraine," pages 274–87 below. Also, the author himself has provided a detailed overview of the ins and outs of these three phases in his book, *The Keystone in the Arch: Ukraine and the Emerging Security Environment of Eastern and Central Europe* (Washington, DC, 1997).

4. Ostankino Television, 10 February 1993; translated in *FBIS Daily Report: Central Eurasia* 11 February 1993.

5. The letter reads in part: "[E]ven prior to the ratification of START I, a whole complex of problems needs to be resolved. This applies in particular to the question of compensation for the nuclear materials that were taken out of the warheads of the tactical nuclear weapons that had been transferred from Ukraine to Russia in the spring of 1992, to the guarantees of destroying these weapons by Russia, and to the enormous financial expenditure on the reduction of the nuclear potential . . . At the same time it would be a mistake to agree to promises of insignificant monetary compensation in exchange for Ukraine's immediate nuclear disarmament. The question of nuclear disarmament, state independence, national security, and territorial integrity cannot become an object for bargaining or "monetary compensations." The text may be found in *FBIS Daily Report: Central Eurasia* 30 April 1993: 51.

6. Former Ukrainian Defense Minister Morozov's memoirs accuse Deputy Prime Minister Valeriy Shmarov of secretly previewing the idea in Moscow and complains of Kuchma's support for the idea at Massandra. Morozov's memoirs were circulated as a campaign pamphlet in Kyiv in early 1994 and published in *Ukrainska hazeta* 1994 (1–4).

7. *Izvestiia* 31 December 1993.

8. A notable exception in academic circles was John J. Mearsheimer, "The Case for a Ukrainian Nuclear Deterrent," *Foreign Affairs* 72(3) Summer 1993: 50–66.

9. The text of the resolution may be found in *Holos Ukrainy* 20 November 1993.

10. Author's interviews in Kyiv, September 1995.

11. The text of the resolution on START ratification was distributed by UNIAR, 3 February 1994.

12. The text of the Trilateral Statement may be found in *RFE-RL Research Report* 3(4) 28 January 1994: 14–15, and below, Appendix E, pages 313–316.

13. *Final Communiqué of the Ministerial Meeting of the North Atlantic Council*, 10 December 1996, NATO Press Office.

14. See the interview with Yeltsin advisor, Dmitriy Riurikov, in *Kievskie vedomosti* 28 April 1995.

15. Author's interviews in Kyiv, September 1995.

16. After the 1994 Trilateral Statement the Defense Department has attempted to offer technical advice on the Black Sea Fleet issue, including dispatching experts on basing agreements, compensation and other issues to talk to both sides. The Ukrainians were eager; the Russians were not so.

7

Canadian-Ukrainian Relations:
Articulating the Canadian Interest

BOHDAN S. KORDAN

The systemic transformation in Eastern Europe brought on by the revolution of 1989 signaled a sea-change in Western geostrategic thinking, ushering in a policy of international engagement to ensure that the political gains in Eastern Europe were not lost. Specifically, it was at the 1989 Paris G-7 Economic Summit that assistance in support of reforms was first mooted and extended to both Poland and Hungary, Canada participating in the effort by contributing a one-time $72 million (all funds are Canadian unless otherwise specified) emergency package aimed at providing debt relief. By 1991, however, it became clear, especially with the need to integrate the Soviet Union into the global political economy, that a more comprehensive approach in support of reform was required. It was within this context that at the London G-7 Summit in that year an extensive program of assistance was announced. In concert with other G-7 partners, and as part of a larger burden sharing plan, Canada committed $150 million in food credits and a further $25 million in technical assistance to the Soviet Union.

The London Summit underscored three aspects of Canada's foreign policy during the critical years that would bridge the collapse of the Soviet Union. First, despite pressure from Canada's domestic East European constituency, especially those who traced their ancestral roots to the territories located in the USSR, Canada remained committed in principle to the political sovereignty and territorial integrity of the Soviet Union. Second, the Summit provided the political framework which made explicit the notion that aid and assistance would be tied directly to the reform process. And finally, the role assigned to foreign assistance at the G-7 London gathering reaffirmed for Canadian policymakers the validity of Canada's post-war strategy which consistently emphasized assistance as an instrument in achieving its foreign policy goals. It also convinced them of the strategy's continuing relevance and utility. All three aspects would shape in part Canada's evolving relationship with an emerging independent Ukraine.

Ukrainian Independence and Canadian Recognition

For Canada, the Soviet Union had always been problematic. A large domestic constituency of East Europeans—reputedly one of every ten Canadians—often pressed the Government of Canada to take a more active stand on a host of issues rooted in nationalist-independence causes and the aspirations held for the peoples of the region. The structure of the post-war system and Canada's international obligations made this neither possible nor likely. Indeed, Canada relied on the American lead in East-West relations and would not depart from the essential tenets of the model governing the Western alliance. But Canada's ideological adherence to the alliance and the worldview underpinning that commitment had some important consequences.

When, in August 1991, the hard-line opponents of Mikhail Gorbachev staged their coup in Moscow, Canada's foreign minister, the Hon. Barbara McDougall, declared that Canada was prepared to accept the change in Soviet leadership as long as the new officials respected existing international agreements. What was of importance to Canada, so the Minister declared, was the process of democratization and not necessarily those who governed.[1] It was an extraordinary statement, failing to make the connection between the nature of leadership and governance. Not surprisingly, it had serious implications in the aftermath of the failed coup and Ukraine's proclamation of independence on 24 August. Despite every attempt to contain the political damage, when confronted by the prospect that the center would not hold and queried as to Canada's official line on Ukrainian independence in the referendum scheduled for 1 December—an important issue given the perceived political weight of the organized Ukrainian-Canadian lobby—the Minister was forced to concede that "[Canada] would look to be early rather than late."[2]

The concession on recognition, although inconclusive, was nevertheless significant, departing as it did from past practice and given the considerable risks involved. This was highlighted during the visit of the Canadian Prime Minister, Brian Mulroney, to the United States when he declared Canada would not only recognize Baltic independence but also "respect the freely expressed wishes of the people of Ukraine" should the basic requirement, a majority vote in the upcoming referendum, be met. By way of contrast, the American president, George Bush, stated that the United States would reserve its decision, since, unlike Canada, it had "special responsibilities."[3] Although Canada had on occasion adopted a number of foreign policy positions which placed it at odds with its American ally, the independence demonstrated was striking in view of the repercussions such a decision would entail. It was also unexpected, since the prime minister's remarks drew an obvious parallel with Québec secession. Indeed, the media quickly focused on the decision's possible consequences and meaning for the Canadian federation.[4] The Prime Minister sought to distinguish Québec separatism from Ukrainian independence by pointing out the differences in historical experience, but ultimately it was an issue Canadian officials would have preferred had not been broached. That it was unavoidable was a natural consequence of rapidly changing events. It was also a problem of its own design, having been brought on by the foreign minister's earlier remarks which placed the electorally sensitive Conservative government of Brian Mulroney in a politically untenable position.

From the perspective of the Department of External Affairs (later Foreign Affairs), the movement toward recognition was interpreted as hastily conceived and imprudent, and consequently resisted. In the wake of the prime minister's remarks, a ministry spokesperson reiterated the view that a positive outcome in the Ukrainian referendum was welcomed, but stated that recognition would not necessarily be immediate. Other conditions would in fact have to be met, including a negotiated settlement with Russia on outstanding issues. When asked about the possible precedent that Ukraine independence might set with respect to Québec, the spokesperson would add that with the exception of the Baltics, "we are not encouraging the other states to leave."[5]

It was the sort of statement that reinforced the charge and popular perception within the organized Ukrainian-Canadian community that the Department was Russocentric.[6] But more accurately, what animated the ministry was the concern that decisions not run ahead of events and that they be designed with the existing policy in mind. Maximally, that policy was to support the position of the alliance which still placed much stock in the Gorbachev leadership, while, minimally, it was to maintain stability in the region. With this in mind, and tempered by the policy advice of her senior officials, when Foreign Minister McDougall visited Ukraine in September 1991 to officiate at the opening of Canada's consulate in Kyiv, not only did she indicate that recognition was "premature," but that the Government of Canada also wished to see "what kind of affiliation [the Soviet republics] will have together and what kind of affiliation they will have with the center."[7] A month later, the minister continued to echo the policy line of the Department noting that Canada would respect the democratic choice of the Ukrainian people, but recognition would take time and depend on a number of considerations which went beyond a simple referendum.[8]

The Minister's remarks attracted the attention of the Liberal parliamentary opposition, which demanded to know whether the government was now "reneging" on its earlier commitment. By way of reply, it was stated that all nations had an obligation "to sign on to certain principles" and Canada could and should expect this from Ukraine: that existing borders would be respected, the rights of minorities guaranteed, and the question of the control and possession of nuclear weapons on Ukrainian territory resolved.[9] Moreover, Ukraine's approach to all three questions would determine the precise nature of Canadian-Ukrainian relations after the referendum and perhaps even recognition itself, as when an official in the Department asserted that recognition would in fact "require" guarantees from the government in Kyiv.[10] It was in this context, therefore, before a final decision could be made, that a preliminary round of diplomatic negotiation and exchange was undertaken with the intent of securing a number of assurances from the Government of Ukraine.

There was, however, a practical aspect to Canada's search for guarantees. The Bush administration, which continued to support Mikhail Gorbachev in the waning days of the USSR and sought to prevent the unraveling of the Soviet

Union with all its possible consequences, had begun pressuring Canada to
refrain from taking any precipitate action.[11] For Canada, increasingly restricted
in its policy options, the efforts at obtaining guarantees were viewed as a
legitimate way to address American concerns, but also their own. From
Ukraine, there appeared mixed signals on the issue of nuclear disarmament,
prompting the prime minister in an interview with *Le Monde* to declare that the
nuclear question had to be resolved before Canadian recognition would be
granted.[12] Anxious to secure Western support for Ukraine's independence bid,
the Chairman of the Ukrainian parliament and the soon-to-be elected President
Leonid Kravchuk, only days before the referendum offered his personal assurance to the Canadian prime minister that the matter would be dealt with in a
manner satisfactory to all.[13] It appeared to be sufficient, for with a vast majority
Ukrainian vote in favor of independence, Canada, on 2 December, became the
second country after Poland and the first Western state to recognize Ukraine,
formally breaking ranks with its Western counterparts.

Engaging an Independent Ukraine: The Assistance-Reform
Nexus and Canada's Foreign Policy Interests

Despite the referendum and the accompanying recognition, Canada would not
establish formal diplomatic relations until Canadian negotiators had an opportunity to talk with officials in Kyiv. Speaking to Parliament, Prime Minister
Mulroney stated that Canadian emissaries had been sent to discuss the disposition of nuclear arms on Ukrainian territory and to convey Canada's desire that
Ukraine sign on to international human rights agreements with their attendant
promise of protection for minorities.[14] The Liberal opposition critic for foreign
affairs, Lloyd Axworthy, on the other hand, remained unimpressed, questioning the prime minister on the delay in extending full embassy status and
diplomatic powers to the Canadian consulate in Kyiv while stressing the urgent
need for economic assistance. This and other related issues, the prime minister
replied, were be dealt with during the course of deliberations with Ukrainian
officials.[15] The response was not meant to be obfuscating. The Mulroney
government, acutely aware of the assistance needs of Ukraine, also understood
the importance of assistance as political leverage and its potential role in
achieving foreign policy objectives.

Foreign assistance had been an integral part of post-war Canadian foreign
policy, with its emphasis on promoting development within a multilateral
framework. By the late 1980s, however, foreign policy was increasingly guided
by political, economic and commercial interests, and assistance as an important
policy instrument was tailored to reflect those concerns. Nowhere was this
made more explicit than during the 1991 planning review of Canadian foreign
policy where key priorities for Canada in the new global order—strengthening
cooperative security, creating sustainable prosperity, and securing democracy
and respect for human values—were identified.[16] Within this framework, the

new Canadian Programme of Assistance to the Former Soviet Union (FSU) and Central and Eastern Europe (CEE), created in the aftermath of the London Summit, would take shape.

The aim of the program was to promote and assist the transition process in the region. Economic conditionality was to become central in evaluating requests for assistance as would good governance considerations. But there were also specific areas that were targeted by the program. The transition from planned to market-based economies was identified as a "principal challenge," while maintaining adequate levels of education, health and public services was also seen as a priority. Technical assistance would be provided to improve within the various states the institutional framework—legal, accounting, and financial—and mechanisms created to facilitate both foreign direct investment and help deal with balance-of-payments support, debt relief, and stabilization. Finally, it was envisioned that the program would also address food and other humanitarian emergency needs.[17] It was an ambitious scheme, but one that it was thought could be leveraged in a way that would create regional stability, force a final resolution of the nuclear weapons question, and lay the foundation for new markets and potential trading partners.

Strategic Intervention: The Mulroney Years

Within the context of the general program of regional assistance, the Canadian foreign minister, Barbara McDougall, on her September 1991 visit to Ukraine announced a $5 million technical assistance package and offered through Canada's Export Development Corporation $50 million in trade credits. It was a good-will gesture, serving as a measure of the potential in future cooperation. The gesture, however, would not have been possible had certain expectations failed to be met. In this sense, assistance was used as an incentive, enabling Canada to secure a hint of those concessions that would later make Ukraine's recognition a reality. Similarly, when in January 1992, after the preliminary diplomatic negotiations regarding treaty obligations and the like were deemed satisfactory and the foreign minister was dispatched to Kyiv to establish formal diplomatic relations, $1.5 million worth of humanitarian assistance was announced, symbolically highlighted by the arrival of a Canadian Forces transport plane laden with emergency medical supplies and hospital equipment. At the same time, promises of real economic aid were made, the minister acknowledging the many "challenges" facing Ukraine.[18] "Help for self-help," however, was the guiding maxim: Canada was prepared to assist those who helped themselves. Implicit in the notion was that the relationship was reciprocating. Need would not be the only criterion determining assistance. Ukraine would have to demonstrate a capacity for reform.

Assistance, consequently, was seen as a strategic instrument in the Canadian diplomatic arsenal used to promote change in Ukraine within a specific range of parameters. In this regard, between 1991 and 1993, several important targeted initiatives with high visibility were undertaken. In addition to the $1.5 million humanitarian assistance package that would primarily address needs related to the aftermath of the Chornobyl nuclear accident, Ukraine was eligible for funding under the $30 million Canadian Nuclear Safety Initiative set up to provide regulatory assistance and utility management for those countries with Soviet RBMK-type reactors. In 1992, Canada co-sponsored the Science and Technology Center in Ukraine, contributing $5 million for the purpose of converting human and military resources engaged in the defense sector and redirecting them to other economically productive activities. Further, in support of business and trade, the Renaissance Eastern Europe Programme was enlarged to include Ukraine and a number of other states of the fomer Soviet Union, while in January 1993 a people-to-people program, Partners in Progress, was established to utilize community expertise and channel interest. Finally, Canadian policy advisors in key areas of support to the Government of Ukraine were specially funded and a Canadian Cooperation Office was opened in Kyiv, in May 1993, to help facilitate contacts and assistance.

These were strategically important interventions which during the critical years that followed the Soviet collapse created heightened expectations in Ukraine. Yet, overall, Canada's financial commitment was minuscule and in no way approximated what was generally conceded as necessary in addressing even the most basic of transition-related needs. Arguably, Canada's meager contribution to Ukraine reflected the low levels of assistance to the region in general, with only $75 million approved by the cabinet in 1992. Even so, Canadian assistance to Ukraine paled in comparison with that directed toward Russia during the corresponding period. In 1992, credit in the amount $100 million—later increased to a rotating line of credit of $2 billion—was extended to Russia for the purchase of Canadian goods and services while a large number of projects in the energy sector were supported by Canada. Furthermore, during the April 1993 summit between President Bill Clinton and Boris Yeltsin in Vancouver, the Canadian prime minister, caught up in the euphoria of the moment, announced a doubling of aid to Russia, to which the Liberal opposition responded by describing Ottawa's policy as "one-sided."[19]

There were profound reasons for the inverse relationship, primarily linked to the political structure of Soviet Union, its collapse, and the uncertainty to follow. The rapid dissolution of the USSR brought to a head the problem of the centralized nature of the former Soviet state. In Ukraine, both weak infrastructure and political inexperience made the process of diplomatic and political interaction with the West difficult. Given the unsteady nature of the Ukrainian state and lack of historical legitimacy, it was not surprising that its reliability and validity, although never openly questioned, was in doubt. Consequently, when the Minsk agreement of December 1991 was struck between Russia, Ukraine and Belarus, leading to the creation of the Commonwealth of Independent States (CIS), the change was considered a positive development by Canada's foreign minister and met with considerable relief.[20]

Stability, from the outset, was key to Canada's concerns. Moreover, because of the uncertainty, any innovation was welcome, including the CIS as a supranational structure. That the prospects for the region were unclear was reinforced by developments in Ukraine. Having originally agreed to the May 1992 Lisbon Protocol, the failure of Ukraine's Parliament to ratify the START I and Nuclear Non-Proliferation Treaty (NPT) agreements was disconcerting. The dispute with Russia over the Black Sea Fleet was equally seen as destabilizing. Meanwhile, in Canada, the inability of ministry officials to obtain even basic information from the new Embassy of Ukraine in Ottawa was neither encouraging nor helpful in creating the necessary climate in which a cooperative relationship could develop.[21]

The difficulties in the relationship and the accompanying skepticism would translate on the Canadian side into neglect that further exacerbated the problem. Canada's diplomatic presence in Ukraine, which had been operating out of a hotel suite since 1990, continued to do so until early 1994. Furthermore, staffing was inadequate, consisting at any one time of only a handful of career officers and local support staff. The absence of official Canadian support was felt by those hoping to do business in Ukraine, who would describe the Canadian diplomatic effort as "pathetic," a view that resonated with local staff who attributed the shortcomings of Canadian diplomacy in Ukraine to "incompetence" at External Affairs.[22] That two years after independence documents and supplies continued to be sent by the ministry identifying its diplomatic post as the "Canadian Consulate General, Kiev USSR" simply reinforced the impression.[23] A testament to the state of Canadian-Ukrainian relations, it was nevertheless surprising, given the repeated claims that the relationship was "special" and Ukraine was of "strategic" importance to Canada.

In the absence of real reform in Ukraine and from the perspective of hoping to maintain stability in the region, Russia was a preferred alternative. It did not mean that Russia was an attractive alternative. The situation there was as desperate if not more volatile than in Ukraine. But Russia was big, promised opportunities, and was at least a "known quantity." Canada, accordingly, would steer its efforts toward Russia.[24] Lloyd Axworthy, however, was of the view that a more balanced approach to the region was necessary and as the Liberal foreign affairs critic, advocated in a policy platform statement, that Canada avoid using a penalizing strategy which negatively linked assistance to concessions. The argument was for a constructive approach to diplomacy, that Canada should act as an "honest broker" and take the lead by offering inducements to encourage nuclear weapons compliance while furthering the transition in Ukraine.[25]

The position of the Liberal Party of Canada as articulated by Axworthy was significant because, although not departing from the essential model that emphasized the linkage between assistance and Canada's geostrategic interests, it recaptured Canada's traditional foreign policy focus. Its importance, however, also lay in that the Liberal Party would form the next government, having secured the majority of parliamentary seats after a stunning victory in the October 1993 Federal General Election. With the Liberal victory, a veteran of the Liberal party scene, the Hon. André Ouellet assumed the post of foreign minister, and with this a new phase in Canadian-Ukrainian relations was inaugurated.

Canadian-Ukrainian Interests: Enhancing the Relationship

During the election, the Liberals had campaigned on the promise of restoring Canada's foreign policy independence. The Western alliance, to be sure, continued to be the foundation upon which the architecture of post-Cold War security would rest, but Canada's role within the alliance would be tailored to meet specific national interests and needs. Consequently, a strategy of selective engagement was adopted, focusing on specific domains while establishing priorities that would advance Canadian geostrategic, commercial and political interests.[26] The new policy would emphasize balance. It was also designed with an eye toward a number of domestic developments, considerations that would serve generally as a backdrop to policymaking in Canada at the time. Electoral gains by the populist Right and the corresponding shift in public discourse resulted in pressure for increased transparency and accountability in the decision-making process. In the foreign policy arena, this meant that Canadian initiatives would have to be rigorously defined, purposeful and aim for maximum impact while not necessarily putting further pressure on existing resources. Equally, to ensure policy transparency, public input through consultation would become a political objective of the new Chrétien Liberal government.[27]

These were important developments that had immediate consequences for Canadian-Ukrainian relations. The foreign minister, André Ouellet, in public remarks to the Ukrainian-Canadian community indicated that there would be "an enhanced relationship" with Ukraine, but that its success would depend on the "help" of the community. Further, he hoped to consult with the community and build their ideas and concerns into the policy.[28] The stated aim of the Liberal government, in effect, was to allow for greater community participation in the implementation of some of the elements of the assistance program, as in fact it would. In August 1994, responsibility of the executive management of the newly created Canadian-Ukrainian Partners Programme (CUPP), which sought to transfer Canadian expertise and assistance to Ukraine, devolved to the Ukrainian Canadian Congress under a government contract, marking a real shift in policy development, planning and delivery.[29]

The change in government policy was no less remarkable in terms of engagement at the state-to-state level, the interests between Canada and Ukraine being increasingly seen as parallel. The impasse over the nuclear weapons and security issues which had been escalating between Ukraine and the West, for instance, prompted Ouellet at the November 1993 Conference on

Security and Cooperation in Europe (CSCE) meeting of foreign ministers in Rome to offer to mediate between the U.S., Russia, and Ukraine in the dispute over START I and NPT ratification.[30] Moreover, in the spirit of mediation, he encouraged his Ukrainian counterparts to consider security in terms other than the nuclear option—to participate, for example, in NATO's Partnership for Peace program, while entering into a relationship with other security-based intergovernmental agencies.[31] More significantly, he recommended that Ukraine strengthen bilateral relations with its natural allies.

In light of the complementary interests between the two states, it was suggested that Canada was just such a partner and would do what it could during the critical transitional period.[32] Consequently, when Ukraine requested help in its first multi-party elections, a $2.5 million package was extended consisting of technical and material assistance in support of the electoral process.[33] Ouellet also announced, in April 1994, $11.5 million in assistance for three specific projects: Dnipro River Rehabilitation (environmental management); the Osvita Medical Project (maternal and infant health care); and a package for the purchase of emergency medical supplies and vaccines.[34] This was in addition to $15 million, allocated in response to Ukraine's decision finally to denuclearize, to help Ukraine in the disarmament process and ensure that it moved quickly to implement START I.[35] Without question, the $15 million allocation was a vote of confidence in Ukraine's decision, but was also a reaffirming statement on the part of Canadian officials who were of the view that the mutual interests between the two countries could best be served by nurturing the relationship. It was with some pride, then, that officials would later state that it was "Canada's special relationship with Ukraine" which supported the international efforts that finally convinced Ukraine to accede to the NPT.[36]

With the January 1994 signing of the Trilateral agreement on nuclear weapons by Ukraine, Russia, and the U.S., and the Ukrainian Parliament's ratification the following month of the START I Treaty and the Lisbon Protocol, real possibilities for Ukraine opened up. For the Western alliance, resolution of the issue was a critical step in restoring a balance of power, as Ukraine's acquiescence finally signaled that it was both prepared to work within a prescribed framework and to accept the responsibilities which followed unconditionally from its role within. Ukraine's decision to denuclearize was a calculated risk and widely recognized as such. Western governments reciprocated by extending immediate aid—a specific allocation of US$200 million to assist Ukraine with the reform of its energy sector and the closure of the Chornobyl nuclear power station[37]—while also communicating that Ukraine could gain access to much needed US$4 billion in international financing should it demonstrate a renewed commitment to market reform. In this regard, it was at the 1994 Naples Economic Summit that a proposal for a G-7 sponsored conference on Partnership for Economic Transformation in Ukraine was endorsed.

Significantly, the issue of support for Ukraine at the Naples Summit was championed by Canada which offered to host the fall conference in Winnipeg, the historical center of Ukrainian-Canadian life. Canada's initiative in the matter as well as the location were both symbolically important. For one, it represented Canada's clear desire to assume a leadership role in the multilateral initiative. But by choosing Winnipeg it was also an indication that diaspora involvement would be key to Canada's contribution, for only by leveraging the potential of the one million strong Ukrainian-Canadian community could Canada increase its stake under existing budgetary constraints and retain a lead in the international effort at assisting reform in Ukraine.[38]

This did not mean a lessening of Canada's bilateral commitments to Ukraine. Indeed, during the Winnipeg conference, which the newly elected Ukrainian President Leonid Kuchma attended, several bilateral agreements on assistance and cooperation were signed, increasing Canada's relative commitments to Ukraine.[39] To meet these new obligations, an amount of $57.3 million was budgeted. This included a new $20 million line of credit through the Export Development Corporation, a $13.5 million grant to assist Ukraine with its balance of payments, and the remainder for technical assistance in the areas of business management training, retooling personnel in the nuclear field, and for the storage of spent nuclear fuel.[40] With the conclusion of the Winnipeg conference, Canada's commitment totaled $140 million, consisting largely of a mix of bilateral technical and humanitarian assistance packages, multilateral and regional initiatives, balance of payment support and commercial credits.[41] By January 1995, total Canadian assistance to Ukraine had increased to approximately $170 million and of this sum bilateral technical assistance accounted for $96.6 million.[42]

An element seen as vital to the reform process and given considerable play at the Winnipeg conference was the role assigned to trade and foreign investment. The Canadian-Ukrainian agreements on taxation and investment signed in October underlined the importance attached by both countries to this dimension of the relationship. It was also a theme readily picked up by Ukraine's president, Leonid Kuchma. In a speech to Canadian business concerns during his Canadian sojourn, Ukraine's head of state stressed that economic reform was his administration's priority. He acknowledged the structural obstacles in Ukraine inhibiting trade and hoped that recent measures on currency regulation and export control would help facilitate export sales and stimulate production and growth. But he also noted that in crises lay opportunities and encouraged Canadian businesses and venture capital to take advantage of the moment, one that would serve their own and Ukraine's interests while further strengthening Canadian-Ukrainian relations.[43]

These were buoyant expectations but the reality bore testament to the less than full confidence that Canadian investors and commercial interests expressed in the current Ukrainian economy. Despite an Inter-governmental Trade and Commerce Agreement which established a framework of GATT-compatible rules for the conduct of trade and commercial relations between the two countries, as well as a Joint Declaration on Special Partnership, commercial and trade activity was minimal. For all of 1994, a paltry $7.3 million in goods were exported to Ukraine, and from January to November of the same year only $17.4 million worth of Ukrainian imports made their way onto the Canadian market.[44] Financing of joint ventures emphasizing development in Ukraine was available through the Renaissance Programme, but by 1995 only forty such initiatives received funding. As for investment opportunities, these were reserved for those companies whose planning and outlook for Ukraine was long-term and who were able to adapt and cope in the uncertain Ukrainian economic environment with its complex legislation on ownership and shifting tax policies. By the end of 1995, the list of major Canadian companies doing business in Ukraine was small, although there was a mix of interesting players including Northland Power, Magna International, Seagram's, Ault Foods, and a number of capital risk ventures which focused on oil recovery and the development of the potentially lucrative off-shore oil reserves.[45]

Trade under the Liberal administration was viewed as a legitimate and necessary part of Canadian foreign policy activity in the new global environment. The inability to translate the potential in the historical link between Canada and Ukraine into economic opportunity prompted the Canadian government to consider a high-level mission in early 1996 to stimulate trade. The new foreign minister, the Hon. Lloyd Axworthy, led a delegation that would included some seventy senior business representatives in October 1996. The aim of the trade mission, following an earlier Saskatchewan provincial initiative of a similar kind, was to stimulate commercial activity by providing a context for contracts and agreements to be made, and through senior level discussion, in the form of the newly established Intergovernmental Economic Commission, help support at the policy level business and trade cooperation.[46]

During the Axworthy mission, trade deals worth over $600 million were concluded. The expectation was that this would deepen the economic relationship between the two countries, with the private sector picking up the lead. With this in mind, while in Ukraine, the Minister encouraged participation in the proposed Canadian-Ukrainian Business Initiative (CUBI), a major prairie-based trade forum scheduled for June 1997. CUBI was an important step, for although the Government of Canada was closely involved on the coordinating side through its Western Diversification Office, a federal agency, ownership of the project and its ultimate success rested with the Ukrainian-Canadian community.[47] The event, attended by two hundred entrepreneurs from Ukraine as well as an official delegation that included the Ukrainian Prime Minister Pavlo Lazarenko, built on the earlier Axworthy trade initiative with approximately $800 million in contracts and agreements being negotiated.[48] Its success, however, was overshadowed by rumors of the imminent dismissal of the Ukrainian prime minister, for alleged corruption. His removal from office, within days of leaving Canada, did little to improve the confidence of Canadian investors, identifying concretely the problems of doing business in Ukraine and the efforts still required in moving the democratic process forward.[49]

The importance assigned by the Canadian government to the organized community as a necessary and vital link in Canadian-Ukrainian relations was reflected in the increased commitment to the Canadian-Ukrainian Partners Programme with its "people to people" focus. With a budget allocation of $3.9 million, the 1994–95 program had witnessed the placement of 160 volunteer professionals in Ukraine, while forty Ukrainian officials were brought to Canada for training during the same period.[50] Evaluated at year's end in 1995, the program's success[51] translated into a renewed two-year mandate and more than a doubling in the federal commitment, with an initial $8.9 million being provided for additional placements and exchanges. After a strategic review, however, the focus of the new phase shifted from the simple transfer of skills and creation of linkages to project development and "strategic institution building."[52] CUPP would still rely on community participation and be volunteer-driven, but the rearticulation of the program's objective followed the need to meet the more focused policy goal of increasing the institutional capacity for reform in Ukraine. It was an expression of both the desire to maximize the effectiveness of assistance and a recognition of the deepening crisis in Ukraine.[53] Projects to be funded would continue to target the priority sectors of health, public administration and civil society, yet they would require institutional partnering on a volunteer basis. Assistance, in effect, would now become cooperation.

With the new policy in place, the federal Canadian International Development Agency (CIDA), which by mid-1995 had taken over responsibility from Foreign Affairs for bilateral technical assistance programs in the region, launched a number of major initiatives in 1996 under CUPP. These included the $5.5 million Small Business and Economic Development Project (previously earmarked in the 1995 budget); a $4 million jointly sponsored project assisting the development of credit unions in Ukraine; a $2.2 million Canadian-Ukrainian Legislative Education Programme; $2.1 million for judicial reform; $2.5 million for the Canadian-Ukrainian Public Sector Reform Project; $0.2 million in logistical support to the organization Help Us Help the Children which provided humanitarian aid to orphanages; $1.2 million for a Non-governmental Organization Development Project; and $1.2 million to help train and develop a notarial profession. In all cases, Canadian partners were non-profit agencies, ranging from the Council of Ukrainian Credit Unions of Canada to the Canadian Bureau of International Education, Association of Canadian Court Administrators, and the Chambres des Notaires du Québec.

By the end of 1996, a total of nearly $111 million in bilateral technical assistance in support of over 100 projects and programs had either been spent or declared, an amount that would increase by mid-1997 to $115.5 million with the announcement of the "Policy Advice for Reform Project." Significantly, the total amount for Ukraine by this time had approximated that extended to Russia. It would constitute a major policy shift, providing substance and meaning behind the oft-repeated claim of the "special" nature of Canadian-

Ukrainian relations. But, arguably, it is also a realistic and logical response given Canada's natural interests in the region, historical foreign policy orientation, and particular political role in the international system.

Conclusion

The shift in the power political structure which accompanied the decline and eventual demise of the USSR did not translate immediately into political support for Ukrainian independence by the international community. Custom and uncertainty resulted in considerable trepidation if not consternation among the majority of Western governments over the prospects of an independent Ukraine. Canada, because of special circumstances, broke ranks but approached the question of its future relations with Ukraine cautiously. Trading foreign assistance for influence, Canada's political leadership expected not only to promote, but potentially to shape certain political outcomes in Ukraine. In many ways, the strategy was informed by broad security-based interests that reflected national concerns but had little effect because of the contradictory politics and hampering internal debate in Ukraine. Moreover, the penalizing character of Canada's strategy which tied foreign assistance to influence served only to muddy relations. And yet foreign assistance was both vital and critical to the reform process.

With a change in government and the ultimate resolution of the nuclear weapons issue, a major policy shift occurred. Stressing a more balanced approach in the region, one that reflected more closely Canada's natural interests, the Liberal administration creatively and effectively leveraged assistance in promoting reform and the transition in Ukraine. Indeed, having set the new approach within the traditional parameters of Canadian foreign policy, but mindful of constraints and realities, the relatively modest budgetary outlays supporting assistance to Ukraine would by all accounts pay enormous dividends. It would place Canadian-Ukrainian relations on a more constructive footing, but also in the context of the specific relationship restore the historical purpose and traditional character of Canadian foreign policy.

NOTES

The author wishes to thank Carol Ann Alphonse, Tonya Kirilenko, Lida Shawarsky, and Ostap Skrypnyk for their assistance and cooperation. A special note of thanks is extended to Jane Jamieson who kindly shared her recent work on Canada's policy of aid and assistance to Ukraine.

1. Ross Howard, "Ottawa Resists Demanding Gorbachev's Return to Power," *Globe and Mail* 21 August 1991; Editorial, *Globe and Mail* 22 August 1991; and John Cruickshank, "Putting a Foot in a Minister's Mouth," *Globe and Mail* 23 August 1991.

2. Stephen Handelman, "McDougall Raises Flag at Consulate in Ukraine," *Toronto Star* 10 September 1991.

3. "Statements by Bush and Mulroney," *New York Times* 27 August 1991.

4. Ross Howard, "Ottawa Crosses Forbidden Line: Mr. Mulroney's Pronouncements About Ukraine Could Have Implications for Québec," *Globe and Mail* 31 August 1991; Edward Greenspoon, "Québec Fears Felt in Ukraine," *Globe and Mail* 5 September 1991; and Jeffrey Simpson, "If Canada Followed the Communists, Things Might Not Stop at Québec," *Globe and Mail* 10 September 1991. For a discussion of Canada's recognition of Ukraine and the government's handling of the question with the Québec situation in mind, see Bohdan S. Kordan, *Other Anxieties: Ukraine, Russia and the West* (Kingston, 1994), 22–30.

5. Ross Howard, "Ottawa Crosses Forbidden Line: Mr. Mulroney's Pronouncements About Ukraine Could Have Implications for Québec," *Globe and Mail* 31 August 1991.

6. See, for example, Orest Nowakiwsky, "Who is Manipulating Canadian Foreign Policy?" and Andrij Hluchowecky, "Kyiv Consulate—Twenty Months and Waiting," *Ukrainian Echo/Homin Ukrainy* 28 August 1991. Canadians working in Ukraine were equally of the view that the Government of Canada was reluctant to engage Ukraine because of "its mania about [preserving] the center." See Edward Greenspoon, "Québec Fears Felt in Ukraine," *Globe and Mail* 5 September 1991. A slightly different take on the subject, but one which echoed this sentiment was the testimony of Professor Lubomyr Y. Luciuk before the House of Commons Standing Committee on External Affairs and International Trade. See *Minutes of Proceedings and Evidence* 11 February 1992: 1130–1250.

7. Jim Sheppard, "McDougall Timid on Ukraine," *Calgary Herald* 9 September 1991. See also Stephen Handelman, "McDougall Calls Ukraine a 'Country' but Awaits Referendum," *Toronto Star* 9 September 1991.

8. Tim Harper, "Canada Tells Ukraine to Honor Rights," *Toronto Star* 20 November 1991.

9. House of Commons. *Hansard,* 28 November 1991, 5505–5506.

10. Tim Harper, "Canada Tells Ukraine to Honor Rights," *Toronto Star* 20 November 1991. The assurances Canada was seeking were presaged in an address by the Chairman of Ukraine's Parliament, Leonid Kravchuk, on 24 September to a joint meeting of The Canada Club of Toronto and the Empire Club of Canada, wherein he emphasized Ukraine's commitment to treaty obligations including human rights and regional security. See Leonid M. Kravchuk, "An Independent Ukraine Counts on Canada's Help," *Canadian Speeches: Issues of the Day* 5(7) 1991.

11. Jeff Sallot, "Canada Recognizes State of Ukraine," *Globe and Mail* 3 December 1991. The U.S. fixation with Gorbachev was paralyzing. As one senior U.S. official noted, rather than dealing with the situation at hand, "The last few weeks have all been about finding a way of persuading the President to dump Gorby." See Kordan, *Other Anxieties,* 44, fn. 11.

12. Tim Harper, "Canada Tells Ukraine to Honor Rights," *Toronto Star* 20 November 1991.

13. House of Commons. *Hansard,* 2 December 1991, 5635–5636;

14. Jeff Sallot, "Canada Recognizes State of Ukraine," *Globe and Mail* 3 December 1991.

15. House of Commons. *Hansard,* 2 December 1991, 5635–5636.

16. Department of External Affairs and International Trade (DEAIT). *Foreign Policy Themes and Priorities: 1991–92 Update,* 16.

17. Ibid., 11–12.

18. "Minister Boosts Ukraine: McDougall Predicts Expanded Relations," *Globe and Mail,* 27 January 1992; and Chrystia Freeland, "Canada Celebrates Start of Full Ties with Ukraine," *Toronto Star* 28 January 1992.

19. Lloyd Axworthy, "Liberal Party Unveils Ukraine Platform," *Ukraine-Canada Policy and Trade Monitor* 1(3) July–October 1993: 11. For an executive summary of the distribution of aid and assistance to the FSU and CEE, see DEAIT, *Task Force on Central and Eastern Europe,* 1992.

20. House of Commons. *Hansard,* 10 December 1991, 6085.

21. This unusual situation would force Department officials to turn to the Ukrainian Canadian Congress (UCC) Information Bureau for information and eventually lead the Department to offer the diplomatic corps at the Ukrainian Embassy orientation sessions on how to operate a mission. Ukrainian Canadian Congress, "National Information Bureau Weekly Report," 1–7 March 1993.

22. Edward Struzik, "Canada Losing Out," *Edmonton Journal,* 30 May 1992; George Nikides, "Consulate in Ukraine a Hotel Suite," *Winnipeg Free Press,* 2 July 1992; and John Gray, "Canadian Diplomacy in Ukraine on Cruise Control," *Globe and Mail* 1 July 1993.

23. Ukrainian Canadian Congress, "National Information Bureau Weekly Report," 23 March–2 May 1993.

24. A seasoned veteran of the Department, in an uncharacteristically frank moment, described the Canadian focus on Moscow as the "Boris and Brian show," attributing the relationship to Mr. Mulroney's desire "to scramble onto the world's largest stage, with leaders such as Russia's Boris Yeltsin, [rather] than on a slightly smaller stage with Canada's natural allies." John Gray, "Canadian Diplomacy in Ukraine on Cruise Control," *Globe and Mail* 1 July 1993.

25. Lloyd Axworthy, "Liberal Party Unveils Ukraine Platform," *Ukraine-Canada Policy and Trade Monitor* 1(3) July–October 1993: 10–12.

26. The new directions for Canadian foreign policy were initially articulated in a Special Joint Parliamentary Committee which was tasked with producing a report that would identify the principles and priorities to guide Canada's international relations. After extensive public discussion, the report, entitled *Canada's Foreign Policy: Principles and Priorities for the Future,* was finally released in November 1994 and served as the basis for the government's statement on foreign policy. See Department of Foreign Affairs and International Trade (DFAIT). *Canada in the World*, 1995.

27. Ibid. The issue of public consultation is explored in T. Draimin and B. Plewes, "Civil Society and the Democratization of Foreign Policy," in M. Cameron and M.A. Molot, eds., *Canada Among Nations 1995: Democracy and Foreign Policy* (Ottawa, 1995), 63–82.

28. "Canada's Foreign Minister Discusses New Relations with Ukraine," *Ukraine-Canada Policy and Trade Monitor* 2(1) Winter 1993–94: 2–7. The offer would later also translate into the creation of a Canadian-Ukrainian Advisory Council.

29. "UCC to Administer Canadian-Ukrainian Partners Programme," *Ukrainian News/Ukrains'ki visti* September 1994. The CUP Programme would grow out of the earlier regional Partners in Progress Initiative and as a response to the enthusiastic involvement of the Ukrainian-Canadian community in the initial program.

30. Canada's acknowledgment of Ukraine's specific security needs were also communicated at the NATO meetings in Brussels and favorably received in community circles. UCC Confidential Briefing Document, "Meeting with the Hon. André Ouellet, Minister of Foreign Affairs," March 1994. For an assessment of Canada's role, see the editorial "Canada's Key Role As Intermediary," *Ukrainian News/Ukrains'ki visti* December 1993.

31. Specifically, an enhanced peacekeeping role was envisioned for Ukraine within the UN mandate as well as the OSCE. Given the need to develop a common understanding of the operational concepts and requirements of peacekeeping, and in view of the technical and planning requirements associated with the operations side of peacekeeping, Canada would provide support to Ukraine under its military training assistance program (MTAP). Within the context of the NATO-sponsored Partnership for Peace, it was thought that MTAP would serve to strengthen the multilateral efforts supporting both regional stability and cooperation in the maintenance of peace and security. The program, which included all of the FSU and CEE, focused on language training at CFB Borden and Ottawa as well as instruction in defense resource management and civil-military relations at the Lester B. Pearson Canadian International Peacekeeping Center. Ukrainian participation in the program would account for the largest share of the $9.4 million 1997 budget. The MTAP is the primary mechanism through which Canadian-Ukrainian defense relations take place, although Canada has also acted as the intermediary for the NATO mission in Ukraine, housing the mission at the Canadian Embassy. See DFAIT. *News Release*, "Canada Signs Agreements With Ukraine," 43 (6 March 1997); DFAIT. "Declaration on Peacekeeping," nd; Department of National Defense (DND), "Canadian-Ukrainian Defense Relations," 1 October 1997; and DND, "Briefing Note—Canadian Military Training Assistance Programme: Partnership for Peace," 14 October 1997.

32. "Canada's Foreign Minister Discusses New Relations with Ukraine," *Ukraine-Canada Policy and Trade Monitor* 2(1) Winter 1993–94: 2–7.

33. The contribution—one quarter and by far the largest share of the total foreign assistance package—could be interpreted simply as part of the Canadian government's general commitment to promoting international democratic development. But its purpose was much more specific. When seeking Ministerial approval for project support, Department officials communicated that the government should accord high priority not only to support democracy in Ukraine, but also as a high profile and tangible measure it would signal Canada's desire to strengthen bilateral relations with Ukraine. There was also some expectation that, at the level of process, fair and free elections might unlock the political stalemate between the Ukrainian President and the legislative arm of the government which had such debilitating consequences. J. Jamieson, "New Directions in the Canadian Foreign Policy/Foreign Assistance Nexus: The Case of the Canadian Assistance Programme to Ukraine" (master's thesis, Carleton University, 1997), 80–81. See also DFAIT. *Canada and the International Promotion of Democracy*, nd; and DFAIT. *Canadian Electoral Assistance in Ukraine*, March 1994.

34. "Ouellet Announces $26.5 Million in Aid for Ukraine," *Ukrainian News/Ukrains'ki visti* April 1994; and "Aid Pledged to Ukraine," *Globe and Mail* 2 April 1994.

35. J. Boulden and D. Cox, *Guide to Canadian Policies on International Peace and Security* (Ottawa, 1994), 39.

36. DFAIT. *Government Response to the Recommendations of the Special Joint Committee Reviewing Canadian Foreign Policy*, 19.

37. The offer of US$200 million was an initial installment of a larger package of US$700 million in grants and US$2.5 billion in loans that would be negotiated between Ukraine, the G-7 and EU countries, leading to an agreement on the eventual closure of the Chornobyl nuclear power facility and the development of alternative energy sources. The agreement was signed in Ottawa in December 1995 by Canada's environment minister on behalf of the G-7 and the European Community. Canada would also sign a separate nuclear cooperation agreement that opened the possibility of sales of Canadian nuclear technology, specifically CANDU reactors, to Ukraine as it considered its future energy options. Peter O'Neil, "Canada, Ukraine Deal Will Shut Down Chernobyl," *Vancouver Sun* 20 December 1995; DFAIT. *News Release*, "Canada and Ukraine Sign Nuclear Co-operation Agreement," 236 (20 December 1995); and "Canada Hosts Signing of G-7 Chornobyl Agreement," *Canada-Ukraine Monitor* 4(1) Spring 1996: 2–3.

38. DFAIT. "Notes for an Address by the Hon. André Ouellet, Minister of Foreign Affairs, at the Conference on Partnership for Economic Transformation in Ukraine," 94/66, 27 October 1994.

39. In addition to a general friendship and co-operation agreement, a number of specific agreements and memoranda of understanding were concluded between the two parties in the economic, military, foreign investment and taxation spheres. For a summary of the agreements and a review of the public statements, see *Canada-Ukraine Monitor* 3(1) Spring 1995.

40. Jeff Sallot, "Ottawa Gives Ukraine $57 Million Aid Package," *Globe and Mail* 25 October 1994.

41. The bilateral technical assistance program had committed $46 million to some 80 projects, of which $26 million had been disbursed by this time. A sum of $13.5 million was also provided for balance of payments support, and another $8.5 million allocated for humanitarian aid. Commercial credits in the amount of $70 million was extended for the purchase of Canadian goods and services, while $5.8 million was to be used for the hiring of Canadian consultants on bank projects in the region as part of a multilateral arrangement. DFAIT, Bureau of Assistance for Central and Eastern Europe. *Canadian Assistance to Ukraine*, October 1994.

42. During the period 1989–95, Ukraine received 19.5 percent of the total bilateral assistance budget allocated for the region. This would compare favorably with the total share of 22.7 percent for Russia which was the largest single recipient among all the FSU and CEE states. A summary of commitments is cited in J. Charnetski, "Analysis of Canadian Public and Private Sector Programmes Active in Commercial, Technical and Humanitarian Assistance to Ukraine" (Ukrainian Canadian Congress, mimeographed), Sections A and F.

43. His Excellency Leonid Kuchma, "Help for Ukraine Offers Opportunity for Canada," *Canadian Speeches: Issues of the Day* 8(8) December 1994: 44–48. See also Olivia Ward, "Ukraine's New President Seeks Aid, Trade in Canada," *Toronto Star* 22 October 1994; and Geoffrey York, "Ukraine's Economy Ripe for Change," *Globe and Mail* 25 October 1994.

44. DFAIT. *Ukraine Economic Profile,* January 1995. In 1995, the figures were only slightly improved with the value of total trade turnover estimated at $63.5m. See statitstical table "Canada Trade with Ukraine by Province, 1995" in *Canada-Ukraine Monitor* 4(2) Summer 1996: 43–44.

45. Martin Mittelstaedt, "Northland Power Signs Kiev Deal," *Globe and Mail* 3 February 1993; Diane Francis, "Canadians Doing Their Bit to Help Ukraine," *Financial Post* 23 December 1993; Glenn Cheater, "Agro-businesses Proceed with Caution on Ukraine," *Financial Post* 8 February 1994; and DFAIT. *Ukraine Economic Profile* January 1995.

46. DFAIT. *News Release,* "Axworthy to Lead Business Delegation to Ukraine," 192 (18 October 1996); and DFAIT, *News Release,* "Axworthy Trade Mission Expands Business Links with Ukraine," 196 (24 October 1996); "Foreign Minister to Lead Trade Mission to Ukraine," *Canada-Ukraine Monitor* 4(3) Fall 1996: 10–11; "Canada, Ukraine Sign Business Deals," *Globe and Mail* 25 October 1996; and Alan Toulin, "Axworthy Mission Sees $600m in Ukraine Deals," *Financial Post* 25 October 1996.

47. See "Canada-Ukraine Business Initiative: Draft Proposal" (Ukrainian Canadian Congress, mimeographed), 9 February 1996; and "Canada-Ukraine Business Initiative: Current Guiding Principles" (Ukrainian Canadian Congress, mimeographed), 7 March 1996.

48. The results of the Ukrainian trade mission are reported in "Special Friendship Brings Business," *Canada-Ukraine Monitor* 5(2) Summer 1997: 2–7; and "Ukrainians Wheel and Deal with Canadian Businesses: CUBI Attracts 200 Ukrainian Business People," *Ukrainian Canadian Congress Headquarters' Bulletin* 45(1) July 1997: 27.

49. Geoffrey York, "Ukraine's PM Dogged by Corrupt Image," *Globe and Mail* 12 June 1997; Jeff Sallot, "Invest in Ukraine Visiting PM Says,"

Globe and Mail 14 June 1997; and Geoffrey York, "Ukraine Stymies Foreign Investors," *Globe and Mail* 16 June 1997.

50.   For a brief survey of CUPP funded activity in 1994–95, see Mykola Switucha, "Giving Ukraine Friendly Assistance," *Ukrainian Canadian Congress Headquarters' Bulletin* 44(1) May 1995: 11–13.

51.   It has been estimated that within a five-year period, between 1991–95, the Partners Programme, whether in its CUPP form or its earlier manifestation as the 1991–93 Partners in Progress Initiative, the Ukrainian Canadian community made an equivalent voluntary contribution of $48.5 million. The figure is cited in "Background Document on Canada-Ukraine Advisory Council" (Ukrainian Canadian Congress, mimeographed), n.d.

52.   See "Canada's Technical Co-operation Programme for Ukraine," *Canada-Ukraine Monitor* 4(1) Spring 1996: 18–19; and "Canada's Technical Co-operation Programme with Ukraine: CIDA Programme Update, 1996," *Canada-Ukraine Monitor* 4(3) Fall 1996: 21. The strategic review led to a planning document for Ukraine which is reproduced in the appendix.

53.   The issue of maximizing effectiveness would eventually lead to a reduction in the role assigned to the UCC in the management of CUPP. The transfer in authority for bilateral assistance programs from DFAIT to CIDA and the corresponding review of CUPP provided the rationale in scaling back the UCC's role in the new strategic assistance plan for Ukraine. It has been suggested that shortcomings attributable to the UCC led to this situation and ultimately an opportunity lost to influence policy with respect to Ukraine. The reasons cited, most notably political inexperience, belie the complex interaction between societal interests and government in the shaping of foreign policy where the agenda setting process is heavily weighted in favor of bureaucratic and departmental interests. For a candid assessment of the Ukrainian-Canadian community's policy-setting ability and the problems which beset it, see J. Jamieson, "New Directions in the Canadian Foreign Policy/Foreign Assistance Nexus," 129–37.

8

Ukraine and Western Europe

OLGA ALEXANDROVA

Most surveys of Ukrainian foreign policy and international politics with respect to Ukraine focus chiefly on such issues as relations between Ukraine and Russia, the fate of nuclear weapons on Ukrainian territory, Ukrainian-American relations, and, more recently, Ukraine's attitude towards NATO and NATO enlargement. Western Europe's Ukraine policy and the European dimension of Ukraine's policy have so far been handled as rather a secondary issue.

When speaking about Europe's policy toward Ukraine and Ukraine's Europe policy, one has to take into account that there are a number of questions still unanswered, or that have been answered quite differently by the Ukrainian party on the one hand, and by the European party on the other. The key questions here are: What does this dimension mean for Ukraine itself, and what does it mean for Europe or the West in general? How much does Ukraine matter to Europe? What is the nature of its significance? From the European standpoint, is Ukraine a borderland between Russian and Europe, or does it belong to Europe? Other fundamental questions could, for instance, be formulated as follows: Do Western Europe, East Central Europe, and Eastern Europe really have common interests? What are these interests? What is Ukraine's place in the architecture of Europe? What is the most helpful attitude for Europe to adopt towards Ukraine? Should Europe hold out the possibility of integration into Western institutions, or try to implant the idea that the European Union (EU) and NATO membership are not for Ukraine? Or should Europe maintain a studied ambiguity that avoids any commitments?

On the Threshold of Ukrainian Independence: Establishing Patterns

Ukraine, one of the largest states in Europe, located in the geographic center of the continent, still remains a rather unknown entity for many Europeans. During the first years of its independence, Ukraine was either underrepresented in Western public opinion, or present only in connection with the issue of nuclear weapons (and nothing can mobilize Western public opinion so negatively as the nuclear issue) or the conflicts with Russia. After the demise of the Soviet Union, Ukraine had great difficulty in asserting itself as an independent actor in international relations. The West was ill-prepared to meet the end of the Soviet Union and to deal with its successor states. The West, evidently, had and, perhaps, still has its own Ukrainian problem.[1] But to show the Western stereotypes and patterns of behavior with respect to Ukraine that later proved so difficult to overcome, and in a definite sense still persist, one has to begin with the period prior to the dissolution of the USSR in December 1991. The extreme reserve of the Western powers especially towards Ukraine grew out of the respect for—indeed fixation with—Mikhail Gorbachev that characterized Western policy until December 1991. At best, the West viewed Ukraine and other Soviet republics as "irrational children" whose "national interests" were somehow always "menacing."[2] Officials at the Ukrainian Ministry of Foreign Affairs complained that their activities at that time were undisguisedly hampered by Western governments which were afraid of encouraging separatism in the Soviet Union.[3]

Western reluctance to accept Ukraine is well exemplified by the very first attempt of the Ukrainian leadership to engage in European affairs as an independent actor. In November 1990 Leonid Kravchuk appealed to the summit meeting of the Conference on Security and Cooperation in Europe (CSCE) in Paris for an independent Ukrainian participation separate from the Soviet delegation, but because all CSCE members had to assent to the change, and Gorbachev and Soviet Foreign Minister Edvard Shevardnadze refused to allow Ukraine to be represented separately, then Ukrainian Foreign Minister Anatoliy Zlenko withdrew from the Soviet delegation in protest while the Western leaders concurred silently.[4] In 1991, the West was in general opposed to Ukraine's independence.[5] This was demonstrated not only by U.S. President George Bush in his "Chicken Kiev" speech, in which he condemned "suicidal nationalism" and averred that freedom and independence were not the same.[6] Douglas Hurd, then British foreign secretary, delivered in March 1991 in Kyiv one of the clearest warnings about what he called "destructive impulses of old nationalism" and stopped just short of stating that he opposed the idea of Ukrainian independence.[7] During his talks with Ukrainian officials in Kyiv in October 1991, then German Foreign Minister Hans-Dietrich Genscher also could not conceal his disapproval of Ukraine's decision to refrain from signing Gorbachev's Union Treaty.[8] French President François Mitterrand stated during Gorbachev's last official visit to France as Soviet president in October 1991 that it was important that the Union, desperately defended by Gorbachev, should prevail in the end.[9]

On the eve of the 1 December referendum on independence in Ukraine, officials in the European capitals declared that their governments were not planning to move quickly toward recognition of Ukrainian independence in case of a pro-independence vote and would not respond directly to a reported shift in U.S. policy. Diplomatic recognition and the establishment of diplomatic relations did not occur until Soviet President Mikhail Gorbachev had resigned on 25 December 1991. The European Community (EC) member states declared that their possible recognition of the newly independent states was contingent on their acceptance of criteria issued by the EC on 16 December 1991. "Being strict with Ukraine is simply a matter of prudence, for the whole

of Europe," wrote the British weekly *The Economist*.[10] The EC cri
cluded such issues as observance of human rights, treatment of minorities,
renunciation of violence, etc. On this basis, the Federal Republic of Germany
finally recognized Ukraine as an independent state on 26 December and France
on 27 December 1991. The rest of the European Community recognized
Ukraine and seven other former Soviet republics on 31 December 1991, the
day after the new Commonwealth of Independent States (CIS) agreed in Minsk
on a common strategic nuclear command. "The recognition by the European
Community and USA of Ukraine as an independent state finally took place
[. . .] after months of patronizing remarks and demands made by the West,"
commented Serhiy Holovatyi.[11]

In retrospect one can state that some of the problems that the West confronts
today in its policy towards Ukraine (the lag in democratic reforms and economic
transformation, Chornobyl etc.) are to some degree the consequence of the
West's own neglect in those early days. These problems could probably have
been more easily solved if Ukraine had found more understanding of its wish to
be gradually but steadily integrated into European political and economic
structures and in that way had come under definite obligations toward the West.

1991–1993: A Period of Neglect and Annoyance

After the Soviet Union had disappeared, the earlier fixation on the USSR and
Mikhail Gorbachev was uncritically transposed to Russia and Boris Yeltsin.
Western policymakers considered Ukraine to be marginal and of lesser importance. The perception persisted in the West that Ukraine fell within Russia's
"legitimate sphere of influence" and, thus, was only a limited actor in European
and international politics. As Alexander Motyl has written:

> It was evident throughout much of 1992 that Western policymakers still
> would have preferred the revival of some form of maximally centralized
> union. Their unrealistically optimistic assessment of the Commonwealth of
> Independent States and its chances of survival, their continued preference for
> dealing almost exclusively with or through Moscow on important issues, and
> their willingness to tolerate Russia's expropriation of Soviet overseas prop-
> erty suggested that the non-Russian successor states still did not matter.
> Western attitudes toward Ukraine were especially disturbing since they re-
> vealed an inability to recognize the dilemmas of a young nation having to
> come to terms with its former imperial master.[12]

The young Ukrainian diplomacy did not have access to influential circles and
lobbies in foreign offices, parliaments, and political parties in Western Europe.
As one Ukrainian diplomat put it, "the European dimension of Ukraine's policy
started at point zero."[13] The absence of an influential Ukrainian diaspora in
Europe was another factor in Western Europe's relative disinterest in Ukraine:
though there are Ukrainian communities in Great Britain and Germany, they
are far smaller and less influential than those in Canada or the United States.

Immediately after the demise of the Soviet Union, the West's complete absorption in the rosy prospects of a new relationship with Russia combined with a lack of knowledge about the other newly independent states, led to a period of neglect. "Ukraine has been losing the propaganda war," wrote Volodymyr Lanovyi, then deputy prime minister and minister of the economy of Ukraine.[14] The only question that really interested the West at that time was what would happen to the nuclear weapons on the territory of the former Soviet Union. During the two years following Ukraine's independence, the West, led by the United States, was totally preoccupied with only one problem: the fate of the former Soviet nuclear arms stationed on Ukrainian territory. For a long time, Ukraine was considered by Western policymakers chiefly as a proliferation problem and as an impediment to nuclear disarmament. This overriding concern with nuclear weapons, however justified, has sometimes—particularly immediately after the dissolution of the Soviet Union—been exaggerated, and it has at times overshadowed other security considerations and diverted attention from other threats. In respect to the West's preoccupation with nuclear weapons, Sherman Garnett has noted: "Washington's early focus on these [nuclear] ambitions obscured or distorted the real security problem, which is to ensure Eurasian stability in a time of great turmoil and transition. It is the breakdown of stability within and between the countries like Ukraine and Russia that threatens the region as a whole, as well as existing nuclear command and control structures and the security of nuclear technology and knowhow in Eurasia."[15]

In the Russo-Ukrainian disputes over tactical nuclear weapons, over the repayment of the Soviet debt (Ukraine wanted to pay its own share), even over the Black Sea Fleet, the West very often tended to see not Russia, but Ukraine as being unpredictable and unreasonable. During these initial, extremely important years of its statehood, Ukraine was internationally almost completely isolated and virtually ostracized. It was very often overlooked that, with respect to territorial and border disputes, Ukraine is a status quo power while Russia appears as a revisionist power, and that the realization of this fact is very important for security in the whole of Europe. As a result of the Western neglect, Ukraine's initial illusions about close relations with the West and Western support gave way to deep disappointment. Even though the country is now gradually emerging from the shadow of Russia, the West for a long time failed to appreciate the foreign policy of this East European country in its full scope.

The West Turns Its Attention to Ukraine

Only after this initial period of neglect did the West begin to recognize Ukraine's significance and its potential role in European affairs. A discernible Western policy shift towards Ukraine first began to emerge in 1994. Western politicians seemed to have come at last to a realization that the policy of "beating up on Ukraine"[16] was counterproductive, both with regard to nuclear disarmament and economic transformation. A number of factors influenced this shift in the Western attitude towards Ukraine:

• the bloody events of October 1993 in Russia and the subsequent parliamentary elections in December 1993 which brought success to the nationalist Vladimir Zhirinovsky and enhanced doubts in the West about Russia's smooth transition to democracy;

• the increasingly assertive Russian foreign policy, in particular towards the "near abroad," and its great-power posturing;

• the ratification of the START I Treaty by the Ukrainian Parliament (Verkhovna Rada) in November 1993;

• the Trilateral agreement of January 1994 between the United States, Russia, and Ukraine on the withdrawal of strategic nuclear weapons stationed on Ukrainian territory and the ratification of the Nuclear Non-Proliferation Treaty by the Parliament in November 1994;

• a peaceful transition of power through parliamentary and presidential elections in Ukraine in spring–summer 1994;

• the launching of a program of economic reforms by the newly elected president, Leonid Kuchma, in October 1994;

• the shift in U.S. policy from a "Russia first" policy to a policy of "geopolitical pluralism," which in turn influenced the West European policies to pay more attention to the non-Russian NIS;

• the Ukrainian position, independent of and different from the Russian stand, on eastward expansion of NATO;

• the adoption of a new constitution by Ukraine in June 1996.

Nevertheless, the shift in Western attitudes toward Ukraine was slow, prudent, and reserved (the only European official to visit the newly elected President Kuchma was the Finnish Foreign Minister Pekka Haavisto, who came to Kyiv first in October 1994).

The reconsideration of Western positions towards Ukraine included such significant changes as a shift in perception of Ukraine from a security challenge to a partner in new European security design; the shift from (very modest) financial aid to elaborate programs of economic assistance to reforms. It has become almost commonplace for Western politicians to affirm that Ukraine is crucial for stability on the European continent, and that uncertainty in Ukraine would reverberate throughout Europe: in September 1995 British Foreign Secretary Malcolm Rifkind called Ukraine a "strategic pivot" in the post-Cold War order.[17] Nevertheless, Western attitudes towards Ukraine remain rather equivocal. Many Europeans appear to be still undecided what to do with Ukraine, whether it is a "real country" and a part of Europe or not. Unfortunately, despite official Western rhetoric, there persists among many Western politicians and analysts a viewpoint that sees Ukraine first and foremost instrumentally as a buffer between Russia and "Europe proper," as a strategic barrier between them.[18]

But not only were the West Europeans rather reserved in their attitude towards Ukraine—Ukraine itself, especially under its first president, Leonid Kravchuk, neglected the European direction of its politics and concentrated its international activity (Russia aside) substantially on developing its relations with the United States. In July 1994, on the eve of the second round of presidential elections, Leonid Kuchma sharply attacked President Kravchuk's foreign policy. With regard to Ukraine's Europe policy, Kuchma defined the optimistic declarations by Foreign Minister Zlenko as "imitating integration with Western Europe."[19] Since 1995, Ukraine has concentrated increasingly on trying to become integrated into European structures.

Since independence, Ukraine's foreign policy has displayed continuity in the most important issues and approaches, even if some accents have shifted. Ukraine has become more active and more insistent in the European direction of its policy since 1995. The year 1997 was especially successful in strengthening Ukraine's links with Europe and with international organizations. The new formula of the "two-track" Ukrainian foreign policy—"cooperation with the CIS, integration into Europe"[20]—clearly sets the priorities. This new Ukrainian policy toward Europe is undoubtedly a sign of Ukraine's growing self-confidence in international politics, of its emancipation from Russia. One of the main challenges to confront the Ukrainian leadership in its foreign policy course lies in resolving the deep-rooted contradiction between the desire to create a state with a stable European future and the country's inescapable economic ties with the territory of the former Soviet Union. Ukraine as a "normal" European state would like to integrate into European structures, even as it realizes that this is still a very remote goal. The Ukrainian leadership under President Leonid Kuchma has attempted to pursue a more differentiated foreign policy than its predecessor and has been especially anxious to improve bilateral relations with the other member countries of the CIS and with the Baltic states, with the countries of East Central Europe and with some newly industrializing nations of Asia and Latin America. However, its relations with Russia on the one hand and with the leading Western powers and European organizations on the other continue to occupy the focal point of Ukrainian foreign policy.

Theoretically, the Ukrainian leadership has four options with regard to the foreign and security policy it wants to pursue:

1. very close ties in one form or another with Russia, which seems to be at present unacceptable;

2. an alliance with other successor states to the former Soviet Union without Russia. Ukraine has pursued a very active policy towards other CIS states, but an alliance appears to be an unrealistic option;

3. close cooperation or even an alliance with the Western powers, especially with the U.S., Germany, or both;

4. an ambitious, but risky policy of maintaining a balance betw
and the West.

It seems that Ukraine under President Kuchma attempted at first to implement the fourth option, but has since inclined more and more towards close
cooperation with the Western powers with the long-term goal of an alliance.

Bilateral Relations

Ukraine's bilateral relations with countries of Western Europe have taken
shape along two patterns that are characteristic for the West European approach
to Ukraine in general. The first, represented (together with the United States)
by Germany, the United Kingdom, and the Netherlands, proceeds from the
assumption that Ukraine is crucial for European security and, hence, more
decisive and extensive assistance and cooperation should be a major part of
Western strategy. The second pattern, represented in the first instance by
France, proceeds from the conviction that if the West has to choose between a
partnership with Russia and Ukrainian independence, it should choose Russia.

Through the end of 1994, Ukrainian foreign policy, in its attempts to develop bilateral relations, found itself confronted with a reserved and reluctant
position of most West European states. These relations were limited to the
friendship and cooperation agreements that Ukraine concluded with France, the
United Kingdom, Germany, Italy, and Spain. These agreements were, of
course, very important for Ukraine as a base on which to build future relations,
but they represented, nevertheless, a rather modest and not very binding form
of political and economic cooperation, cultural exchanges, and humanitarian
assistance.[21]

Ukraine and Germany

Germany as an economic great power in Europe came naturally to the forefront
of Kyiv's interest. Germany was seen as an anchor in the safe European haven.
Taking into account the very ambivalent experiences of the past, it is remarkable how positive the view of Germany is among the Ukrainian population. In
public opinion polls Germany is rated higher than the U.S. or Russia.[22] Representatives of the Ukrainian elite see no threat to Ukraine from Germany,
whereas 11 percent of them perceive the United States as a security threat.[23]
On the other hand, of all West Europeans, the Germans, for a number of
reasons, are probably the most interested in Ukraine. At the same time, German
policy in Eastern and East Central Europe remains for historical reasons a
rather touchy issue. From the German point of view, there are two very important, critical factors in the German-Ukrainian relationship. First, during the
First and the Second World Wars, German policy towards Ukraine had inevitably an anti-Russian character. Today, because of the heavy burden of history,

Germany must by all possible means avoid any suspicion of an anti-Russian policy, any impression that its relations with Ukraine are directed against Ukraine's neighbors, primarily Russia or Poland. Second, due to its geographic location and economic might, Germany will in any case play an important role in Eastern and East Central Europe. For historical reasons, it is in Germany's interest, as well as in the interest of East Central European countries and Germany's West European allies, that Germany does not conduct its own *Ostpolitik* but does everything possible to develop a pan-European policy towards the region. From the very beginning, Germany tried to handle the relations to the newly independent states as a European problem. There were speculations in Ukraine, as well as in Russia and Poland, that Germany was prepared to build its *Ostpolitik* on the basis of preferential German-Ukrainian relations and even envisioned a "special relationship" between Germany and Ukraine as a counterweight to the alleged Russo-French alliance. Equally erroneously, some Ukrainian policymakers cherished hopes that Germany would see Ukraine as a partner in containing the influence of the United States (!) and Russia in East Central Europe.[24] However, it must be admitted that such options for German policy can seem not only undesirable, but also extremely unrealistic.

Symbolically, the very first visit by President Leonid Kravchuk to the West was to Bonn in February 1992. Kyiv attempted to court Bonn by inviting—unsuccessfully, as it it turned out—ethnic Germans living in Kazakhstan to settle in Ukraine. Chancellor Helmut Kohl's visit to Kyiv in June 1993 two-and-a half years (!) after the demise of the Soviet Union, was the first visit to Ukraine by such a high-ranking Western politician. During that visit, Chancellor Kohl and President Kravchuk signed "A Joint Declaration on Principles of German-Ukrainian Relations." From the Ukrainian point of view, it was particularly important that both parties committed themselves to respect the principles of sovereignty, inviolability of borders, and renunciation of force. In August 1993, German Defense Minister Volker Rühe visited Kyiv. During that visit, Germany and Ukraine signed an agreement on military cooperation. The accord called for exchanges of specialists, ship visits, and information exchanges on training. Chancellor Kohl proclaimed in Kyiv that Germany would not give preference to Russia over Ukraine. But, though Bonn has claimed that it conducts a well-balanced policy towards Ukraine and Russia, the latter remains undoubtedly the focal point of German *Ostpolitik*.

Bonn has played a key role within the European Union in promoting greater economic assistance to Ukraine. When Germany held the chairmanship in the EU, it tried to promote a special EU assistance program for Ukraine. A Ukrainian-German Commission on Economic Cooperation was founded in February 1992, during the visit to Kyiv by German Minister for the Economy Jürgen Möllemann. Ukraine received approximately half of its foreign aid from Germany. After the collapse of the Soviet Union, Ukraine was, together with Russia, among the recipients of German financial aid originally destined for the

Soviet Union in accordance with the Soviet-German Treaty of Oct
Ukraine received about 2.7 billion deutschmarks, or 3 percent of app___
90 billion deutschmarks, including 755 million deutschmarks for construction
of apartments for and education of soldiers of the Soviet Army withdrawn from
East Germany. Because of previous economic ties between the Ukrainian SSR
and the German Democratic Republic, German trade relations are relatively
elaborate in comparison with other Western countries.[25] Germany is the biggest exporter to Ukraine among Western countries (7.6 percent of all exports to
Ukraine in January–December 1997) and together with the U.S., the biggest
Western importer of Ukrainian goods (4.0 percent in the same period).[26] Total
volume of trade between the two countries reached 3.8 billion deutschmarks.[27]
In the years 1992–1995, the German government gave export loan guarantees
within the framework of the HERMES AG insurance fund for German firms
exporting goods and services to Ukraine for about 1.6 billion deutschmarks.
But, compared with 1993, insurance funds from HERMES to Ukraine were cut
almost by half, from 562 million deutschmarks to 300 million deutschmarks
per year. Ukrainian officials have discussed with German government officials
and representatives of HERMES AG the possibility of placing Ukraine in the
group of countries with a lower risk rate. Ukraine's position in the fifth (highest
ranking) group of export risks significantly raises the price of imported goods
for Ukrainian consumers and is not in the interest of German firms which
export their products to Ukraine. Of all CIS countries, HERMES has moved
only Russia and Turkmenistan to the fourth risk group.[28] By 1997 the German
investments in the Ukrainian economy stood at 182.9 million dollars or 13
percent of the total sum invested.[29] At the beginning of 1996, 512 German
firms were operating in Ukraine, of which 460 were German-Ukrainian joint
ventures. One hundred sixty-five offices of German firms (117 in Kyiv, 8 in
Odesa, 5 in Dnipropetrovsk, and the remainder in other cities) were registered
in Ukraine.[30]

Ukraine and Great Britain

The initial period of the British policy towards Ukraine corresponds with the
general Western approach described above. Bilateral activity was limited to a
few exchange visits. President Kravchuk visited London in summer 1992.
Malcolm Rifkind, then secretary of state for defense, visited Ukraine in December 1992 and September 1993. During his second visit, a memorandum of
understanding was signed which envisaged cooperation between the defense
ministries of the two countries and consultations on such issues as the management of armed forces in a democratic society. In December 1995, President
Kuchma paid a visit to London, during which he and Prime Minister John
Major signed a British-Ukrainian Joint Declaration. This visit was praised in
Kyiv as a breakthrough in British-Ukrainian relations. Prime Minister Major
and Prince Charles visited Ukraine in 1996.

A modest shift in Britain's policy towards Ukraine began in 1994. In April 1994 Douglas Hurd, then British foreign secretary, visited Ukraine. It was his third visit to Kyiv since March 1991. In September 1995 Malcolm Rifkind visited Ukraine again, this time as British foreign secretary. That visit and Rifkind's statements on the crucial importance of Ukraine for European security represented, perhaps, a turning point in Britain's attitude towards Ukraine. Subsequently, Malcolm Rifkind was even more emphatic in his statements on Ukraine. During his visit in Washington in March 1997, he stated that Ukraine shapes Europe's geopolitical situation more than any other country and that Ukraine's eventual admission to NATO is crucial to overcoming the Soviet legacy in Europe.[31] In February 1997, British Defense Secretary Michael Portillo continued the tradition of his predecessor and paid a visit to Ukraine. Portillo and his Ukrainian counterparts agreed to establish regular exchanges of visits between British and Ukrainian military personnel. Moreover, he urged Ukraine to seek a special relationship with NATO.

London has tried to formulate a more comprehensive approach towards Kyiv that includes economic and technical assistance. But limited financial resources reduce British influence. Like most other Central and East European countries, Ukraine benefits from Britain's Know-How Fund, which provides technical and legal assistance for restructuring former communist societies. In the years 1992–1995, Great Britain was the third largest (after the United States and Germany) Western investor in the Ukrainian economy; in 1996, however, it was overtaken by the Netherlands. In mid-1997, British investments reached 130.9 million dollars or 7.9 percent of total foreign investments in Ukraine.[32] The trade turnover between the two countries remains very low. In January–December 1996, British exports to Ukraine grew by 31.5 percent compared with 1996.[33] In 1992–1996, British investments reached 94.8 million dollars or 6.8 percent of the total foreign investments in Ukraine.[34] Notwithstanding the rather modest level of bilateral interaction, Ukraine considers Great Britain as its "strategic partner."[35]

Ukraine and France

Relations between France and Ukraine were and remain lukewarm since Ukraine became independent, as one Ukrainian commentator put it, France was always a weak point of Ukraine's policy in Europe.[36] Ukrainian officials, inexperienced in international politics as they were, believed quite naively that France would see independent Ukraine as an ally against possible German hegemony.[37] France, however, traditionally has conducted a Russophile policy, and it has taken a very cautious stand on Ukraine. France has evidently supported a Western approach towards Ukraine (and other post-Soviet states) that stipulates that if the West faces a dilemma between maintaining peace with Russia and upholding independence of the other successor states of the former Soviet Union, the West can and should opt only for preferred relations with

Russia. This approach actually contradicts France's role as one of the guarantors—together with other nuclear powers—of Ukrainian security. Traditionally inclined toward centralization, French politicians have, apparently, particular difficulties in coming to terms with Ukrainian independence. Former President Valéry Giscard d'Estaing even ventured a remark in February 1993 that Ukraine's independence was no more justified than would be that of France's Rhône-Alpes region.[38]

In June 1992, Presidents Leonid Kravchuk and François Mitterrand signed a treaty on Friendship and Cooperation. That was the first such treaty between Ukraine and a West European state.[39] Mitterrand called Ukraine "a one hundred percent European state."[40] Though the treaty covered cooperation in a large number of areas, including the military, communications, energy, the environment, space technology, and healthcare, and called for meetings between the foreign ministers of the two countries "at least twice a year" and summits "by mutual consent," it remained rather a kind of declaration of intent. In April 1996, the Chairman of Ukraine's Parliament, Oleksandr Moroz, paid a visit to Paris, on what turned out to be a very unsuccessful mission. Moroz's French interlocutors were only interested in when the last nuclear warheads would leave Ukraine and when the Chornobyl reactor would be closed. They were not at all interested in Ukraine's financial difficulties connected with the closure of the reactor.[41]

President Kuchma visited France first in January–February 1997. Thus, France was the very last of the G-7 states that the Ukrainian president visited. Before that, President Kuchma and French President Jacques Chirac had only one encounter with each other in April 1995, and this, very symbolically, took place in Moscow. Kuchma's meeting with Chirac was the first ever French-Ukrainian summit. Kyiv has hoped that France would exercise its influence in European institutions in order to promote their engagement with Ukraine. The two governments have set up a high-level joint commission for trade and economic cooperation. However, France lags behind most other major industrial powers in terms of trade with and investment in the newly independent states. Nuclear power engineering, transport, oil refining and gas supplies, nature protection, conversion of military-oriented enterprises, iron and steel industry are considered as the most promising areas of French-Ukrainian cooperation. Contacts have been established between the French government and the French nuclear establishment to assist Ukraine in improving security in its nuclear power plants. There has been very slow growth in trade between both countries since 1994. In 1997, the total trade turnover between them reached 450 million dollars, with a negative trade balance of over 150 million dollars for Ukraine.[42] According to a report of the Ukrainian Ministry for Foreign Economic Ties and Trade, there were 81 companies backed by French capital in Ukraine as of 1 October 1996. Total French investment amounted to almost 22 million dollars, an extremely modest sum compared with the 20 million dollars invested by small Switzerland or the 120 million dollars in Dutch investments.[43] However, it seems that France now wants to expand ties with Ukraine both on a bilateral basis and within the European Union. During French Foreign Minister Hubert Vedrine's visit to Kyiv in July 1998, the two countries agreed to create a special high-level cooperation mechanism folliwing the example of Kuchma-Gore and Kuchma-Kohl commissions.[44]

Ukraine and the Netherlands

The Netherlands deserve mention alongside such European powers as France, Germany and Great Britain because this relatively small country is very actively engaged both politically and economically in Ukrainian affairs. Anders Aslund has singled out the Netherlands as a country that, together with Germany, demonstrated its commitment to reform in Ukraine and called the indifference of most European countries "shocking."[45] In March 1996, Prime Minister of the Netherlands Wim Kok paid a visit to Ukraine and, with President Kuchma, signed "A Joint Declaration on the Principles of Relations" between the two countries. This document determined the main areas of cooperation in both political and economic terms. The best prospects in their bilateral cooperation lie in energy, agriculture, ecology, electronics, telecommunication and conversion. In 1996 more than 30 Ukrainian-Dutch companies operated in Ukraine, and the Netherlands ranked seventh among the West European countries in terms of volume of trade with Ukraine. In 1995, the Netherlands was the third biggest donor country to render financial assistance to Ukraine. By the end of 1995 Dutch financial assistance to Ukraine totaled approximately 37 million dollars.[46] The program of economic cooperation between the Netherlands and Ukraine for 1997 envisaged that Dutch technical aid to Ukraine would reach approximately 9.4 million dollars.[47] In 1997, it became the second biggest (!) investor in the Ukrainian economy. In mid-1997 Dutch investments in Ukraine reached 160.2 million dollars or 9.7 percent of the total foreign investment in that country.[48] Richard Malpas, the governor of the sixth leading European bank, the Dutch bank ING Barings, said during a meeting with President Leonid Kuchma that his bank has embarked on a long-term program of cooperation with Ukraine. Ingbank has offered to finance a part of the Ukrainian-Russian trade and to help Ukraine penetrate international securities markets.[49] The Netherlands represents Ukrainian interests in the International Monetary Fund (IMF) and in the World Bank.

Ukraine and Italy

Ukrainian-Italian bilateral activities began rather late, but seem to be gathering momentum. In May 1995, President Kuchma visited Italy. During this visit, the first inter-governmental agreement on friendship and cooperation in the history of Ukrainian-Italian relations was signed. In October 1996, Italy's President Oscar Luigi Scalfaro paid a visit to Kyiv. During this visit the two presidents agreed to set up a joint commisssion on trade and economic cooperation. In February 1997, Italian Prime Minister Romano Prodi visited Kyiv. On 25 February 1997, the Italian Parliament ratified the Partnership and Cooperation Agreement concluded between the European Union and Ukraine.

Especially lively are Italian-Ukrainian trade relations. Italy is in second place after Germany among West European countries in the amount of trade turnover with Ukraine. In 1997, this reached 795.4 million dollars and had grown by 19.8 percent in the one year since 1996.[50] There has been a surge of interest among Italian companies in the Ukrainian market, especially in communications, automobile production, the energy sector, and small business development. Romano Prodi was accompanied to Ukraine by representatives of twenty-four leading Italian companies and banks. One of the most ambitious projects involving Italian and Ukrainian participation is the envisioned construction of the so-called Cretan transportation corridor from Trieste via Slovenia, Hungary, and Ukraine to Kazakhstan and China. As of 1 October 1996, 172 companies backed at least partially by Italian capital operated in Ukraine. The size of Italian investments reached, however, only a modest 22.6 million dollars, but it almost doubled compared to the previous year. Out of this total, 9.1 million dollars were invested in trade, 3.8 million dollars in the food industry.[51]

$$* \quad *$$
$$*$$

During the period from 1992 to 31 December 1996, foreign investments in the Ukrainian economy reached 1.4 billion dollars. This equals 27.5 dollars per capita. In the years 1992–1995, the biggest foreign investments came from the United States (245.3 million dollars, or 17.5 percent of the total), Germany (182.9 million dollars or 13 percent), the Netherlands (119.2 million dollars or 8.5 percent), Great Britain (94.8 million dollars or 6.8 percent), and Cyprus (72.9 million dollars or 5.2 percent).[52] According to the Federal Department of Foreign Economic Affairs of Switzerland, improvements in the investment climate in Ukraine promoted a doubling—to 20 million dollars—of Swiss investments in Ukraine's economy. By 1996, Switzerland was ranked fifth among foreign countries in terms of the volume of investments in the Ukrainian economy. Twenty offices representing Swiss companies are registered in Ukraine.[53]

One other aspect of Ukraine's bilateral relations with the West European states should be mentioned. The frequency and density of state visits by high ranking officials have always been considered as attributes and unmistakable indicators of the level of bilateral relations. From this point of view, the general picture of Ukraine's bilateral relations with West European countries in the years 1992–1996 appears rather gloomy. Not only the years of neglect (1992–1993), but even the years 1994–1995 were a fallow period in this respect. Intensification in official visits began only in 1996. Nevertheless, only Germany and the United Kingdom reveal a frequent exchange of high ranking visitors with Ukraine. Especially symptomatic is the case of France: neither the French president, nor any French prime minister has yet visited Ukraine. With the exception of Germany and Great Britain, few other West European countries have revealed a readiness to engage in Ukrainian affairs. Rhetorically, European leaders do recognize that Ukraine is a European state, and one important for European security, but few are truly ready to implement this recognition in everyday politics. Western guarantees were never extended to Ukraine. One of the main misunderstandings between Ukraine and its Western partners consists in that the West has made it clear that before entering Western structures Ukraine must solve its disputes with Russia, while Ukraine, on the contrary, hopes to solve its "Russian problem" by entering the Western sphere of interest.[54]

Ukraine and European Organizations

A major role in Ukrainian foreign policy conceptions and official declarations was always assigned to the integration of the country into the European and the global community of nations and into international organizations. Ukraine regards itself as a European state with regional interests, but without any global claims. Ukraine as a "normal" European state would like to integrate into European structures, even as it realizes meanwhile that this is still a very remote goal and assumes its chances realistically. Ukraine's proximity to Russia makes the issue of possible Ukrainian membership in the European Union (EU), the Western European Union (WEU), and NATO sensitive for all parties concerned. At the same time, Ukraine has manifested its interest in finding a role in international institutions and in the settlement of conflicts in Europe, and in developing economic and technical links which foster economic restructuring and regeneration of the country. Kyiv values close ties with the EU both for economic and political reasons. Since 1994, Ukraine's cooperation with various international organizations—with the Organization for Security and Cooperation in Europe (OSCE), the Council of Europe, the European Union, the International Monetary Fund, and NATO—has increased noticeably in intensity and significance. But the main problem is that Ukraine is unlikely to become a member of the European Union, the Western European Union or NATO in the foreseeable future. In his speech at the Economic Summit of the East Central European countries in Salzburg in July 1996, President Kuchma presented a very ambitious program of Ukrainian participation in the European integration process, with a claim for a regional East Central European great power status. His program included the following demands of security guarantees for Ukraine:

• unequivocal assurances by the European Union, NATO and the WEU that their doors will remain open not only to Hungary, Poland, and the Czech Republic, but also to other states that would like to join later as well;

- a special NATO-Ukrainian relationship;
- Ukraine's status of "associated partner" of the WEU that would "re-establish the historical justice of the rightful return of Ukraine to Europe";
- a "partial" associated membership of Ukraine in the EU, with special reference to the political and military-political sphere;
- involvement of Ukraine in the political dialogue between the European Union and East Central European countries.[55]

The most striking characteristic of this program is Ukraine's self-identification as an East Central European country, an identification that other East Central European countries, the West European powers, and Russia seem to be unwilling at the moment to share.

Ukraine and the European Union

Somewhat complicated at the practical level are Ukraine's relations with the European Union. In 1992–1993, during the first period ("the period of neglect"), relations between Ukraine and the European Community (EC) were rather formal. Ukraine did not announce its intentions to join either the EC or the WEU. The European Community for its part explicitly made the development of relations with Ukraine contingent on Ukraine's compliance with the START I and the Nuclear Non-Proliferation Treaty (NPT). But already in 1993, Ukraine began negotiations with the EC on a Partnership and Cooperation Agreement. In May 1994, Ukraine was the first CIS state to sign a Partnership and Cooperation Agreement (PCA) with the European Community.[56]

The objectives of the partnership were formulated in Article 1 of the Agreement as follows:

- to provide an appropriate framework for political dialogue allowing the development of close political relations;
- to promote trade, investment and economic relations;
- to provide a basis for mutually advantageous economic, social, financial, technological and cultural cooperation;
- to support Ukrainian efforts to consolidate its democracy and to complete the transition into a market economy;[57]

Although the Agreement provides for the creation of a free-trade zone after 1998, it falls short of the Association Agreements with the East Central European and Baltic states that envisage their full membership in the European Union. The improbability that the European Union would grant Ukraine an "associate-partner" status in the near future hampers substantially Ukraine's chances to achieve another goal, that is, to join the Central European Free Trade Agreement (CEFTA), because the EU's "associate-partner" status is one of the conditions for joining CEFTA. Recently, especially after the appoint-

ment of Borys Tarasyuk as the new foreign minister, the Partnership and
Cooperation Agreement has apparently been considered as already obsolete,
and EU associate membership has become one of the main goals of Ukrainian
diplomacy in Western Europe. Representatives of that country do not miss any
occasion to request that Ukraine be granted associated membership in order to
pave the way for full-fledged membership in the future. But the European
Union has serious reservations about this idea and is not ready to look further
than the Partnership and Cooperation Agreement in its relations with Ukraine.

In June 1995, an Interim Agreement that gives Ukraine most favored nation
status in trade with the EU was signed between the European Union and
Ukraine. It came into force on 1 February 1996. In accordance with the Interim
Agreement, a Ukrainian-European Union Committee was founded as an official institution to monitor economic and trade cooperation between the EU and
Ukraine. This is an interim committee which will function until the formation
of the Union for Cooperation between Ukraine and the European Union.[58]
However, there are still doubts, especially among EU experts, that Ukraine
would be ready to become a free-trade zone after 1998. The main problems are
Ukraine's poor economic performance, the necessity to adapt Ukrainian legislation to European norms, and fears of internal instability in Ukraine. In December 1996, the European Union adopted a special action plan to provide
support for Ukraine's new reform program. This plan included the following
provisions:

- supporting democratic reforms and development of a civil society;
- supporting economic reforms and development of trade and economic
cooperation;
- strengthening the political dialogue and supporting Ukraine's participation
in the European security architecture;
- supporting regional cooperation;
- strengthening treaty relations, especially within the framework of the Partnership and Cooperation Agreement;
- reforming the energy sector.

Cooperation of the post-Soviet states with the European Union has at least two
dimensions: political and economic (the third dimension, cooperation in the
security field, should rather be considered within the framework of the WEU).
Politically, of special importance from the Ukrainian point of view was the
European Union's repeated expressions of support for Ukraine's national security and territorial integrity. During the aggravation of separatist conflict in
Crimea in May 1994, the EU articulated in a special declaration its respect for
Ukraine's sovereignty and territorial integrity. In November 1994, the Euro-
pean Union adopted a common position on Ukraine. As EU officials stress,
Ukraine is the only CIS or East Central European country to be the subject of
such a formalized expression of political interest on the part of the European

Union.[59] This common position includes the following objectives and priorities:

- to establish strong political relations with Ukraine;
- to lend its support to the independence, sovereignty and territorial integrity of Ukraine;
- to express support for initiatives to ease tensions in Crimea within the context of sovereignty, and territorial integrity;
- to support reform policies, particularly in the field of energy with a strong emphasis to nuclear safety and the closure of the Chornobyl reactor.

In December 1996, as the verbal conflict between Russia and Ukraine over the Black Sea Fleet escalated again, Ireland, which then held the chairmanship in the European Union, made a statement on behalf of the EU criticizing the inflammatory resolution of the Russian State Duma and the Federation Council on Sevastopol, and once again supported the independence, sovereignty, and territorial integrity of Ukraine.[60]

The draft document "A Conception of Foreign Economic Relations [of Ukraine]" prepared in 1995 and debated in fall 1996 in the Ukrainian Parliament sets relations with the European Union as the second priority of Ukrainian foreign economic policy, just behind the CIS and Baltic states, with top priority given to ties with Germany, Italy, Spain, and Greece.[61] The economic dimension of cooperation between the European Union and Ukraine includes trade, assistance, and aid. From the very beginning it was evident that opening the EC/EU's market to trade with Eastern Europe from Czechoslovakia to Ukraine was the surest way to help the post-communist countries in transforming their economies. But, precisely on this issue the EC/EU was and remains especially reluctant. One of the main reasons is that the goods these countries produce in greatest quantities are products on which the EC/EU was and still is most protectionist—agricultural products and steel, for instance. Though the European Union officially sees Ukraine as having the "potential" to become an important political and economic partner of the Union, a number of EU members have adopted and continue to display a more restrained and reluctant attitude towards Ukraine. So, for instance, though the Partnership and Cooperation Agreement between the European Union and Ukraine was signed as far back as May 1994, it took the member states almost four years to ratify it. The PCA entered into force only on 1 March 1998. Ukrainian politicians are becoming increasingly frustrated with some EU member states" coolness toward Ukraine and warn that a gap could grow between Ukraine and the West unless the European Union fosters better relations with Kyiv.

One of the objectives of the PCA is to boost mutual trade. The European Union is the biggest trade partner of Ukraine beyond the CIS borders. In 1996, the total volume of trade between Ukraine and the European Union reached 4.1 billion dollars. Trade with the EU countries amounts now to about 15 percent of Ukriane's entire foreign trade volume,[62] but almost half of the EU's trade with Ukraine falls on two countries only, Germany and Italy.[63] The Ukrainian government is now finalizing its concept for developing relations with the European Union. A lowering of tariffs on Ukrainian goods by the EU member countries, as well as recognition of the transitioned status of the Ukrainian economy are among the main goals of this concept. Agreements with the European Union on trade in nuclear materials and agricultural products are to be finalized. Ukraine will insist that the EU quotas for its textile and iron-and-steel industry production be increased.

Trade cooperation between Ukraine and the European Union still suffers from the EU's anti-dumping measures. Due to pressures from domestic producers, the EU member states continue to classify Ukraine, together with Russia and the other CIS members as well as the Baltic states, as "non-market" economies, against which the World Trade Organization (WTO) allows a unilateral imposition of antidumping sanctions. As a non-member of the WTO, Ukraine cannot claim protection against such measures. Negotiations should be held on the imposition of EU anti-dumping duties against Ukrainian goods. As a result of these sanctions, many Ukrainian goods which are foreign-currency earners already are or will be barred from the EU's markets. Since 1991, the European Union imposed anti-dumping duties against fifteen classes of Ukrainian exports. Antidumping legislation affected almost 10 percent of the total trade turnover between Ukraine and the European Union. Compared with 1991, although Ukraine's exports to the EU increased significantly, export revenues from trade with the EU countries which resorted to anti-dumping measures dropped 2.2 times.[64] Together with Belarus, Georgia, Japan, Pakistan, South Korea, and Turkey, Ukraine is among the seven countries most affected by the EU's antidumping sanctions.[65] Ukraine has a negative trade balance with the European Union amounting to over 1 billion dollars. Consultations are also to start with Germany, Great Britain, and the Netherlands on the formation of a free-trade area. The government also intends to bring Ukrainian legislation in line with EU standards; to promote agreements between branches of industry which would facilitate the access of Ukrainian goods to the EU markets.[66]

Since 1995, Ukraine has begun to receive significant international financial aid. While the IMF and the World Bank committed a total of 3.4 billion dollars in loans, 1.5 billion dollars of which were slated for 1996, the European Union was ready to provide in 1996 a rather modest 260 million dollars, and the European Bank for Reconstruction and Development (EBRD) 80 million dollars. Anders Aslund writes that the European Union turned out to be a major stumbling block with regard to financial aid to Ukraine; its lack of interest was astounding.[67] The EU supports the process of economic reform mainly through the Tacis program. The main sectors of Tacis assistance include nuclear safety, enterprise reform, human resources development, agriculture and private sector development. In the years 1992–1995 the European Union committed through the Tacis program 236 million ecus for Ukraine.[68] In the years 1996–1999, the volume of assistance within the framework of the Tacis program should reach 538 million ecus.[69] Since 1991, the EU has provided a total of 3.17 billion ecus for the support of economic reform in Ukraine, in particular for the modernization and safety of the energy system. Of that sum, 1.9 billion ecus have been provided by the EU member states (mostly by Germany) and 1.27 billion ecus have been granted by the Union.[70] The European Union is ready now to support Ukraine with a special action plan within the framework of the Partnership and Cooperation Agreement. One of Ukraine's handicaps in its relations with the European Union was until recently that the EU did not yet legally recognize Ukraine as a country with a transitional type of economy. That recognition came only in July 1996.

The not so bright economic situation in the 1990s in most EU member states and the preoccupation of the EU with its own internal problems, in particular with the Monetary Union, hinder an active EU policy towards Ukraine. The situation in the European Union is additionaly aggravated by the position of the southern members of the Union that primarily see in East Central and East European aspirants for EU membership competitors for the EU's subsidies. The EU-Ukrainian relationship has not developed easily. Ukrainian criticisms of the EU's policy includes, among others, reproaches for not considering Ukraine as a potential member of the Union and reducing cooperation with it to dispensing aid, and for not inviting Ukraine to participate in the European Conference, a forum of the European Union and the EU's aspirants.

Ukraine and the Western European Union

Relations between the Western European Union, the defense arm of the European Union, and Ukraine have been, at least until recently, non-existent.[71] But, Kyiv showed a rather early interest in obtaining at least observer status in the WEU Assembly.[72] More recently, Ukraine has become more insistent on developing ties with the WEU and has even declared its desire to become an associated member.[73] However, until now the WEU has not considered Ukraine as a possible applicant for "associate partner" status because, according to its rules, this status can be granted only to those states that have concluded association agreements with the European Union (six East Central European and three Baltic states) and therefore are considered potential EU members. The WEU regards Ukraine's neutrality and membership in the CIS as incompatible with its aspirations for "associate partner" status as a preliminary to WEU membership. The paper "Ukraine and European Security" presented at the Parliamentary Assembly of the WEU in June 1996 stated that the WEU intended to carry on a constant dialogue with Ukraine, but could not impart a new character to its relations with Kyiv in the present situation. This could change if Kyiv made a decision to abandon its neutral status and to leave the CIS.[74]

In September 1996, the WEU Secretary General José Cutileiro visited Kyiv. On this occasion, Ukraine and the WEU issued a joint communiqué. President Kuchma told Cutileiro that Ukraine should be granted the "associate partner" status already gained by former Warsaw Pact states, and that Ukraine wants eventually to join the WEU itself.[75]

Ukraine and NATO

The issue of the Ukrainian-NATO relationship extends, of course, beyond the theme "Ukraine and Western Europe." But as NATO is to become one of the pillars of the future European security system, this relationship is of essential importance for all parties concerned. During the last few years, Ukrainian policymakers were increasingly inclined to consider NATO as the guarantor of security and stability in Europe and as the core structure of the future European security system, and consequently to cooperate closely with this structure. Ukrainian conceptions of a European security architecture attached special importance to NATO. Ukraine was the first state of the CIS to sign up for the "Partnership for Peace" (PfP) program. As a participant in the PfP, it signed a cooperation agreement with NATO that went beyond the normal PfP framework. Now, the Ukrainian leadership feels that their country's security needs have already outgrown the relatively narrow scope of the PfP program and strives for the development of the NATO-Ukrainian cooperation beyond the PfP framework.

Ukraine's willingness to engage in close cooperation with NATO went hand in hand with its position on the issue of NATO's eastward opening. The Ukrainian leadership's initial reservations against the extension of NATO were not based on any perceptions of their country being threatened. NATO was not seen as a potential threat to Ukraine. Rather, those reservations were the result of fears of a constellation arising which could have adverse consequences for Ukraine. NATO's commitment to expand eastward raised a new set of dilemmas for Ukraine, where many officials feared that early NATO expansion to East Central Europe would leave Kyiv more vulnerable to Russian pressure, and the country could find itself pinned between two blocs. Ukraine would have preferred an "evolutionary" NATO eastward enlargement and a "soft integration" of the East Central European states into NATO. More recently, however, Ukrainian decision makers have not excluded the possibility of a "gradual" rapprochement between NATO's and Ukraine's positions and of the revision of Ukraine's non-block status. One of the most important shifts in the Ukrainian security conception consists of redefining Ukraine's non-block status as consistent with close cooperation with NATO. Rapproachment with NATO is considered now as a basic component of Ukraine's strategy to join European and Euro-Atlantic economic, political, and security institutions.

Even the option of Ukrainian membership of NATO in the future is now seen by some politicians as desirable, since it would contribute to the process of Ukrainian integration into Europe and thus accord with the wider integration process. The Ukrainian leadership has harbored fears, as have the Baltic states, that the agreement between Russia and NATO could result in a tacit creation of spheres of influence as the price for NATO's eastward enlargement, with Ukraine falling "naturally" into the Russian sphere of influence. The determinant political forces in Kyiv increasingly turned to NATO in an effort to establish ties which were as close as possible. The result of these efforts was the signing of a "Charter on a Distinctive Partnership between the North Atlantic Treaty Organization and Ukraine" on 9 July 1997. There had been a lengthy prior search for an appropriate term to describe the relations between NATO and Ukraine. The Ukrainian side advocated "special relations," whereas NATO wanted to avoid the term. The Charter is aimed at creating a framework for the extension of close relations between the two sides. In the Charter the NATO member states promise to support Ukraine with respect to its sovereignty, political independence, territorial integrity, inviolability of borders, and its democratic development and economic prosperity, which are addressed as key factors for stability and security in Central and Eastern Europe and for the intensification of Ukraine's integration into all European and Euro-Atlantic structures.

The NATO-Ukraine Charter was generally very highly rated (sometimes almost euphorically) by the Ukrainian foreign policy establishment. In many respects, however, the Charter has a primarily symbolic character. For almost all Ukrainian politicians and analysts the main significance of the Charter is the recognition of Ukraine as an eastern Central European state. In respect to Ukrainian Europe-oriented policies the importance of the term "eastern Central European" as opposed to "Eurasian" cannot be overrated. Whether the NATO-Ukraine Charter will be filled with real content and implemented will depend on a variety of external and internal factors and, last but not least, on the behavior of the West.

Conclusion

Geographically and politically Ukraine is situated between Russia and Europe. Paradoxically, this is concurrently the strong and the weak point of the country's geostrategic position. On the one hand, due to this position, Ukraine is essential for European stability. On the other hand, this same position makes Ukraine especially vulnerable in its sense of security. To solve its security problems, Ukraine needs support from and cooperation with the international community—first of all with the European institutions. But the West will be able to help the country only if it solves its own "Ukrainian question," i.e., the formulation of a new comprehensive policy towards Ukraine. During the years since independence, Ukraine has managed to develop from a potential risk factor to European security into a European security asset.[76] The recent trend in the West has been to place increased emphasis on bolstering the security and economy of Ukraine. The West should demonstrate that it does not perceive Ukraine as an extension of Russia nor as an appendage of Western and East Central European security.[77] The "Partnership for Peace" and the Partnership and Cooperation Agreement with the European Union have given Ukraine a firmer anchor in the West, but how and where Ukraine fits into the wider security framework in Europe, its precise role and position, remain to be determined.

Ukraine still finds it difficult to convey clearly what role it envisages for itself in Europe. Ideally, Ukraine should prefer to develop balanced relations, to the same extent and importance with Russia and the West as well. But Ukraine's even-handed cooperation, especially in the security field, with Russia and the West cannot and will not meet Russian expectations. This represents one of Ukraine's fundamental dilemmas in its foreign and security policies. However, Ukraine has manifested its interest in playing a role in international institutions and in conflict resolution in Europe, as well as developing economic links that foster economic restructuring and regeneration of the country. Kyiv values close ties with the European institutions both for economic and political reasons. Assisting Ukraine's economic transition and political reforms and a more decisive cooperation on the part of the European Union and the Western European Union should be a major part of Western strategy. However, the future of Ukraine's relations with its western neighbors will depend to a large extent on how successfully the country carries out its political and economic reforms. Ukraine's recent undeniable foreign policy successes find themselves in a growing discrepancy with the increase in political problems at home, the growing number of government crises, the strained relationship between the executive and the legislature, and the inability of the leadership to carry out far-reaching economic reforms. If the reforms take hold, Ukraine will become a more attractive economic and political partner; should they fail, however, Ukraine and the European states will increasingly go their separate ways.

NOTES

1. Alexander J. Motyl, *Dilemmas of Independence. Ukraine after Totalitarianism* (New York, 1993), 180; Peter van Ham, *Ukraine, Russia and European Security: Implications for Western Policy* (Paris, February 1994), 33–34 [=Chaillot Papers 13].

2. Serhiy Holovatiy [Holowaty], "Ukraine in the After-the-Soviet Union Days," in Dick Clark, *United States–Soviet Relations: Building a Congressional Cadre.* Tenth Conference, 15–20 January 1992, The Aspen Institute, (Queenstown, MD, 1992), 49–50.

3. *The Economist* 15 June 1991: 28.

4. *Izvestiia* 9 November 1990; *Neue Zürcher Zeitung* 8 December 1990.

5. John Edwin Mroz and Oleksandr Pavliuk, "Ukraine: Europe's Linchpin," *Foreign Affairs* 75(3) May–June 1996: 58.

6. "Bush Wants Improved Relations with Soviet Republics" USIS, *U.S. Policy Information and Texts* 104 (2 August 1991): 5.

7. *The Times* 21 March 1991.

8. Vera Tolz, "Weekly Record of Events," *Report on the USSR* 3(43) 25 October 1991: 37.

9. *International Herald Tribune* 29 November 1991.

10. *The Economist* 7 December 1991: 14.

11. Holovatiy, 49–50.

12. Motyl, 179–80.

13. Oleksandr Kupchyshyn, "Spivrobitnytstvo—z SND, intehratsiia—z Ievropoiu," *Polityka i chas* 1996(7): 13.

14. *International Herald Tribune* 9 April 1992.

15. Sherman W. Garnett, "The Sources and Conduct of Ukrainian Nuclear Policy," in George Quester, ed., *The Nuclear Challenge in Russia and the New States of Eurasia* (NY–London, 1995), 126 [=The International Politics of Eurasia].

16. So one U.S. diplomat, as quoted in *Financial Times* 7 May 1993.

17. *Financial Times* 5 September 1995.

18. See, for instance, F. Stephen Larrabee, "Ukraine's Balancing Act,"*Survival* 38(2) Summer 1996: 143–65, in particular, 145, 159.

19. Quoted in Bohdan A. Osadczuk-Korab, "Die Aussen- und Innenpolitik der Ukraine in jüngster Zeit," in Wolfdieter Bihl et al., *Russland und die Ukraine nach dem Zerfall der Sowjetunion* (Berlin, 1996), 167 [=Abhandlungen des Göttinger Arbeitskreises, 12].

20. Kupchyshyn, 13–16.

21. Bohdan Lupiy, *Ukraine and European Security: International Mechanisms as Non-Military Security Options for Ukraine* (Frankfurt a.M., 1996), 93–94 [=Euro-Atlantic Security Studies,3]

22. *Den'* 29 July 1997

23. *Den'* 18 June 1997.

24. Dmytro Vydrin, "Naidem li obshchii iazyk? Obiazany!" *Viche* 9 (August 1994): 70.

25. Peter van Ham, 42.

26. Calculated according to the Economist Intelligence Unit, *Country Report Ukraine* 2nd Quarter (1998): 26.

27. *Uriadovyi kur'ier* 30 May 1998.

28. *Faks-postup* 2(22) 29 May 1996.

29. *Zerkalo nedeli* 7 (15–21 February 1997).

30. *Faks-postup* 2(23) 5 June 1996; II(43) 23 October, 1996.

31. As quoted in *Jamestown Monitor* 11 March 1997.

32. See Volodymyr Sidenko, "Proryv u Ievropu—iakym chynom?" *Polityka i chas* 1997(11): 26.

33. Calculated according to the Econtomist Intelligence Unit, *Country Report Ukraine* 2nd Quarter (1998): 26.

34. *Zerkalo nedeli* 7 (15–21 February 1997).

35. *Polityka i chas* 1996 (5): 86.

36. Tor Bukkvoll, *Ukraine and European Security* (London, 1997), 73 [=Chatham House Papers]; *Zerkalo nedeli* 5 (1–7 February 1997).

37. Dmytro Vydrin, 70.

38. As quoted in Peter van Ham, 44.

39. ITAR-TASS, 16 June 1992.

40. *Izvestiia* 17 June 1992.

41. Bukkvoll, 73.

42. *Den'* 25 July 1998; The Economist Intelligence Unit, *Country Report Ukraine* 2nd Quarter (1998):26.

43. *Faks-postup* 3(4) 31 January 1997. According to the Ukrainian government newspaper *Uriadovyi kur'ier* (1 February 1997), as of the end of 1996 French investments amounted to 10.9 million dollars only, or one (!) percent of all foreign investment in Ukraine.

44. *Zerkalo nedeli* 30 (25–31 July 1998).

45. Anders Aslund, "Eurasia Letter: Ukraine's Turnaround," *Foreign Policy* 100 (Fall 1995): 139, 140.

46. *Faks-postup* 2(11) 13 March 1996.

47. *Faks-postup* 3(1) 6 January 1997.

48. See Volodymyr Sidenko, "Proryv u Ievropu—iakym chynom?" *Polityka i chas*, 1997(11): 21.

49. *Faks-postup* 3(1) 6 January 1997.

50. Calculated according to the Economist Intelligence Unit, *Country Report Ukraine* 2nd Quarter (1998): 26.

51. *Faks-postup* 2(44) 30 October, 1996.

52. *Zerkalo nedeli* 7(124) 15–21 February.

53. *Faks-postup* 2(12) 20 March 1996.

54. Oleg Strekal, *Independent Ukraine: The Search for Security* (Ebenhausen, March 1995), 54 [=IAI/WP-Projektpapier, 3].

55. *Uriadovyi kur'ier* 11 July 1996.

56. "Partnership and Cooperation Agreement Between the European Communities and Their Member States, and Ukraine."

57. Ibid.

58. *Faks-postup* 2(19) 8 May, 1996.

59. R. Verrue, "Ukraine and European Security. Outline of Intervention," in Gerhard Gnauck, Steffen Sachs eds., *Die Ukraine und die europäische Sicherheit. Bericht über eine Konferenz des Aspen Instituts* (Berlin, 8–10 April 1995).

60. *Uriadovyi kur'ier* 24 December 1996.

61. Oles' Tyshchuk, "Plan Osyky: Dyktat na rynkakh do 2000 roku," *Post postup* 10 (17–23 March 1995).

62. *Uriadovyi kur'ier* 6 June 1998.

63. See Volodymyr Sidenko, "Proryv u Ievropu—iakym chynom?" *Polityka i chas* 1997 (11): 21.

64. *Faks-postup* 3(9) 7 March 1997.

65. *Faks-postup* 2(43) 23 October 1996.

66. Ibid.

67. Aslund, 139, 140.

68. Ibid.

69. *Vseukrainskie vedomosti* 31 July 1996.

70. Die Europäische Union, *Ukraine—Aktionsplan* (Bruxelles, December 1996).

71. Peter van Ham, 49.

72. Ibid.

73. "Nova arkhitektura bezpeky v Ievropi nemozhlyva bez Ukrainy. Vystup Prezydenta Ukrainy L.D. Kuchmy na Asamblei ZES 4 chervnia 1996 roku," *Polityka i chas* 1996 (7): 3–7.

74. Ośrodek Studiów Wschodnich, *Wiadomości* 121 (23 June 1996): 7.

75. *The Economist* (28 September 1996): 40.

76. Guido Lenzi and Laurence Martin, eds., *The European Security Space. Working Papers by the European Strategy Group and the Institute for Security Studies of Western European Union* (Paris, 1996), 12.

77. Gerard Snel, "At the Border of European Security: The Case of Ukraine," in David Carlton, Paul Ingram, and Giancarlo Tenaglia (eds.), *Rising Tension in Eastern Europe and the Former Soviet Union* (Aldershot, 1996), 128.

9

Ukraine and the Middle East

OLES M. SMOLANSKY

Speaking in January 1995, Ukrainian Foreign Minister Hennadiy Udovenko noted that, under President Leonid Kuchma, Ukraine's foreign policy would be more active, more dynamic, more pragmatic, and more predictable than under his predecessor, Leonid Kravchuk. It would also be better designed to serve Ukraine's national interests. As one manifestation of this projected dynamism, Udovenko cited Kuchma's foreign travels which had taken the president to the United States, Canada, Turkmenistan, and Georgia. However, he had not yet visited any of the Middle Eastern states. (Kravchuk, in contrast, during his term in office, had visited Iran, Turkey, Israel, Egypt, and Tunisia.)

Udovenko also listed the regions of the world in which Ukraine had displayed an interest. They were—in descending order of importance—Russia and the "Commonwealth of Independent States" (CIS), the West, the Persian Gulf countries (including Iran), the Asia-Pacific region, Latin America, and Africa. Among the non-Persian Gulf Arab states, Udovenko mentioned Egypt, Algeria, Morocco, and Tunisia but made no reference to Israel.[1] In April 1995, the foreign minister explained that Ukraine was trying to establish and expand "economic relations with as many states as possible" but added that, in the Middle East, Ukraine's presence was "limited."[2]

Udovenko's successor as foreign minister, appointed in April 1998, Borys Tarasyuk, made no public reference to the Middle East in the first months of his tenure. Instead, he has expressed his determination to pursue "the course, outlined by the President, aimed at Ukraine's integration into European and Euro-Atlantic structures." Tarasyuk also embraced the notion that Kyiv's foreign policy would continue to be guided by " . . . Ukraine's interests. Everything else . . . is a matter of secondary importance." By emphasizing Europe and the Euro-Atlantic region in his initial public pronouncement, the new foreign minister let it be understood that Ukraine would attempt to shift the emphasis in its foreign policy away from Russia and the other ex-Soviet republics to the West—a major modification to the approach espoused by Udovenko.[3] But even though Tarasyuk had not yet publicly addressed the subject of the Middle East, it stands to reason that Ukraine will continue to pursue an active policy in the region.

Nature of Ukraine's Interest in the Middle East

In retrospect, there can be no doubt that the Middle East is regarded as very important to independent Ukraine because of its geographic location and because of its potential economic and political significance to Kyiv.

Geographic Location

In 1992, Viktor Nahaichuk, then head of the Near and Middle East Department of the Ukrainian Ministry of Foreign Affairs, described the Middle East as "one of the nerve-centers in world affairs." Home of over 200 million people, inhabiting 18 states, and rich in mineral resources, the Middle East was important to Kyiv as a "geographically strategic area, . . . situated in the immediate vicinity of Ukraine's southern borders."[4] Other officials, including Yevhen Mykytenko, who replaced Nahaichuk as head of the Foreign Ministry's Near and Middle East Department after the latter's appointment as Kyiv's ambassador to Egypt, mentioned also the importance to Ukraine of the sea-lanes, passing through the Turkish Straits and the Mediterranean. Iran, in particular, and Ukraine were seen as links in a potentially important land or land-sea route, linking Asia and Europe.[5]

Economic Factors

1. Potential Source of Fuel. Many Ukrainian officials have noted that some Middle Eastern and North African states were among the world's largest producers of petroleum and natural gas—commodities in short supply in Ukraine and which, therefore, had to be imported from abroad. Minister of Foreign Economic Relations, Serhiy Osyka, put it this way: "In light of the need to find alternative energy sources and diversifying imports, the government will contribute to the deepening of trade and economic relations with Near and Middle East countries."[6] Ukraine has indeed attempted to establish close working relations with some of these states (Iran, the United Arab Emirates [UAE], Saudi Arabia, and Kuwait) by opening embassies and maintaining lively interstate dialogues. However, as time passed and the hoped-for flow of Middle Eastern fuel failed to materialize, Kyiv scaled down its expectations. Speaking in early 1997, the deputy head of the coal, oil, and natural gas department of the Ministry of Economics described Azerbaijan and Iran as Ukraine's "most realistic suppliers of crude in the future.[7]

2. Potential Source of Capital. Upon his appointment as ambassador to the United Arab Emirates in 1993, Oleh Semenets explained that the Ukrainian mission would be hard at work exploring "the possibilities of . . . receiving credits" from that oil-rich Persian Gulf state. Osyka, too, referred to the petroleum-producing countries of the Middle East as a major source of capital,[8]

and it may be safely assumed that attempts to attract Middle Eastern capital were also made in Turkey, Iran, Kuwait, Saudi Arabia, and, possibly, Libya. In the ensuing years, Kyiv continued its efforts to attract capital from the Middle East. For example, during his 1997 visit to Cairo, Deputy Foreign Minister Kostiantyn Hryshchenko attempted to "draw . . . Egyptian investment into the construction and modernization of tourist complexes and hotels in Ukraine."[9]

3. Trade. In addition to possible sources of fuel and capital, the countries of the Middle East were also perceived as potential markets for Ukraine's industrial and agricultural products. Some states, including Iraq and Libya, were reminded that, prior to the dissolution of the USSR, it was Ukraine—rather than the other Soviet republics—that maintained close economic relations with them.[10] The unmistakable implication was that Ukraine was ready to start where the USSR had left off. For instance, in mid-1996, a Ukrainian government delegation visited Baghdad and offered "to supply food . . . in exchange for oil." One member of the delegation noted that the Iraqi crude was of a higher quality and much cheaper than the oil imported from Russia. In a similar fashion, Kyiv was also trying to barter Ukrainian agricultural products for two million tons of Iranian oil.[11]

4. Technical Cooperation. Some Arab states expressed an interest in this type of interaction and Kyiv, as a rule, was happy to oblige—in principle. A few examples will illustrate this point. As early as February 1992, then Minister of Economics Oleksandr Minchenko met with a visiting Kuwaiti delegation and offered to send 600,000 Ukrainian oil and gas industry workers, who were employed in Russia at the time, to help rebuild Kuwait's fuel industry. It will be recalled that much of it was destroyed during the Iraqi occupation.[12] In April 1993, commenting on his tour of the Persian Gulf, then Prime Minister Kuchma said that the governments of the Gulf states were interested in securing Ukrainian assistance in such diverse economic pursuits as exploration and extraction of fuel; construction of pipelines and dams; development of metallurgical industry; and shipbuilding.[13] In August 1994, the Libyan chargé d'affaires complained about the lack of progress in developing bilateral relations, but noted that "hundreds of Ukrainian specialists" were working in his country. A few months later, during a meeting with an Egyptian government delegation, Udovenko said that Ukraine remained interested in sending its specialists to help develop the Egyptian economy. According to the foreign minister, its most promising sectors were: "geological prospecting, irrigation, [and] ore-dressing . . . ."[14]

In mid-1996, as noted, a Ukrainian government delegation, led by Yevhen Dovzhok (then head of Ukrderzhnaftohazprom, a state concern in charge of the oil and gas industries), visited Iraq. In the course of a press-conference, Minister of Oil 'Amir Muhammad Rashid noted that his country was determined to expand its industrial base and that "the prospects for cooperation between Iraq and Ukraine are great." Rashid explained that Ukraine's need for fuel and

Iraq's need for "transferring . . . industrial expertise" created a solid basis on which to expand relations between the two states. According to a member of the Ukrainian delegation, the sides signed a protocol of intent "to cooperate in the oil and gas industry, in particular to develop oil fields in Iraq and prospect for new deposits."[15]

Otherwise, in 1995, Kyiv and Tehran concluded an agreement for the construction in Iran of approximately one hundred AN-140 turboprop passenger planes under Ukrainian license. The terms of the contract were not disclosed. In 1996, Iran and Russia renewed a contract (signed initially by Iran and the USSR) to build a nuclear power plant at Bushehr. Ukraine became part of the deal by agreeing to supply a million-kilowatt turbine to the project. Finally, in mid-1997, Ukraine and Iran entered into an agreement providing for "cooperation in the spheres of oil and gas." Under its terms, Kyiv undertook to deliver "equipment and machinery" for use at Iran's fuel production sites and promised to send Ukrainian specialists to help in the construction of pipelines.[16]

5. <u>Potential Arms Market</u>. It was generally acknowledged that independent Ukraine had inherited from the Soviet Union both a sizable capacity for weapons production and a vast arsenal of modern arms. For this reason, it was natural that many officials favored Ukraine's entry into the international "arms bazaar" in an attempt to acquire hard currency and to cement economic cooperation with other states. For example, in March 1992, deputy chairman of the Parliament, Volodymyr Hrynov, announced that Ukraine would attempt to "export arms," provided that they would not be transferred to the so-called "hot spots and to countries which have not signed corresponding international agreements and conventions."[17] A few months later, however, Nahaichuk added that "Ukraine does not want to base its policy [in the Middle East] on the arms trade." Nevertheless, some (unnamed) Arab countries had expressed an interest in purchasing arms, and Nahaichuk saw no reason why Kyiv should refuse them. Similar sentiments were also expressed by then Prime Minister Kuchma.[18] Conversely, it was acknowledged that the process of modernizing or converting defense-related industries to civilian production would require a considerable outlay of money. Government officials were hoping that the sale of arms would provide some of the necessary funds to assist Ukraine in this painful process. Kyiv's most important initiative to date has been participation in the annual weapons fair, held in Dubai (UAE). It was there, at IDEX-95, that Ukraine unveiled its new M-84 diesel-powered tank (otherwise known as T-80 UD) which was subsequently purchased by Pakistan.[19] Another important agreement provided for the purchase by Iran of "more than ten An-74T-2000 military transport aircraft . . . for use by the Iranian armed forces." The terms of this contract were not disclosed.[20]

Among the other countries with which Kyiv attempted to establish cooperation in the "military-technical area," were embargo-stricken Iraq and Libya as well as Egypt and Jordan. For example, in a report on then Prime Minister Pavlo Lazarenko's 1997 visit to Cairo, it was noted that Egypt was one of the world's leading importers of arms. Since its armed forces were "largely equipped with former Soviet weapons manufactured in Ukraine," Kyiv was in a position to offer Cairo some "mutually beneficial projects." In fact, Lazarenko suggested that the sides sign appropriate agreements to that effect. Instead, they merely "agreed that . . . deliveries of Ukrainian weapons, special equipment and spare parts" to Egypt as well as "overhauls and modernization of Egyptian weapon systems and possible construction of military infrastructure facilities are very promising."[21]

In April 1998, Defense Minister Oleksandr Kuzmuk traveled to Jordan and met with the country's top political and military leaders. According to the Jordanian media, the sides "reviewed the regional situation . . . , aspects of bilateral cooperation, and friendly bilateral relations." Common sense suggests that the reference to broadening "cooperation in the military sphere," contained in the Jordanian account, referred to Kuzmuk's efforts to persuade Amman to purchase Ukrainian weapons.[22]

Political Factors

Partly to assist in its pursuit of the economic goals by establishing normal working relations with the states of the Middle East and North Africa and partly to promote Ukraine's image as an independent power in the international arena, Kyiv has striven to enhance its visibility in that part of the world by means of presidential visits (supplemented by visits of government delegations), of establishing embassies, and of conducting dialogues on political problems of mutual interest. Kyiv appeared to have been pleased with its early diplomatic efforts. Returning from his April 1993 tour of the Persian Gulf states, then Prime Minister Kuchma was convinced that "the East understands us better than the West or America. Perhaps this is so because 20–30 years ago, they were in a situation similar to ours."[23]

In any event, as noted, President Kravchuk had visited Iran, Turkey, Egypt, Tunisia, and Israel, while President Kuchma paid state visits to Israel and Turkey. These were supplemented by numerous visits on the ministerial and sub-ministerial levels.

Ukrainian embassies are functioning in Turkey, Iran, Israel, Jordan, Saudi Arabia, the United Arab Emirates, Kuwait, Egypt, and Tunisia. In 1995, Kyiv announced its intention to open an embassy in Libya as well but, presumably for political reasons, has not done so yet. In contrast, a Libyan chargé d'affaires arrived in Ukraine in 1995. The relative modesty of Kyiv's effort is not difficult to understand. Starting from "zero" and lacking human and financial resources for a large-scale "diplomatic offensive," Ukraine had no choice but to exercise restraint in the matter of opening embassies. Kyiv, therefore, picked its partners carefully, weighing their respective potential for serving Ukraine's economic and political interests. Thus,

- in the Persian Gulf, Iran, Saudi Arabia, the UAE, and Kuwait—all important oil producers—were chosen because of their presumed economic
importance to Ukraine.
- Egypt and Tunisia were regarded as "bridges to the Arab East and North
Africa."[24]
- Turkey, a major Black Sea power, has rendered valuable political support
in helping Ukraine resist Russian encroachments in that region. Ankara
has also developed into an important economic partner.[25]
- Finally, Ukraine's interest in Israel has rested on a number of factors
which, in the Middle Eastern context, were quite unique. For one thing, some
300,000 Ukrainian citizens of Jewish descent had emigrated to Israel, establishing an important link between the two states that could not be duplicated
anywhere else in the Middle East. Moreover, since Israel possesses an advanced economy with a highly sophisticated technological base, it has been felt
in Kyiv that Ukraine could benefit greatly from close economic cooperation
between the two states.[26] Last but not least, Israel possesses a unique entry into
the legislative and executive branches of the U.S. government and has, therefore, been seen by Ukrainian leaders as a unique and valuable communications
conduit between Kyiv and Washington.[27]

Humanitarian and Security Factors

In addition to geography, economics, and politics, Ukraine's interest in the
Middle East has also been conditioned by a set of other interests which can best
be described as humanitarian and security concerns. Included in this broad
category are such items as education—with thousands of students from Middle
Eastern countries attending Ukrainian universities and technical colleges—as
well as efforts to combat drug smuggling and international terrorism. Agreements to that effect have been signed with several Middle Eastern states.[28]

Problems and Difficulties

Fuel

In connection with Ukraine's fuel situation, it is important to remember that by
the mid-1990s, the country's annual fuel consumption amounted to some 30
million tons of petroleum and 100 billion cubic meters (c.m.) of natural gas. In
the meantime, the domestic production of fuel fell to 4 million tons of oil and
18 billion c.m. of gas per year. This amounted to approximately 10 percent of
the annual consumption of oil and 20 percent of the annual consumption of
natural gas, making it necessary for Kyiv to import the rest. "In line with the
pattern established during the late Soviet period, Russia has been
supplying . . . [some] 90 percent of Ukraine's annual oil and 60 percent of its

annual gas requirements. The remaining 20 percent of gas imports have . . . been [delivered by] Turkmenistan."[29]

In an effort to deal with what amounted to Russia's stranglehold on Ukraine's economy, Kyiv decided in early 1992 to begin looking for alternate sources of fuel. Initially, as noted, the Persian Gulf countries, particularly Iran, recovering from its eight-year conflict with Iraq, as well as war-torn Kuwait were singled out as the most likely partners. In fact, the initial agreements, providing for the supply of Iranian fuel (4 million tons of oil and 3 billion c.m. of natural gas a year) were signed in January and February 1992. Other agreements of this type followed in the ensuing years.[30]

Some problems connected with the delivery of Middle Eastern fuel were noticed in Kyiv early on. For example, on the crucial issue of payment, it was noted that Ukraine would need to come up with between $6 and 8 billion a year for oil alone. This amount was even more staggering if one kept in mind that, in 1991, Ukraine's exports had netted the national treasury but some $50 million. Nor did anyone have any idea where the money required to pay for Ukraine's fuel deliveries would come from. One analyst who had recognized the problem lapsed into wishful thinking, expressing the hope that the "government's dynamic foreign political and economic activity" would somehow take care of the payments problem.[31] It did not, and, in retrospect, could not have, as attested to by Kyiv's chronic indebtedness to Russia and Turkmenistan for their fuel deliveries to Ukraine.

In addition to insurmountable financial problems, Ukraine also ran into major logistical and technical difficulties in connection with the purchase of Middle Eastern fuel. Specifically, Ukraine possessed neither a sizable tanker fleet, nor adequate terminals to receive large amounts of fuel,[32] nor the refining capacity to process huge quantities of Iranian oil which, like the Russian petroleum produced in the Urals, has a high content of sulphur.[33]

To be sure, Kyiv did come up with numerous proposals designed to remedy some of these problems. More prominent among them have been the construction of a new oil terminal at Pivdennyi (near Odesa) as well as of several pipelines. Specifically, the new oil terminal is to have an estimated annual capacity of 40 million tons, serving not only as a port of entry but also as a transshipment point for Middle Eastern petroleum bound for Europe. In 1994, the cost of the project was estimated at $1.3 billion. For economic as well as political and ecological reasons, progress on the terminal's construction has been slow. As a result, the work is nowhere near completion in spite of Kyiv's repeated assurances that the Pivdennyi terminal would soon be ready to receive Middle Eastern petroleum.[34] More recently, Chairman of the Executive Committee of Ukrnaftoterm (the company in charge of the terminal construction) Anatoliy Nyhreskul insisted that the Pivdennyi terminal was ready to receive up to 12 million tons of oil a year. He later added that the "priority complex" of the terminal was to be made "operation[al]" in the third quarter of 1999, while the first stage—in the fourth quarter" of that year. He estimated the cost of the first stage at $1.35 billion.[35]

Closely related to this effort have been Kyiv's attempts to participate in the construction of several pipelines, designed to expedite the delivery of Middle Eastern fuel to Ukraine and, by using and enlarging the existing Ukrainian pipeline network, to Europe as well. In fact, should any of these pipelines materialize, Ukraine would also benefit handsomely by collecting fuel transit fees. In any event, Kyiv has entered into agreements to participate in the construction of the following pipelines:

- Iran-Azerbaijan-Russia-Ukraine oil and gas pipelines;
- Turkmenistan-Iran-Turkey-Europe gas pipeline;
- Kuwait-Turkey oil pipeline;
- Turkey-Ukraine oil pipeline; and
- Azerbaijan-Georgia-Ukraine oil pipeline.[36]

The problem with these projects is that none of them have materialized. The reasons for the failure to complete, or even to begin, the construction of the pipelines fall into two categories: economic/financial and political.

In examining economics first, it is obvious that all of the major fuel-related projects (i.e., the pipelines as well as the terminal) are capital-intensive under-takings which require an initial investment of billions of dollars. As it turned out, none of the countries with which Ukraine attempted to cooperate (Iran, Turkey, Azerbaijan, Turkmenistan, Georgia, and even Kuwait) could afford to spend large sums of money on such projects, no matter how profitable they might turn out to be in the future. And efforts to obtain capital from Western sources have so far proved unsuccessful. To be sure, Ukraine is in a position to supply pipes and compressor stations, as well as expertise, but that is not enough to undertake projects of such magnitude. Moreover, it should be borne in mind that these Ukrainian products are considered to be qualitatively inferior to their Western and Asian counterparts, explaining, in part, why Kyiv lost the tender to construct the projected Azerbaijan-Georgia pipeline.

On the political plane, one of the main reasons why some of these schemes have yet to materialize has been Russia's opposition. For example, aware of the fact that the transshipment of Caspian Sea region petroleum and natural gas has the potential of bringing in billions of dollars into the Russian treasury, Mos-cow has insisted that the Caspian fuel be pumped through the pipeline network located on Russian territory and not outside it. In addition, potential economic losses were likely to result in political setbacks as well. That is to say, Russia's political influence in the former Soviet republics—widely regarded in Moscow as essential in terms of preserving the country's great power status—would also be undermined severely, as other regional and extra-regional powers moved in to fill the vacuum, created by Russia's pullback. For these reasons, Moscow has opposed the construction of new pipelines which would bypass Russian territory, particularly if this should benefit Ukraine, the Kremlin's main rival in the "Near Abroad."[37] Though never publicized, official Kyiv seems to have been reluctant to provoke Moscow's ire, as demonstrated, in part, by Ukraine's foot dragging in the matter of completion of the Odesa fuel terminal and of the Turkish pipeline.[38] The latter project, to be sure, will become viable only after the UN lifts its economic embargo on Iraq, enabling Baghdad to resume the flow of petroleum to Turkey's Mediterranean terminals, but its potential importance should not be underestimated.

Trade

Ukraine's efforts to develop extended commercial relations with the countries of the Middle East and North Africa (with the notable exception of Turkey) have not been overly successful. In some instances (e.g., Libya and Iraq), Kyiv's freedom of action has been circumscribed by the United Nations embargoes. Problems on the Arab side of the Persian Gulf and elsewhere, in contrast, have been of a different nature. As explained by Ambassador Semenets in 1994, the development of economic and commercial relations between Ukraine and the United Arab Emirates was made difficult by that country's "mature market," characterized by limited local consumption and high competition. Yet, the UAE was a major regional trade center and, if Kyiv were serious about making headway in the Persian Gulf region, it had to bring to the United Arab Emirates personnel who were highly skilled in economic and commercial matters. In addition, Ukrainian enterprises and companies had to establish offices in the UAE and to enter into close contacts with the local intermediary companies. Semenets went on to say—and this applies to all Ukrainian officials and businessmen operating abroad—that "over the years of transition toward market relations, we should have assimilated the culture of conducting business and, simply, human relations. . . . [The] absence [of this culture] scares away potential partners." Semenets concluded that "the deficiencies in public relations that the Ukrainian Embassy and local businessmen have experienced with Ukrainian producers and ministries, which as a rule do not even find it necessary to respond to requests for information, point to their lack of interest in contacts, if not something worse."[39]

Another problem that has been cited often by both Ukrainian and foreign officials is the absence of a legal basis for engaging in bilateral trade and commerce. The two items that have usually been mentioned in this connection are: protection of investments and avoidance of dual taxation. Over the past few years, some agreements addressing these and related issues have been signed by Ukraine and a number of Middle Eastern and North African states. Nevertheless, many problems remain.[40] Otherwise, some countries have periodically accused Ukraine of foot-dragging in implementing agreements. The Iranians have done so in connection with the delivery of fuel and the Turks in connection with the oil-pipeline.[41] The Libyans in 1994 charged that the Ukrainian government commission, created for the purpose of promoting coopera-

tion between the two states, had done nothing. The problem of non-implemen-
tation of the existing agreements has also been acknowledged by Ukrainian
officials.[42]

In fairness, it should be noted that not all the blame should be assigned to
Ukrainian functionaries. Many of their Middle Eastern counterparts, too, have
acquired a well-earned reputation for procrastination and unreliability. Thus,
during Prime Minister Lazarenko's March 1997 visit to Egypt, he suggested
that the pace of the signing of "documents encouraging export and import
operations and mutually granting the most favored nation status in trade and
economic relations" be stepped up. President Hosni Mubarak concurred, instructing the appropriate government agencies to complete the draft of "a free
trade agreement between the two countries which . . . had been 'shelved' in the
depths of Egyptian [government] departments for two years."[43]

In any event, in retrospect, it is possible to speak of a veritable flurry of
initial Ukrainian diplomatic activity in the Middle East which took the form of
visits and of the signing of agreements, memoranda, protocols of intent, etc.—
all designed to promote cooperation and to improve relations. Early enthusiasm
was often followed by a period of inertia and lack of action. Occasionally,
renewed efforts would be made, mostly as a result of high-level visits. Sometimes action did follow, but many times it did not. In retrospect, Iran tops the
list of Ukraine's Middle Eastern partners in terms of the number of agreements
signed as well as of agreements that have not been implemented, while Turkey
has emerged as Kyiv's most active economic partner in this part of the world.

To sum up, as Deputy Premier Anatoliy Kinakh observed in May 1996 in
connection with Ukrainian-Iranian relations, many bilateral agreements have
"remained just paperwork with no visible signs of [ever] being implemented."
Kinakh singled out "predominantly bureaucratic obstacles" as an important
reason for the lack of cooperation between Ukraine and Iran. As Kyiv Radio
put it, he "blamed faulty and imperfect mechanisms for implementing the
agreements and the involved government officials' inadequate skills for the
deplorable situation."[44]

Trade Turnover	1993	1994	1995	1996	1997
Morocco	$ 2.5m	$6m[45]			
Egypt			$30m	$120m[46]	$204m[47]
Iran	$30m	$50m	$34m	$100m[48]	$140m[49]
Israel		$60m	$100m	$100m[50]	
Turkey			$125m	$1b[51]	

Though the dollar figures presented above are modest, they indicate that the
pace of economic interaction between Ukraine and the countries of the Middle
East has picked up significantly over the past few years. This is true of Iran
and, particularly, of Turkey and Egypt. Still, in terms of their relative potential,

it is clear that much room for improvement remains. As noted in the account of Lazarenko's visit to Egypt, favorable conditions exist for doubling the trade turnover between the two states "in the near future."[52]

Politics

On the political front, as in economics, Ukraine's record in the Middle East has also been mixed. For example, on the vital issue of independence, Ukraine encountered no major problems and was relatively promptly recognized by all of the Middle Eastern and North African states. Kyiv also established diplomatic representation in most of the states that were judged to be important to Ukraine. In other words, all of the Middle Eastern and North African countries have endorsed Ukraine's status as an independent and sovereign state. However, with respect to the related issue of territorial integrity or, more precisely, of the ambiguous status of Crimea, most relevant bilateral documents contain no reference to it. Notable exceptions to this rule are Turkey and Israel; both have repeatedly stated that Crimea must remain an integral part of Ukraine.[53] In the case of Iran and particularly of the Arab states, the official silence on this issue can be attributed to their unwillingness to offend Russia over an issue that, in the final analysis, is of no vital interest to them.

Otherwise, during the early—and quite intense—stages of Ukrainian-Iranian relations, Tehran attempted—and failed—to drive a wedge between Ukraine on the one hand and Turkey and the United States on the other. In return, Iran tried to boost Ukraine in its competition with Russia by means of offering to supply oil and to help build pipelines.[54] In retrospect, however, as already noted, none of this activity amounted to much. To be sure, the potential for Ukraine's cooperation with Turkey and Iran remains, fueled by their common distrust of Russia and by their shared desire to weaken Russian influence in the Transcaucasus and Central Asia. (Iran's initial support of Russia in the matter of the exploitation of Caspian oil was but a tactical maneuver, dictated, in part, by Moscow's willingness to supply Tehran with nuclear reactors and by Azerbaijan's refusal to cooperate with the Islamic Republic, and does not invalidate the above proposition). As yet, however, this commonality of interests has not been translated into significant political and economic results.

In fact, it is possible to speak of a marked decline in Iranian-Ukrainian relations, caused by Kyiv's refusal to participate in the construction of the above-mentioned nuclear power plant at Bushehr. The sale of a one million kilowatt turbine, valued at $45 million, and the expectation of future orders for turbines seemed to offer Ukraine important economic advantages. However, in March 1998, under intense U.S. pressure, the Kuchma administration pulled out of the Bushehr deal. Tehran, objected, but to no avail.[55]

The incident did little to enhance Ukraine's reputation as a reliable trading partner, but, in Kyiv's defense, it must be said that, dependent as Ukraine had become on American support, Kuchma had no choice but to bow to

Washington's wishes. He tried, but failed, to assure Tehran that Kyiv had no intention of "abandoning cooperation with Iran"—the Iranian foreign minister "indefinitely" postponed his planned June 1998 visit to Ukraine.[56]

Shifting the focus, in the early stages of the Kuchma administration, Udovenko proposed the creation of a "triple alliance" between Ukraine, Israel, and the United States. He never explained the meaning of the term but denied that he had advocated a military or an economic alliance, directed at "third countries." Then, during his November 1996 visit to Israel, Kuchma spoke of a "strategic partnership" between Kyiv, Jerusalem, and Washington. The Ukrainian press explained that, as Israel was America's "strategic partner" in the Middle East, Ukraine, with its strong pro-U.S. bent in its foreign policy, could well become America's "strategic partner" in Eurasia. Proceeding from this, Kyiv hoped that the three states would cooperate with each other to the fullest extent possible. It was also reported that Israel endorsed this idea but that Washington remained silent.[57]

In the context of Middle Eastern politics, Ukraine adopted a stand on both of the major regional issues: the Arab-Israeli conflict and the Iraq-Kuwait dispute. With respect to the first, Kyiv originally adhered to the old Soviet position which called on the antagonists to accept the UN Security Council Resolutions 242 and 338. (It will be recalled that these documents required Israel to withdraw from Arab territories, occupied in 1967, in exchange for comprehensive peace and guarantees of security for all of the involved parties). In 1993, Kravchuk explained that, at the United Nations, Ukraine had traditionally defended the "Palestinian people and their legitimate rights" which included the Palestinians' right "to have their own independent state."[58] In line with this approach, Kyiv endorsed the Oslo accords and, more specifically, the 4 May 1994 Israeli-Palestinian agreement as an "important step toward Middle East peace." Its signing, the Ukrainian Foreign Ministry statement said, "provide[d] an exceptional chance . . . [to end] the planet's longest conflict and to start a new era . . . [in inter-regional] relations . . . ."[59] In the ensuing years, Kyiv continued to adhere to an "even-handed" approach to the Israeli-Palestinian problem, calling on both sides to continue negotiations in order to find a "mutually acceptable compromise."[60]

In the case of the Iraq-Kuwait conflict, Kyiv originally lent its moral support to the beleaguered shaykhdom, calling for the release of the Kuwaiti captives and upholding Kuwait's request for the demarcation of the border with Iraq.[61] To a significant degree, Kyiv's interest in Kuwait was prompted by the possibility of Ukraine's participation in restoring the shaykhdom's shattered petroleum industry. After such hopes failed to materialize, Kyiv began exploring the possibility of economic cooperation with Iraq. This activity, which reached a marked crescendo in the summer and fall of 1996, led to the signing of a "protocol of bilateral cooperation" but has not, as yet, resulted in any concrete action.[62]

Partly responsible for this state of affairs has been Ukraine's attempt to project itself onto the Middle Eastern scene by taking a stand on a crisis which occurred in late summer 1996 as a result of Baghdad's successful attempt to reestablish its military presence in the Kurdish "safe haven" of northern Iraq. After the United States retaliated by bombarding radar installations in southern Iraq, Foreign Minister Udovenko, in an apparent attempt at evenhandedness, noted that "any military means of resolving the conflict . . . [were] not conducive to" a peaceful settlement of the Middle East crises. In an official statement, issued soon afterwards, the Ministry of Foreign Affairs expressed Kyiv's deep concern about the Iraqi events and called on the parties involved "to refrain from further use of force in the region, observe the corresponding UN decisions on Iraq strictly, and establish a political dialogue between the Iraqi government and Kurdish factions."[63] Then, in an apparent attempt to dispel the impression that Kyiv was equating the Iraqi and American actions, Udovenko suggested that Baghdad's attack had been prompted by a desire to scuttle "the Middle East peace process." This, the minister explained, concerned Ukraine because of its location "near the region" and because Kyiv could not remain "indifferent to the fate of 300,000 Ukrainian Jews in Israel." To assist in calming the situation, Kyiv offered to send Ukrainian observers to northern Iraq.[64] Not surprisingly, there were no takers. It is difficult to see what precisely Udovenko was trying to accomplish by this diplomatic demarche. While Washington may have been pleased, Baghdad was not. As a result, the budding relationship between Ukraine and Iraq has since been put on hold by Saddam Hussein.

It is conceivable that Baghdad's adverse reaction to this Ukrainian stand influenced Kyiv's position in the Iraqi crisis of late 1997–early 1998. Specifically, in November 1997, the Iraqi government accused American members of the UN weapons inspection team of espionage and refused to allow them to continue participating in the team's activities. As demands for the use of force began circulating in Washington and London, Kyiv adopted a cautious wait-and-see policy. The Ministry of Foreign Affairs denounced Iraq for its "unconstructive actions" but withheld comment on the "possibility of unilateral use of force by the United States."[65]

As the crisis continued to escalate, the United States reinforced its military presence in the Persian Gulf in preparation for possible massive air strikes against Iraq. Among the permanent members of the UN Security Council, only Great Britain was solidly in Washington's camp. The others—France, Russia, and China—opposed the use of force against Baghdad. In this tense situation, Ukraine chose to support the powers opposed to the United States. Then Foreign Minister Udovenko, arriving in Cuba in February 1998, was quoted by the Russian news agency ITAR-TASS as saying that Ukraine's "position on settling the Iraq crisis coincides with that of Russia: the most important thing is not to allow a military conflict to arise." In addition, Udovenko also "offered the services of Ukrainian experts who could join the commission and take part in on-the-spot investigations."[66] Foreign Ministry spokesman Nahaichuk amplified Udovenko's statement by saying that Ukraine favored a peaceful resolution to the Iraq crisis and regarded the "use of force . . . [as] undesirable and admissible only under extreme circumstances . . . ." The clear implication was that this had not been the case in Iraq. Nahaichuk further explained Kyiv's stand in this fashion: "Our position must not be influenced by bilateral relations with other countries but by our own national interests." Since the Middle East is situated in close proximity to Ukraine, he concluded, Kyiv was working to maintain "peace and stability in the region."[67]

Even upon reflection, it is not entirely clear what specific Ukrainian national interests Nahaichuk had in mind. To be sure, taking a pro-Russian (and anti-American) position in an international crisis was bound to play well in Moscow—with which relations had improved in 1997 as a result of the Kuchma-Yeltsin summits—as well as in Baghdad. What is not certain is what concrete benefit Kyiv expected to gain in those two capitals, as Moscow remained Moscow, and Baghdad, even under the best of circumstances, could not be expected to provide tangible benefits to Ukraine for a long time to come.

Hence, one possible explanation of Kyiv's stance is that it represented an attempt by Kuchma to use the Iraq crisis for domestic political purposes. With the parliamentary elections looming, his administration may have tried to steal some of the thunder of the anti-Western leftist forces which were expected to solidify their majority position in the Supreme Council. Even so, it was probably not wise to antagonize Washington—the superpower without whose support Ukraine is not likely to survive economically—over an issue in which no vital Ukrainian national interests were involved, the pronouncements of the Foreign Ministry notwithstanding. In short, by taking a stand in opposition to the projected American use of force, Kyiv displeased Washington without gaining any appreciable benefits in either Baghdad or Moscow.

Otherwise, Kyiv has generally adhered to the position developed earlier in the decade: with respect to Iraq and Libya, countries with a "negative image in the international arena" on which the United Nations had imposed "certain sanctions," Ukraine's bilateral relations with them would develop "in conformity with the UN decisions."[68] In line with this stance, Kyiv has "categorically" denied allegations of government-sanctioned arms sales to these two states.[69]

Conclusion

An article, which appeared in *Post-Postup* (Lviv) in January 1995 and was devoted to Ukraine's foreign policy, noted that while Kravchuk attempted to integrate Ukraine with Europe, Kuchma initially sought cooperation with both the CIS and the United States. As the newspaper put it, Kuchma wanted "to live" within the CIS but to use the United States and the West generally to help finance Ukraine's economic development. Kuchma succeeded in Washington (though not in Moscow) but discovered that even substantial infusions of Western capital had little positive effect on Ukraine's internal socioeconomic situation. In any event, because of the continuing Russian pressure on Ukraine, the paper argued against a pro-Western orientation and advocated instead an "alliance with the Muslim world which share[s] Ukraine's apprehension of Russia and . . . its intentions."[70] This is an entertaining but unrealistic idea— Ukraine cannot rely on the Muslim world to bail it out of trouble, as the experience of Kyiv's relations with the states of the Middle East clearly illustrates.

On balance, Ukraine has not been, and should not try to become, a major actor in Middle Eastern affairs because it lacks the means to influence them in any meaningful manner. Nor should this come as a surprise, as even Russia, with its long history of significant involvement in the Middle East, has now been reduced essentially to the role of spectator. Whether this state of affairs will ever change, remains to be seen. One thing is clear, however. In order to derive major economic advantages from its association with the Middle East— and this should be a high national priority—Ukraine will first have to straighten out its own economy as well as the mindset of many of its officials. Unfortunately, as everyone is aware, this is a very tall order indeed.

NOTES

1. Interview with *Moloda Halychyna* (Lviv), 21 January 1995, as quoted in Foreign Broadcast Information Service (FBIS)-SOV, 30 January 1995: 43–44.

2. Interview with *Demokratychna Ukraina* (Kyiv), 18 April 1995, as quoted in FBIS-SOV, 27 April 1995: 45–56.

3. Kyiv Radio, 17 April 1998, and 18 May 1998, as quoted in FBIS-SOV-98-107 and 138.

4. Kyiv Radio, 3 June 1992, as quoted in FBIS-SOV, 4 June 1992: 63–64.

5. Interview with *Holos Ukrainy* (Kyiv) 15 February 1995, as quoted in FBIS-SOV, 21 February 1995: 41. On Iran, see Kyiv Radio, 23 May 1996, as quoted in FBIS-SOV, 23 May 1996: 37.

6. Interview with *Kievskie vedomosti* (Kyiv), 7 October 1995, as quoted in FBIS-SOV, 18 October 1995: 60–61. For details, see interview with Oleksandr Sverdlov, a high official at Ukrderzhnaftohazprom, in *Odesskie izvestiia* 5 July 1996, as quoted in FBIS-SOV, 12 July 1996: 38–39.

7. Kyiv Radio, 24 April 1997, as quoted in FBIS-SOV-97-114.

8. Kyiv Radio, 19 October 1993, as quoted in FBIS-SOV, 20 October 1993: 70. On Osyka's statement, see n. 6.

9. Moscow Radio, 23 September 1997, as quoted in FBIS-SOV-97-266.

10. See Udovenko's statement during a meeting with an Egyptian delegation. Kyiv Radio, 17 January 1995, as quoted in FBIS-SOV, 18 January 1995: 41.

11. Moscow Radio, 9 and 16 July 1996, as quoted in FBIS-SOV, 10 July 1996: 35; and 19 July 1996: 34.

12. Moscow Radio, 27 February 1992, as quoted in FBIS-SOV, 28 February 1992: 50.

13. Article by Vladimir Skachko, *Nezavisimaia gazeta* (Moscow) 24 April 1993.

14. Kyiv Radio, 26 August 1994, and 17 January 1995, as quoted in FBIS-SOV, 30 August 1994: 30; and 18 January 1995: 1. For more recent material, see the account of Deputy Foreign Minister Hryshchenko's September 1997 visit to Cairo. Moscow Radio, 23 September 1997, as quoted in FBIS-SOV-97-266.

15. Baghdad Television, 7 July 1996, as quoted in FBIS-NES, 8 July 1996: 21; and Moscow Radio, 9 July 1996, as quoted in FBIS-SOV, 10 July 1996: 35.

16. Moscow Radio, 9 June 1997, and Lviv Radio, 7 July 1997, as quoted in FBIS-SOV-97-160 and 97–188. On Bushehr, see *Vremia* (Kharkiv) 14 March 1998, as quoted in FBIS-SOV-98-089.

17. Moscow Radio, 28 March 1992, as quoted in FBIS-SOV, 1 April 1992: 47.

18. Moscow Television, 2 June 1992, as quoted in FBIS-SOV, 3 June 1992: 46. For Kuchma's statement, see n. 13.

19. See an extensive report by Kyiv Radio, 13 March 1995, as quoted in FBIS-SOV, 15 March 1995: 57.

20. Moscow Radio, 23 September 1997, as quoted in FBIS-UMA-97-266.

21. Vasyl Yurychko, *Vseukrainskie vedomosti* (Kyiv) 1 April 1997, as quoted in FBIS-SOV- 97-066.

22. Amman Television, 26 April 1998, as quoted in FBIS-NES-98-116.

23. See n. 13.

24. See Kravchuk's interview with *al-Hayat* (London), 9 December 1993, as quoted in FBIS-SOV, 13 December 1993: 78. The motives for the opening of the embassy in Tunis are not clear to this author.

25. For more details, see my "Ukrainian-Turkish Relations," *The Ukrainian Quarterly* 51(1) Spring 1995: 5–34.

26. For some details, see an interview with Yevhen Mykytenko, Kyiv Radio, 27 February 1996, as quoted in FBIS-SOV, 27 February 1996: 40–41.

27. On this point, see Moti Bassok, *Davar* (Tel Aviv), 17 September 1995, as quoted in FBIS-NES, 20 September 1995: 51.

28. For some examples, see Amman Radio, 26 April 1998, a quoted in FBIS-NES-98-116 on education; Tehran Radio, 17 November 1997, a quoted in FBIS-TDD-97-321 on drug smuggling; and *Ukraina moloda* (Kyiv) 16 August 1997, as quoted in FBIS-TOT-97-239 on terrorism.

29. See my "Ukraine and the Fuel Problem: Recent Developments," *The Ukrainian Quarterly* 52(2–3) Summer–Fall 1996: 143.

30. Serhiy Hutsalo, *Uriadovyi kur'ier* 11 (March 1992): 7. For more details, see my "Ukraine's Quest for Independence: The Fuel Factor," *Europe-Asia Studies* 47(1) 1995: 67–90; and "Ukraine and Iran," in Alvin Z. Rubinstein and Oles M. Smolansky, eds., *Regional Power Rivalries in the New Eurasia: Russia, Turkey, and Iran* (Armonk, NY, 1995), 65–92.

31. See Hutsalo, n. 30.

32. The maximum capacity of the old Odesa terminal is 4 million tons a year.

33. The only refinery capable of doing so is located in Kremenchuk.

34. For some details, see Olena Hubina, *Molod' Ukrainy* 23 September 1994, and Dmytro Chobit, *Holos Ukrainy* 23 November 1995, as quoted in FBIS-SOV, 28 September 1994: 50; and 28 November 1995: 61–64.

35. *Nezavisimaia gazeta* 6 May 1997, and Moscow Radio, 19 August 1997, as quoted in FBIS-SOV-97-231.

36. For more details, see my "Ukraine and the Fuel Problem," 165–67.

37. See, for example, Yuriy Yurov, *Khreshchatyk* (Kyiv) 17 March 1995, as quoted in FBIS-SOV, 29 March 1995: 62–63. See also articles by A. Baneva and A. Volyntseva in *Kommersant-Daily* (Moscow) 14 and 29 April 1995.

38. For some details, see Sergei Kiselev, *Nezavisimost'* (Kyiv) 13 November 1996, as quoted in FBIS-SOV-96-237-S; and article by Oleh Dudkin, read on Kyiv Radio, 17 August 1997, as quoted in FBIS-SOV-97-229.

39. Interview with *Uriadovyi kur'ier* 30 June 1994, as quoted in FBIS-SOV, 7 July 1994: 23–24.

40. On these points, see Osyka, n. 6; the announcement of the signing of a trade agreement by Ukraine and the UAE (Kyiv Radio, 20 March 1995, as quoted in FBIS-SOV, 21 March 1995 51); a report on Osyka's visit to Israel (Kyiv Radio, 17 May 1995, as quoted in FBIS-SOV, 18 May 1995: 53); and a report on Ukrainian-Jordanian negotiations (*Jordan Times* [Amman] 27–28 July 1995, as quoted in FBIS-NES, 28 July 1995: 47).

41. On Iran, see my "Ukraine and Iran," 73–77. On Turkey, see Kyiv Radio, 25 July 1995, as quoted in FBIS-SOV, 25 July 1995: 62–63.

42. See interview with the Libyan chargé d'affaires, Kyiv Radio, 26 August 1994, as quoted in FBIS-SOV, 30 August 1994: 30. For Ukrainian self-criticism, see statement by Deputy Prime Minister Anatoliy Kinakh, Kyiv Radio, 23 May 1996, as quoted in FBIS-SOV, 23 May 1996: 37.

43. See n. 21.

44. See n. 42.

45. Rabat Radio, 8 April 1995, as quoted in FBIS-NES, 10 April 1995: 25.

46. See n. 21.

47. Interview with Ambassador Ivan Kuleba, *Ukraina moloda* 15 May 1998, as quoted in FBIS-SOV-98-145.

48. Kyiv Radio, 28 June 1996, as quoted in FBIS-SOV, 28 June 1996: 36, and statement by Udovenko, Tehran Radio, 10 June 1997, as quoted in FBIS-SOV-97-161.

49. Tehran Radio, 10 February 1998, as quoted in FBIS-NES-98-041.

50. Kyiv Radio, 6 September 1995, as quoted in FBIS-SOV, 6 September 1995: 54, and Andrei Kapustin, *Nezavisimaia gazeta* 18 April 1997.

51. Ukrainian Ministry of Statistics. Data on Ukraine's Trade in 1994, as quoted in FBIS-SOV, 24 February 1995 (Supplement): 65. The $1 billion figure for 1995 was cited by President Suleyman Demirel. See Iuliia Mostovaia in *Zerkalo nedeli* (Kyiv): 30 November 1996.

52. See n. 21.

53. See statements by then Foreign Minister Shimon Peres, Kyiv Radio, 16 June 1994, and by the Turkish chargé d'affaires, Kyiv Radio, 1 August 1994, as quoted in FBIS-SOV, 17 June 1994: 30; and 2 August 1994: 32.

54. For some details, see my "Ukraine and Iran," 71–72.

55. See Moscow Radio, 6 March 1998, as quoted in FBIS-SOV-98-065 and Tehran Radio, 9 March 1998, as quoted in FBIS-NES-98-068.

56. Moscow Radio, 24 March 1998, and Kyiv Radio, 18 June 1998, as quoted in FBIS-SOV-98-083 and 169.

57. See Moscow Radio, 12 July 1995, as quoted in FBIS-NES, 13 July 1995: 52 and Mostovaia in *Zerkalo nedeli*.

58. Interview with *al-Hayat* 9 December 1993, as quoted in FBIS-SOV, 13 December 1993: 78.

59. Kyiv Radio, 4 May 1994, as quoted in FBIS-SOV, 5 May 1994: 40.

60. See account of a visit by a Palestinian Legislative Council delegation. Kyiv Radio, 21 January 1998, as quoted in FBIS-SOV-98-021. For a Foreign Ministry statement, see Kyiv Television, 31 July 1997, as quoted in FBIS-SOV-97-212.

61. See the text of the joint communiqué, issued on the occasion of Prime Minister Kuchma's visit to Kuwait. Kuwait KSC Television, 18 April 1993, as quoted in FBIS-NES, 19 April 1993: 17.

62. For details, see Lviv Radio, 3 July 1996, and Baghdad Television, 7 July 1996, as quoted in FBIS-SOV, 3 July 1996: 38 and FBIS-NES, 8 July 1996: 21.

63. Kyiv Radio, 3 September 1996 and Moscow Radio, 4 September 1996, as quoted in FBIS-SOV, 4 September 1996: 33 and 5 September 1996: 31.

64. Kyiv Radio, 5 September 1996, as quoted in FBIS-SOV, 6 September 1996: 34.

65. *Kievskie vedomosti* 20 November 1997, as quoted in FBIS-SOV-97-328.

66. Moscow Radio, 16 February 1998, as quoted in FBIS-SOV-98-047.

67. Moscow Radio, 17 February 1998, as quoted in FBIS-SOV-98-048.

68. See Mykytenko's interview, cited in n. 5.

69. See, for example, the 9 December 1996 statement by the Ministry of Foreign Affairs, FBIS-SOV-96-238, and interview with the chairman of the State Export Control Service of Ukraine in *Nezavisimost'* 9 September 1997, as quoted in FBIS-SOV-97-267.

70. *Post-Postup* (Lviv) 30 December 1994, as quoted in FBIS-SOV, 10 January 1995: 21–22.

10

Ukraine and Asia: Diplomacy and Prospects in the Contemporary World

JIANG CHANGBIN

There is every reason to consider that the creation, existence, and rapid development of Ukraine as a new, fully independent and sovereign state is one of the most important, positive events of modern history.

Ukrainian independence brought not only the realization of long cherished dreams and aspirations of the Ukrainian people, but opened new perspectives for peace and progress for all mankind. Through its voluntary renunciation of nuclear weapons, Ukraine has demonstrated by example the possibility for the elimination, once and for all, of all nuclear weapons—the most colossal and dangerous threat to human existence. The international community has underestimated the significance of this Ukrainian example, often viewing it as submission under pressure from the United States and Russia. This is a delusion. Such pressure existed earlier and still exists now with respect to other countries. Despite such pressure, India and Pakistan still conducted nuclear weapon tests in May and June 1998, and some other countries are still trying to develop nuclear weapons—against the common wish of mankind and the tendencies of modern historical development.

Over the more than six years of its existence as an independent state, Ukraine obviously has achieved greater success in the sphere of external and international relations than in its internal and domestic policy. How is this phenomenon to be explained? Briefly stated, in its external relations Ukraine has had more freedom: it is easier to maintain its policy of active neutrality; inside the country, however, Ukraine has been constrained by the difficult legacy of the former Soviet Union. When Ukraine succeeds in throwing off this legacy, it will certainly begin to develop swiftly and grow into "another France," a country it resembles in many ways.

Asia, generally speaking, is a "virgin land" for Ukrainian diplomacy. But in Ukraine's approach to this vast region, adjustment in relations with its neighboring countries, especially with Russia, and also with the West must be considered. At the same time, Ukraine cannot be limited in its diplomatic activity. It must maintain full independence and freedom of action in these new areas of its foreign relations.

Ukrainian politicians, economists, and scientists have understood this well and acted almost irreproachably. A convincing example is the successful development of relations between Ukraine and the People's Republic of China, although naturally there still exists a great potential for further development of mutual relations between them. It is important to take into account that Ukraine and China have no strategic and political contradictions between them, and they derive real benefits from their mutual relations. Furthermore, both countries share certain similarities in their historical fate, making it easier for them to find a common language. Both countries trust in peace, and see no mutual threat from each other. And, finally, both countries need domestic and international political stability for their development in the future.

All these factors are fully applicable to most countries of East, South, and Southeast Asia as well. Thus, it is possible to look at Ukraine's relations with this vast continent with full optimism.

A Nation Calling for Justice and Affection

The author was very much surprised while reading a news account of Ukrainian President Leonid Kuchma's visit to Poland. The article stated that some ordinary Poles could not recognize the Ukrainian national flag as late as 1996.[1] He was struck with the realization that it was not enough to recognize Ukrainian independence politically: the international community must possess more knowledge about this nation. If people in a nation as close to Ukraine as Poland could show such gaps in their knowledge about their neighbor, then it is natural that nations in Asia would posses even less familiarity with Ukraine. If we draw concentric circles around Ukraine, knowledge of the country diminishes as the distance from the center increases.

Nevertheless, even distant peoples share similar criteria for historical judgment and harbor similar national sentiments. Since August 1991, the people of the Eastern Hemisphere had been watching the drastic changes in the territories of the former Soviet Union with shock and surprise. After the attempted putsch in Moscow (19–21 August 1991), the Ukrainian Verkhovna Rada declared independence on 24 August 1991—a decisive factor in the later breakup of the Soviet Union. On 1 December 1991, Ukraine conducted a national referendum in which 90 percent of the people favored independence and elected the first Ukrainian president, Leonid Kravchuk. The Belavezha Agreement on 8 December 1991 and the Alma-Ata (Almaty) Agreement on 21 December 1991 legally ended the existence of Soviet Union, and President Mikhail Gorbachev resigned on December 25.

What, then, is Ukraine? Can Ukraine exist as an independent nation in the long run? There were natural questions to ask. The first reaction to Ukrainian independence in Asia has been a strong desire to understand Ukraine's history and its current situation and make attempts to befriend this newly emerging state.

In a relatively short time, many people realized that Ukraine and Russia are two different, independent nations. But knowledge and understanding take much longer to develop. Many confused the history of Ukraine with the history of Russia. Others were misled by biased Soviet historiography that presented, for example, the annexation of Ukraine to Russia in the seventeenth century as a "reunion."[2] The ten-volume *History of Ukraine-Rus'*, written by the most brilliant Ukrainian historian Mykhailo Hrushevskyi at the beginning of the twentieth century, banned in the USSR, was totally unknown in the East. It was only in the late Soviet period that matters started to improve. But even the minor improvements initiated by Western publications had a very limited circulation, and failed to fill the void of Ukrainian history. It thus remains a fundamentally important task for scholars to bring about a correct understanding of Ukrainian history to the East.[3]

Knowledge of Ukrainian history was so distorted that the world failed to appreciate the strong desire of the Ukrainians to gain independence. As late as 1 August 1991, then U.S. President George Bush made mistakes in this regard during his visit to Kyiv, calling the Ukrainian capital the "mother of all Russian cities," and criticized Ukrainians favoring independence as promoting "suicidal nationalism." Both comments offended national sentiments and were resented and protested by the Ukrainians.[4] The independence of Ukraine achieved in 1991 is a genuine national liberation. Ukraine revealed itself, and the world should understand and support the newly independent state. It should respect Ukrainian national feelings and the country's sovereignty and territorial integrity. In brief, Ukrainian's hard-won independence is a symbol of human society's embrace of justice, equality, reason and prosperity. What other goals could have been nobler than that?

Ukrainian-Chinese Relations

In history, especially in modern times, both China and Ukraine have endured painful and humiliating experiences. Therefore, it is relatively easy for the two nations to reach consensus, to understand and to support each other. It is not a coincidence that the Chinese-Ukrainian relationship has been at the forefront of Ukraine's relations with Asian nations. Both, China and Ukraine are actively pursuing an independent, neutral and non-aligned diplomatic policy. Both nations seek international peace and stability. Nevertheless, Ukraine may choose to join NATO and the European Union (EU) in the future, while China has announced that it would never join any military or political bloc. There is no doubt that similar interests and shared experiences will play a central role in Chinese-Ukrainian relations. Differences that exist between the two nations are defined by their internal structures and external situations, which should play a very minor role in their mutual relations.

Knowledge of Ukraine in China is still at a low level, lower even than Ukraine's knowledge of China, despite the fact that the two nations had links long before their establishment of formal diplomatic ties. Even before 1917, Ukrainian communities, with a population exceeding one thousand people, existed in northeastern China and in the city of Shanghai. Harbin had a Ukrainian club; Shanghai had Ukrainian organizations as well. In 1918, the Ukrainian National Republic established a consulate in Harbin. At that time there were Ukrainian schools, Orthodox churches, national homes, associations and Ukrainian newspapers.[5] Among the Chinese, however, from the general public to the intellectuals, very few understood the difference between Ukraine and Russia. Only a handful of Chinese intellectuals possessed some familiarity with Ukraine and in some small measure introduced Ukraine to the Chinese people.[6] For example, the Chinese were able to read works by such famous writers and poets as Taras Shevchenko. Chinese readers appreciated their talent and sympathized with their fate. However, official Soviet propaganda played an important role in the Chinese people's understanding of Ukraine. Many Chinese regarded writers like Shevchenko as representatives of the anti-tsarist movement, without realizing that they are primarily symbols of the Ukrainian nation.

Chinese intellectual circles started to broaden their understanding of Ukraine in the 1970s, when they first gained access to the works of Ivan Dziuba and Petro Shelest.[7] Soon, Chinese scholars undertook the study of ethnic problems in the Soviet Union; such studies were represented by the works of Ruan Xihu.[8] In the meanwhile, works of Soviet dissidents and Western scholars (and also Eastern European scholars) began to circulate in China.[9] Many Chinese scholars in the 1980s, however, had to go to the West to study nationality problems in the USSR because of the prevailing hostility between China and the Soviet Union. The first Ukrainian-Chinese dictionary was not published until 1990.[10] The first institution for Ukrainian studies, the Ukrainian Research Office, was established in Wuhan University in the mid-1980s; it focused on the study of Ukrainian history, culture, and language.[11]

Even though one can detect a gradual increase in Ukrainian studies in China, even before Ukraine's independence, its limitations were pronounced. Neither Chinese intellectuals nor the political leadership expected that the Soviet Union would dissolve so quickly and Ukraine would become independent in such a short time. Thus, Ukrainian studies were not a pressing issue in their minds. This also shows that Chinese scholars failed to appreciate the severity and depth of social crises and ethnic conflicts within the Soviet Union.[12]

From the late 1980s through the early 1990s, opinion in China about the drastic changes in East Europe and the former Soviet Union republics was divided. Some believed that these changes represented historical reaction and social degeneration. Others felt that they were a natural result of social change and a progressive phenomenon in accordance with historical development. It is worth emphasizing that the Chinese government, under the leadership of the late Deng Xiaoping, adopted proper political and diplomatic policies in dealing with those countries. These policies played a decisive role in the development of Chinese-Ukrainian relations. Although China is a socialist country, in its treatment of the East European and formerly Soviet nations it took a principled position not to differentiate nations according to their social system and ideology.[13] Ever since the East European visit of Chinese Foreign Minister Qian Qichen in 1989, and the deputy foreign minister-level negotiations in Eastern

Europe headed by Tian Zengpei in August 1990, China has fostered a smooth relationship with nations in the region, with the exception of some problems with Latvia.[14] The relationship with Ukraine is a special case in point.

On 27 December 1991, the Chinese foreign minister, Qian Qichen, announced recognition of the new independent Ukraine and began negotiations on the establishment of formal diplomatic relations.[15] At the end of December 1991 and the beginning of 1992, a Chinese delegation, headed by the Economic and Trade Minister Li Lanqing and Deputy Foreign Minister Tian Zengpei, visited Ukraine and adjacent countries to discuss issues related to the formation of diplomatic ties. On 4 January 1992, the Chinese government appointed its ambassador to Russia, Wang Jinqing, as a plenipotentiary representative to Ukraine to sign the communiqué announcing the establishment of diplomatic relations.[16] The communiqué declared that China and Ukraine would develop bilateral and friendly cooperation on the basis of five principles: mutual respect for each other's sovereignty and territory integrity; mutual non-aggression; mutual non-interference in each other's internal affairs; equality and mutual benefit; and, lastly, peaceful coexistence. The Ukrainian government recognized the stand of the People's Republic of China on its territorial integrity and would conduct official relations with the only legal government of China, the People's Republic. It also promised never to establish an official relationship with Taiwan in any form. The Chinese government in turn confirmed its respect for the territorial integrity of Ukraine and supported its efforts of maintaining independence and developing its economy.[17]

After the communiqué, relations between the two nations began their gradual development. In March 1992, Ukraine and China exchanged ambassadors extraordinary and plenipotentiary. In August 1992, the deputy chairman of the Standing Committee of the National People's Congress, Sai Fuding, led a congressional delegation to Ukraine. Qingdao in China and Odesa in Ukraine became sister cities. From 29 October to 3 November 1992, Ukrainian president Leonid Kravchuk paid a state visit to China at the invitation of Yang Shangkun, president of the People's Republic. During his visit, President Kravchuk met Yang Shangkun, Jiang Zemin, the secretary general of the Chinese Communist Party, and Premier Li Peng. The two heads state signed twelve documents regarding bilateral cooperation in the political, economic, cultural, health, and civil air communications fields. The Chinese government also decided to provide Ukraine with commodity loans amounting to 50 million yüan. Besides his stay in Beijing, President Kravchuk also visited Shanghai and Shenzhen.[18] His visit gave a powerful to impetus Ukrainian-Chinese of bilateral relations.

High-level exchanges between Ukrainian and Chinese leaders continued unabated. On 12–16 April 1993, the speaker of the Ukrainian Parliament, Ivan Pliushch, led a delegation to China. On 6–7 September 1993, Qian Qichen, vice premier and foreign minister, visited Ukraine, as did Li Peng, Chinese premier, on 18–19 April 1994. On 6–8 September 1994, Jiang Zemin, president of the

People's Republic of China, paid a state visit to Ukraine and signed a joint declaration, which summarized the previous friendly bilateral agreements and laid the groundwork for future long-term cooperation. Both nations have realized the huge potential of their mutual cooperation to serve their national interests. As was remarked by a senior Ukrainian scholar and diplomat, Leonid Leshchenko, "for Ukraine, China is a strategic partner . . . for China—Ukraine is an important partner. Ukraine is attractive because of its strong industrial and intellectual potential, trade, economic and scientific potential and increasing political influence on the European continent."[19] On 4 December 1994, China became the first country to offer Ukraine nuclear security assurances.[20] In June 1995, Chinese Premier Li Peng again visited Ukraine. On 3–8 December 1995, the second president of Ukraine, Leonid Kuchma, paid a widely heralded state visit to China. The heads of state signed a joint communiqué, reiterating the fundamental principles of the first communiqué and enlarging the spheres of mutual cooperation. Ukraine showed great interest in the reform experience of China; many Ukrainian delegations visited Shenzhen and Shanghai. President Kuchma's visit significantly promoted the political, economic, scientific and cultural links between two countries. In fact, international media showed their interest in the visit even before President Kuchma headed to China.[21] From 21 to 25 December 1997, the newly appointed Ukrainian prime minister Valeriy Pustovoitenko, visited China for the first time, also visiting Shenzhen and Shanghai. Besides these high-level visits, there were many more ministerial exchanges during this period.

It must be emphasized that in China's relations with other countries, Taiwan is a highly sensitive issue. The Chinese government's stand on Taiwan is well-known to the world community. China cannot establish diplomatic relations with any country unless that country recognizes that there is only one China and that Taiwan is part of China. China does not object to social, economic, and trade relations on a grassroots level between Taiwan and other nations. However, China strongly opposes any official relationship between Taiwan and any nation with diplomatic relations with China.[22]

No major problem has ever arisen between China and Ukraine concerning Taiwan. However, some small problems warrant caution among those concerned about the Ukrainian-Chinese relationship. On 7–8 April 1992, Taiwanese authorities sent air shipments of medicine and medical equipment worth 15 million dollars to Ukraine. On this occasion, a number of Taiwanese officials, headed by Zhang Xiaoyan of the Taiwanese government (vice-foreign minister), visited Ukraine. The purpose of the visit was to negotiate the opening of offices in Ukraine and Taiwan with the hope of eventually establishing diplomatic relations with Ukraine. In this, the Taiwanese officials hoped that Ukraine would emulate Latvia and eventually upgrade the Taiwan office into a "Republic of China Delegation."[23] From 30 to 31 August 1992, Kyiv was the sight of the first "Ukraine-Taiwan Economic Cooperation Conference." Although the conference was jointly hosted by Ukrainian and Taiwanese economic research institutes, Jiang Bingkun of the Taiwanese government (vice-minister of the Economic Ministry) participated at the head of a delegation.[24] The author was in Ukraine at the time for research purposes and became very concerned about the implications of these developments for Ukrainian-Chinese relations. On 20 May 1992, he went to hear the debate in the Ukrainian Parliament and had a frank discussion with the chairman of the Foreign Committee of the Ukrainian Parliament, Dmytro Pavlychko. The main points of the discussion stressed that the Ukrainian-Chinese relationship must be treated on a strategic level and that the majority in Parliament believes Ukraine should not sacrifice a friend like the People's Republic of China, even though a minority of deputies favor diplomatic ties with Taiwan. During the dinner hosted by the Chinese ambassador that night, Pavlychko also emphasized that among the many countries recognizing Ukraine, China accounts for one-quarter of the world's population. Recognition by China reinforces the fact that Ukrainian independence is genuine and irreversible. The author felt relieved after such comments. In late August 1996, however, a visit to Ukraine by Lian Zhan of the Taiwanese government (vice-president) led to a small setback in Ukrainian-Chinese relations. The Chinese government reacted by canceling the scheduled visit to Kyiv of a Chinese government delegation, headed by Li Tieying, director of the National Economic Reform Committee. Nevertheless, a special visit to Beijing by the Ukrainian minister of the interior in September 1996 repaired the damage.[25] Despite the sensitive nature of the Taiwan issue, Ukraine and China solved it by negotiations, without resorting to public pronouncements, ensuring the smooth development of their bilateral relations.

Developments in Ukrainian-Chinese economic and trade cooperation are also extensive. In 1992, when Ukraine and China established diplomatic relations, the bilateral trade exceeded $100 million; China exported $81.15 million and imported $23.45 million, gaining a large surplus.[26] Bilateral trade developed very quickly and by the end of 1994, the total volume exceeded $800 million.[27] In 1997, bilateral trade amounted to over one billion dollars and the trade structure changed as well.[28] Ukraine now enjoys a huge surplus as it exports metal, chemical products, and heavy equipment, while importing consumer goods from China. In addition, Ukraine exported a considerable amount of goods via a third country—Russia. Hence, the actual trade with China well exceeded one billion dollars. As long as the bilateral trade runs smoothly, by the end of the century, the volume may reach $3 billion. In the author's view, Ukraine would benefit significantly if it ceased to use Russia as an intermediary. Ukraine and China should also reinforce their fundamental bilateral economic and trade laws and regulations, and cooperate in such areas as the construction of ports, improvement in the banking system in accordance with international standards, the establishment of a risk insurance system, increasing efficiency, and improvement in after-sale service and training. In the long run, all these form an indispensable infrastructure for economic relations.

Alongside developments in political and economic relations between Ukraine and China, scholarly and cultural exchanges between the two nations surged also. In April 1992, the vice chairman of the Science Committee of the Chinese State Council visited Ukraine and signed a governmental scientific cooperation agreement, which formed a good beginning for intellectual discourse between the two countries. It appears evident that both parties are not satisfied with having to communicate in Russian and have put strong emphasis on learning each other's language, history and current affairs. Many teaching programs and research centers have been established in these fields at universities and other scholarly institutions of Ukraine and China. Already many of the staff at the Ukrainian Embassy in Beijing are graduates of the Kyiv Chinese Language School.[29] On 28 April 1993, the Beijing Foreign Affairs Research Society voted to establish a Ukrainian Studies Committee in Beijing and elected the author as president. On 29 July 1993, the inauguration of the Ukrainian Studies Committee took place in Beijing during the visit of Ukraine's minister of culture, Ivan Dziuba, who is well known to Chinese intellectuals. Minister Dziuba and the Ukrainian ambassador to China delivered warm speeches on the occasion, to which universities and research institutions all sent their representatives. The overseas edition of the Chinese newspaper People's Daily, reported on the event extensively.[30] In August of 1993 and 1996, the International Association of Ukrainian Studies held its second and third conferences in Lviv and Kharkiv respectively. Many Chinese scholars participated and delivered papers at both conferences, and the president of the Ukrainian Studies Committee in Beijing was elected a member of the International Association's organizational committee.[31] Ukrainian and Chinese scholars also helped organize two conferences entitled "Ukraine-China: On the Path of Cooperation," the first held in Kyiv in 1993 and the second in Beijing in 1995. Collections of papers delivered at the two conferences were published subsequently in both languages.[32] The conferences received extensive coverage by Ukrainian, Chinese, and Canadian media.[33] There was a general consensus that the conferences had very positive benefits, especially for Chinese scholars, expanding significantly their knowledge and understanding of Ukraine. Following the appearance of the already mentioned Ukrainian-Chinese dictionary, Professor Liu Dong of the Ukrainian Research Center at Wuhan University published the textbooks *Elementary Ukrainian* and *Chinese-Ukrainian Conversation Manual*, the first such textbooks in Ukrainian to be published in China.[34]

These are but a few examples of cultural intercourse between China and Ukraine, which also includes many exchanges in science, education, culture and arts. In sum, Ukrainian-Chinese relations in all fields are highly promising.

Ukraine's Diplomacy with Russia and the West: An Assessment and Implications for the East

With the passage of time independent Ukraine has demonstrated its vitality and strength to the world. Contrary to the predictions of doomsayers, independent Ukraine has survived and developed successfully without Russia. Over the past six years, the international community has benefited significantly from Ukraine's independence, as for example, when Ukraine voluntarily gave up the nuclear weapons based on its territory.

As an independent nation, however, Ukraine has run into a series of challenging domestic problems. Some have been of its own making. Some are the historical legacy of the former Soviet Union. Others were caused by misunderstanding and mistrust on the part of some Eastern and Western powers. Burdened by its past and misunderstood by certain nations, Ukraine has had to follow a difficult path since independence. Politically, in the early years many predicted that Ukraine would be engulfed by civil war or secessionist movements. Instead, Ukraine has maintained a stable political environment and an increasingly strong national entity. After the major recession of 1993–1994 Ukraine's economy started to pick up, and shows strong promise in the long term, even though currently it fares worse than many other Eastern European and former Soviet nations.[35] With over 100 minority groups residing on its territory, Ukraine has experienced no nationality conflict thanks to its flexible ethnic policies.[36]

Ukraine has made great strides in its foreign policy. After seven years of hard work, its diplomacy has reached a new stage of maturity, as demonstrated by a variety of diplomatic achievements through 1998. In many cases its diplomacy has been nothing less than brilliant. As an independent, peace-loving nation, Ukraine has focused its diplomatic efforts on relations with Russia, the United States, Europe and other adjacent nations. This in turn promotes its relationship with Asia.

First and foremost, the importance of Ukraine's denuclearization cannot be overemphasized. This set an excellent example for the international community. It also laid the groundwork for Ukraine's peace-promoting diplomacy. Moreover, it had important consequences for the world, including the future of Asia. Many experts believe that Ukraine's decision to become a nuclear-free nation was made under pressure by the United States and Russia. In the author's opinion, however, the decisive factor was Ukraine's commitment to a peace-promoting policy. Ever since independence, Ukraine demonstrated its determination not to use force to threaten other nations. When the USSR dissolved, Ukraine possessed a nuclear arsenal second only to the United States and Russia.[37] It had every right not to give up these nuclear weapons. Instead, Ukraine renounced its nuclear weapons and turned them over for dismantling and destruction. Unfortunately, the international community has not rewarded Ukraine well for its unprecedented action—a gross injustice. As President

Kuchma once remarked: "Ukraine voluntarily gave up all its nuclear weapons. But what did we get in return? A good image? We cannot live on a good image."[38] Still, Ukraine's peace-loving action achieved much in other respects. It created a favorable, peaceful international environment crucial to its development. In the long run, this would promote Ukraine's economy and benefit its diplomacy.

On 31 May 1997, Ukrainian President Kuchma and Russian President Yeltsin signed in Kyiv the long-delayed Russian-Ukrainian treaty on friendship, cooperation and partnership, in Kyiv, which in principle resolved such disputed issues as Ukrainian sovereignty over Sevastopol, the Black Sea Fleet, normalization of bilateral economic and trade relations.[39] Ukraine's evolving relationship with NATO has undoubtedly contributed to its improvement in relations with Russia. On 9 July 1997, the Ukrainian president and leaders of the sixteen NATO member states formally signed a special partnership charter regarding Ukrainian-NATO relations. Although only a political document without legal power, the charter represented a major leap for Ukraine into the process of European security integration. President Kuchma noted that the document helped further democratization of Ukraine's domestic political life and enabled Ukraine to participate actively in the solution of international problems. NATO secretary Javier Solana called the charter "a clear symbol of a new Europe."[40]

Between 1996 and 1997, Ukraine achieved major successes in relations with many European and Asian countries, even apart from the breakthroughs in its relations with Russia, the United States and NATO. At the end of 1996, the Ukrainian prime minister signed a series of important military and economic cooperation agreements during his visit to Georgia. On 24 March 1997, President Kuchma and the president of Azerbaijan, Heidar Aliyev, signed a comprehensive package of cooperation agreements which foresaw that Ukraine would soon receive oil from Azerbaijan. Other interested parties included Turkmenistan, Uzbekistan, and Turkey.[41] The series of bilateral agreements made with these countries may lead to a "European-Asian Alignment," which could cause a headache for Russia unless it gives up its excessive demands on the Black Sea coastal nations.[42] On 2 June 1997, Ukrainian President Kuchma and Romanian President Constantinescu signed a treaty of cooperation, ending protracted negotiations between them. Moreover, on 27 May 1997—the very day when Yeltsin signed a Russian-NATO charter with Western leaders in Paris—Ukraine, Poland, and the three Baltic states met in Tallinn to study the establishment of a "Baltic-Black Sea Alignment."[43] In 1997, other states such as Moldova and Belarus have sought neighborly cooperation with Ukraine.[44]

Clearly, Ukraine has achieved much through its diplomatic activities with the West, and this provides a solid foundation for its relationship with the East. It would be hard to imagine how Ukraine could promote its relationships with the East without having established smooth relations with its near neighbors and the west.

What then, is the current state of Ukrainian-Asian relationship?

Asia: The New Frontier of Ukrainian Foreign Policy

Between 26 December 1991 and 28 January 1992, all major countries of Asia recognized Ukrainian independence. To give an overview of Ukraine's diplomatic relations with countries of this vast continent it is best to take a regional approach and look briefly at East, South, and Southeast Asia.

In East Asia, North Korea recognized Ukrainian independence on 26 December 1991 and opened its embassy in Kyiv in September 1992; the first North Korean ambassador to Ukraine submitted the diplomatic credentials on 17 January 1994.[45] On 30 December 1991, South Korea extended recognition to Ukraine and the two countries established diplomatic relations on 10 February 1992. In November 1992 South Korea opened its embassy in Kyiv and on 10 October 1995, the first South Korean ambassador submitted his diplomatic credentials. In October 1997, Ukraine opened its embassy in Seoul and the first Ukrainian ambassador to South Korea submitted his credentials on 18 November 1997. Japan recognized Ukraine on 28 December 1991 and established diplomatic relations on 28 January 1992. The Japanese embassy opened in January 1993 and the first ambassador submitted his diplomatic credentials on 31 May 1993. Ukraine opened its Tokyo embassy in March 1995, but the first Ukrainian ambassador submitted his diplomatic credentials to Japan as late as 10 February 1998.

In South Asia, India recognized Ukraine on 26 December 1991 and the two countries established diplomatic relations on 17 January 1992. Although Ukraine opened its New Delhi embassy and appointed its first ambassador shortly thereafter, India opened its Kyiv embassy relatively late and accredited its ambassador only on 9 February 1997. From Pakistan recognition came on 31 December 1991 and the establishment of diplomatic relations on 16 February 1992. Ukraine was first to open its embassy and appoint its ambassador. Pakistan opened its Kyiv embassy relatively late and its first ambassador submitted his diplomatic credentials on 21 October 1997.

In Southeast Asia, the major countries recognized Ukrainian independence as follows: Thailand on 26 December 1991; Vietnam—27 December 1991; Indonesia—28 December 1991; Malaysia—31 December 1991; Singapore—2 January 1992; the Philippines—24 January 1992. In terms of diplomatic representation, these countries may be divided into two groups. First, the following countries and Ukraine have opened embassies in each other's capitals: Indonesia in June 1994 and Ukraine in Jakarta in June 1996; Vietnam in June 1993 and Ukraine in Hanoi in August 1997. Secondly, the ambassadors to Ukraine from such countries as Singapore, Thailand and The Philippines are posted in Moscow, and the Malaysian ambassador in Poland.

It is worth emphasizing that the year 1997 was especially significant in Ukraine's development of diplomatic relations with the countries of Asia. In the course of the year the first ambassadors of India, Malaysia, Pakistan, Indonesia, Thailand, the Philippines, and Vietnam submitted their diplomatic credentials in Kyiv, as did the first Ukrainian ambassadors to Japan and South Korea. Moreover, the exchange visits between Ukraine and the countries of the region at the levels of heads of state, premiers and vice premiers, ministerial, business and industrial leaders have been on the rise. For example, in 1997 President Leonid Kuchma visited China, Japan, Vietnam, and South Korea. Thus, by 1998 Ukraine's relations with the major countries of Asia were well along toward complete normalization.[46]

In these developments it is important to note that in Asian eyes Ukraine differs significantly from Russia. Ukraine did not become the recognized legal successor to the former Soviet Union. Russia did, and inherited both the advantages and disadvantages of the predecessor state. On the one hand, Russia inherited the strength and international importance of the USSR, including more favorable diplomatic positions. For instance, embassies of the former USSR in other countries automatically became Russian embassies. On the other hand, Russia inherited Soviet disputes with many other countries and some other negative legacies, which are a burden on Russia.

Ukraine, however, when it broke away from the Soviet Union, inherited no problems whatsoever within East Asia or any other Asian region. No political or territorial dispute, and no economic or cultural conflicts exist between Ukraine and the countries of the continent. Thus, Ukraine is in a good position to develop relationships in a region that is widely acknowledged as the most promising in the world as it enters the twenty-first century.

Indeed, there exists an unprecedented historical opportunity for Ukraine to develop its relations with Asian countries to their true mutual advantage. First and foremost, Ukraine has no direct security conflicts or related problems with the region. Second, Ukraine's relations with the East differ fundamentally from Russia's: historically, Ukraine has had no political, military or territorial disputes in Asia, and thus enjoys a superior geopolitical situation. Third, the Ukrainian economy is highly complementary to that of Asian countries and thus it also enjoys superior geoeconomic conditions. Fourth, as is already evident, the more knowledge each side has of the other, the stronger is the desire for cooperation between Ukraine and Asian countries. And fifth, since the East does not have such a mechanism for political, economic and military integration as the European Union, Ukraine can emphasize bilateral relations with countries in this region.

Ukrainian-Chinese relations have been discussed in detail. Let us now survey briefly Ukrainian relations with several other selected Asian countries.

Japan is a major power, especially a major capitalist economic power, in East Asia and in the world—even despite recent problems in its political and economic system. The harsh reality is that Japanese consumer goods have flooded Ukraine, but Japanese investment and technological transfer in Ukraine has been very limited. Japanese trade protectionism has been a problem for many countries, and even nowadays, Japan still values commercial interest above all else, despite its ambition to become a political power. The

Japanese government has concentrated its economic aid on eight former Soviet republics: Azerbaijan, Armenia, Georgia, Kazakhstan, Kyrgyzystan, Tajikistan, Turkmenistan, and Uzbekistan; Ukraine and others have been largely excluded. This shows that Japan is primarily concerned about its own economic interest, especially guaranteeing fuel supplies in the future.[47] Ukrainian-Japanese relations have not developed to their full potential because the two countries' economies are not complementary and also because the Ukrainian investment environment still needs to be improved. Once the investment climate improves and foreign investment and technological transfers can be guaranteed, it is likely that Ukraine will attract huge amounts of Japanese capital and advanced technology. In that case, both Ukraine and Japan will benefit. Chinese-Japanese trade relations can serve as an example. The good news is that Ukrainian-Japanese bilateral diplomatic relations improved considerably in 1997, a good sign for future economic and trade relations.

South Korean-Ukrainian diplomatic relations improved in 1997, even though South Korea was suffering through an economic crisis. South Korea was one of the East Asian economic "miracles," and has reached a high level of economic development. It also made large foreign investment and technological transfers. As a result of the abrupt economic crisis that set in 1997, South Korean investments in foreign countries plunged. However, the crisis is one of the developmental process, and South Korea is likely to recover soon and develop perhaps even more quickly. Before the crisis, South Korea provided Ukraine with special financial aid for the construction of the Ukrainian embassy in Seoul and was undertaking some joint ventures in Ukraine, especially in the automobile industry. Forty-five members of the South Korea Parliament have formed a "South Korean-Ukrainian Relations Improvement Group."[48]

In South Asia, India is a developing country with strong growth potential recognized by the international community. In recent years, India has enjoyed a high annual growth rate in its economy; its investment environment is as good as that of East Asia and is becoming more and more open. Both India and Pakistan have developed and tested nuclear weapons and have not signed either the Nuclear Non-proliferation Treaty (NPT) or the Comprehensive Test Ban Treaty. The nuclear issue is a sensitive area of relations with India in which Ukraine should avoid getting entangled. India has been dissatisfied with Ukrainian sale of conventional weapons to Pakistan.[49] But sales of conventional weapons are common in today's world and a much less sensitive issue than proliferation of nuclear weapons. The United States, Russia, Germany, and a number of other countries have vastly dominated the conventional weapons market.[50] In comparison, Ukrainian sales are inconsequential and especially understandable given its economic difficulties. As long as Ukraine handles well the conventional weapon sale issue Indian-Ukrainian relations should improve. In 1997, the Indian ambassador arrived in Ukraine and submitted his diplomatic credentials, a sign that the problem has not significantly affected Ukrainian-Indian relations.

Pakistan is a less powerful country than India and faces many political and economic difficulties. Especially, Pakistan has serious and complicated territorial disputes with India, the Kashmir issue being particularly sensitive. Thus, Pakistan strongly emphasizes improving its military power, though its focus is primarily defensive vis-à-vis India. Ukraine, in its turn, focuses much effort on the industrial use of military technology. In 1996 Ukraine signed a conventional weapon sale contract with Pakistan amounting to $580 million in 1996, primarily for 320 T-80Y tanks.[51] It is to be hoped that Ukrainian-Pakistani economic relations will gradually shift to production and technical transfers of nonmilitary goods.

Ukrainian relations with the countries of Southeast Asia—Indonesia and Thailand in particular—are very promising, judging by the efforts they have made to strengthen ties to Ukraine in recent years. However, these countries have faced major economic difficulties since 1997 and also, like Japan, are waiting for improvements in the investment climate in Ukraine. Other major nations in South and Southeast Asia such as Sri Lanka, Myanmar (Burma), and Nepal also have unrealized potential in their relations with Ukraine. In all these cases the scope for diplomatic and, especially, economic relations will increase with a richer and more prosperous Ukraine.

Conclusion

Over the past six years, many critics focused their attention more on Ukraine's negative features and domestic difficulties than its foreign policy achievements. It is true that the country is indeed experiencing hard times. Still, the critics frequently overlook the positive side of the domestic scene. The passage of the new constitution in 1996 affirms that Ukrainian politics is on the right track. The Ukrainian government has dealt most successfully with ethnic relations, and the turbulence predicted by many, especially in Eastern Ukraine, never materialized.[52] Institutional development has progressed, and the central government is becoming more experienced and stronger. Even in the reform of the economy—Ukraine's weakest point—gradual improvements have been noticeable since the nadir of 1993–94.

Many international critics complain about the slow pace of reform in Ukraine as well as its corrupt bureaucracy. On this one can agree, but only partially. Ukraine inherited a heavy economic burden from the central planning system of the former Soviet Union. Furthermore, Ukraine lacks the many ample resources of Russia. Excessively hasty, perhaps ill-conceived reforms may cause social upheavals. The problem of an inefficient bureaucracy and rampant corruption, however, is of paramount importance because it may change the fate of the new nation. Still, such phenomena exist not only in Ukraine, but are common in all transitional economies, including Russia and China. The key is for the government to emphasize and strengthen the rule of law, react to citizens' complaints, and to strike a heavy blow against corruption and bribery.

Whatever Ukraine's failings or failures in the domestic sphere, on the international arena Ukraine has already made a historic mark. It has regulated its relationships with its direct neighbors, with many of whom there were long historical antagonisms. This is a great achievement. It has emancipated itself from the rule of Russia and has proceeded to develop bilateral relations with Moscow on the basis of full equality. It has also established links with the West—both in North America and Europe—that are bound to increase with time. All this has also made possible the establishment and ever more rapid development of relations with the countries of Asia, in the first instance China. And finally, the world community is indebted to Ukraine for its unprecedented disavowal of nuclear weapons and their elimination from its territory.

The author is convinced that these achievements truly entitled Ukraine to an "independence bonus" in the international community. This, unfortunately, Ukraine has not yet received. But Ukraine has every right and every precondition to gain a proper place in the world community of nations in the twenty-first century. I believe that day will come eventually.

NOTES

1. H. Johnson, "Ukraine Did Not Earn Respect Despite its Large Territory and Population," *Business Daily* 5 September 1997. According to the article, the Ukrainian flag was flown upside down during President Kuchma's call on Pope John Paul II.

2. For an example of political misuse of such historical interpretations, see Anatoly Dobrynin, *In Confidence: Moscow's Ambassador To America's Six Cold War Presidents (1962–1986)* (New York, 1995), 615.

3. For Chinese readers, promising examples of such works are Zenon Kohut, "The Myth of a Unitary Russia and Russian-Ukrainian Relations," and Zhao Yunzhong, "The Essence of Mid-Seventeenth Century Russian-Ukrainian Relations," *1995 Zhong-Wu Hezuo Zhi Lu Guoji Yantaohui Lunwen Ji* [China-Ukraine: Paths of Cooperations. Papers of the 1995 International Conference], published in Beijing in 1995 jointly by the Beijing Ukrainian Studies Committee and the Canadian Institute of Ukrainian Studies, University of Alberta. These two essays discuss the distorted propaganda surrounding the history of Russian-Ukrainian relations and the myth of a unitary Russia.

4. Jack F. Matlock, *Autopsy on an Empire: The American Ambassador's Account of the Collapse of the Soviet Union* (New York, 1995), 564–71. After completing this article, the author learned that the book has been published in Chinese (Beijing, 1996): materials here quoted appear on pages 660–68 and 955.

5. Gu Zhihong, "Chinese-Ukrainian Relations," *Wukelan Guoqing Chu Tan* [Preliminary Discussions on Ukraine], vol. 2, Chapter 11 (manuscript), 90; edited by the Institute of Eastern Europe and Central Asia, Chinese Social Science Academy, 1994. To the best of the author's knowledge, the following are some of the Ukrainian publications held in the Chinese Hilongjiang Provincial Museum: *Dalekyi skhid; Zasiv; Mandzhurs'kyi visnyk;* and others. It is claimed that a total of twenty-two Ukrainian publications appeared in Harbin, Shanghai, Qingdao, and Manchuria, during that period; none of them was in Chinese. See Y. Malytskyi, "Ukrainian Publications in China," *1993 Zhong-Wu Hezuo Zhi Lu Guoji Yantaohui Lunwen Ji* [China-Ukraine: Paths of Cooperations. Papers of the 1993 International Conference] (Beijing, 1994).

6. For instance, articles written by Long Dajun in the 1920s in the magazine *Dongfang* [The East] focused attention on Ukraine. The articles are relatively objective, if not systematic or comprehensive.

7. Ivan Dziuba [Dzyuba], *Internationalism or Russification? A Study in the Soviet Nationality Problem* (New York, 1974); Chinese translation from the English: Beijing, 1972. Petro Shelest, *Ukraino nasha radians'ka* (Kyiv, 1970); Chinese translation: Beijing, 1974.

8. Ruan Xihu, et al., *Su Lian Minzu Wenti de Lishi yu Xianzhuang* [History and Status quo of Ethnic Problems in the Soviet Union] (Beijing, 1979).

9. Among them may be mentioned Ivan Maistrenko, *Natsional'naia politika KPSS v ee istoricheskom razvitii* (Munich, 1978); Chinese translation: Beijing, 1983. Frantisek Silnitsky, *Natsional'naia politika KPSS v period s 1917 po 1922 god* (Munich, 1978). Roy Medvedev, *Let History Judge: The Origin and Consequences of Stalinism* (New York, 1974); Beijing, 1983. Although this book only partially discusses ethnic problems, it is a good reference for understanding the maladies of the former Soviet Union.

10. *Ukrains'ko-kytais'kyi slovnyk/Wukelanyu Hanyu Cidian* [Ukrainian-Chinese Dictionary], comp. by the Institute of Lexicography of Heilongjiang University (Beijing, 1990).

11. The work of the Research Office was initially limited by a shortage of qualified staff. After the breakup of the Soviet Union, it was expanded into the Ukrainian Research Center of Wuhan University, with many achievements now to its credit.

12. These problems were well presented and analyzed, for example, in Zbigniew Brzezinski, *The Grand Failure: The Birth and Death of Communism in the Twentieth Century* (New York, 1989); Chinese translation: Beijing, 1989. Few if any at that time believed the author regarding the demise of the Soviet Union.

13. Ed. Tian Zengpei, *Gaigekaifang Yilai de Zhongguo Waijiao* [Chinese Diplomacy from Reform and Opening to the Outside World] (Beijing, 1993), chapter 5.

14. Ibid., 323. On 12 September 1991, China established diplomatic relations with independent Latvia. Later, China withdrew its embassy from Riga because Latvia violated the terms of Chinese-Latvian diplomatic relations by forming consular level relations with Taiwan. Later Latvia severed official relations with Taiwan and China resumed its diplomatic relations with Latvia.

15. Ibid., 312.

16. Ibid., 312–13.

17. Ibid., 311.

18. Ibid., 322–23.

19. Leonid Leshchenko, "Ukrainian-Chinese Political Cooperation: Nature and Prospects," *1995 Zhong-Wu Hezuo Zhi Lu Guoji Yantaohui Lunwen Ji* [China-Ukraine: Paths of Cooperations. Papers of the 1995 International Conference].

20. Ibid., 102. The nuclear powers gave their security guarantees on 5 December. See Anatoliy Pliushko, Ukrainian ambassador extraordinary and

plenipotentiary to China, "Three Years of Cooperation: Achievements and Prospects," *Wukelanxue Yanjiu* [Ukrainian Studies] (Beijing) 1995 (4): 6.

21. See, for example, Agence France-Presse, Beijing, 3 December 1995.

22. It is interesting to note that the premises of the Ukrainian embassy in Beijing used to house the embassy of another country, which first established diplomatic relations with China and then with Taiwan, leading China to sever relations with that nation.

23. Cheng Chuankang, "Medical Aid to Ukraine," Lianhe Bao [United] (Taiwan) 7 April 1992.

24. UNIAN, Kyiv, 31 August 1992.

25. ITAR-TASS, Beijing, 14 September 1996.

26. Tian, *Gaigekaifang Yilai,* 323.

27. Anatoliy Plyushko, "Three Years of Cooperation," 6.

28. Statistics provided to the author by the Embassy of Ukraine in China.

29. The author had the opportunity to visit and and observe the school in 1993.

30. See Jiang Changbin, "Working Tirelessly to Promote Chinese-Ukrainian Friendship: A Summary of Achievements of the Ukrainian Studies Committee in Beijing in its Second Year," *Wukelanxue Yanjiu* [Ukrainian Studies] (Beijing) 1995 (4): 1–2.

31. The present author, who was the first president of the Ukrainian Studies Committee in Beijing, has retired from the post and was named honorary president of the Ukrainian Studies Committee in Beijing at that time. The current president is Zhang Zhen, who participated in and delivered a paper at the Third International Ukrainian Conference at Kharkiv.

32. The first international conference: "Ukraine-China: Paths of Cooperation," was held in Kyiv from 30 August to 3 September 1993. The proceedings were published in Ukrainian in Kyiv in 1994, *Ukraina-Kytai: Shliakhy spivrobitnytstva. Materialy konferentsii.* A parallel edition was published in Chinese: *1993 Wu-Zhong Hezuo Zhi Lu Guoji Yantaohui Lunwen Ji.* The second conference was held in May 1995 at Beijing. The Ukrainian delegation was headed by the former vice-premier and member of Parliament Mykola Zhulynskyi. The proceedings of this second conference were published jointly by the Ukrainian Studies Committee in Beijing and the Canadian Institute of Ukrainian Studies: *1995 Zhong-Wu Hezuo Zhi Lu Guoji Yantaohui Lunwen Ji* (Beijing, 1995).

33. See, for example, Mykola Zhulynskyi, "Rozdumy bilia pidnizhzhia hory Sianshan," *Holos Ukrainy* 1 August 1995, and the report of professor

Peter J. Potichnyi, *Holos Ukrainy* 16 August 1995. The symposiums were extensively covered by Ukrainian and Chinese TV stations.

34. *Jichu Wukelanyu* [Elementary Ukrainian] (Wuhan, 1995), 315; *Zhongguo-Wukelanyu Huihua Shouce* [Chinese-Ukrainian Conversation Manual] (China, 1996), 191.

35. Reuters, Kyiv, 31 December 1997. The news release pointed out that in 1997, Ukraine's GDP fell by 4 percent but the currency, the hryvnia, remained stable despite the sorry state of economy and turbulence of world capital markets.

36. Oleksandr Piskun, "Ethnic Policy of the Independent Ukraine," *1995 Zhong-Wu Hezuo Zhi Lu Guoji Yantaohui Lunwen Ji* (Beijing-Edmonton, 1995). Piskun is a former associate minister for ethnic affairs of Ukraine. He now is a member of the Ukrainian Parliament.

37. Chen Youyi, "Ukrainian Military Power," in Li Jingjie and Dong Xiaoyang, *Wukelan Zonghe Guoli yu Zhanlue Diwei* [Ukrainian Comprehensive National Power and Strategic Position] (Beijing 1995), 26.

38. Interview with President Kuchma, "'Image kann man nicht essen': Der Ukrainische Präsident Leonid Kutschma über die NATO, das Verhältnis zu Deutschland und die wirtschaftlichen Nöte seines Landes," *Focus* 1997 (29).

39. ITAR-TASS, Kyiv, 31 May 1997.

40. ITAR-TASS, Madrid, 9 July 1997.

41. ITAR-TASS, Kyiv, 24 March 1997. On Ukrainian-Turkish associations and foundations of their modern friendship, see Natalia Mhitaryan, "Ukraine-Russia: Path of Cooperation," *Eurasian Studies* (Turkey), Summer 1996.

42. Valerii Nikitin, "Moskva i novyi troistvenyi soiuz: Zapad zainteresovan v ukreplenii strateticheskogo al'iansa Kiev-Tbilisi-Baku," *Nezavisimaia gazeta*, 24 December 1996. It may be noted that on two occasions, 29 August 1995 and 9 February 1998, Georgian president Edvard Shevardnadze claimed that there had been attempts to assassinate him; he also implied that the masterminds behind the attempts were not in Georgia, but Moscow. See "Russian Meddling in Transcaucasia," *Intelligence Digest* 13 February 1998.

43. Maksim Yudin, "V Talline sozdaetsia 'Baltiisko-chernomorskii blok,'" *Izvestiia* 28 May 1997.

44. ITAR-TASS, Moscow, 8 May 1997. Iuras' Karmanov, "Minsk peresmatrivaet vneshnepoliticheskii kurs," *Nezavisimaia gazeta* 5 June 1997.

45. Due solely to "limited funding," North Korea withdrew its Kyiv embassy in December 1997. The two countries maintain their diplomatic relations, however.

46. The author is grateful for relevant data provided by the Embassy of Ukraine in Beijing.

47. ITAR-TASS, Tokyo, 17 January 1998.

48. Ia. Pylypenko, "Perspekty ukrains'ko-pivdennokoreis'koho spiv-robitnytstva," *Reitynh* 26 June 1996. The author of the paper also expects that Ukraine's income in foreign exchange would increase significantly if Ukraine could sell 90 percent of its merchandise directly to the Asia-Pacific region; this equally would be applicable to Sino-Ukrainian relations.

49. Indian weaponry is partly produced in India and partly imported from Russia and other former Soviet Union republics. The scale of these transactions is much larger that that of Pakistan.

50. Gennadii Kliuchikov and Vladimir Lartsev, "Kto pravit na 'rynke smerti'?" *Kievskie vedomosti* 16 September 1997.

51. Met'iu Kaminski [Matthew Kaminski], "Voenno-promyshlennyi kompleks Ukrainy ishchet pokupatelei svoei produktsii," *Izvestiia* 29 October 1996. The same article reports that Ukraine sold Sri Lanka four A-32 military transportation airplanes and 200 ten-ton trucks to India.

52. Chrystia Freeland, "East Ukraine Forsakes Russia," *Financial Times* 5 August 1997.

11

Ukraine and the Southern Hemisphere

TARAS KUZIO

As a relatively new independent state Ukraine has sought to extend its diplomatic activity and to diversify its foreign trade into regions of the world with which it previously had had little contact and experience. A main priority for Ukraine has been to break into the markets of the developed world—North America and the Europe. Two problems, however, have thwarted a major breakthrough into these markets: the sub-standard quality of Ukrainian goods (a legacy of the Soviet era), and the protectionism of the North American Free Trade Agreement (NAFTA) and the European Union (EU).

Ukraine, therefore, has also not neglected targeting second world countries of the Southern Hemisphere—in Latin America, Sub-Saharan Africa, and to a lesser extent Oceania. Although a relatively large Ukrainian diaspora exists in Australia (similar in size to that in the United Kingdom at approximately 30,000), there has been little development in Ukraine's relations with Oceania. (Ukraine still has only a consulate, not an Embassy, in Australia.) Geographic distance, traditionally close ties to the British Commonwealth coupled with the closeness of the East Asian market have all inhibited the development of Ukraine's ties with Oceania.

Diversification of Foreign Trade: In Search of Economic Security

The evolution of Ukrainian foreign policy towards the Southern Hemisphere (including the second and developing worlds) has proceeded without the intention of carving out for itself spheres of influence or to fulfill great power ambitions. Instead, the link between Ukraine's evolving foreign policy and national security rests upon two areas. First, is the need to develop alternative sources of energy. Here Ukraine became the initiator of the new Georgian-Azerbaijani-Moldovan-Ukrainian (GUAM) axis within the Commonwealth of Independent States (CIS).[1] By becoming the main channel for Azerbaijani (and possibly Central Asian) energy into Europe, Ukraine clearly hopes that the transit charges it will earn will more than offset its annual energy costs.

Secondly, Ukrainian national security dictates that it diversify its foreign trade away from its inherited over-reliance upon Russia and the CIS. Since 1995–1997, when Ukraine obtained security assurances from the world's declared nuclear powers and NATO, Ukraine can afford to focus upon developing its economic interests within its foreign policy. These, "should always,"

President Leonid Kuchma believes, "dictate the political course of any country."[2] After the recognition of the last two portions of Ukraine's frontiers by Russia and Romania, respectively, in May–June 1997 Kuchma outlined the main tasks ahead in the following manner:

> Having completed the process of the recognition of Ukrainian sovereignty on the part of its neighbors and the entire world, the Foreign Ministry must concentrate its efforts on establishing the country's economic independence.[3]

The formation of a "real security belt around Ukraine" gave Ukraine the possibility of focusing upon, "resolving domestic problems, including problems relating to the national economy."[4] By focusing upon the country's foreign economic interests, Ukraine would be able to end its economic crisis and implement a radical program of economic reform.[5] Looking at this in a different manner, improving the pace and quality of political and economic transformation domestically would, in turn, provide the means to change the vectors of Ukraine's foreign policies away from over-dependence upon Russia and the CIS.[6]

Greater focus upon Ukraine's foreign economic interests has led to an interest in furthering or developing new ties to second world countries. In many of these countries the policies of political and economic transformation were similar to those currently being undertaken by Ukraine. As Yuri Shcherbak, Ukrainian Ambassador to the United States and Ukraine's diplomatic representative in Mexico, pointed out, both sides understood that transformation and privatization of their economies meant that Ukraine and Mexico were undergoing similar processes.[7] Ukraine has been particularly impressed with the successful transformations undertaken during the last twenty years in Brazil and Chile.

The experience of regional integration for Latin American states within the North American Free Trade Agreement (NAFTA) is also obviously of interest to Ukraine in its relations with the CIS, the Central European Free Trade Area (CEFTA), the Central European Initiative (CEI), as well as the European Union.[8] The experience gained by Latin American countries during the economic and political transformation of their region during the 1980s and 1990s is therefore also of close interest to Ukraine, which is in the throes of a far more complicated "four-pronged" transition:[9]

> To a large extent the historical experience of the countries of Latin America in the transformation of their national economies, in resolving problems of regional economic integration, in the development of multi-faceted relations and their self-realization on the level of subjects of international economic relations could become 'food for thought' for Ukraine in helping it to define its own model of joining the world economy.[10]

Relations between the United States and Mexico on the one hand and Ukraine and Russia on the other, are also comparable to a certain degree, the Ukrainian delegation to Mexico found in September 1997. In both cases relations were improving after some earlier difficulties. But a Ukrainian commentary believed that the "elder-younger brother" syndrome did not exist in American-Mexican relationship because "both peoples had never lived in one state."[11] Nevertheless, psychologically Latin American countries had greater empathy with Ukraine than with Russia, seeing a close similarity between Russia's and America's arrogant and great power attitudes towards their respective "Near Abroads." Latin American countries with whom Ukraine most closely cooperated refused to deal with Central and Eastern Europe through the G7. Instead, they preferred to deal directly with them on a bilateral basis.[12] Latin American countries often backed Ukrainian initiatives and enthusiastically supported Hennadiy Udovenko's candidacy for president of the UN Assembly in 1997–1998.

In addition, there are close parallels between the struggles for independence of Latin American states and Ukraine. Whereas Ukraine only celebrated its seventh anniversary of independence in 1998, Mexico began its independence struggle in 1810. Nevertheless, "in a similar manner to the Ukrainian people, the Mexican path to final independence was difficult and long."[13]

Ukraine and Latin America

Ukraine's relations with Latin America are a relatively new development. President Leonid Kuchma visited Latin American countries with a large delegation for the first time as late as October 1995. The Organization of American States (OAS), however, had invited Ukraine to become a permanent observer earlier, and it attended an OAS meeting in this capacity for the first time in June 1994. Until 1995 Ukraine's political and economic relations with Latin America were largely of a "symbolic character," with trade amounting to only a small fraction of its real potential. Therefore:

> The Ukrainian state has come to force the problem of developing its own, fundamentally new—in contrast to the Soviet-imperial—model of economic relations with the countries of Latin America. In the first instance, they should be based upon clearly defined and comprehensively developed Ukrainian economic interests in this region.[14]

Ukraine has diplomatic ties with nineteen Latin American countries, while being recognized by twenty-one. The department to deal with these countries was created as late as 1994, and was included within the European and American Directorate of the Ministry of Foreign Affairs. A major problem for Ukraine in developing its foreign policy, as for most former dependencies of an imperial power, has been two-fold. First, is the financial burden of establishing embassies and foreign trade missions (Ukraine, like other non-Russian successor states of the former USSR, never received a single former Soviet building located outside the USSR, all of which were taken over by the Russian Federation). The second problem was the lack of experts and analysts, translators and interpreters, and diplomats familiar with these new regions into which Ukraine wanted to expand its foreign relations. All of the information pertaining to Soviet foreign trade and the research institutes devoted to world regions were located in Moscow. Ihor Tumasov, head of the Latin American department of the Ukrainian Ministry of Foreign Affairs, complained that, "therefore, Ukraine began to build its relations with Latin America practically from ground zero."[15] The process of creating a pool of experts and support staff would take another five or more years, Tumasov believed. This process was being undertaken at the Diplomatic Academy (established in 1996), the Institute for International Relations (Kyiv State University), and the Institute for World Economy and International Relations (National Academy of Sciences).

Ukraine is interested in developing its relations with Latin America for seven interrelated reasons:

1. the similarities of their transformation processes to democracies and market economies;

2. problems of organized crime and corruption;

3. the trafficking in narcotics;

4. trade and economic relations;

5. maintaining existing markets (for example, Ukrainian tractors and televisions were exported to Cuba in the Soviet era);

6. creating new markets for Ukrainian products and services;

7. obtaining diplomatic support in the UN and other international institutions.

Only three countries have thus far established permanent diplomatic representations in Kyiv—Cuba, Argentina, and Brazil. (Chile has established a trade mission, but no Embassy.) Ukraine has embassies in the same three countries in Latin America, which also represent Ukrainian interests in other countries in the region. The remainder of the Latin American countries were initially represented in Ukraine by their embassies in Moscow—a legacy of the Soviet period. Ukraine has since successfully persuaded most Latin American countries that lack direct diplomatic presence in Kyiv to transfer their representation of Ukrainian interests from their Moscow embassies to Central Europe. The reasons for this were two-fold. First, Ukraine argued that Latin American embassies would not obtain "objective" information on Ukraine based in Moscow. Secondly, the use of Latin American embassies in Central Europe to represent Ukrainian interests would clearly define Ukraine as a "European"—in contrast to a Eurasian—country. Chile, Ecuador, and Colombia, for example, were now represented in Ukraine through their embassies in Prague, Vienna, and Warsaw, respectively.[16] Tumasov believed that henceforth, "Latin American countries began to understand that Ukraine and Russia were two different matters, and one could not completely understand the Ukrainian situation sitting in Moscow."[17]

President Kuchma's whirlwind tour of Latin America in October 1995 included its three most important countries—Brazil, Argentina, and Chile. Kuchma met with the Ukrainian communities in all three states (that in Chile is relatively small). Argentina, Brazil, Uruguay, and Paraguay have the largest Ukrainian diasporas in Latin America, largely descended from arrivals from western Ukraine between the 1890s and the 1930s.[18] In Argentina and Brazil, the Ukrainian diasporas number close to 300,000 each, and play a strategic role in facilitating diplomatic cooperation and economic trade between Ukraine and their countries of residence. On 22 June 1995 a Ukraine-Brazil Society was established in Kyiv headed by the secretary of the Presidential Administration, S. Drizhchanym. The Ukrainian diaspora in Brazil also established a Brazilian-Ukrainian Chamber of Commerce. In Argentina a "Friends of Ukraine" parliamentary group was established. During President Kuchma's visit to Argentina he laid flowers at the unveiling of the Taras Shevchenko monument in the Ukrainian Park in Buenos Aires and attended services in the Ukrainian Greek-Catholic and Autocephalous Orthodox churches. In Argentina in 1993 an Argentinian-Ukrainian Chamber of Commerce was established while in 1995 an Institute for Argentinian-Ukrainian Friendship was created that has helped to cement academic links. One of its first projects was the establishment of a Center for Ukrainian Studies at the University of Buenos Aires.

In Brazil a treaty on Friendly Relations and Cooperation was signed, as well as an agreement on trade and economic cooperation, a joint declaration on the peaceful use of space, and a protocol on consultations between both countries' foreign ministries. Diplomatic representations exist in both countries from 1995. As in many other Latin American countries both sides were interested in expanding their then small trade turnover of only $6.3 million in 1994. These included non-ferrous metals, energy, transportation, information technology, the foodstuffs industry, pharmaceuticals, and the environment.

President Kuchma signed a Declaration on Principles of Relations with Argentina, as well as a similar agreement on trade and economic cooperation and a declaration on peaceful cooperation in space. A Joint Declaration was signed by both countries during President Kuchma's visit to Argentina, together with economic and trade agreements. Direct trade turnover amounted to $11 million at the time, although the actual value of Ukrainian goods exported to Argentina amounted to some $50 million which were mainly conducted through middlemen. A joint venture on air transport was established and economic cooperation in the fields of fisheries, automobiles and machinery are likely to represent future areas of cooperation. Meanwhile, Chile could become Ukraine's main partner in Latin America with regard to research into, and the peaceful use of, space technology.[19]

President's Kuchma's visit to Latin America in 1995 represented Ukraine's first ever diplomatic foray into this region at such a high level and led to the dynamic development of mutual relations. After his visit to these three countries, another seven Latin American countries stated their interest in forging ties and exchanging high-ranking officials. In October 1997 alone, five delegations visited Kyiv from Brazil representing banking, military and political interests.

The Argentinean foreign minister, Guildo Di Tella, paid an official visit to Ukraine in October 1996 which focused upon economic and trade cooperation. Ukrainian foreign minister Hennadiy Udovenko stressed the importance of building these bilateral relations "without intermediaries," since Ukraine, "was losing too much because of them."[20] Areas of cooperation between Ukraine and Argentina included water power, mining, shipbuilding, sea and air links as well as jointly opening up the Antarctic continent. A joint communiqué issued during the visit pointed to migration, space, scientific, technical and agricultural areas which would bring forth fruitful cooperation.

A Ukrainian delegation headed by President Kuchma visited Mexico in September 1997 in another bid to expand economic ties. The Ukrainian side once more stressed the importance of direct trade and not through Russian intermediaries—again a legacy of the Soviet era. President Kuchma noted that, "I hope that the agreements signed on partnership and cooperation in science, engineering, and technologies will be filled with real substance to benefit each side".[21] The delegations signed a declaration on the principles of their relations and cooperation, a memorandum on consultations of matters of concern, education and culture and an agreement on visa-free travel for holders of diplomatic passports. The Mexican Tourist Board opened its office in Kyiv in January 1998 to entice Ukrainians to visit their country. Besides furthering bilateral relations it was hoped that greater trade and cooperation could be expanded between the Black Sea Economic Cooperation Agreement and the Southern Common Market.

A Ukrainian industrial exhibition was held in Mexico City in 1998. The Mexicans demonstrated a keen interest in furthering cooperation in energy-related issues, Ukrainian turbines and hydroelectric power plants. A number of joint ventures were created or discussed during President Kuchma's visit, including with the Bancomext Bank for foreign trade, the Pemex oil company, trade and tourism. A problematical area remains hot-rolled steel products, whose export to Mexico led it to impose a 29.6 per cent anti-dumping duty on Ukrainian products in 1995 (Mexican steel manufacturers demanded that this be raised to 64 per cent). Nevertheless, steel products make up 90 per cent of all Ukrainian exports to Mexico, accounting for over $10 million in value in the first six months of 1997.[22] Ukrainian tractors are also a possible alternative in Mexico to more expensive American ones.[23]

In October 1997 a delegation of the Lower Chamber of the Brazilian parliament, led by the chairman of the Brazil-Ukraine group, Paulo Cordeiro, visited Ukraine. At the time of the visit trade turnover stood at only a pitiful $150 million, but then Ukrainian parliamentary speaker, Oleksandr Moroz, assured his hosts that, "the Ukrainian parliament will provide for the necessary legal basis for business relations between the two states."[24] Areas for fruitful cooperation between Brazil and Ukraine include power engineering, shipbuilding, aircraft engineering and banking. Cordeiro, the delegation's head, believed that Ukrainian technology and equipment were of international standards. A visit during the same month by the governor of the Brazilian state of Parana, Jaime Lerner, where the bulk of the Brazilian Ukrainian diaspora live, discussed joint cooperation in power engineering and railroad construction.

Ukraine and Africa

Africa, especially sub-Saharan Africa, represents virgin territory for Ukrainian diplomacy.[25] Within the Ukrainian Foreign Ministry, African affairs lie within the competency of the Directorate on Asia, Pacific, the Middle East, and Africa, responsible for 108 countries in all.[26] The majority of African countries recognized Ukraine's independence as early as 1992, and established diplomatic relations soon thereafter. Nevertheless, in sub-Saharan Africa Ukraine maintains embassies only in South Africa and Guinea, though Parliament (the Verkhovna Rada) has agreed to the opening of additional embassies in Nigeria and Senegal. Only South Africa maintains an embassy in Kyiv.

The African countries, like the Arab world, are important for Ukraine from the viewpoint of military specialists who aid them in economic matters, technical assistance, and the provision of expertise in such areas as medical services. Within sub-Saharan Africa, the greatest degree of cooperation exists with South Africa, although half of Ukraine's trade turnover comes from Guinea (bauxite). Many African countries have large populations, but an arid climate and/or poorly developed agricultural sectors. These are large potential markets for Ukrainian primary products.[27]

Ukraine and Oceania

Although Australia has a relatively large and dynamic Ukrainian community, the growth of political and economic ties between Australia, New Zealand, and Ukraine since 1992 has been slow and uneven. Two major drawbacks which have hampered the growth of mutual ties have been the distances involved and the socio-economic crisis in Ukraine. In 1996 Australia only exported a meager $10.3 million worth of goods to Ukraine, while importing only $2 million. This is in stark contrast to the approximately $200 million worth of wool that Australia exported to Ukraine when it was a constituent part of the USSR.

In August 1994 Ukraine's then Deputy Foreign Minister Oleksandr Makarenko led a trade delegation to Australia and initialed a "Trade and Economic Cooperation Agreement" (that is still not functioning). Ukrainian parliamentary delegations visited Australia in 1995 and March 1997 and an Australian delegation visited Ukraine in 1995. An invitation was issued to Ukrainian President Leonid Kuchma to visit Australia.[28]

Conclusions

Ukraine's foreign relations with the southern hemisphere are a relatively recent development, more energetically pursued by President Kuchma than by his predecessor. The main factor pushing Ukraine to expand its relations with these regions are economic, especially the need to improve the country's national security by diversifying its foreign trade away from Russia and the CIS. Two other factors also play a role in the development of Ukraine's relations with the second and developing worlds. First is the similarity of their experiences—the struggle's for independence; the normalization of relations with the former imperial power and/or regional hegemon; combatting corruption and organised crime; democratization and the creation of a market economy. The second is obtaining diplomatic support in international forums and organizations on such issues as territorial integrity. Both in the short and medium terms, all these factors are likely to drive Ukrainian foreign policy in the Southern Hemisphere.

NOTES

1. *Delovoi Mir* 23 October 1997.

2. *Vechirnyi Kyiv* 1 February 1996.

3. President Kuchma speaking to the Council of Regions, Kyiv (*Interfax* 19 June 1997).

4. President Kuchma speaking to the Investment Council, Kyiv (*Uriadovyi Kur'ier* 4 October 1997).

5. President Kuchma speaking to the diplomatic corps, Kyiv (*Uriadovyi Kur'ier* 14 January 1997).

6. Volodymyr Horbulin, Secretary of the National Security and Defence Council, "Natsional'na bezpeka Ukrainy ta mizhnarodna bezpeka", *Politychna dumka* 1997(1): 88. Oleksandr Derchachov of the University of the Kyiv Mohyla Academy agrees with the link made by Kuchma and Horbulin between the domestic reform process and the need to concentrate on Ukraine's foreign economic interests. See his "Ukrains'ka zovnishnia polityka pislia madryds'kykh niuansiv," *Narodna armiia* 29 July 1997.

7. See Volodymyr Tronenko, "Meksykans'ki uroky reformuvannia", *Polityka i chas* 1996 (4): 48–52 and "Pro shcho domovleno v Meksiko," *Uriadovyi kur'ier* 2 October 1997.

8. See Ievhen Svynarchuk, "Kozhen—dlia potreb usikh," *Polityka i chas* 1997 (3): 52–57.

9. See T. Kuzio, "Ukraine's Four-Pronged Transition," in T. Kuzio, ed., *Contemporary Ukraine. Dynamics of Post-Soviet Transformation* (Armonk, NY, 1998), 165–80. The "four-pronged" transition refers to economic and political reform, state and nation-building.

10. Volodymyr Tronenko, "Nam zanovo vidkryvaty Latyns'ku Ameryku," *Polityka i chas* 1995 (6): 72.

11. *Uriadovyi kur'ier* 30 September 1997.

12. Interview with Ihor Tumasov, head of the Latin American department of the Ukrainian Ministry of Foreign Affairs, Kyiv, 23 October 1997. Tumasov recalled how in March 1997 the Chilean minister of foreign affairs had been met by all high-ranking leaders in Kyiv. When he then traveled to Moscow, Prime Minister Viktor Chernomyrdin found only thirty minutes of spare time to see him. Such arrogance and disrespect for small and, in Russian eyes, non-strategic countries as Chile only served to confirm among Latin American countries that Russia viewed itself like the U.S.

13. "Ukrains'ki prapory v meksykans'kii stolytsi," *Uriadovyi kur'ier* 30 September 1997.

14. Tronenko, 72.

15. Interview with I. Tumasov, Kyiv, 23 October 1997.

16. Ibid.

17. Ibid.

18. See Volodymyr Budiakov, "Nashchadky emihrantiv: Ukrains'ka diaspora v Latyns'kii Amerytsi," *Polityka i chas* 1994 (6): 68–70, Oleh W. Gerus, "Ukrainians in Argentina: A Canadian Perspective", and Serge Cipko, "The Legacy of the "Brazilian Fever": The Ukrainian Colonization of Parana," *Journal of Ukrainian Studies* 11(2) Winter 1986: 3–18 and 19–32 respectively.

19. On President Kuchma's tour of Latin America see *Polityka i chas* 1995 (12): 70–77.

20. UNIAN, 30 October 1996.

21. *Interfax* 26 September 1997.

22. *Infobank* 25 September 1997.

23. See Yuriy Valuiev, "Meksyka daleka i blyz'ka," *Chas* 2–8 October 1997.

24. *Interfax* 10 October 1997.

25. The Arab countries of North Africa are treated above in the article by Oles Smolansky, "Ukraine and the Middle East," 171–90.

26. On Africa see Victor Hura, "V poshuku stratehii rozvytku," *Polityka i chas* 1995 (5): 18–20.

27. Interviews with Petro Kolos, Deputy Head of the Directorate on Asia, Pacific, Middle East, and Africa and Yuriy Savchenko, head of the Department on Africa, Ukrainian Ministry of Foreign Affairs Kyiv, 23 October 1997.

28. "Ukraine Country Brief" (Canberra: Australian Foreign Office, n.d.). My thanks go to Halyna Koshcharsky for procuring me this document

Part II

National and Regional Security

12

Ukraine's Armed Forces and Military Policy

JOHN JAWORSKY

When the Soviet Union collapsed in 1991 one of the most urgent challenges facing the leaders of the former Soviet republics, now independent states, was deciding the fate of the military and military-related personnel, equipment, and infrastructure on their territory. Similar challenges had arisen in a wide range of (usually post-imperial) situations. However, Ukraine began to create its own armed forces in 1991 in a very distinctive and complex setting.

The second echelon status of the Soviet Union's three military districts on the territory of Ukraine meant that a disproportionately large number of the USSR's armed forces personnel—approximately 750,000 individuals—were stationed in this republic in 1991, as were numerous personnel in other military-type formations (e.g., border troops, internal security troops, etc.) and a large volume of sophisticated military equipment. A significant portion of the Soviet Union's military-industrial complex (MIC) was located in Ukraine,[1] as were many military educational institutions and a large number of the Soviet Union's nuclear warheads. In short, just as Ukraine played a significant role in the Soviet military effort, it bore a heavy burden after 1991 in dealing with the Soviet military legacy.

Western concerns about the way in which Ukraine would handle this legacy centered on the fate of the nuclear warheads in Ukraine when it declared independence. As a result, few observers noted that the creation of the Ukrainian Armed Forces (UAF) was in itself a dramatic development. It played a crucial role in ensuring the success of the state-building process in Ukraine, and in undermining plans to create a Moscow-dominated collective security system after the formation of the Commonwealth of Independent States (CIS). The survey below focuses on the general context of the emergence of the UAF, the challenges facing this institution, and the overall significance of military developments in Ukraine.

Background

Ukrainians were heavily represented among the professional military cadres of the Soviet Armed Forces (SAF), and were considered conscientious and reliable. According to a widespread stereotype, they were capable disciplinarians who made effective junior officers and deputy commanders.[2] Thus, none of the various efforts in the West to assess the "ethnic factor" in the SAF ever pointed to Ukrainians as a significant source of actual or potential problems within the military. Most of these studies lumped Russians, Ukrainians, and Belarusians together in one single Slavic category, for there appeared to be no good reasons to differentiate among these groups.

The image of Ukrainians as loyal "younger brothers" of the dominant Russian population of the Soviet Union coincided with another stereotype, also widespread in the West, of Ukraine as a generally peaceful, obedient, and conservative backwater of the USSR. However, certain state policies demonstrated that the central authorities were aware of and concerned about the potential for unrest in Ukraine, including possible unorthodox behavior by military personnel of Ukrainian background. For example, the pattern of political repression following World War II showed that activists in the Ukrainian national rights movement were singled out for special attention by the state's coercive apparatus.[4] In addition, it appears that there was a "glass ceiling" for ambitious officers of Ukrainian background in the SAF and, after World War II, relatively few Ukrainians were appointed to the most senior command posts in the Soviet military.[5]

From the perspective of the leaders of a centralized, authoritarian state preoccupied with maintaining domestic stability, the great attention devoted to a relatively small number of Ukrainian dissidents, and concerns about the loyalty of senior military personnel, were justified. As soon as local conditions permitted, many former dissidents, including individuals recently released from detention, resumed their political activities. Their initial demands included greater autonomy for Ukraine, more rapid introduction of democratic political practices, and changes in cultural and linguistic policies. However, beginning in 1989 nationalist and national-democratic circles in Ukraine began to advance more ambitious demands and discuss a variety of military-related grievances. These included the poor conditions of service for officers and conscripts, and the dangers they faced in regions of growing ethnic conflict in the Soviet Union. At the same time articles discussing the possible establishment of a Ukrainian military began to appear in publications sponsored by these circles.[6]

After the anti-communist opposition, including a number of former dissidents, won nearly a third of the seats during the March 1990 elections to the Ukrainian Supreme Soviet (Verkhovna Rada), it set the tone for many of the parliamentary debates which followed. Thus the Declaration of State Sovereignty adopted in July 1990 clearly stated that the Ukrainian SSR had the right to establish its own armed forces. Little was done during the twelve months following this declaration to implement formally this Declaration's clauses concerning the military. However, military issues continued to be of concern to the nationalist and national-democratic opposition. For example, the links they had established to certain military officers serving in Ukraine led to the creation of the Union of Officers of Ukraine, which held its first Congress in July 1991, shortly before the abortive coup attempt of August 1991.[7]

In the aftermath of this coup attempt what had appeared to be fringe activities assumed great significance. On 24 August 1991, in its proclamation of Ukraine's independence, Parliament (Verkhovna Rada) stressed the country's helplessness when faced, during the coup, with the possible use of military force. As a result, the parliament resolved to create a Ukrainian defense ministry headed by Major General Kostiantyn Morozov, appointed on 3 September, and place all military formations deployed on Ukraine's territory under its jurisdiction.[8]

Building Ukraine's Armed Forces: Initial Successes

One of the greatest—and, to date, most poorly recognized—successes accompanying the drive for Ukraine's independence was the rapid and peaceful transformation of the Soviet military units on its territory in the fall of 1991 into an independent military force. In the fall of 1991 the Ukrainian Parliament approved a package of draft laws on national defense, and by the end of December 1991 the legal basis for the UAF had been firmly established. This was followed, early in 1992, by the administration of an oath of loyalty to the military personnel on Ukraine's territory, and those who refused to swear this oath were provided with funds to leave Ukraine.[9]

Thus, by the time the Soviet Union formally ceased to exist and the CIS came into being, Ukraine had already created the framework for its own armed forces and was the first state within the CIS to establish an independent military. Russia's armed forces did not come into being until May 1992, after the great majority of the military officers on Ukrainian territory had sworn an oath of loyalty to Ukraine and it became clear that the country's leaders would refuse to engage in collective security arrangements dominated by Russia.[10]

This emphasis on establishing an independent military was not surprising in the overall context of a normal state-building process. Given Ukraine's limited (and incomplete) experience of independence in modern times, in 1991–92 a great deal of attention was devoted to rapidly acquiring the most significant attributes of statehood, including the establishment and maintenance of an independent military capability. The salience of this issue was particularly great in view of the large number of military personnel located on Ukraine's territory when it became independent, for they could have posed a serious threat to the country's sovereignty if they had not been rapidly and effectively subordinated, through clear lines of authority, to the Ukrainian government. Thus, the politicians who prompted Ukraine's independence frequently underlined the disastrous consequences of the failure to organize a cohesive army during the turbulent civil war period of 1918–21, which was characterized by conflicts among a confusing array of military and paramilitary forces in Ukraine.

Given the circumstances in which Ukraine emerged as an independent state, it is not surprising that the process of building the UAF was difficult and at times controversial. What *is* surprising is that the actual creation of the UAF took place in a peaceful fashion and did not provoke significant protests among the military personnel on Ukraine's territory or effective counteractions in Moscow. There were several reasons why the process of establishing the UAF was so successful and, at least in the short term, relatively "painless":

- A small but cohesive, dedicated group headed by Kostiantyn Morozov, Ukraine's first minister of defense, worked energetically and persistently to establish a framework for the UAF in the fall of 1991.
- All nationalist and national-democratic forces in Ukraine were united in supporting the creation of the UAF and the general means chosen to carry out this project—that is, administering an oath of loyalty to all military personnel in Ukraine rather than attempting to create a Ukrainian military from scratch.
- Conservative forces in Ukraine opposed to the disintegration of the USSR were greatly disoriented by the dramatic developments which followed the August 1991 coup attempt and were unable to organize a coherent opposition to the creation of the UAF.
- The unsettled political situation in Moscow in the fall of 1991, and the accompanying disorientation in the senior ranks of the Soviet military, did not permit a coherent political or military response by Moscow to developments in Ukraine.

Thus, the abortive coup attempt of August 1991 and its political aftermath led to the opening of an unprecedented "window of opportunity" for Ukraine in the fall of 1991. At the time, the great majority of senior military commanders in Ukraine opposed the creation of the UAF.[11] However, vigorous action by a determined core group headed by Morozov and supported by Leonid Kravchuk, chairman of the Parliament and soon to become Ukraine's president, and the national-democratic politicians who dominated the political scene in Ukraine at the time, quickly laid a firm foundation for the establishment of the UAF following Ukraine's independence referendum of 1 December 1991 and the creation of the CIS on 8 December. The only significant failure accompanying this process was the inability, or unwillingness, of Ukraine's leaders to immediately establish firm control over the Black Sea Fleet units stationed in Crimea and the infrastructure supporting the Fleet's activities.

In turn, the unexpected strength of the drive for Ukraine's independence, and the determination which its leaders demonstrated to establish an independent military capability, kept the Soviet military command off balance throughout the fall of 1991. Even after the CIS was created, Marshal Evgenii Shaposhnikov and his associates failed to understand that setting up a unified collective defense structure for the CIS was irrelevant to Ukraine's new national security goals. Thus, security policy was the most contentious issue at the CIS Minsk meeting of 30 December 1991. Specifically, Ukraine's refusal at this meeting to accept a CIS collective security arrangement led to an agreement confirming the right of each member state to create its own armed forces.[12]

In short, Ukraine's emphasis on establishing its own armed forces played an essential role in the country's overall state-building effort, sparked similar developments among other CIS member states, and fatally undermined Moscow's efforts to promote a highly integrated CIS collective security system. However, once Ukraine's armed forces were established they faced a number of serious challenges in the areas of finances, personnel, and restructuring.

Reality Sets In: The Challenges of Independence

Finances

The massive military presence in Ukraine during the Soviet period was an integral component of the USSR's hypertrophied and highly centralized, integrated, military effort. Thus, the first and foremost military-related challenge faced by Ukraine's leadership was coping with the enormous financial burden of reducing, reforming, and restructuring the Soviet military personnel, equipment, and infrastructure on Ukraine's territory. However, the resources available to pursue these goals were limited. The USSR's disintegration had been accompanied by widespread optimism in Ukraine concerning the economic future of the newly independent country, but these expectations proved unwarranted. Ukraine's independence led to an acceleration of the economic decline that had begun well before 1991, and this had a dramatic impact on military reform plans.

During the crucial period when they were first being established, the UAF were provided with quite generous funding. According to one estimate, in 1992 almost twenty percent of Ukraine's state budget was consumed by military-related expenditures, and this figure did not include expenditures on conversion.[13] However, it is difficult to get a clear picture of funding for the UAF in 1992–93 because of the chaotic state of budgetary planning in the fledgling Ukrainian state. As Col. Gen. Vitaliy Radetskyi, Ukraine's second minister of defense, commented, during this period the UAF essentially existed without a budget.[14]

Following this period of relative largesse there was a dramatic reduction in funding for the UAF. Between 1992 and 1995 the budgetary funds which the UAF received, as a percentage of funds requested, fell from 43.8 percent to 21.8 percent. In 1996 per capita spending on Ukraine's military was $15, compared to $113 in Russia and $674 in France, a country similar in size and population to Ukraine.[15] These funds barely sufficed to pay (usually with considerable delays) military personnel and provide them with basic necessities, and according to Defense Minister Oleksandr Kuzmuk, in 1997 the UAF received only 38 percent of the funds needed to ensure their normal functions a result the military has accumulated a number of significant debts. mple, in the fall of 1997 Ukraine's railway companies refused to transport military shipments until outstanding debts were cleared.[17] Shortfalls in funding for the military have been largely a result of the poor state of Ukraine's economy after independence. However, they also reflect the relatively weak influence of Ukraine's military within the corridors of power in Kyiv. It is not considered a significant actor in domestic politics, and it has not mounted effective opposition to continued cutbacks in military spending.[18]

A number of additional factors made it difficult to use existing financial resources in an effective fashion and thus further complicated an already complex situation. For example, because of Moscow's highly centralized control over the military, in the fall of 1991 Ukraine's government lacked basic information concerning the nature and extent of the military-related resources on the territory under its formal control. Since Moscow was unwilling to provide Kyiv with this information, Ukraine's new Defense Ministry had to prepare quickly an inventory of these resources.[19] In the meantime a significant volume of military stores and equipment was quietly transferred from Ukraine to Russia in late 1991 and early 1992.[20] Control over military equipment has remained poor, and most of the illegal weaponry circulating in Ukraine has been stolen from military stores.[21]

Other significant problems associated with the Soviet legacy included the structure and location of the military forces on Ukraine's territory and Ukraine's role in the Soviet Union's military-industrial complex, which reflected the USSR's military priorities rather than those of the new Ukrainian state. Thus, there was a disproportionately heavy concentration of troops and support facilities in Ukraine's western regions (the Carpathian Military District during the Soviet period) and also in some parts of the old Odesa Military District (especially Crimea), whereas there was a relatively limited military presence in the eastern regions of the old Kyiv Military District. Similarly, although a large part of the Soviet Union's military-industrial complex was located in Ukraine, it served the needs of a highly integrated defense industry. Only a limited range of military goods could be produced by Ukraine in the absence of components from other former Soviet republics, especially the Russian Federation.[22]

Last but not least, the resources allotted to Ukraine's military were often used in an inefficient fashion. The reasons for this included, among others: a lack of clarity concerning the contours of Ukraine's military doctrine and the new tasks to be assigned to the military; the Ukrainian Defense Ministry's lack of experience with financial and budgetary matters, and primitive accounting practices within the military; the continuous emergence of crisis situations which hampered effective medium- and long-term planning; widespread corruption within the military; and funding decisions which were not based on a realistic assessment of Ukraine's future military needs. For example, Ukraine was unable to negotiate a mutually convenient price for the sale, to Russia, of the strategic bombers found on Ukraine's territory in 1991. A large amount of scarce funds has been expended by Ukraine to maintain these bombers, but by 1997 Russia had lost all interest in them.[23]

The consequences of underfunding were predictable. Conditions of military service, for both officers and troops, gradually deteriorated, and have had a significant impact on the prestige of military service as well as the morale and political restiveness of military personnel. Almost all budgetary funds allotted to the military go to pay for salaries and to cover the basic needs of military personnel.[24] Thus, only very limited funds are available to maintain old or purchase new military equipment for the UAF. A large part of its equipment is already outdated[25] and the poor state of Ukraine's economy, as well as the unpredictable levels of future funding for the military, have made it impossible to introduce any long-range plans to provide the UAF with new equipment.[26] This has led to a gradual deterioration in the combat readiness of UAF units, which is further exacerbated by a lack of funds to provide military personnel (e.g., pilots) with the training time they need to maintain their skills, and to conduct frequent, large-scale military exercises.[27]

Chronic underfunding of Ukraine's military thus has seriously affected, and will continue to affect, attempts to restructure the UAF and its supporting infrastructure. For example, rapid downsizing of the military has been hampered by poor job opportunities in other sectors of Ukraine's economy and the state's financial obligations to those released from service. Redistributing the military resources on Ukraine's territory has been held up by the great expense of developing the appropriate infrastructure in the regions where it is lacking. Finally, reforming Ukraine's military-industrial complex, by encouraging conversion or closing production cycles so that Ukraine can produce the military goods it needs and also sell them abroad, are expensive processes which have received only limited support from Ukraine's weak economy.

This gloomy picture is slightly attenuated if one considers the various strategies which have been adopted to ensure that the military continues to function in spite of the difficult circumstances described above. For example, instead of purchasing new military equipment the UAF have taken advantage of the large volume of equipment stored on Ukraine's territory (because of its second echelon status) during the Soviet period. Military commanders often enter into various agreements, both formal and informal, with local administrative officials to ensure that the personnel in the units under their command are provided with foodstuffs, heat, and other essential services. In return, military personnel are assigned to bring in the harvest, work as laborers on construction sites and public works projects, help deal with the aftermath of natural disasters, etc.[28] Many military units are also engaged in their own agricultural activities, growing vegetables and tending livestock on military farms.[29]

The military has also been given considerable freedom to procure non-budget funds to complement state funding. In April 1997 President Leonid Kuchma approved a program which was to restructure the administration of the

UAF's activities, encouraging a more effective use of resources allotted to the military and allowing the UAF to derive greater benefits from the commercial use of military property (e.g., transport aircraft, health care facilities, etc.) made redundant as a result of downsizing.[30] Military-based "businesses" began operating (often in a legal gray zone) well before this program was introduced. However, a more consistent effort now has been made to provide a framework for such activities, with the aim of ensuring the proper use of military property and preventing the resulting profits from lining the pockets of corrupt officials. Non-budget funds have already been used to provide 2,700 officers and their families with apartments.[31]

Some of these practices bring only short-term benefits, or divert UAF personnel from military-related activities. Most significantly, the engagement of some military personnel in commercial activities has seriously affected morale, as opportunities to benefit from such activities vary greatly within the military. Abuses have been inevitable, especially in view of primitive accounting practices within the UAF and poor supervision of the new commercialization program.[32] However, the various survival strategies adopted by the military have helped to ensure that an already difficult situation does not degenerate even further. For example, the notable increase in UAF training activities and maneuvers in 1997 has been attributed to increases in the income from the military's commercial activities.[33]

Personnel

The consequences for UAF personnel of the consistently poor funding noted above have been predictable. Both conscripts and officers usually live in poor, sometimes atrocious, conditions. According to some press reports, in certain garrisons conscripts have such poor diets that they have suffered from malnutrition. Poor diet, combined with substandard sanitary and housing conditions, has contributed to widespread health problems among conscripts, who in many cases are already in poor physical condition when they begin their military service. A relatively small percentage of draft-age youth (according to one estimate, 11.5%) are conscripted, an increasing percentage of those who are drafted have a limited educational background, and draft evasion is common.[34] The quality of the conscript pool is further affected by the selection of the healthiest and most physically fit conscripts by the National Guard and other domestic security formations. Last but not least, as a result of downsizing and the decreasing size of the conscript pool, Ukraine has an increasingly "top-heavy" military over-staffed with senior officers and, like other post-communist militaries, the UAF suffers from a lack of capable and well-trained junior officers.[35]

Wage payments to military personnel, low to begin with, are often delayed for months on end and are insufficient to provide for family needs. In addition, in many garrisons officers' wives have great difficulty finding employment to supplement their husbands' meager wages. Another major grievance voiced by military personnel is the lack of appropriate housing. In December 1997 almost 70,000 officers and their families did not have their own accommodations, and over 33,000 retired and reserve officers were on waiting lists to receive housing. They live in barracks and other communal quarters, and in 1997 the state budget only allowed for 800 new apartments to be assigned to military personnel to help deal with this housing shortage. In these difficult circumstances individual officers have adopted a variety of survival strategies. These include relying on support from relatives, raising crops and livestock on garrison territory specially assigned to this purpose, moonlighting, etc.[36]

The end result of such problems has been high levels of demoralization within the UAF. Among its manifestations are: a steady decrease in the prestige of military service; frequent attempts to evade conscription by draft-age youths; and desertion. The educational level of conscripts has decreased sharply since 1993, and a variety of pathological phenomena which were found in the SAF continue to exist in the Ukrainian military. They include practices generally subsumed under the polite title of "non-statute relations" (the abuse of military personnel, such as the brutal hazing of new conscripts popularly known as *didivshchyna*); suicides among military officers who cannot make ends meet or are placed on lengthy waiting lists for housing;[37] alcoholism and drug abuse; etc.[38]

Western press reports on conditions in Russia's armed forces frequently dwell on the problems faced by their personnel; however, these are also widespread in the UAF as well. In fact, the wages and living conditions of some of Ukraine's military personnel have been markedly inferior to those of their counterparts from Russia. In Crimea, where military personnel from the two countries have been in close contact over an extended period of time, these differentials played a significant role in determining the allegiance of these personnel when Ukraine was establishing its naval forces.[39]

In these demoralizing circumstances there is a great temptation, among all military personnel, to engage in corrupt practices. Corruption has been fuelled by the behavior of certain senior officers who have clearly abused their positions to enrich themselves, and additional "inspiration" has been provided by well-publicized examples of blatant and widespread corruption in society at large. Corrupt practices within the military include, among others, embezzlement, the theft and sale of military property (including firearms), the illegal use of conscript labor on construction projects (e.g., building elaborate country homes for senior officers), accepting bribes from the parents of potential conscripts, and the smuggling of illegal migrants across Ukraine's western borders. Efforts have been made to control these and other corrupt practices within the military; however, these efforts have been inconsistent and appear to have had limited success.[40]

The logical response to many of these problems is to reduce the number of personnel in the UAF, with the aim of creating a smaller and better-equipped military force more suited to the country's needs. However, rapid personnel reduction was initially hampered by fears of protest by those slated to be ousted, a lack of job opportunities for former officers, and the cost of downsizing—in particular, the cost of a commitment that those released after a certain period of service would be provided with housing and other benefits. Some retraining opportunities have been made available to former officers; however, the number of spaces in job training programs has been limited, and these programs have been of the greatest interest to the best and the brightest in the UAF rather than its deadwood.[41]

In spite of these concerns a considerable downsizing has, in fact, already taken place. In late 1997, some 386,000 military personnel served on Ukraine's territory,[42] approximately half the number present on the same territory in 1991. However, the savings achieved by this reduction have not been great in view of the state's financial obligations to those released from service, and have not significantly offset the great expense of maintaining what is still a large and unwieldy military presence with a disproportionate number of officers.[43] Thus, although Minister of Defense Kuzmuk had earlier stated that 350,000 active duty personnel was the optimal size of the UAF, on 9 December 1997 President Kuchma unexpectedly called for a further reduction of armed forces personnel. Some of the downsizing is to be achieved by releasing from service those officers assessed, by a special attestation commission, as unfit for service, which would reduce the costs associated with downsizing.[44] In addition, the number of conscripts drafted for service in the UAF is to be reduced, as is the number of students admitted to institutions of higher military education. As a result of all these cutbacks, by the end of 1998 Ukraine's Ministry of Defense is expected to comprise 320,000 military personnel and 80,000 civilian personnel.[45]

Last but not least, the peaceful and relatively uneventful emergence of the UAF does not mean that its officer corps has worked together cohesively to further Ukraine's defense goals. A significant number of Soviet officers (approx. 10,000) serving in Ukraine in 1991 did not wish to swear a new oath of allegiance and left Ukraine for other former republics.[46] However, many who remained in Ukraine had only a limited commitment to the new state. Some, especially those with family roots outside Ukraine, joined the UAF expecting that it would be part of a highly integrated CIS collective security system. Others, for a variety of personal reasons, simply wished to complete their service peacefully and retire in Ukraine.[47]

These varying motivations for service in the UAF were reflected in serious divisions of opinion, within the officer corps, concerning the geopolitical stance to be taken by Ukraine. Other issues of controversy included the desirability of civilian defense ministers (only one had a civilian background); the relationship between the Ministry of Defense and the General Staff; and the desirability of decentralizing administration of the military formations on Ukraine's territory. Last but not least, frequent changes in the post of defense minister—four since independence to date—have contributed to cleavages within the senior ranks of the UAF, for each minister had his distinct priorities and introduced a number of major personnel changes within the military.

Ukraine's first defense minister, Kostiantyn Morozov (appointed 3 September 1991), resigned his post after vigorous disagreement with President Leonid Kravchuk following the controversial 1993 Massandra meeting between the presidents of Ukraine and Russia. This meeting had been called to discuss the fate of the Black Sea Fleet, and Morozov considered that Kravchuk had made unwise and unwarranted concessions to the Russian side. So strongly did Morozov feel about this issue that he decided he could not continue as defense minister. Morozov's successor Vitaliy Radetskyi, suspected of encouraging military personnel to support the candidacy of incumbent President Leonid Kravchuk during the 1994 presidential elections, was relieved of his office following the victory of Leonid Kuchma.

However, the most serious controversies surrounded the figure of Valeriy Shmarov. Prior to his appointment in October 1994, Shmarov had occupied senior positions within Ukraine's military-industrial complex, and his goals as minister were to accelerate reform within this important but stagnant sector of Ukraine's economy, as well as within the UAF in general. His appointment also represented an attempt to promote greater civilian control over the military. However, Shmarov's civilian background was resented by the professional military UAF hierarchy. Some of Shmarov's efforts to bypass senior figures in the conservative military bureaucracy were probably justified, but the secretive fashion in which he prepared his reform plans quickly alienated the central apparatus of the Ministry of Defense, the General Staff, and military district commanders. As a result of the ensuing conflict, Chief of Staff General Anatoliy Lopata lost his post in February 1996. In July 1996, a military professional, General Oleksandr Kuzmuk, replaced Shmarov as defense minister.[48] This represented a setback in plans to introduce full civilian control over Ukraine's military.

However, Ukraine's first three defense ministers all left their posts quietly, and eventually all were "rehabilitated."[49] Certainly, none of the controversies noted above led to a politicization of the military comparable to that which has accompanied the activities of senior military figures in Russia. Since Ukraine's senior military personnel have been unwilling to become involved in domestic political disputes, the UAF never assumed the role of an actual or potential power-broker as did the Russian military prior to the debacle in Chechnya. This quiescence is particularly noteworthy in view of the tremendous resource constraints under which the UAF have operated in recent years and the difficulty of predicting the nature and direction of political developments, in a turbulent domestic and intentional environment, that will have a dramatic impact on the fate of Ukraine's military.

Restructuring

The way in which, and extent to which, the Soviet military legacy in post-Soviet Ukraine has been restructured and reformed has been influenced by an array of domestic and foreign policy considerations. The domestic considerations include: financial and personnel constraints (some of them discussed above), which have led to a postponement of all plans to establish gradually a professional military; domestic controversies concerning the status, treatment, and future of various service branches, as well as internal security formations not included within the regular military; controversies concerning the locus of political control over the state's coercive institutions; the virtual absence of "think tanks" in Ukraine which could apply autonomous expertise to help resolve contentious issues; and regional pressures in Ukraine to maintain, eliminate, or transform (e.g., to serve commercial interests) certain elements of the Soviet military legacy on Ukraine's territory.

The main drawback of the military restructuring process in Ukraine has been its narrow focus and the way in which long-term objectives have been neglected or sacrificed because of short-term exigencies dictated by severe economic constraints. The emphasis has been on implementing limited reforms within the military, largely connected to downsizing, rather than conducting a restructuring process based on a fundamental review of the geostrategic, political, socio-economic, scientific-technical, and legal implications of reforming all military and military-related institutions in Ukraine.[50] A comprehensive framework document outlining Ukraine's national security priorities was approved by Ukraine's parliament in January 1997.[51] However, little has been done to date to create the integrated national security system proposed by this document.

For example, as noted above, plans for the downsizing of military personnel were extended and accelerated in 1997 and early 1998 as a result of continuing shortfalls in state funding. However, the new downsizing plans were announced in the absence of a clear, long-term personnel development plan. This has contributed to further demoralization within the UAF, especially since the civilian defense establishment (approximately 100,000 people) has been relatively unaffected by the budget and personnel cutbacks of recent years.[52] Earlier, morale within the military was also seriously affected by the way in which Ukraine's first (and, to date, only) civilian defense minister, Valeriy Shmarov, attempted in 1995 to force through quickly a sweeping plan to restructure the UAF. This plan, which would have resulted in a significant decentralization of control over the regular armed forces, was drawn up in considerable secrecy by a small group of individuals and had to be scrapped when it encountered significant opposition within and without the military.[53]

Restructuring efforts have also been complicated by the specific nature of the military infrastructure inherited by Ukraine. For example, Ukraine inherited an extensive network of military education institutions that far exceeded the country's needs. Various efforts have been made to reform this educational infrastructure, but these efforts have met with strong resistance. It has become, therefore, exorbitantly expensive to educate officers in these institutions, which are heavily staffed and consume a large percentage of Ukraine's military budget.[54]

Last but not least, few attempts have been made to coordinate the activities of the regular military with those of domestic security formations such as the National Guard and border troops, and prevent duplication of the infrastructure supporting these organs of state coercion. Some commentators have also pointed to growing resentment within the regular military because of the higher wages, better living conditions, and superior equipment provided to the personnel serving in domestic security formations, which have not undergone the same harsh cutbacks faced by the regular military.[55]

A number of important challenges remained unsolved in the sphere of civil-military relations. These include: clearly defining the relationship between the Ministry of Defense and the General Staff;[56] allowing for greater parliamentary oversight of the military; improving the judicial and other mechanisms of redress available to military personnel with serious grievances; ensuring that the public is better informed about developments within the military; and preventing politicization of armed forces personnel (which, however, remains quite low). Little has been done to institutionalize firm and effective control of civilian institutions over the military.[57]

Restructuring efforts have also been shaped by certain foreign policy considerations. The goal of Ukraine's security policy "is a defensive one: to preserve a favorable external situation that supports, or at least does not interfere with, state-building and internal consolidation."[58] In line with this goal Ukraine's leaders have stressed the need to create a smaller, more mobile military that could effectively forestall regional security threats. However, achieving this goal is complicated by Ukraine's regional security environment.

Ukraine emerged as an independent state at a time of great regional instability, when its neighbors, in particular Russia, were also attempting to define their regional identity and geopolitical orientation. In general, Russia's politicians have not been satisfied with normal state-to-state ties with Ukraine. They have pursued a broader agenda of integration, including integration in the military sphere,[59] which is backed by several significant levers of influence— in particular, Ukraine's heavy reliance on imports (especially fuel) from and exports to Russia. This integrationist agenda is also supported by several left-wing parties in Ukraine and part of the country's population.[60]

Ukraine's political leadership has consistently placed a strong emphasis on defending the country's sovereignty by creating and maintaining an independent UAF, promoting a positive relationship with NATO, and avoiding entanglements in Moscow-sponsored military integration projects. At the same time, it has generally avoided taking dramatic steps that would strongly antagonize Russia's political leadership and pro-integration forces in Ukraine. This helps explain the ambiguity of Ukraine's military doctrine and the stress on the country's neutrality. However, the tensions inherent in this "creative ambiguity," combined with the indecisiveness of Ukraine's political leadership and the domestic constraints noted above, have led to military policies characterized by inertia and a general adherence to the status quo.

For example, few substantive efforts have been made to shift troop concentrations and modify the military infrastructure that was in place in 1991 to reflect the defensive focus of Ukraine's security policy and provide for a more balanced distribution of forces. The prime reason is the significant expenses and general disruption this would entail. Such moves, however, would also antagonize those forces in Ukraine and Russia that favor the coordination of their states' military policies and strongly condemn any actions or statements which imply that Russia could be considered a potential enemy.

The reasons for the Ukrainian leadership's initial hesitation and vacillation concerning the fate of the Black Sea Fleet in Crimea similarly included domestic considerations such as limited ambitions to build up a strong navy, the expense of maintaining the Fleet and its infrastructure, and Kyiv's ineffective regional policies, which limited its influence over developments in Crimea and, especially, the naval base of Sevastopol. Decisive steps to establish full control over the BSF were also deterred by the vigorous (and often extremist) rhetoric voiced by many of Russia's politicians on the need to maintain a long-term military presence in Sevastopol and Crimea in general.[61]

In view of the problems listed above, the enthusiasm that drove those behind the creation of the UAF has largely faded away, and demoralization within the ranks has understandably affected the ability of the UAF to act as a "school of patriotism." A Social-Psychological Service (SPS) had initially been established to coordinate political socialization activities within the UAF (e.g., reviving Ukrainian military traditions, fostering the use of the Ukrainian language within the military, encouraging patriotism, etc.) and counteract nostalgia for the "good old days" when military personnel served in a powerful and privileged Soviet military. However, attempts to dispel such nostalgia and quickly develop a distinct institutional identity for the UAF by promoting Ukrainian patriotism were often crude and counterproductive. For example, much of this work was conducted by political officers formerly employed by the Main Political Administration of the SAF, who had difficulty quickly recasting themselves as experts in Ukrainian culture and history. In addition, many senior UAF officers, steeped in Soviet military traditions, resented attempts to impose what they considered to be the rather parochial form of "hurrah-patriotism" promoted by the Social-Psychological Service and its head, Volodymyr Muliava.[62] After much criticism, Muliava was replaced and the Social-Psychological Service was renamed the Main Administration for Educational Work. However, the work of this new institution does not appear to represent a significant improvement over that of its predecessor.[63]

A Balance Sheet

There is a sharp contrast between a portrayal of the creation of the UAF as a success story and the many dire problems faced by the UAF after the initial euphoria of independence had passed. However, there are reasons for guarded optimism concerning the further development of the UAF.

First and foremost, the military has not played a significant role in domestic politics. Calm has generally prevailed in the relations among Ukraine's military, societal, and political institutions, and representatives of the military have not had a significant influence on the state's defense policies. Many of the problems faced by the UAF are similar to those faced by other post-Soviet militaries; in particular, Russia's armed forces. However, levels of politicization are much higher among Russia's military personnel. Reasons for this situation include the very different contexts in which Ukraine's and Russia's armed forces were established; the way in which Russia's armed forces have been used as pawns in domestic politics; the rhetoric and practice of intervention by Russia's armed forces in the domestic affairs of neighboring states; and the presence in Russia of senior military officials with a prominent public profile.[64] Because of the relative quiescence of Ukraine's military, further restructuring can likely proceed without fears that the military could oppose this process and play an active role in the country's politics.[65]

In Ukraine, as in Russia, the regular military and internal security formations no longer possess the monopoly on the means of violence which was characteristic of the Soviet period. Thus, various paramilitary formations can have a significant impact on domestic politics, and this has been the case in Georgia and throughout the North Caucasus.[66] However, paramilitary groups are not particularly active in Ukraine. For example, those behind attempts to promote a Cossack revival in Ukraine have generally demonstrated a greater interest in Cossack history and traditions, and using them to promote Ukrainian patriotism, than in the use of Cossack units to fulfill a military or paramilitary role.[67] In contrast, the leaders of Russian Cossack formations in the North Caucasus, and some politicians in Moscow, have expressed a strong interest in the incorporation of Cossack paramilitary organizations into state service.[68]

One should not dismiss the disruptive potential of paramilitary formations, as illustrated by the activities of UNSO (Ukrains'ka Natsional'na Samooborona—Ukrainian People's Self-Defense Forces) the only sizable organization of this kind in Ukraine. A small number of UNSO members have been involved in several regional conflicts (e.g., in Chechnya and Abkhazia) beyond Ukraine's borders, and UNSO leaders have threatened to step up their activities directed against Russia if relations between the two countries seriously deteriorate.[69] However, to date the domestic political role of UNSO has been limited, and it does not currently pose a serious threat to the domestic order in Ukraine.

Even in the best of circumstances, for several years to come Ukraine's economy will remain weak and the UAF will continue to be starved for resources. However, a number of measures have allowed the UAF to receive some new military equipment, engage in various training exercises, and maintain a certain (albeit minimal) level of combat readiness. For example, troops from Ukraine have played an active role in peacekeeping efforts (e.g., in the former Yugoslavia and Angola), and in a wide variety of military exercises sponsored and financed by the Partnership for Peace program.[70] Some cities and regions of Ukraine have assisted the UAF by "adopting" military units and raising funds (a practice called *shefstvo*) to help provide them with equipment. Thus, in the first half of 1997 Ukraine's naval forces received two million hryvnias from various municipal and oblast administrations.[71]

In addition, Ukraine's extensive network of underutilized military-educational institutions has begun to train sizable contingents of military personnel from other former Soviet republics, especially those countries (Georgia, Uzbekistan, Turkmenistan, Moldova) that lack appropriate training facilities and are reluctant to send these personnel to Russia for training. Thus, in March 1998, some 750 cadets from Turkmenistan were studying in three institutions of higher military education in Ukraine, and this figure was expected to grow to over 1,000.[72] The expense of training these personnel has been deducted from Ukraine's debts to these countries, or bartered for military equipment and spare parts not available in Ukraine.[73] Among other initiatives, Ukraine has provided Georgia's fledgling navy with several small ships, education and training for its military personnel; an agreement with Georgia was signed in the fall of 1997 to form a joint peacekeeping battalion which could also be used to help guard the Euro-Asian transit corridor that crosses Georgian territory, and is important for the transport of Caspian oil. In turn, Ukraine is to receive three Sukhoi-25 fighters produced in Georgia, and may use Georgia's aircraft repair facilities to help modernize its air force.[74]

Ukraine has also begun to gain significant revenues from its involvement in the international arms market. Ukraine's initial attempts to break into this market were hampered by Moscow's monopoly on the expertise needed to operate effectively in this highly competitive sphere. However, in 1996–97 Ukraine began to achieve some notable successes in the arms market, the breakthrough being an agreement to supply Pakistan with tanks from the Malyshev factory in Kharkiv.[75] There was considerable speculation, especially in the Russian press, that Ukraine would be unable to fulfill this contract. However, all technical problems have been overcome, and representatives of Ukraine's military-industrial complex have recently succeeded in finding alternative sources, most of them within Ukraine, for various tank components which originally came from Russia.[76] Ukraine has also begun to close the production cycle for certain military goods (e.g., small arms) which it earlier had been incapable of producing,[77] and a number of contracts have been signed (with countries such as Egypt and Ethiopia) to modernize the old Soviet equipment in their arsenals.[78] An increasing proportion of the military equipment produced in Ukraine incorporates innovations introduced after 1991, and over twenty foreign firms are involved in joint military production projects with Ukrainian firms.[79]

As a result of this, Ukraine has become one of the leading arms exporting countries. The products and areas of expertise which are of the greatest interest to foreign customers include: tanks and armored personnel carriers; transport aircraft and aircraft engines; naval vessels of all kinds; radar systems; and artillery systems.[80] Some military-related technologies developed during the Soviet period (e.g., rocket boosters and other space technology) are also finding a civilian market abroad.[81] However, representatives of the United States have expressed concern in connection with Ukraine's plans to produce, for domestic use, military equipment (e.g., ballistic missiles with a range of 300–500 km) which could be of great interest to countries such as Libya and Iran.[82] In addition, although Russia and Ukraine are cooperating in several arms projects (e.g., the production of the An-70 military transport plane and the S-300 air defense missile system), competition between Russia and Ukraine for certain arms markets has been very stiff.[83]

Such survival strategies, and successes in the arms trade, have provided Ukraine's military with some flexibility during a prolonged and difficult restructuring process. However, they cannot serve as a substitute for a turnaround in Ukraine's economy. Although levels of politicization in Ukraine's military remain low, its personnel is unlikely to remain aloof from the political process if the country's economy, and their status and well-being, continue to deteriorate.

Apart from their practical concerns about their standard of living Ukraine's military personnel, and especially the senior officers who were trained and advanced their careers in the USSR, suffer from a certain identity crisis largely based on memories of the privileged status and global role of the military in the Soviet Union. Thus, survey results indicate that a sizable number of Ukraine's officers continue to support military integration efforts within the CIS rather than a gradual rapprochement with NATO.[84] Such sentiments are particularly troubling given persistent efforts by Moscow to retain Ukraine within Russia's sphere of influence and to promote military integration efforts between the two states. This was reflected in the very hostile reaction in Russia to Ukraine's sponsorship of the 1997 Partnership for Peace "Sea Breeze" exercises off the coast of Crimea, which led to certain changes in the conduct of the exercises.[85]

However, the most important factor facilitating the emergence of a new and more stable identity for the UAF is the passage of time. In spite of the rapid downsizing of the military in the last few years, a small but steady stream of personnel who completed their military education during the post-independence period is now joining the UAF, already trained and socialized in a new environment.[86] In addition, comparisons between the Russian and Ukrainian militaries do not always favor Russia. The living and working conditions of military personnel vary considerably throughout the vast expanse of Russia, and in some regions of the country they are worse than those faced by most of Ukraine's officers and conscripts. Russia's military personnel have also been seriously demoralized and politicized as a result of the poorly planned and executed military operation in Chechnya in 1994–1996, attempts to involve the military in domestic political disputes (e.g., during the bitter conflict between the executive and legislative branches of government in October 1993), and the great hostility of much of the local population in neighboring countries (e.g., Tajikistan and Georgia) where Russian troops have been stationed.[87]

The massive and debilitating problems that face Russia's military are widely known throughout the post-Soviet region. Thus, it is doubtful whether the UAF personnel who support (at least in opinion polls) Ukraine's participation in CIS military integration efforts led by Moscow truly feel that this would solve the many challenges facing the UAF. Rather, the likely motivation is a naive nostalgia for the certainty and stability of the Soviet past, fed by intense dissatisfaction with the nature and consequences of military reform efforts in Ukraine and the very great socio-economic problems faced by UAF personnel. Certainly there does not appear to be a determined and cohesive lobby, within the UAF, for consistent support of CIS military integration programs.

Nonetheless, such programs continue to be vigorously promoted by politicians and military officials in Moscow.[88] In fact, Moscow's insistence on maintaining a long-term naval presence in Sevastopol, in the form of the Russian portion of the Black Sea Fleet, is likely motivated by hopes that it could act as a spearhead of future military integration efforts. One should not dismiss the possibility of success of an East Slavic (Russia, Ukraine, and Belarus) variant of the military integration scenario promoted by Moscow. It could, for example, come about if Ukraine's economy continues to stagnate, Russia's economy rapidly recovers, and dissatisfaction with the results of Ukraine's independence leads to widespread public unrest that is ably exploited by pro-integration forces. However, even if pro-integration tendencies in Ukraine gain strength, they can be balanced by the growing attractiveness of various forms of cooperation with countries to the west of Ukraine and the regional organizations to which they belong, or aspire to belong—in particular, NATO.

These countries and organizations can offer support and assistance that will promote the rapid modernization of Ukraine's military without posing direct threats to the UAF's institutional autonomy or Ukraine's sovereignty, and Ukraine's civilian and military leaders are keenly aware of the benefits of such cooperation.[89] The pattern of Ukraine's participation in military exercises, and other forms of bilateral and multilateral military cooperation, underlines the extent to which Ukraine's leadership has stressed the need to cooperate with NATO's Partnership for Peace (PfP) program[90] as well as with Ukraine's immediate neighbors to the west, in particular Poland.[91] Some aspects of this cooperation have been institutionalized in the Charter on a Distinctive Partnership between the North Atlantic Treaty Organization and Ukraine, signed on 9 July 1997 during a NATO summit in Madrid.[92]

Discussions of Ukraine's military-related cooperation with NATO and its non-Russian neighbors usually stress the benefits that Ukraine can gain from such interactions. However, Ukraine can, in turn, make a significant contribution to regional security by becoming more involved in peacekeeping missions in countries such as Moldova (Transdniester republic) and Georgia (Abkhazia), where Russia's dubious "peace-keeping" activities have been discredited. The leaders of both Georgia and Moldova have strongly supported such a peacekeeping role for the UAF. In addition, Ukraine can play a significant role in repairing and modernizing the military equipment on the territory of those states which will be joining NATO in the near future. In view of the substantial military restructuring expenses faced by these countries, those sectors of Ukraine's military-industrial complex which can meet NATO standards can provide a low-cost alternative to the purchase of expensive equipment from traditional NATO suppliers.[93]

The existing support within the UAF, Ukraine's political elite, and society at large for greater military cooperation within the CIS is largely driven by memories of the supposed glories of the Soviet Union's Red Army, and a great deal of inertia. It is generally "soft" support, and how it is expressed will depend heavily on domestic economic and political developments within Ukraine and Russia, and the unpredictable state of economic and political relations between the two countries. In contrast, support for an autonomous Ukrainian military and its cooperation with countries to the west of Ukraine is based on a pragmatic evaluation by Ukraine's political leadership of the historical legacy of Russian-Ukrainian relations and the continuing unwillingness of much of Russia's political elite to accept fully Ukraine's independence. In these circumstances, those who supported the decision of Ukraine's leaders in 1991 to develop and maintain an independent military capability, and currently promote military cooperation with Ukraine's western neighbors, are acting in accordance with the political imperatives which drive all states eager to maintain and defend their independence.

NOTES

1. According to one estimate Ukraine "inherited" 30 percent of the USSR's MIC and 20 percent of the MIC's research centers. See Volodymr Iurchyk, "Osoblyvosti viis′kovo-ekonomichnoi polityky Ukrainy v umovakh formuvannia rynkovykh vidnosyn," *Rozbudova derzhavy* 6 June 1997: 20.

2. Alexander R. Alexiev and S. Enders Wimbush, eds., *Ethnic Minorities in the Red Army: Asset or Liability?* (Boulder, 1988), 151–53.

3. For a survey of some of the research on the "ethnic factor" in the Soviet military, see Teresa Rakowska-Harmstone, "USSR" In *Warsaw Pact: The Question of Cohesion,* Phase II, vol. 3, ORAE Extra-Mural Paper No. 39, Teresa Rakowska-Harmstone et al., eds. (Ottawa, 1986), 171–84.

4. John Jaworsky, "Dissent, Ethnonationalism, and the Politics of Coercion in the USSR," Ph.D. dissertation (Carleton University, 1990), 251–55.

5. "Interviews." Interviews conducted with Kostiantyn Petrovych Morozov, former Minister of Defense of Ukraine (Cambridge, Massachusetts, 1995).

6. A. M. Rusnachenko, *Na shliakhu do natsional′noi armii (1989–1991)* (Kyiv, 1992), 4–9; and Taras Kuzio, "Civil-Military Relations in Ukraine, 1989–1991," *Armed Forces and Society* 22(1) Fall 1995: 26–34.

7. Taras Kuzio, "Ukrainian Civil-Military Relations and the Military Impact of the Ukrainian Economic Crisis" in *State Building and Military Power in Russia and the New States of Eurasia,* Bruce Parrott, ed. (Armonk, 1995), 169–70.

8. John Jaworsky, *The Military-Strategic Significance of Recent Developments in Ukraine* (Ottawa, 1993), 79–80 [Operational Research and Analysis, Directorate of Strategic Analysis, Department of National Defence, Project Report no. 645].

9. Bohdan Pyskir, "The Silent Coup: The Building of Ukraine's Military," *European Security* 2(2) Spring 1993: 149–55.

10. Dale Herspring, *Russian Civil-Military Relations* (Bloomington, 1996), 155–63.

11. "Interviews."

12. Herspring, *Russian Civil-Military Relations,* 157.

13. Oleksandr Honcharenko, et al., "Kontseptsiia natsional′noi bezpeky Ukrainy. Problemy i perspektyvy rozbudovy," *Viis′ko Ukrainy* 1993 (5): 9.

14. *Kievskie vedomosti* 9 April 1994 and *Ukrains'ka hazeta* 20 January–2 February 1994.

15. O. F. Belov, *Natsional'na bezpeka Ukrainy, 1994–1996 rr.: Naukova dopovid' NISD* (Kyiv, 1997), 77.

16. *Zerkalo nedeli* 7 December 1997.

17. *Den'* 18 October 1997.

18. Roy Allison, "Military Factors in Foreign Policy," in *Internal Factors in Russian Foreign Policy,* edited by Neil Malcolm et al. (Oxford, 1996), 232.

19. As late as 1997, Russian defense officials were still refusing to provide their Ukrainian counterparts with information concerning the locations in Ukraine where chemical weapons were stored prior to the collapse of the Soviet Union. See *Den'* 7 June 1997.

20. Interviews.

21. *Den'* 27 November 1997.

22. Jaworsky, "Dissent, Ethnonationalism . . . ," 93–96.

23. *Den'* 18 September 1997, 24 October 1997; and *Izvestiia* 7 October 1997.

24. According to one estimate 80 percent of the military's budget is used to cover wages. See *Ukraina moloda* 15 October 1996.

25. Iurchyk, "Osoblyvosti viis'kovo-ekonomichnoi polityky . . . ," 22.

26. *Den'* 11 December 1997.

27. Taras Kuzio "Crisis and Reform in Ukraine—Part 1," *Jane's Intelligence Review* 8(10) October 1996: 449; and *Nezavisimost'* 21 June 1997, 4 July 1997.

28. *Den'* 17 December 1997.

29. Kostiantyn Khivrenko, "Viis'kovi khliboroby," *Viis'ko Ukrainy* 1997 (5–6): 24–25.

30. See, for example, the article in *Vseukrainskie vedomosti* (3 July 1997) on the various services provided (for a fee) to the civilian population by the Main Clinical Hospital of Ukraine's Ministry of Defense. However, some of the recent attempts to ensure the cost-effectiveness of the commercial use of military property (e.g., the civilian use of military transport planes) have apparently been bungled, leading to the partial loss of a significant market. See *Den'* 5 June 1997.

31. *Ukrains'ke slovo* 15 May 1997; and *Zerkalo nedeli* 7 December 1997.

32. *Kievskie vedomosti* 6 August 1997.

33. *Ukraina-Ievropa-Svit* 29 November 1997.

34. The growth in the unpopularity of military service appears to have bottomed out in 1997, largely because of very poor job opportunities in the civilian sector. This has been reflected in growing competition for admission to military educational institutions See *Den'* 18 July 1997 and 13 November 1997.

35. On plans to introduce, with American assistance, a new system for training sergeants and other junior officers for the UAF see *Ukrains'ke slovo* 15 May 1997. Also see Kuzio "Crisis and Reform in Ukraine—Part 1," 449; *Vechirnii Kyiv* 22 April 1996; *Nezavisimost'* 11 April 1997; *Fakty* 4 October 1997; *Vseukrainskie vedomosti* 8 October 1997; *Den'* 30 July 1997, 27 November 1997.

36. *Nezavisimost'* 16 July 1997; and *Den'* 12 July 1997, 6 December 1997, 25 December 1997; and *Vechirnii Kyiv* 4 December 1997.

37. In 1997, 107 UAF military personnel committed suicide. See *Den'* 17 February 1998.

38. *Den'* 4 November 1997, 9 December 1997, 18 December 1997, 17 February 1998; *Vseukrainskie vedomosti* 19 February 1997, 26 March 1997, 2 April 1997, 24 June 1997; and, *Zerkalo nedeli* 14 December 1997.

39. Nikolai Savchenko, *Anatomiia neob'iavlennoi voiny* (Kyiv, 1997); and Kuzio "Crisis and Reform in Ukraine—Part 1," 450.

40. *Kievskie vedomosti* 29 January 1996, 6 August 1997; and, *Den'* 25 September 1997, 7 October 1997.

41. *Ukraina-Ievropa-Svit* 31 January 1998; *Vechirnii Kyiv* 11 February 1998. Regular reports on, and advertisements for, these retraining programs are regularly published in the journal *Viis'ko Ukrainy*. See, for example, *Viis'ko Ukrainy* 1997 (5–6): 26.

42. *Zerkalo nedeli* 7 December 1997.

43. According to an official of the presidential administration's Military Inspection Office, in late 1997, there was one officer for every four soldiers and sergeants in the UAF. See *Den'* 12 March 1998.

44. *Den'* 25 December 1997, 4 February 1998, and 14 March 1998.

45. *Ukrains'ke slovo* 1 January 1998.

46. Pyskir, "The Silent Coup . . . ," 139–61.

47. Kuzio, "Ukrainian Civil-Military Relations," 166–67; and Roy Allison, "Military Factors . . . ," 242.

48. Details concerning the controversies surrounding the figure of Shmarov can be found in a series of transcripts of trial proceedings initiated by Shmarov against the newspaper *Vechirnyi Kyiv*, accused of slandering

Shmarov, in the following issues: 14 May, 18–22 and 25–29 June, 2–5, 9–13, 16, 18–20, and 23–24 July.

49. In 1996 Morozov was assigned to Brussels to coordinate Ukraine's military cooperation programs with NATO and the West European Union, in 1995 Radets'kyi was appointed to head the Main Military Inspection unit of the Ministry of Defense, and Shmarov continued his military-industrial complex reform activities.

50. *Zerkalo nedeli* 1 November 1997.

51. *Zerkalo nedeli* 18 January 1997.

52. *Zerkalo nedeli* 7 December 1997; and *Ukraina-Ievropa-Svit* 13 September 1997.

53. Kuzio, "Crisis and Reform in Ukraine—Part 2," *Jane's Intelligence Review* 8(11) November 1996: 496–97; and Serhii Markiv, "Ukraine Adopts Military Reform Program," *Prism* 3(3) 21 March 1997: pt. 2.

54. Ukrainian Center for Peace, Conversion and Conflict Resolution Studies,"Problems of the Armed Forces and the Military-Industrial Complex of Ukraine and Civil Control over their Activities." [Excerpt from electronic version of report at following web site: http://www.public.ua.net/˜potekhin/ucpccrs/vpk_e.htm], Kyiv, 1997, 5; and *Den'* 19 March 1998.

55. *Ukraina-Ievropa-Svit* 13 September 1997, 7 February 1998; and *Den'* 30 July 1997.

56. In August 1997 a resolution of Ukraine's Cabinet of Ministers attempted to clarify this relationship. However, Minister of Defense Kuzmuk has failed to implement its provisions fully, and has insisted that the General Staff continue to be fully subordinated to the Minister of Defense. See *Den'* 6 August 1997, 29 August 1997.

57. *Ukraina-Ievropa-Svit* 11 October 1997, 7 February 1998.

58. Sherman W. Garnett, *Keystone in the Arch: Ukraine in the Emerging Security Environment of Central and Eastern Europe* (Washington, DC, 1997), 43

59. Frank Umbach, "The Role and Influence of the Military Establishment in Russia's Foreign Policy and Security Policies in the Yeltsin Era," *The Journal of Slavic Military Studies* 9(3) September 1996: 479–88.

60. *Den'* 26 June 1997, 21 August 1997.

61. James Sherr, "A New Storm over the Black Sea Fleet," Occasional Brief 51, Conflict Studies Research Centre (Sandhurst, 1996), 1–4.

62. Jaworsky, *The Military-Strategic Significance . . .* , 112–13.

63. "Ukraini ne potribni bezbatchenky u pohonakh," *Viis'ko Ukrainy* 1996 (9–12): 10–13.

64.   John Jaworsky, "Civil-Military Relations in Russia and Ukraine," *The Harriman Review* 9(1–2) Spring 1996: 114–16.

65.   Roy Allison, "Military Factors in Foreign Policy," 232.

66.   Stephen F. Jones, "Adventurers or Commanders? Civil-Military Relations in Georgia Since Independence," in *Civil-Military Relations in the Soviet and Yugoslav Successor States,* Constantine P. Danopoulos and Daniel Zirker, eds. (Boulder, 1996), 35–52.

67.   For an overview of the role of Cossack traditions in Ukraine, see Frank Sysyn, "The Reemergence of the Ukrainian Nation and Cossack Mythology," *Social Research* 58(4) Winter 1991: 844–64; and Serhii M. Plokhy, "Historical Debates and Territorial Claims: Cossack Mythology in the Russian-Ukrainian Border Dispute," in *The Legacy of History in Russia and the New States of Eurasia,* S. Frederick Starr, ed. (Armonk 1994), 147–70. One of the leaders of Ukraine's Cossack revival advocated a (limited) paramilitary role for Cossack formations, but this proposal did not have much substance, and was politely rebuffed by Ukraine's President Kuchma and his associates. See *Visti z Ukrainy* 19–25 January and 29 June–5 July 1995.

68.   Roman Laba, "The Cossack Movement and the Russian State, 1990–1996," *Low Intensity Conflict and Law Enforcement* 5(3) Winter 1996: 400–401.

69.   Taras Kuzio, "Radical Nationalist Parties and Movements in Contemporary Ukraine Before and After Independence: The Right and its Politics, 1989–1994," *Nationalities Papers* 25(2) June 1997: 233–34.

70.   *Vseukrainskie vedomosti* 26 June 1997.

71.   *Vseukrainskie vedomosti* 22 July 1997; and *Den'* 17 December 1997.

72.   *Den'* 4 March 1998.

73.   *Den'* 16 August 1997, 20 February 1998, 11 December 1997.

74.   *Nezavisimaia gazeta* 30 October 1997; *and Den'* 31 October 1997; and Reuters, 31 October 1997.

75.   *Den'* 11 June 1997.

76.   *Den'* 1 August 1997; and *Kommersant-Daily* 18 March 1998.

77.   Stefan Korshak, "Ukraine: Locally Produced Pistols Boost Trade," *RFE/RL Weekday Magazine* 22 January, 1998; and, *Den'* 13 March 1998.

78.   *Vseukrainskie vedomosti* 26 June 1997.

79.   *Den'* 29 January 1998; *Zerkalo nedeli* 21 March 1998.

80.   *Den'* 2 October 1997, 15 October 1997, 29 October 1997, 5 February 1998. 24 December 1997; *Zerkalo nedeli* 21 December 1997; and, *Ukraina-Ievropa-Svit* 21 June 1997.

81. Victor Zaborsky, "Ukraine's Niche in the US Launch Market" *World Affairs* 159(2) Fall 1996: 55–63; *Den'* 24 June 1997, 25 June 1997, 30 July 1997; *Vseukrainskie vedomosti* 5 June 1997; *Nasha respublika* 22 August 1997; and, Robert Lyle, "Russia/Ukraine: Sea Launch Venture to Aid Dying Aerospace Companies," *RFE/RL Weekday Magazine* 5 June 1997.

82. *Kyiv Post* 15 May 1997; and, *Den'* 21 June 1997, 6 March 1998.

83. *Den'* 23 July 1997; *Nasha respublika,* 18 July 1997; and, *Kommersant-Daily,* 22 April 1997.

84. *Ukraina-Ievropa-Svit* 13 September 1997; and, Allison, "Military Factors . . . ," 257.

85. *Ukraina-Ievropa-Svit* 30 August 1997, 13 September 1997.

86. *Holos Ukrainy* 27 June 1996; and, *VV* 18 July 1997.

87. Robert H. Epperson, "Russian Military Intervention in Politics 1991–1996," *The Journal of Slavic Military Studies* 10(3) September 1997: 90–99; and, Iuri Chernavin, "The Status of the Army in Russian Society," *The Journal of Slavic Military Studies* 9(4) December 1996: 733–41.

88. *Krasnaia zvezda,* 15 May 1997; and *Nezavisimaia gazeta,* 15 May 1997; and *Den'* 27 August 1997

89. On Ukraine's "Westpolitik" see Sherman W. Garnett, "Reform, Russia and Europe: The Strategic Context of Ukraine's NATO Policy" in *From Madrid to Brussels: Perspectives on NATO Enlargement,* Stephen J. Blank, ed. (Washington, DC, 1997), 73–90.

90. Although Ukraine's military has actively participated in a wide range of PfP activities, the General Staff of the UAF has been criticized for not making better use of the opportunities provided by the full range of PfP programs. See *Den'* 29 July 1997.

91. A Polish-Ukrainian joint battalion has existed since 1996, but its existence was fully formalized only in November 1997. There are plans to establish similar battalions with Romania, Slovakia, Hungary, and Georgia. See *Den'* 28 November 1997.

92. Olga Alexandrova, "The NATO-Ukraine Charter: Kiev's Euro-Atlantic Integration," *Aussenpolitik* 48(4) 1997: 325–34.

93. *Jamestown Foundation Monitor*, 23 March 1998.

13

Ukraine's Place in European and Regional Security

F. STEPHEN LARRABEE

The emergence of an independent Ukraine is one of the most important geopolitical events resulting from the collapse of the Soviet Union. With a population of 52 million people, Ukraine is too populous and territorially too large and centrally located to be ignored. Its stability and prosperity have a direct bearing on regional security and European security more broadly. In an important sense, Ukraine is the cornerstone—the "keystone in the arch"—of the new European security architecture.[1]

An independent Ukraine transforms the geopolitics of Europe. The reincorporation of Ukraine into Russia or a Russian-dominated security system would have a major impact on European security, bringing the shadow of Russian power back to Central European borders. As Zbigniew Brzezinski has noted, without Ukraine Russia ceases to be a Eurasian empire. But if Russia regains control over Ukraine, Russia regains the potential to become a powerful imperial state again.[2] With Ukraine's loss of independence, Poland would be transformed into the geopolitical pivot on the eastern frontier of a united Europe. Hence, how Ukraine evolves will have a critical influence on the evolution of the post-Cold War security order in Europe.

This survey examines Ukraine's foreign and security policy since 1991. The first section focuses on the nexus between domestic and foreign policy. Subsequent sections analyze Ukraine's relations with Russia; ties to the United States and Europe, including the European Union and NATO; relations with Central and Eastern Europe; and Ukraine's role in the Baltic-Black Sea area. A final section examines Ukraine's future security options and their implications.

The Domestic Context of Ukrainian Foreign Policy

The main strategic challenge facing Ukraine is the need to create a benign external environment that will allow Ukraine to focus its attention on its real security challenges. These challenges are largely *internal* and center around the need to create a stable democratic political system and a viable market economy.

Despite significant progress to date, Ukraine is still a "state in the making."[3] Unlike Poland, Hungary and other former members of the Warsaw Pact in Eastern Europe, Ukraine existed as a state only for a few brief years after World War I. Thus, when the Soviet Union collapsed in 1991 a new state had to be created virtually from scratch. This significantly complicated Ukraine's transition and made it more difficult than the transitions elsewhere in Central Europe.

Moreover, the process of state-building had to take place against the background of great economic, regional, and ethnic diversity. Western Ukraine had been part of the Habsburg empire. Its compact Ukrainian ethnic and linguistic composition, political culture and level of economic development differ significantly from that of Eastern Ukraine, which had been under tsarist Russian rule and is predominantly Russian-speaking. These economic, ethnic, and regional differences have greatly complicated the process of state-building and the development of a truly Ukrainian national consciousness and foreign policy.

The greatest threat to Ukraine's independence is not military but economic—in particular, the lack of a coherent economic reform program. The failure to pay sufficient attention to this fact was one of the most serious mistakes made by both Ukrainian and Western policymakers in the initial period following Ukrainian independence. This failure nearly led to the collapse of the Ukrainian economy in 1993, as inflation reached 10,000 percent a month.

The economic reform program introduced by the newly elected President Leonid Kuchma in 1994 brought the economy back from the edge of collapse and helped to restore Western confidence in Ukraine, at least temporarily. However, many of its most important provisions, especially those regarding privatization, have been blocked or watered down by the Parliament, which has been dominated by anti-reformist forces. Corruption also has become increasingly widespread.

The price for reducing high inflation has been a major "payments arrears" crisis. Most of this indebtedness is between enterprises, but workers and pensioners by the late 1990's were owed about $3 to $4 billion by public and private utilities. These problems have reduced the confidence of Western governments and investors in Ukraine and made it difficult for Ukraine to attract large foreign investment. Many Western companies have scaled down or closed their operations in Ukraine because of the poor investment climate.

Addressing the issue of economic reform is crucial. Unless Ukraine begins to take the issue of economic reform more seriously, Western economic and political support could begin to erode and Ukraine's ability to integrate into Euro-Atlantic structures could be imperiled. This, in turn, could make Ukraine more vulnerable to outside pressures, particularly from Russia, which still has considerable economic leverage over Ukraine.

Relations with Russia

The most pressing external challenge facing Ukraine has been the need to regulate its relations with Russia. The break-up of the Soviet Union left a number of unresolved issues, including the division of the Black Sea Fleet, the demarcation of the Russian-Ukrainian border, the status of Crimea and Sevastopol, and the restitution of normal trade relations. Russia and Ukraine have also differed over the nature of the Commonwealth of Independent States (CIS) and NATO enlargement.

The root cause of many of the differences between Russia and Ukraine lies in Russia's ambiguous attitude toward Ukrainian statehood. Many Russians, including many Russian democrats, have difficulty in accepting Ukraine as an independent state. They regard Ukrainian independence as "temporary" and hope that Ukraine will eventually return to a "fraternal Slavic compromise"— that is, an integrated relationship involving relations which are far closer than normal state-to-state ties. Hence, until May 1997, Russia procrastinated on signing a state-to-state treaty which would recognize Ukraine's borders as permanent and make integration more difficult. Even after the signing, the treaty still faced strong opposition in the Russian Duma.

Russian-Ukrainian relations have also been burdened by differences over the Black Sea Fleet.[4] In June 1992, Russia and Ukraine agreed on an equal division of the fleet and other related assets. At a summit in Massandra in September 1993, Ukraine agreed to sell Russia a portion of its share of the fleet in order to reduce its energy debt to Russia. A final agreement, however, was held up by differences over where the fleets would be based and the terms governing the lease for Russian ships. Russia wanted to use Sevastopol as a base for its share of the fleet, while Ukraine wanted to avoid any agreement that might weaken its claim to sovereignty over Sevastopol. Both sides also differed over the duration of the leasing agreement, with Russia pressing for a much longer lease.

A third area of contention has been economic policy. Ukraine is heavily dependent on Russian energy supplies, especially oil and gas. The Russian energy company Gazprom has repeatedly cut off gas supplies as a result of Ukraine's failure to pay its energy debts, causing serious disruptions in the Ukrainian economy. Ukrainian officials have tended to see such disruptions as politically motivated. Russian officials, on the other hand, have claimed such disruptions are simply designed to force Ukraine to pay its debts.

Russia's decision in October 1996 to impose a 20 percent sales tax on Ukrainian goods and quotas on sugar also caused friction between the two countries. These restrictions resulted in a virtual trade war between Russia and a sharp drop in Ukraine's trade with Russia.[5] Ukrainian officials tended to regard these restrictions as part of a growing policy of economic intimidation by Russia. Russia, on the other hand, argued that these restrictions were a response to Ukraine's policy of "dumping" its cheaper products on the Russian market.

A fourth source of friction has been related to the Commonwealth of Independent States (CIS). Russia has tried—unsuccessfully—to turn the CIS into a cohesive political, economic, and security organization with some supranational structures. CIS integration has become—at least rhetorically—an important *leitmotiv* of Boris Yeltsin's foreign policy. In September 1995, Yeltsin signed a decree calling for increased efforts to promote closer cooperation within the CIS, including in the defense field. The edict specifically directed the CIS states to develop a collective security system along the lines of the 15 May 1992 Tashkent Treaty on Collective Security and to unite in a defensive alliance on the basis of their common interests and military-political objectives.[6] It also called on CIS states to refrain from participation in alliances and blocs aimed against member states. While little progress has been made in implementing policy, leading Russian officials continue to emphasize the need to create a CIS security system and alliance.[7]

Ukraine, on the other hand, has taken a very reserved position toward relations with the CIS. While Kyiv has actively pursued economic cooperation with the CIS, it has rejected any form of political, economic, or military integration. Ukraine joined the CIS Inter-State Economic Committee but it is not a member of the Customs Union and Payments Union and it is only an associate member of the Economic Union. Kyiv has also refused to join the Inter-Parliamentary Assembly and the Tashkent Treaty on Collective Security, which it regards as an effort by Russia to create a Russian-dominated defense alliance that would constrain Ukraine's sovereignty and independence. In short, Ukriane has adopted a "minimalist" approach to CIS cooperation. It wants to see the CIS transformed into a loose mechanism for economic cooperation, nothing more.

Finally, Russia and Ukraine have been at loggerheads over NATO enlargement. Russia has firmly opposed enlargement as a matter of principle. Moscow grudgingly went along with the inclusion of Poland, Hungary, and the Czech Republic in the first round of enlargement, largely because it could not prevent it. However, it is opposed to a future wave of enlargement that might include the Baltic states and Ukraine. Ukraine, by contrast, has asserted the right of any country to choose its security orientation. While at the moment Ukraine has opted for non-bloc status, it has not excluded the option of joining NATO at a later date (see below).[8]

These issues have led to periodic friction between Russia and Ukraine since 1991. Relations have been burdened in particular by Russia's refusal to recognize officially Ukraine's borders and by differences over the Black Sea Fleet. While these issues were finally regulated in the Treaty of Friendship and Cooperation in May 1997 (see below, pages 319–29), the Russian Duma has on several occasions called into question Ukrainian sovereignty over the city of Sevastopol in the Crimea, as have several leading Russian politicians such as Moscow's Mayor Yurii Luzhkov. Although Yeltsin has been careful to dissociate himself from such statements, the statements have reinforced Ukrainian fears of Russian intentions.

However, since early 1997, bilateral relations have significantly improved. After a delay of nearly three years, the two sides finally signed a Treaty of

Friendship, Cooperation and Partnership during Yeltsin's state visit to Kyiv in May 1997. Valid for ten years, with a possibility to be renewed for another ten years, the treaty officially recognizes the "immutability of existing borders"— one of Ukraine's key demands—ending the cat and mouse game that Moscow had played since 1991 regarding the recognition of Ukraine's borders.

This is an important gain that clearly enhances Ukrainian security and independence. Russia had previously insisted that CIS borders should be "transparent" and undemarcated, as in Soviet times. It had also demanded that "external" CIS borders should be protected jointly, with the participation of Russian border troops. Thus, the treaty gives legal substance to Russia's rhetorical recognition of Ukraine's territorial integrity and removes Crimea and Sevastopol as points of contention in Russian-Ukrainian relations.

At the same time, in a separate accord, the two sides regulated the remaining details of the division of the Black Sea Fleet. Under the accord, Russia received four-fifths of the fleet. Ukraine also agreed to lease port facilities at Sevastopol to Russia for twenty years. The agreement represented important gains for Ukraine. While Russia is allowed use of the facilities at Sevastopol, the accord underscores Ukrainian sovereignty over the city (it is the facilities which are leased, not the actual territory itself).

The Friendship and Cooperation Treaty also contains some important gains for Russia. For instance, it obliges the two sides not to make any kind of agreement with third parties directed against the other party. It also obligates each side not to allow its territory to be used to the detriment of the security of the other party. Russia could conceivably argue that this clause prevents Ukrainian membership in NATO. However, this constraint is more hypothetical than real. The treaty is valid for only ten years and it is unlikely that Ukraine will be ready to join NATO before then, if at all.

In short, the treaty and accords on the Black Sea Fleet contain important provisions which should serve to strengthen Ukrainian security and self-confidence over the long run. The treaty by no means ends all differences between Moscow and Kyiv. Both countries still do not see eye-to-eye on many issues, particularly ties to the CIS and NATO enlargement. But the treaty does eliminate several important irritants in relations and should help to put bilateral relations on a firmer footing in the future, thereby giving Ukraine a greater sense of security over the long run.

The treaty also vindicates President Kuchma's effort to pursue a "balanced" policy and his contention that strong ties to the West are not inconsistent with—and could, in fact, contribute to—better relations with Russia. Yeltsin's decision to go to Kyiv and finally sign the Friendship and Cooperation Treaty—after a three-year delay—was primarily motivated by his desire to counter Ukraine's growing ties with the West, especially NATO and the United States. The visit was thus an implicit acknowledgment that Moscow's hard-line policy on the border issue had failed and that a new, more conciliatory policy was needed to forestall a stronger tilt toward the West by Ukraine.

Since the signing of the treaty, Ukrainian-Russian relations have continued to improve. At an informal summit at Zavidovo in mid-November 1997, Yeltsin and Kuchma agreed to eliminate the value-added tax (VAT) imposed on Ukrainian goods in October 1996. Yeltsin also agreed that an annual quota of 600,000 tons of Ukrainian sugar could be exempted from the 25 percent surcharge imposed by Russia on Ukrainian sugar in May 1997.[9] These moves could lead to a significant increase in Ukrainian exports to Russia—perhaps by as much as 20 to 25 percent—and a visible growth in the volume of trade, which declined by 18 percent during 1997, mostly as a result of the VAT.

The two presidents also agreed to set up a "Strategic Consultative Group on Russian-Ukrainian Relations." The group, composed of key presidential and governmental aides, and cochaired by Sergei Yastrzhembsky, Yeltsin's foreign policy coordinator, and Oleksandr Razumkov, the Deputy Head of Ukraine's Defense and Security Council, is charged with managing the bilateral relationship. The fact that the group is chaired by Yastrzhembsky and Razumkov suggests that the two presidents want to keep control of bilateral relations firmly in their own hands.

Yeltsin, in fact, appears to regard Kuchma as a guarantor of good Russian-Ukrainian relations. In February 1998 he virtually endorsed Kuchma for reelection in 1999, stating that to ensure good Russian-Ukrainian relations, "the first thing to do is not to change the presidents, given that we have established friendly personal relations. If you change presidents, you may be in for a change of relations."[10] His remarks seemed designed to give Kuchma an electoral "shot in the arm," especially among the Russian-speaking population in Eastern and Southern Ukraine.

However, it is too soon to conclude that Russian-Ukrainian relations are on a permanent upward swing. There is strong opposition to the Friendship and Cooperation treaty in the Russian Duma, which has postponed ratification of the treaty several times. The Black Sea Fleet accords also face strong opposition in the Ukrainian parliament. In addition, Ukraine and Russia remain at odds over a host of other issues, including the legal status of the Azov Sea and Kerch Strait, the division of former Soviet assets, NATO enlargement and the transit of Caspian oil and gas.

As long as Kuchma and Yeltsin remain in power, these problems are not likely to cause a major disruption of relations between the two states. However, the political future of both men is uncertain. Kuchma faces a difficult election in October 1999, while Yeltsin's health is poor. If Yeltsin were to become incapacitated or if he were to be succeeded by someone like Yurii Luzhkov, the popular mayor of Moscow and an undeclared candidate for president in the year 2000, Russian-Ukrainian relations could face difficult times again. Luzhkov has repeatedly asserted Russia's claim to Sevastopol.[11] His election could lead to an escalation of Russian-Ukrainian tensions.

Moreover, the situation in Crimea—the majority of whose population is ethnic Russian—remains highly fragile. Economically, the peninsula is worse off than most of the rest of Ukraine. If the Crimean economy continues to stagnate, while Russia's takes off, this could reignite separatist pressures. Some Russian politicians like Luzhkov might be tempted to exploit these pressures for their own political purposes.

The greatest threat to Ukraine's independence, however, comes not from Russia but from Ukraine's internal weakness and failure to carry out a coherent policy of economic reform. Unless Ukraine implements a coherent reform program, it will remain heavily dependent on the Russian market—and on Russian goodwill. The real danger, as James Sherr has noted, is not that Ukraine will turn eastward, but that it will involuntarily drift in that direction as a result of its failure to modernize its economy and the comparative ease of doing business in a new Russian market.[12] Thus, how well the Ukrainian leadership uses the current breathing space to relaunch economic reform will have a critical impact not only on relations with Russia but on Ukraine's future more broadly.

Relations with the United States

Ukraine's effort to regulate its relations with Russia has been accompanied by an active *Westpolitik*. This attempt to forge closer ties to the West and Euro-Atlantic structures has intensified markedly since 1994. This diplomatic effort to expand ties to the West reflects a conscious strategic choice on Ukraine's part, and is all the more significant because President Kuchma had emphasized the importance of strong ties to Russia during his 1994 electoral campaign.

The centerpiece of Kyiv's *Westpolitik* has been an effort to develop close ties to the United States. The U.S. is the only country powerful enough to counter Russia's strategic weight. It also brings important economic and political assets to the table. Hence, Ukraine has been anxious to obtain U.S. support for its independence and foreign policy goals.

In the initial period after the proclamation of Ukrainian independence, the U.S. essentially pursued a "Russia first" policy and concentrated most of its attention on Russia. Ukrainian security concerns were given short shrift and were largely subordinated to U.S. concerns about nuclear proliferation.[13] Ukraine was seen as a "spoiler" because of its reluctance to give up the nuclear arsenal left on its soil after the collapse of the former Soviet Union.

The U.S. preoccupation with the nuclear issue created serious strains in U.S.-Ukrainian relations. First, it put emphasis on the nuclear issue to the virtual exclusion of other issues. In effect, U.S.-Ukrainian relations were reduced to a single issue. Second, it tended to reinforce the predisposition of many Ukrainian officials to hang onto nuclear weapons or use them as a bargaining chip. Many Ukrainian officials feared that if Ukraine gave up nuclear weapons, the U.S. would no longer pay attention to Ukraine.

The preoccupation with the nuclear issue, moreover, tended to obscure the fact that the main threats to Ukrainian security were not military but economic, particularly the failure to implement a serious program of economic reform. In the spring of 1993, U.S. policy underwent an important shift.[14] Thereafter the U.S. began to link nuclear disarmament with incentives for broader U.S. economic and political engagement—a policy which many critics within the U.S. government and outside had been advocating for some time. At the same time, Ukraine's own economic weakness increased Ukraine's desire for economic and security assistance and made it more willing to resolve the nuclear issue.

Russia also began to recognize that Ukraine's economic weakness was a mixed blessing. This weakness provided not only an opportunity to pressure Ukraine to align its policy closely with Russia's, but also presented important risks to Russia's own security. If Ukraine imploded, Russia's security would be directly affected. Moreover, Russia faced severe economic problems of its own and was in no position to take over Ukraine's failing economy. Thus Russia slowly and grudgingly came to recognize that the nuclear issue could not be resolved bilaterally with Ukraine but required trilateral cooperation and the involvement of the United States.

This recognition paved the way for the cooperation that led to the signing of the Trilateral Statement in January 1994—which committed Ukraine to eliminate all strategic nuclear missiles on its soil—the ratification of the SALT I Agreement by the Ukrainian Parliament in February 1994, and the ratification of the Nuclear Non-Proliferation Treaty (NPT) in November 1994. These agreements defused the nuclear issue and removed it as an irritant in U.S.-Ukrainian relations. At the same time, the election of President Leonid Kuchma in July 1994 and his introduction of a comprehensive reform program helped to restore U.S. confidence in Ukraine and resulted in a substantial influx of U.S. assistance to the country. Ukraine is the third largest recipient of U.S. foreign assistance after Israel and Egypt. The U.S. also used its influence to press international financial institutions like the World Bank and International Monetary Fund, as well as its European allies, to provide assistance to bolster Ukraine's reform efforts.

Since 1994 the U.S. and Ukraine have taken important steps to broaden and institutionalize their relationship. At the end of 1996 the two countries agreed to set up a special binational commission chaired by Vice President Gore and President Kuchma. Modeled after the Chernomyrdin-Gore Commission in Russia, the Kuchma-Gore Commission meets twice a year and is composed of four working groups—foreign policy, security, trade and investment, and sustainable economic cooperation (which includes special sub-groups on energy, environmental issues and science and technology). The Commission provides an important institutional mechanism for developing the newly emerging "strategic partnership" between Washington and Kyiv and helps to ensure that the relationship receives ongoing high-level attention.

However, despite the significant improvement in ties since 1994, U.S.-Ukrainian relations remained marred by several issues. One has been Ukraine's missile technology policy. While Ukraine has destroyed or returned to Russia the missiles left on its territory after the collapse of the Soviet Union, it has refused to renounce the right to build ballistic missiles of more than 300 to 500 km range carrying warheads of 500 kg or more on the grounds that it faces a threat from Russia. The U.S. has made a willingness to forgo production of these missiles a precondition for supporting Ukraine's application to join the Missile Technology Control Regime (MTCR).[15]

A second, more serious, problem is Ukraine's sales of missile technology to China and "rogue states" such as Iran and Libya. At the end of 1996, reports surfaced in the U.S. press that Ukrainian firms had agreed to sell missile technology to Libya.[16] Ukraine has also reportedly sold SS-18 components to China.[17] These sales have raised concerns within the U.S. government as well as in the U.S. Congress. If Ukraine fails to tighten controls on its sales of missile technology, this could seriously undermine Congressional support for Ukraine.

Ukraine's plans to sell turbines to complete a Russian-built nuclear power plant in Iran also created difficulties in bilateral relations.[18] However, during the visit of U.S. Secretary of State Madeleine Albright to Kyiv in March 1998, Ukraine agreed to abandon the sale.[19] In return, the U.S. offered a substantial compensation package including small business loans, import-export credits, military space cooperation, and the prospect of future access to U.S. nuclear fuel.

Ukraine's abandonment of the turbine sale removed an important irritant in bilateral relations. The most important obstacle to better relations, however, is the stagnation of the economic reform process. The slowdown of the reform process has undercut support for Ukraine in the U.S. Congress. Unless more is done to reinvigorate the reform process, Congressional support for Ukraine could be endangered. The U.S. could also become less willing to encourage international financial institutions like the International Monetary Fund to support Ukraine. This could significantly diminish the chances for Ukraine to receive much needed financial assistance in the future, increasing its internal difficulties and reducing its room for maneuver in foreign policy.

Ties To Europe

While Ukraine's relations with the United States have significantly improved sice 1994, relations with Europe and the European Union have not advanced so rapidly. Ukraine has not been a major strategic priority for most European governments. Many European governments were initially hesitant to support Ukraine too openly for fear of antagonizing Russia and did not feel it was a "real" country. Many continue to regard it as part of Russia's "sphere of influence" and and question whether it is really a part of "Europe."

Ukraine's initial reluctance to give up its nuclear weapons also slowed the development of ties between Europe and Ukraine. Like the United States, the EU made the development of relations contingent on Ukraine's willingness to sign the NPT and ratify the START I agreement. Thus relations with the EU were largely frozen until 1994, when Ukraine ratified START I and signed the NPT.

The ratification of the START I agreement and the signing of the NPT opened up new prospects for an expansion of ties to Europe, especially the European Union. In June 1994, Ukraine signed a partnership agreement with the EU—the first such agreement between the EU and a CIS state. The agreement granted Ukraine most-favored nation status and contained a commitment to consider establishing a free-trade zone in 1998 if Ukraine exhibited sufficient progress in developing a viable market economy. However, unlike the association agreements signed with Eastern Europe and the Baltic states, the accord with Ukraine made no mention of possible EU membership.

Relations with the EU, moreover, have developed slowly. The EU's main concern has been nuclear safety. The bulk of the EU's financial assistance to Ukraine has been allocated to support the closing of the nuclear reactor in Chornobyl. Very little has gone to modernize the Ukrainian economy or help Ukraine gain better access to EU markets, which Ukraine badly needs. The volume of EU trade with Ukraine is relatively small, especially in comparison to that with Russia.

The Chornobyl issue has been a serious irritant in Ukraine's relations with the EU. In December 1995, Ukraine signed a Memorandum of Understanding with the EU and G-7 in which it agreed to close the Chornobyl plant by the year 2000. In return, the EU and G-7 promised over $1 billion to assist Ukraine in closing Chornobyl and help it construct two new facilities—built to Western standards—at Rivne and Khmelnytskyi. However, implementation of the agreement has been delayed by difficulties over financing the construction of the two reactors.[20] These delays have created an atmosphere of mistrust between the sides. Ukraine has warned that further delays in the construction of the two reactors would force it to keep Chornobyl open after the year 2000.

Ukraine has made deepening relations with the Western European Union (WEU) an important strategic objective. In August 1996, Ukrainian Foreign Minister Hennadiy Udovenko proposed that relations between Ukraine and the WEU be strengthened through, inter alia, Ukrainian involvement in WEU peacekeeping operations, Ukrainian observers attending training exercises, and the appointment of Ukrainian liaison officers to various WEU headquarters.[21] Kyiv has also requested associate partnership status (the status currently enjoyed by the Baltic states, Slovenia, and the former East European members of the Warsaw Pact). However, the WEU so far has refused Ukraine's request because associate partnership status is linked to prospective accession to the EU and Ukraine is not considered a prospective EU member.

One of Ukraine's problems is that it lacks a strong patron within the EU to champion its cause. Germany has been one of the few European countries to pay serious attention to Ukraine. Chancellor Helmut Kohl has visited Ukraine twice in an effort to underscore Germany's support for independence. Germany is also Ukraine's second largest Western trade partner, behind the United States. But Germany's top priority is Central Europe, especially Poland. Bonn has also been careful to ensure that its relations with Ukraine do not in any way jeopardize good relations with Russia.

Great Britain has been one of the few other European countries to show a strong interest in Ukraine. Former Defense Minister Malcolm Rifkind even went so far as to hint that Ukraine might someday become a member of NATO. Britain has supported Ukrainian economic development through the Know-How Fund, which provides financial assistance to small businesses in Ukraine and other activities in the financial and banking sectors.

With the exception of Britain and Germany, however, few European countries have shown strong interest in Ukraine. While many EU members agree, in principle, that preserving an independent Ukraine is important, few are willing to commit scarce resources to support it. The danger is that the slow pace of economic reform in Ukraine could further diminish the willingness of many European states to provide assistance to Ukraine. Thus, how well Ukraine addresses its economic problems will have a major impact on Ukraine's relations with Europe and its ability to forge closer ties to European institutions, especially the EU, over the long run.

Ties to NATO

While Ukraine officially maintains a non-bloc status, Kyiv's attitude toward NATO has undergone an important evolution since independence. Initially, many Ukrainian officials were opposed to NATO enlargement, fearing that it would create new dividing lines in Europe and lead to increased Russian pressure on Ukraine. However, Russia's hard-line opposition to enlargement and Kyiv's desire to improve relations with the West contributed to a gradual shift in Ukrainian attitudes toward NATO enlargement. During 1995 Kyiv dropped its opposition to enlargement and since then it has increasingly come to feel that Central European membership in NATO is in Ukraine's own interest and will strengthen Ukraine's security.

Ukrainian officials, however, want to see a gradual or "evolutionary" process of enlargement that takes into consideration the security interests of non-member states, especially Ukraine.[22] A slow timetable, Ukrainian officials believe, would give Ukraine time to stabilize and reduce the chance that it would become a buffer between Russia and NATO. It would also enable the European security system to evolve and provide time for NATO's overall transformation.

In effect, Ukrainian strategy is designed to buy time and keep all options open. Currently, Ukraine has no intention of applying for NATO membership. Ukrainian officials know that such a move would heighten Russian feelings of vulnerability and could upset the relatively cooperative relations with Russia that have begun to emerge since Yeltsin's visit to Kyiv in May 1997. They also know that Ukraine has little chance of being admitted to NATO at the present moment. As Foreign Minister Borys Tarasyuk, Ukraine's former Ambassador to NATO, has noted:

> Seeking membership now would just devalue our position in Europe: the door is not opening, so why should we lose respect for ourselves and ask for membership? If we can be sure that the door will open, then we should think about [membership]. But that process will take time and we should [meanwhile] find a proper form of cooperation between Ukraine and NATO.[23]

However, Ukrainian officials have been careful not to slam the door entirely to NATO membership. During his visit to Latvia in May 1995, President Kuchma stated that a policy of neutrality was "nonsense" in light of NATO enlargement and Ukraine's own geographic position. Ukraine, as he put it, was "not Switzerland."[24] Similarly, during his visit to NATO headquarters in September 1995, then Foreign Minister Udovenko stressed that Ukraine reserved the right to become a member of any political-military structure that showed promise of becoming an integral part of the new European security structure.[25] Volodymyr Horbulin, Kuchma's national security adviser, has also stated that he did not exclude the possibility that Ukraine would become a member of NATO someday.[26]

The more open attitude toward NATO and possible NATO membership down the line has been accompanied by a concerted effort since 1994 to strengthen ties to the Alliance. Ukraine was the first CIS state to join PfP and it has been one of the most active and enthusiastic participants in Partnership for Peace (PfP) exercises. Ukraine also has a liaison officer at Supreme Headquarters Allied Powers Europe (SHAPE) in Mons (Belgium) and in May 1997 a NATO information office was opened in Kyiv.

In particular, Ukraine has pushed for a "special relationship" with the Alliance that would go considerably beyond the framework of PfP. These efforts culminated in the signing of the Ukraine-NATO Charter on a Distinctive Partnership at the Madrid Summit in July 1997. While the Charter does not provide explicit security guarantees, it calls for the establishment of a crisis consultative mechanism that can be activated if Ukraine perceives a direct threat to its security.[27] It also foresees a broad expansion of ties between NATO and Ukraine in a number of key areas such as civil-military relations, democratic control of the armed forces, armaments cooperation and defense planning. Thus, the Charter establishes a deeper relationship with Ukraine than with any non-NATO member with the exception of Russia.

Moreover, the Charter has already brought some positive benefits for Ukrainian security. Rather than leading to more hostile relations between Russia and Ukraine, as many critics of NATO enlargement predicted, Ukraine's efforts to strengthen its ties to NATO have contributed to the emergence of the more conciliatory Russian policy toward Ukraine, evident since Yeltsin's visit to Kyiv in May 1997. As noted earlier, Yeltsin's decision to go to Kyiv and sign the long-delayed Russian-Ukrainian Friendship and Cooperation treaty was in large part motivated by a desire to counter Ukraine's growing rapprochement with NATO and reflected a recognition that Russia's delaying tactics were driving Kyiv more strongly into the arms of the West.

For the foreseeable future, however, the Charter probably represents the limits of Ukraine's relations with NATO. While some members of the Ukrainian elite favor membership in NATO in the long term, a large part of the elite, especially in the more Russified parts of Eastern Ukraine, is opposed to NATO membership and favors closer ties to the CIS instead.[28] In addition, Ukraine has a long way to go before it meets the economic and political criteria for membership. Much more would have to be done to eliminate corruption in the economy and stabilize democracy. Civilian control of the military is also considerably weaker in Ukraine than elsewhere in Central Europe.

Moreover, NATO will need time to consolidate the first round of enlargement and decide how to proceed with the next stage. This may take considerable time. NATO will also have to decide how far it can expand without losing its military effectiveness and political cohesion. Finally, Russian sensitivities will need to be managed. Russia is likely to vigorously oppose Ukrainian membership in NATO, which it regards as a threat to its security.

None of this implies that Ukraine will never become a member of NATO, but membership is not likely in the next decade. Over the longer term, Ukraine's prospects for membership will depend on many factors that are hard to predict—internal developments within Ukraine, NATO's evolution and Russia's transformation. Hence, unless there is a significant deterioration in Ukraine's security environment, Ukraine's main efforts in the coming years are likely to be devoted to strengthening ties to NATO through enhanced PfP, increasing interoperability with NATO forces, and giving concrete content to elements of the Ukrainian-NATO Partnership Charter signed at Madrid.

The Central European Connection

As part of its effort to strengthen its European orientation and establish closer ties to the West, Ukraine has sought to expand ties to Central Europe and emphasize its "Central European" identity. This effort, however, has proven problematic. With the exception of Poland, most Central European countries do not really consider Ukraine a Central European country, either politically or culturally. Moreover, Ukraine is considerably less advanced economically than Poland, Hungary, and the Czech Republic. Thus, initially there was strong opposition to including Ukraine in regional groupings like the Visegrád triangle or the Central European Initiative (CEI).

Some of Ukraine's early foreign policy initiatives, moreover, such as the proposal to create a Central European Security Zone, launched by former President Leonid Kravchuk at the CSCE meeting in Prague in April 1993, had a negative echo in Central Europe.[29] The proposed security zone—which would have included Ukraine, Belarus, the Baltic states, Moldova, and the former East European members of the Warsaw Pact but not Russia—seemed designed to entice the Central European countries into an openly anti-Russian alliance. They were thus reluctant to support the Ukrainian proposal. In addition, many Central European officials feared it would result in the creation of a special security zone in Central Europe and weaken their prospects for eventual membership in NATO.

Ukraine's proposal in June 1996 to create a nuclear-free zone in Central Europe also received a cool reception in Central Europe. The proposal reflected Ukrainian fears about the possible deployment of nuclear weapons on the territory of prospective new NATO members such as Poland, Hungary, and the Czech Republic. However, it was seen by many East European countries, especially Poland, as a "trap" which, if accepted, would weaken the significance of any security guarantee from NATO and complicate Poland's entry into NATO.[30] Hence Warsaw flatly rejected the proposal, much to Ukraine's embarrassment.

However, since 1994 Ukraine has made important progress in strengthening ties to Central Europe. In June 1996 Ukraine joined the Central European Initiative (CEI), a regional grouping of ten Central and Southern European countries designed to promote greater regional economic and political cooperation. Ties to the Central European Free Trade Association (CEFTA), which includes Poland, Hungary, the Czech Republic, Slovakia, and Slovenia, have also been strengthened. In January 1998, President Kuchma was invited to attend the annual summit of Central European Presidents in Levoča, Slovakia—the first time such an invitation was extended to a Ukrainian leader. These developments have helped to tie Ukraine more closely to Central Europe and strengthened its Central European identity.

At the same time, Ukraine has made a conscious effort to expand bilateral relations with the countries of Central and Eastern Europe, especially Poland.[31] Historically, relations between Ukraine and Poland have been characterized by considerable tension and mistrust. However, over the last few years the two countries have succeeded in overcoming their past animosities and developing remarkably cordial relations. In May 1992, they signed a treaty of friendship and cooperation. In the treaty both sides affirmed the inviolability of the borders and renounced all territorial claims against one another.[32]

The treaty paved the way for a broad improvement in political relations. An important step in this process was taken in May 1997 with the signing of the "Declaration on Understanding and Unity" (see below, pages 317–18) The Declaration is aimed at eradicating past historical grievances and deepening the approchement that has taken place in recent years. Both sides hope that the Declaration will lead to a process of reconciliation similar to that which occurred between France and Germany after World War II and more recently between Germany and Poland.

Military ties have also intensified. The two countries have set up a joint peacekeeping battalion, to be located in Przemyśl (Poland) near the Polish-

Ukrainian border. Drawn from a Ukrainian mechanized division in the Carpathian military district and a Polish tank brigade, the joint battalion is expected to be fully operational in 1998 and is intended to be used in international peacekeeping operations under NATO and UN aegis. The formation of the battalion underscores the growing links between the two countries in the military-security area.

Some Polish politicians have even begun to talk about the emergence of a "strategic partnership" between Poland and Ukraine. While such claims are somewhat exaggerated, they nonetheless underscore the far-reaching process of rapprochement that has taken place between the two countries since 1990. If this process continues, it could radically transform the geopolitics of Central Europe, ending centuries of animosity and rivalry that have greatly contributed to instability and insecurity in the region.

Moreover, Poland serves as Ukraine's gateway to the West. Closer Ukrainian-Polish ties help to anchor Ukraine more tightly to the West and facilitate Kyiv's gradual integration into Euro-Atlantic institutions, thereby strengthening Ukraine's European orientation over the long term. Hence, it is strongly in the West's interest to encourage closer Polish-Ukrainian collaboration.

Ukraine's outreach to Central Europe, however, has not been limited to Poland. Relations with Hungary have also improved significantly since 1990. In 1990 the two countries signed a declaration on minority rights—an important concern for Budapest, since there is a large Hungarian minority (160,000) living in Ukraine. The Hungarian minority in Ukraine is relatively well treated. As a result, the minority issue has not been a source of tension in Hungarian-Ukrainian relations in the way it has been in Hungary's relations with Slovakia and Romania. The two countries also signed a treaty of friendship and cooperation in 1991, which contains provisions for the inviolability of borders and a renunciation of any territorial claims.

Ukraine's relations with Romania, on the other hand, have been marred by outstanding territorial differences over northern Bukovina and Chernivtsi as well as southern Bessarabia and Serpent Island, which were annexed by the USSR and attached to Ukraine at the beginning of World War II.[33] These differences led to periodic tensions in relations after 1991. However, relations have witnessed a visible improvement since early 1997. In June 1997, Ukraine and Romania signed a Treaty on Cooperation and Good Neighborly Relations. The treaty contains important provisions regarding the inviolability of frontiers, effectively laying to rest Romanian territorial claims against Ukraine. The treaty also contains important provisions for the protection of minorities. In an appendix to the treaty both sides agreed to the demilitarization of Serpent Island.[34]

The treaty ended four years of difficult and often acrimonious negotiations. It was facilitated, in particular, by Romania's desire to obtain membership in the EU and NATO. With the approach of the NATO summit in Madrid in July 1997, the Constantinescu government wanted to be able to present Romania's candidacy in the best possible light in order to enhance its chances of being included in the first round of enlargement. This gave Romania a strong incentive to regulate outstanding differences with both Hungary and Ukraine. Thus Ukraine indirectly benefited from the process of NATO enlargement, even without applying for membership itself.

The treaty opens up new prospects for cooperation between Ukraine and Romania. The current Romanian government sees a stable, democratic, and independent Ukraine as a major asset and is intent on playing a more active role in fostering cooperation with Ukraine, especially in the economic and cultural field.[35] Some Romanian officials, in fact, believe that Romania can play the same type of constructive, stabilizing role in the South vis-à-vis Ukraine that Poland is playing in the North.

These developments have helped to strengthen Ukraine's ties to Central Europe and Europe more broadly. These ties are likely to become more important, moreover, as the countries of Central Europe—especially Poland—are increasingly integrated into the EU and NATO. With Poland in NATO, Ukraine will have a "spokesman" for its interests inside the Alliance. This will help to ensure that the Alliance considers Ukraine's security concerns even more carefully in its internal deliberations.

Ultimately, however, the success of Ukraine's effort to forge closer ties to Central Europe—and Europe more broadly—will depend on the pace of economic and political reform in Ukraine. If Ukraine's economy begins to stabilize, Ukraine will become a much more attractive partner for Poland and other countries in Central Europe. This could lead to a significant expansion of economic and political ties—possibly even eventual membership in the Central European Free Trade Agreement. But if reform falters and Ukraine fails to develop a healthy market economy, the gap between Central Europe and Ukraine will grow and Ukraine's prospects for joining Euro-Atlantic institutions will diminish, leaving it more isolated and vulnerable to outside pressures.

Baltic-Black Sea Cooperation

Ukraine has also promoted the idea of Baltic-Black Sea regional cooperation. As originally conceived and promoted by former President Kravchuk, the basic idea was to create a grouping of independent states extending from the Baltic to the Black Sea as a bulwark against Russian domination. However, the idea has elicited little enthusiasm among countries in the Baltic region. The Baltic states and Poland are more interested in developing strong ties to the EU and NATO, which they see as the most effective means of enhancing their security. The union between Belarus and Russia has also diminished the feasibility of creating such a regional grouping.

Nevertheless, while downplaying the Baltic-Black Sea regional cooperation concept, Ukraine has sought to forge closer ties to the Baltic states. For Ukraine, the Baltic connection offers an indirect means of strengthening ties to the West and avoiding isolation. The Baltic states, in turn, have a strong stake in the maintenance of an independent Ukraine, which imposes important de facto constraints on Russia's imperial ambitions. However, the Baltic states are likely to eschew anything that resembles a regional alliance with Ukraine. Such a move would complicate relations with Russia and could lead to increased Russian pressure on all three Baltic states.

Turkey and the Black Sea, on the other hand, are becoming areas of increasing strategic importance for Ukraine. Ukraine and Turkey share a number of common interests: both countries are concerned about Russia's efforts to increase its influence in the Caucasus. Turkey also plays an important role in the development and transport of energy resources, especially oil, in the Caspian Sea and Middle East. In June 1997, the two countries signed an agreement for the construction of a pipeline between the port of Çeyhan on Turkey's Mediterranean coast and its Black Sea port of Samsun. From there the oil will be delivered by tanker to the Ukrainian port of Odesa. The pipeline could help Ukraine reduce its dependence on Russian oil. However, work on the project has been held up because of lack of funds and the refusal of the Ukrainian parliament to ratify some sections of the agreement.

Military and security cooperation has also increased. During the visit of Turkish Prime Minister Mesut Yilmaz to Ukraine in February 1998, the two countries agreed to upgrade their relationship and to increase cooperation in the energy and security fields.[36] This evolving "strategic partnership" could become an important geo-political factor in the Black Sea area in the future and act as a counterweight to Russian influence in the region. Ukraine has also expressed an interest in expanding the current military cooperation with Turkey to include Israel.[37]

Ukraine shares Turkey's interest in developing a belt of independent states on Russia's periphery and has recently sought to expand cooperation with Georgia, Azerbaijan, and Moldova. The four countries have formed a special regional group (GUAM). The first official meeting of the group was held in Baku in November 1997. At the meeting the four countries decided to coordinate national policies in a number of areas such as peacekeeping, conflict resolution, energy supplies, and transportation links.[38] The group has also discussed the formation of a joint peacekeeping battalion.

The GUAM cooperation is an interesting new departure in Ukrainian policy. How successful it will be remains to be seen. Nonetheless, it illustrates Ukraine's growing interest in the Caspian region and Caucasus. This interest is driven in large part by Ukraine's desire to reduce its energy dependence on Russia. But it also has broader strategic motivations. Georgia, Azerbaijan, and Moldova all share with Ukraine a desire to avoid Russian domination and expand ties to the West. Hence closer regional cooperation with these countries makes good economic and strategic sense.

Prospects for the Future

Since achieving independence in 1991, Ukraine has made important strides toward regulating relations with Russia and forging closer ties to the West, especially the United States. But many of these positive developments could be undone if the Ukrainian government fails to follow through with domestic reforms, above all the implementation of a coherent economic reform program. Without such a program Ukraine will remain dependent on the Russian market and have difficulty integrating into Euro-Atlantic institutions.

In short, Ukraine's foreign policy options will be heavily influenced by how well it manages its domestic agenda, especially economic reform. If it succeeds in relaunching a coherent program of economic reform, Ukraine stands a solid chance of strengthening its Central European identity and becoming a part of a broader European space and Euro-Atlantic institutions. But if it does not, Ukraine will find it increasingly difficult to maintain the careful balancing act it has pursued since independence and could eventually be forced down the path adopted by Belarus.

NOTES

1. Sherman W. Garnett, *The Keystone in the Arch* (Washington, DC: Carnegie Endowment for Peace, 1997).

2. Zbigniew Brzezinski, *The Grand Chessboard* (New York, 1997), 46.

3. See Sherman W. Garnett, "Reform, Russia and Europe: The Strategic Context of Ukraine's NATO Policy," in Stephen J. Blank, ed., *From Madrid to Brussels: Perspectives on NATO Enlargement* (Carlyle, PA, 1997), 73–90.

4. For a detailed discussion of the negotiations over the Black Sea Fleet, see James Sherr, "Russia-Ukraine Rapprochement?: The Black Sea Fleet Accords," *Survival* 39(3) Autumn 1997: 33–50.

5. Ukrainian trade with Russia dropped 18 percent in the first half of 1997. Exports to Russia dropped 27.5 percent during the same period. See *Jamestown Monitor* 3(157) 26 August 1997.

6. For the text of the decree, see *Rossiiskaia gazeta* 23 September 1995.

7. See the article by Russian Security Council deputy head Leonid Mayorov and Council department chief Dimitri Afinogenov "Vazhneishie napravlenia integratsii,"*Nezavisimaia gazeta* 3 February 1998.

8. Three differences over NATO have come more prominently to the fore since the appointment in April 1998 of Borys Tarasyuk as Foreign Minister. Tarasyuk, who previously served as Ukraine's ambassador to Benelux and NATO, has angered Moscow by taking a more positive attitude toward NATO and NATO enlargement. See Charles Clover, "Moscow Rebukes Kiev Over Praise for NATO," *Financial Times* 9 July 1998.

9. *Jamestown Monitor* 3(216) 18 November 1997.

10. *Jamestown Monitor* 4(36) 23 February 1998.

11. In January 1997 Luzhkov flew to Sevastopol unannounced and infuriated the Ukrainian leadership by stating that Sevastopol was a Russian city and that Ukraine had to negotiate with Moscow over Sevastopol's return. He also criticized the accords on the Black Sea Fleet and reasserted his view that Sevastopol was a Russian city and would remain Russian regardless of the accords. See RFE/RL *Newsline* 43(1) 2 June 1997.

12. Sherr, "Russia-Ukraine Rapprochement?: The Black Sea Fleet Accords," 46.

13. For an excellent discussion of U.S. policy during this period, see Sherman W. Garnett, "The Sources and Conduct of Ukraine's Nuclear Policy," in George Quester, ed., *The Nuclear Challenge in Russia and*

the New States of Eurasia, (London, 1996), 125–51. Also Garnett, *Keystone in the Arch,* 113–24.

14.   For details, see Garnett, *Keystone in the Arch,* 115–19.

15.   Jeff Erlich and Pyotr Yudin, "Ukraine Missile Stance Troubles Russia, US," *Defense News* 2 June 1997; Bill Gertz, "Kiev Entry Into Missile Pact Questioned," *Washington Times* 23 September 1996; Victor Zaborsky, "US, Ukraine Face Missile Impasse," *Defense News* 15 July 1996.

16.   Martin Sieff, "US Officials Express Concern Over Ukraine," *Washington Times* 10 December 1996; Bill Gertz, "Kiev Imperils U.S. Aid With Libya Arms Deal," *Washington Times* 9 December 1996.

17.   Bill Gertz, "Russia, Ukraine Get Stern Missile Warning," *Washington Times* 21 May 1996.

18.   David B. Ottoway and Dan Morgan, "US-Ukraine at Odds Over Nuclear Technology Transfer," *Washington Post* 8 February 1998.

19.   See David Hoffman, "Ukraine Bows to U.S. Pressure," *Washington Post* 7 March 1998.

20.   For details see "West's Policies on Eastern Nuclear Plants 'Misguided,'" *Financial Times* 2 February 1997; Leyla Boulton and Matthew Kaminski, "Ukraine Threatens to Keep Chernobyl Open After 2000," *Financial Times* 20 February 1997; and Leyla Boulton, Kevin Done, and Charles Clover, "ERBD Weighs Price of Ukraine Project against Chernobyl," *Financial Times* 8 April, 1998.

21.   Martinez Cusari, "The Consequences of the Madrid NATO Summit for the Development of WEU's Relations with Central and Eastern European Countries and Russia" (Paris: Assembly of the Western European Union, Document 1585, 5 November 1997), 9.

22.   See Hennadiy Udovenko, "European Stability and NATO Enlargement: Ukraine's Perspective," *NATO Review* 6 (November 1995): 15. For a detailed discussion of Ukrainian Attitudes, see F. Stephen Larrabee, "Ukraine's Balancing Act," *Survival* 38(2) Summer 1996: 143–65.

23.   Boris [Borys] Tarasyuk, "A New Concept of Security," *Transition* 1(13) 28 July 1995: 19–20.

24.   Chrystia Freeland and Matthew Kaminski, "Ukraine May Spoil the CIS Party," *Financial Times* 26 May 1995. *Interfax* 24 May 1995. Reuters, 23 May 1995. See also Kuchma's news conference on 7 December 1994 in which he rejected non-aligned status over the long run: "Yes, indeed it is my personal opinion that Ukraine cannot remain non-aligned. But I want Ukraine to take this decision only when it firmly stands on its own." Kiev

Radio, 7 December 1994. Translated in FBIS-SOV-94-237, 9 December 1994: 33.

25. See "Statement by H. E. Mr. Gennadi Udovenko," Minister for Foreign Affairs of Ukraine at the North Atlantic Council plus Ukraine Meeting, Brussels, 14 September 1995 (mimeographed), 3.

26. *OMRI Daily Digest* 11 (16 January 1997).

27. For the text of the Charter, see "Charter on a Distinctive Partnership Between the North Atlantic Treaty Organization and Ukraine," Appendix I below, pages 340–46. See also David Buchan and David White, "NATO Signs Charter with Ukraine," *Financial Times* 10 July 1997.

28. Popular support for NATO membership varies between 30 and 50 percent. It is considerably stronger among the Ukrainian elite than among the broad masses. According to a poll conducted by the Ukrainian Institute for Public Opinion Research "Socis-Gallup" with the Institute "cultur prospectiv" in Zurich and Humbolt University in Berlin, 50 percent of the elite favor Ukrainian membership in NATO, while only 30 percent of the broad public favor Ukraine joining NATO. See "NATO—ein heikles Thema in der Ukraine," *Neue Zürcher Zeitung* 3 September 1997.

29. For the text of the proposal, see *Gazeta Wyborcza* 24 May 1993. For a detailed discussion, see F. Stephen Larrabee, *East European Security After the Cold War.* MR-254-USDP (Santa Monica, CA, RAND, 1993), 108–109.

30. "Polnische Kritik an Kiewer Plänen für atomwaffenfreie Zone," *Frankfurter Allgemeine Zeitung* 28 August 1996.

31. For a comprehensive discussion, see Antoni Z. Kaminski and Jerzy Kozakiewicz, *Polish-Ukrainian Relations 1992–1996* (Warsaw, 1997). See also "Polnisch-ukrainische Annäherungen," *Neue Zürcher Zeitung* 15 February 1998.

32. For details, see Jan de Weydenthal, "Polish-Ukrainian Rapprochement," *RFE/RL Research Report* 28 February 1992: 25.

33. For a good discussion of these issues, see Garnett, *Keystone in the Arch,* 91–94.

34. For details, see "Kiev und Bukarest paraphieren Grundvertrag," *Neue Zürcher Zeitung* 5 May 1997.

35. In order to increase communication and contacts between the two countries two "Euro-regions" are to be established, which will also include parts of Moldova. Romania has also proposed opening a multinational university in Chernivtsi.

36. "Turkey and Ukraine Advancing Toward an Extensive Partnership," *Turkish Daily News* 14 February 1998.

37. Ibid.

38. *RFE/RL Newsline* 1(168) 26 November 1997.

14

The Denuclearization of Ukraine: Consolidating Ukrainian Security

NADIA SCHADLOW

The nuclear weapons issue has defined and shaped relations between the West and Ukraine since the first days of Ukrainian independence. Despite Ukraine's geopolitical importance, it was the existence of strategic nuclear missiles on Ukrainian territory that brought this newly independent state to American policymakers' abrupt attention in the summer of 1991. Negotiations over the removal of these weapons from Ukraine is fundamentally a tale of how Washington and the West became increasingly aware of the extraordinary implications of Ukrainian statehood.

There were positive ramifications to Ukraine's inheritance of a considerable proportion of the former Soviet Union's nuclear arsenal.[1] Its legacy of 130 older SS-19 intercontinental ballistic missiles (ICBMs), 46 newer SS-24 ICBMs and 40 strategic nuclear bombers (for a total of 1800 nuclear warheads) effectively made Ukraine the world's third largest nuclear power and compelled Washington and Kyiv to engage in intensive diplomatic negotiations for over four years.[2] Both governments were forced to take a crash course in learning to know one another. This had beneficial effects for both countries, particularly for Ukraine. By early 1992 the nuclear issue had forced Washington to recognize the irreversibility of the Soviet breakup and the implications of an independent state the size of France on Russia's borders.

Over time, the United States would come to recognize Ukraine as a state important in its own right, with or without nuclear weapons. By the same token, the negotiations over the weapons' removal forced Ukraine rapidly to confront the challenges of independence and to consolidate critical foreign and defense policy functions and institutions in order to master the complex negotiation process. In addition, the denuclearization process was closely tied to the development of an independent conventional defense establishment in Ukraine and the emergence of substantial U.S.-Ukrainian military and defense contacts.

A review of the denuclearization process will illustrate that it was inextricably linked to the improvement of Ukraine's security. Each phase of the process was used by Kyiv to "buy time" as it worked to consolidate key components of its statehood, particularly its newly emerging relationship with Russia. Ukrainian negotiators became increasingly sophisticated throughout the process, structuring their demands to coincide with the advancement of particular aspects of its security: a stronger economy, more stable relations with Russia, and closer ties with the West.[3]

Stage One: Imperfect Control (June 1991–May 1992)

The denuclearization process can be divided into three fairly distinct phases.[4] Sherman Garnett has aptly described the first phase as one of "romanticism and declarations." During these initial days of independence, and even earlier, the Ukrainian Verkhovna Rada (until independence usually called the Supreme Soviet and subsequently Parliament) issued somewhat confusing nuclear-related declarations. Statements like the July 1990 Declaration of Sovereignty, that noted Ukraine's non-nuclear aspirations, appeared to be driven mainly by the horror of the Chornobyl nuclear power disaster of 1986, rather than a clear strategic rationale for denuclearization.[5] Later, Ukrainian policymakers seemed to recognize the overarching nature of these earlier statements and skillfully backtracked, couching language on Ukraine's nuclear-free status with qualifications like "in the shortest possible time." [6]

This early phase of the U.S.-Ukrainian relationship saw the emergence of themes that were to dominate the denuclearization process over the next three years. By December 1991, following the proclamation of independence confirmed by plebiscite, the creation of a defense ministry, and the popular election of Leonid Kravchuk as Ukraine's first president, it was clear to the United States that Ukraine was determined to use the weapons to its advantage. Among Kyiv's main objectives were to manage and shape its changing relationship with Russia, to negotiate favorable economic benefits, and to ensure that the West recognized Ukraine as a legitimate heir to the former Soviet Union. It is also likely that in this period, the Minsk and Almaty (Alma-Ata) Summits in December 1991 convinced Ukraine that American engagement in Ukrainian-Russian relations would work to Kyiv's advantage and that the weapons assured Washington's continued involvement. By early 1992 it was also clear that Ukraine intended to use the weapons as a bargaining chip for issues related to compensation. A mere five months after Ukraine's referendum on independence in December 1991, some of the key themes that were to dominate the denuclearization process had emerged.

The events of mid-1991 shed light on Washington's decision-making process regarding the most momentous event of the post-war period: the dissolution of the Soviet Union. Indeed, much of the mistrust and misunderstanding that characterized this early denuclearization period stemmed from the months immediately preceding Ukrainian independence. A clear division existed in the United States government that pitted Secretary of Defense Dick Cheney's defense team against Secretary of State James Baker's close advisors, with the latter group often supported by key National Security Council officials. The Baker team, evidently more influential with President George Bush, revealed little appreciation for the historical importance of Ukraine's independence from Russia. Washington was focused virtually entirely on Russia, and as the Soviet Union began to dissolve, on managing the balance between Mikhail Gorbachev and Boris Yeltsin. While expressing empathy for the complicated relations between Yeltsin's Russia and Gorbachev's effort to hold together the Soviet central government, Baker's memoirs on the period virtually ignore the opportunities afforded by an independent Ukraine and consequently, a weaker Russian empire.[7]

The Bush-Baker approach to the possibility of the Soviet republics' achieving independence was manifested in President Bush's infamous speech of 1 August 1991 to the Ukrainian Supreme Soviet. Washington would not try to pick winners and losers in the political competition between the republics, Bush said. He urged the Ukrainian Supreme Soviet to accept the revamped union agreement being championed by Gorbachev and, though acknowledging that freedom was an "inalienable individual right," warned "it was not the same as independence." Most unfortunate, however, was his statement that "Americans will not support those who seek independence in order to replace a far-off tyranny with a local despotism and that the U.S. "would not aid those who promote a suicidal nationalism based upon ethnic hatred."[8] This speech established a legacy of mistrust that was difficult to undo over the next year.

As the Soviet empire dissolved, Washington's main preoccupation with Ukraine, Kazakhstan, and Belarus was that they posed proliferation problems.[9] During this period Baker stressed to Yeltsin and Gorbachev that the U.S. did not want to see the emergence of more nuclear powers.[10] At the same time the Bush Administration held virtually no serious consultations with the Ukrainian leadership. Heated discussions within the U.S. government took place through the fall of 1991 about the possible recognition of Ukraine. The dominant State Department and National Security Council view maintained that recognition should be delayed beyond Ukraine's vote for independence scheduled to take place on 1 December 1991. A number of officials argued that U.S. recognition should be extended only in exchange for a quick removal of the nuclear weapons from Ukrainian soil.[11] Overall, these debates reveal the pervasive "arms control status quo" mentality that seemed to shape many U.S. officials' views about the Soviet Union's dissolution.

Department of Defense officials, supported by Secretary Cheney, argued that the denuclearization of Ukraine, while important, should not be Washington's paramount goal: more important were Ukraine's ultimate independence and the need to develop a full spectrum of contacts with the new state. From the fall of 1991 through the spring of 1992, Secretaries Cheney and Baker discussed these issues often, with Cheney pressing for a broader agenda with Ukraine. The Department of Defense was so persistent with its message that the phrase "Ukrainiacs" was apparently later informally coined to describe those who consistently argued for a broader view of Ukraine. This broader view, however, did not extend to anyone publicly advocating that Ukraine actually retain nuclear weapons. Virtually the only serious public argument for this possibility was made in a *Foreign Affairs* article by a prominent political scientist.[12] This piece was quickly translated into Ukrainian and apparently widely distributed in Ukraine.

The first set of bilateral discussions between the United States and Ukraine occurred in July 1992 over the status of the START I arms control agreement that had been signed one year earlier by President George Bush and Soviet President Mikhail Gorbachev. After years of protracted negotiations, Washington's primary objective was to ensure that the breakup of the USSR did not jeopardize the START agreement. Its recognition of Ukraine was immediately followed by steps to ensure that Ukraine would abide by the terms of the treaty. Indeed, it is likely that the United States issued its invitation to President Leonid Kravchuk to visit Washington in May 1992 in order to set a concrete date to finalize the details of Ukraine's accession to the START Treaty.

Kravchuk's first visit to Washington was structured around a letter that outlined the obligations Ukraine would assume in conjunction with Kyiv's eventual ratification of START. It reiterated Ukraine's intention to become a non-nuclear state and clarified its right to control the non-use of nuclear weapons deployed on its territory—an issue that would reappear throughout the next two years.[13] Another critical commitment was Kravchuk's promise that Ukraine would remove all of the weapons within the seven-year period allowed by the START I Treaty, but that Ukraine will take into account its national security interest in conducting this activity.

Russia, Ukraine, Belarus, and Kazakhstan signed the Lisbon Protocol, which codified Ukraine's, Belarus', and Kazakhstan's accession to the START Treaty on 7 May 1992. The three states thus recognized the "altered political situation resulting from the replacement of the former USSR with a number of independent states."[14] By signing the Protocol, Ukraine agreed to assume the same obligations as the former USSR under the START. This meant that inspection and verification provisions called for by START could continue in the USSR's successor states. In addition, Article V of the Protocol established the critical provision that Ukraine would adhere to the Nuclear Non-Proliferation Treaty (NPT) "in the shortest possible time" and would "take all necessary actions to this end in accordance with their constitutional practices." Thus, the Kravchuk-Bush letter and the Lisbon Protocol codified key points that would continue to appear throughout the negotiations leading to the January 1994 Trilateral agreement.

Throughout this first phase the United States quickly grew to appreciate the importance and influence of the Ukrainian Foreign Ministry. Since the first visit of a senior Ukrainian official to the United States, Defense Minister Kostiantyn Morozov, in April 1992, it was clear that Foreign Ministry officials would play the leading role in the denuclearization process. During this visit the Head of the Arms Control Directorate in the Foreign Ministry, Kostiantyn Hryshchenko, asserted himself—even over the defense minister—as the lead official on issues related to nuclear weapons.[15]

Over time the Ministry of Foreign Affairs, effectively led by Deputy Foreign Minister Borys Tarasyuk, became particularly skilled at negotiating with

the United States and at using the fractured politics of the Ukrainian Parliament
to their advantage. Key executive branch officials, including President
Kravchuk, Foreign Minister Anatoliy Zlenko and Deputy Minister Tarasyuk,
appeared to use some of the Parliament's more radical statements on nuclear
weapons to illustrate that Ukraine's executive branch was in fact pursuing as
tempered and moderate a course as possible. Ukrainian defense officials became involved in the weapons negotiations mainly when the more technical
dismantlement issues became paramount and when military housing problems
emerged on the agenda in 1993.

Stage Two: Leveraging the Weapons (May 1992–January 1994)

The second stage of the denuclearization process began with the completion of
the Lisbon Protocol and ended with the signing of the Trilateral Statement in
January 1994. Though the Lisbon agreement satisfied Washington's initial set
of concerns, namely that Ukraine abide by START and eventually the NPT,
virtually all of the details regarding actual dismantlement remained unresolved.
Of paramount concern to Ukraine was the consolidation of its independence,
the emergence of a stable security situation vis-à-vis Russia, and compensation
for costs associated with the weapons. The weapons on Ukrainian territory
were powerful tools to achieve these ends; they represented tangible emblems
of independence in a nation with few such symbols.

By the summer of 1992 the extraordinary complexity of Ukraine's political
processes became clear to Washington policymakers, and their hopes for early
ratification of START and accession to the NPT dimmed. Ukraine's desire to
be treated as an independent entity precluded any quick resolution of the
nuclear problem. The debate surrounding the ratification of START provided
an opportunity for Kyiv to define itself apart from Russia. Unfortunately, many
of these broader strategic issues became subsumed in the detailed negotiations
over the weapons' removal. The technical negotiations became protracted and
politicized, resulting in a series of frustrating meetings between U.S. and
Ukrainian officials over the next two years. Ukraine became preoccupied with
receiving as much compensation as possible for the weapons, as well as with
stabilizing its relationship with Russia, before the weapons were removed and
their value as leverage was lost.

An important illustration of the growing tension in the Ukrainian-Russian
relationship was the problem of appropriate compensation for the highly enriched uranium (HEU) contained in the warheads of these nuclear weapons—
warheads that were ultimately to be removed from Ukraine and dismantled in
Russia. Ukraine wanted to ensure that by giving up these weapons it would
receive compensation for the highly enriched uranium.[16] In September 1992
the United States and Russia initialed an agreement whereby the U.S. would
purchase the highly enriched uranium contained in Russian nuclear warheads
that were being decommissioned under START. The purpose of this purchase

agreement was to prevent the HEU from reaching other countries and posing a proliferation threat. During these early HEU negotiations, however, the Ukrainian government insisted on receiving 16 percent of the compensation that Russia was to receive.[17] During the HEU talks between Washington and Moscow, Russia vigorously opposed any written commitment that would have clarified the exact terms of compensation to Ukraine, Kazakhstan, and Belarus.

The Department of Defense was aware of this lack of agreement among Russia and the three republics over the HEU compensation issue. The Department argued that the U.S. government should not sign a deal with the Russians until a formula for equitable compensation among Russia, Ukraine, Kazakhstan and Belarus was reached. High-level officials at the Pentagon sympathized with Ukraine's position and doubted Russian intentions to divide the HEU money at a later point. The Pentagon pressured the Energy and State Departments not to finalize the HEU agreement until the compensation issue was resolved.

Some U.S. policymakers at this time argued that the U.S. should not compensate the Ukrainians directly, since that would symbolize Washington's de facto acceptance of Ukrainian control over the weapons. The Defense Department's position ultimately prevailed, however, and Russia was pressured into working out a compensation arrangement before Washington would finalize any HEU purchase. This relatively early intervention by Washington in a Russian-Ukrainian disagreement established a precedent for U.S. involvement in Russian-Ukrainian negotiations that would later culminate in the Trilateral agreement.

When President Bill Clinton came into office following the elections of 1992, the new Administration was determined to move forward on the denuclearization process. It initiated a focused, two-pronged strategy: pressuring the Ukrainian government and Parliament to abide by Ukraine's commitments to ratify START and accede to the NPT, and developing a framework to provide for the removal of the nuclear warheads safely and speedily from Ukraine.

The Administration's new secretary of defense Les Aspin advanced one of these initiatives during his June 1993 trip to Kyiv. He proposed the early deactivation of missile warheads, meaning that Ukraine would remove the dangerous nuclear warheads from the missiles and store them in separate facilities. These warheads would then be transferred to Russia as soon as Ukraine received compensation for the highly enriched uranium they contained. This initiative was designed to begin the warhead removal process independently of the Parliament's prolonged consideration of START and NPT and apart from lengthy debates about the final status of the missiles and silos.[18]

Complicating these goals was the fact that Kyiv was faced with the rather uncomfortable knowledge that the strategic nuclear missiles were of little value militarily. Ukraine's ability to use these weapons on its territory was questionable.[19] The weapons that might actually have provided Ukraine with some real security vis-à-vis Russia had been the shorter-range tactical nuclear weapons, but the last of these had left Ukrainian territory by May 1992.[20] Though Ukraine recognized the very limited military utility of the strategic missiles (which were targeted against the United States), Ukraine quickly moved to assert "administrative control" over them as a means of ensuring command over property on its territory. Furthermore, assertion of ownership of the weapons was necessary to claim rights to their components and for compensation. Kravchuk stated that Ukraine had a right to control the "non-use of weapons on its territory" and that Ukraine would guarantee the physical safety of the weapons.[21] He explained that Ukraine could block an unsanctioned launch of a missile with the use of special signals. He clarified that he did not "strive to obtain the technological ability to enable [an] independent launch [of] the missiles."[22]

Simultaneous with this effort to assert physical control over the weapons was Ukraine's determination to exert control over the negotiations determining their removal. These discussions began in earnest in early 1993 and became known, after their chief Democratic and Republican sponsors in the Senate, as the "Nunn-Lugar talks." The Nunn-Lugar talks were a continuation of discussions about the safe and secure dismantlement of nuclear weapons that had begun between the U.S. and the Soviet Union just prior to the USSR's dissolution. Senators Sam Nunn and Richard Lugar initiated these talks by authorizing funds to provide a beleaguered Gorbachev with resources for the safe dismantlement and transport of nuclear weapons. Secretary of Defense William Perry, who succeeded Les Aspin, and his assistant secretary of defense, Ashton Carter, recognized the value of $400 million authorized by this legislation as important leverage that could be used to speed Ukrainian agreement on the removal and destruction of the strategic missiles.[23]

Two main themes dominated the protracted Nunn-Lugar talks: politics and money. Regarding money, there were serious misconceptions about U.S. promises and actions. Washington withstood much criticism at the time that the U.S. was simply stalling in its provision of real financial aid to Ukraine. The truth is more complicated. While U.S. negotiators did promise large sums of money to Ukraine, Washington could not simply provide Kyiv with cash; U.S. financial assistance was linked to agreements on specific projects on which the money would be spent. For example, compensation for the dismantlement of the SS-19 missiles was linked to the methods by which they would actually be destroyed. Yet for over a year the Ukrainian government was unprepared to make a commitment to specific dismantlement methods. Defense and foreign ministry officials wanted to evaluate every option carefully, including the financial ramifications of each technical procedure. Though some Ukrainian officials acknowledged that the liquid fuel contained in the SS-19s was an environmental hazard, others argued that the fuel could be safely transformed and sold.[24] Failure to achieve a quick resolution of such issues did delay compensation to Ukraine, but this was due to circumstances in both capitals, not ill will on the part of Washington.

Ukraine's highly inflated cost estimates for dismantlement particularly frustrated U.S. officials. This was partly due to the inability of both sides to agree on specific projects and partly due to the general lack of information about the denuclearization process. Estimates coming from Ukrainian deputies and officials ranged from 5 billion dollars, to 2.8 billion dollars, to 175 million dollars.[25] These figures changed so frequently that many in the U.S. government began to take Ukrainian pronouncements less and less seriously.

Further contributing to misunderstandings was the fact that the discussions took place during Ukraine's "state-building" period, in which nascent political structures used the negotiations to assert themselves. Ukrainian executive branch officials tended to use the Parliament's complex deliberation process as leverage to exert pressure on Washington to increase dismantlement aid. Kravchuk was skilled in this technique, as was his successor, Leonid Kuchma. Kravchuk stated that the Ukrainian Parliament had the right to express its views on the nuclear issue just as the U.S. Senate carefully had studied the treaty.[26] At the same time, the Parliament appeared to use its power over START and NPT issues to exert control over the executive branch. Ukrainian deputies and ministers consistently conveyed mixed signals about Ukraine's timetable for the weapons' removal. Yuriy Kostenko, Ukraine's young minister of the environment, articulated a theme that soon became familiar: Ukraine played a role in developing the weapons and deserved compensation on those grounds. Kostenko also argued that "the rate of Ukrainian nuclear disarmament should be interdependent [and the last] strategic missile located on Ukrainian territory should be destroyed when Ukraine's fate has been fused with that of Europe."[27]

Ukraine's negotiating position was also influenced by the presence in Parliament of a very vocal nationalist bloc that often gained the attention of the Western press and kept Kravchuk on the defensive. In April 1993 a bloc of 162 parliamentarians drafted an open letter demanding that Ukraine remain a nuclear state until key compensation issues were resolved. The letter caused much concern throughout the U.S. government and acted as a strong impetus to the Clinton administration's determination to broaden U.S. strategy toward Ukraine. The fate of the weapons was clearly linked to Ukraine's acute economic decline, its increasingly acrimonious relations with Moscow, and internal political discord. It became apparent that Washington's sustained involvement in Ukrainian economic and security issues would be a prerequisite for removal of the weapons. Secretary of Defense Les Aspin's and Ambassador at Large Strobe Talbott's visits to Kyiv in May and June finally established this broader policy approach.

In hearings before Congress, Ambassador Talbott articulated the Administration's commitment to broaden its policy toward Ukraine and reiterated that a democratic, prosperous and secure Ukraine was crucial for stability throughout the former Soviet Union.[28] The Administration also promised to codify this new relationship in a bilateral charter that would be signed once Ukraine acceded to the NPT and ratified START. Another important but often overlooked component in the emerging U.S.-Ukrainian relationship was the strengthening of defense and military contacts between the two countries. In July 1993 the Pentagon and Ukraine's Ministry of Defense signed a Memorandum of Understanding establishing a framework for extensive defense and military contacts between the two institutions. This event highlighted Washington's commitment to help Ukraine restructure its conventional defense forces.

In October 1993 Secretary of State Warren Christopher traveled to Kyiv to pressure the Ukrainian government and Parliament to ratify START and accede to the NPT. He and Foreign Minister Zlenko signed an agreement calling for the dismantling of the 130 SS-19 missiles. Washington agreed to pay 175 million dollars for this process and an additional 155 million dollars in economic aid. During this period some Ukrainian officials began to state that Ukraine should separate consideration of START and NPT and should consider the SS-24 missiles in a separate category than the older SS-19 weapons. The SS-24 missiles had been assembled in Ukrainian plants and many Ukrainians viewed these missiles as important parts of Ukraine's heritage.

The main elements of the denuclearization process began to fall into place by the fall of 1993. Washington had broadened its policy toward Ukraine, and Ukrainian executive branch officials were managing to appease the U.S. by beginning the early removal of the most dangerous components of the weapons—the nuclear warheads. Ukrainian officials also managed to avoid direct confrontation with the Parliament by delaying concrete action on missile dismantlement, thereby allowing the Parliament to continue deliberations on the treaties.

On 18 November 1993 the Parliament finally acted, albeit ambiguously, on START. It voted 254 to 9 (out of 440 deputies) to ratify START and the Lisbon Protocol, but with the reservation that Ukraine would not yet accede to the NPT as a non-nuclear state.[29] Reportedly, the Parliament was concerned that the NPT did not contain any provisions for dealing with successor states to the USSR. It also insisted that no action be taken on any of its decisions until Ukraine received proper compensation. Most troubling to Washington, however, were the Parliament's statements that Ukraine would destroy only thirty-six percent of the launchers on its territory and forty-two percent of the warheads. Deputies apparently wanted to treat the SS-24 missiles separately.

Overall, the Parliament demanded compensation for the tactical weapons removed from Ukraine the previous year, foreign financial assistance for disarmament, binding security guarantees, and recognition of Ukraine's existing borders. The statement also reaffirmed Ukraine's ownership of the weapons. These demands essentially codified the key elements of what would soon become the Trilateral Statement: security guarantee, financial compensation, and compensation for the fissile material which the U.S. was paying Russia to remove. The vote revealed Kyiv's determination to develop a comprehensive approach to denuclearization that would address central Ukrainian security concerns.

As news of the Parliament's vote reached Washington, there was a great deal of internal government debate about appropriate U.S. responses.[30] Some advocated taking a tougher line toward the statement, citing concerns about the statement's implications for the non-proliferation treaty. Key National Security Council officials ultimately prevailed, however, pushing the Administration to respond positively. The government publicly interpreted the events as concrete action on START and noted that bilateral talks would continue to resolve outstanding issues. This was the message conveyed to the Ukrainian Embassy in Washington and by Ambassador William Miller in Kyiv.

This November vote must be understood within the context of deteriorating Ukrainian-Russian relations. Throughout 1993 tensions between Russia and Ukraine were high. The Massandra summit in September revealed disturbing implications for Ukraine, namely that bilateral resolution of important issues like the Black Sea Fleet and compensation for the warheads would be very difficult to achieve.[31] Furthermore, tensions over Crimea were constant, with Russian Duma deputies publicly questioning the status of Sevastopol and even asserting Russian ownership of the city. In addition, Moscow was issuing statements about its determination to protect Russians living abroad.

During this period Moscow also appeared to be trying to undermine the West's confidence in Ukraine by accusing Kyiv of maintaining unsafe facilities for the storage of the nuclear warheads. Ukrainian Deputy Foreign Minister Tarasyuk dismissed these accusations as false and as examples of Russian pressure on Ukraine. And indeed, Washington did not gather enough evidence to substantiate Russia's claims. These rising tensions reinforced Ukraine's determination to link a resolution of the nuclear weapons issue to an improvement in Ukrainian-Russian relations as a whole and to keep the U.S. involved in this complicated process.

As awareness of this important linkage grew in Washington, the United States intensified its negotiations over the key elements of the Trilateral agreement. First, the United States worked to influence the Russian Foreign Ministry to accede to security guarantee language acceptable to the Ukrainians. The Russians were pressing strongly for language that would have guaranteed Ukraine's borders only within the context of the CIS; this position was unacceptable to Ukraine, and Washington eventually persuaded Moscow to accept language based on previously established principles.[32] Throughout this process, the Ukrainians used the phrase "security guarantees," while the U.S. used the word "assurances." This issue was never openly resolved and the differences in phraseology were artfully dodged by negotiators. Parallel to these talks were the ongoing discussions about the HEU compensation.

The final Trilateral Statement was signed by the presidents of the United States, Ukraine and Russia in Moscow on 14 January 1994. The main provisions of the agreement consisted of three main elements.[33] First, the agreement outlined the timetable for the transfer of the nuclear warheads from Ukraine to Russia. Ukraine agreed to complete this process over the seven-year period contained in the START agreement. Kyiv also agreed to the early deactivation of the SS-24 warheads. Second, Russia agreed to compensate Ukraine for the HEU removed from the warheads. In exchange for this HEU, Ukraine would receive low enriched uranium rods from Russia.[34] The U.S. underwrote this exchange with an advance payment of 60 million dollars to Russia so it could begin immediate shipment of the much needed LEU fuel rods to Ukraine. Third, the agreement contained security assurances for Ukraine that would be provided by the U.S., Russia, and the United Kingdom once Ukraine fully acceded to the NPT as a non-nuclear state. These assurances provided the strongest language on the recognition of Ukraine's existing borders with Russia.[35] Finally, the agreement pledged an expansion of technical and financial assistance. Thus, the Trilateral agreement had forced Russia to concede Washington's involvement in Moscow's relations with Kyiv. In doing so, Moscow was compelled, through this process, to recognize the equality of all the signatories. The agreement stated that each country would deal with each other as "full and equal partners."

Stage Three: The Trilateral Legacy

Though the Trilateral Statement was a momentous achievement, the denuclearization process was by no means complete. The third phase only began following the January declaration. A number of key challenges remained. First, the missiles and nuclear warheads were still located on Ukrainian soil. Second, the Parliament had yet to accede to the NPT treaty. And third, Ukraine had not yet moved closer to resolving its real security problems: it continued to suffer from serious economic weakness that would continue to keep Ukraine vulnerable to Russian pressure. Indeed, Ukraine had little choice in accepting the Trilateral agreement: it remained in a weak position so long as President Kravchuk did not embark on an economic reform program. Nonetheless, the January agreement provided a needed mechanism for stabilizing Kyiv's relations with Moscow.

For the most part, the removal of the nuclear warheads proceeded relatively smoothly. Early problems regarding the delivery of nuclear fuel rods from Russia to Ukraine were resolved, partly with Washington's assistance. The main obstacle to smooth U.S.-Ukrainian relations was the Ukrainian Parliament's continued resistance to the NPT Treaty. This may have been due to its desire to preserve some negotiating leverage over Russia, as efforts to reach a bilateral friendship treaty had again failed and the Black Sea Fleet problem remained unresolved and tense.

During the spring of 1994 U.S. diplomacy focused on pressuring Ukraine to accede to the NPT by the time of the NPT review conference in early 1995. That was Vice-President Al Gore's main message during his August stopover in Kyiv.[36] Key deputies in the Parliament, however, remained reluctant to accede to the NPT until security guarantees were forthcoming. The situation was a bit of a conundrum: the U.S. had provided Ukraine with such assurances in the Trilateral agreement, but that agreement specified that the assurances would not go into affect until Ukraine had acceded to the NPT. This issue illustrates the often cyclical and frustrating nature of the entire denuclearization process.

The United States was careful to complement this NPT focus with repeated commitments to assist Ukraine with economic reform. During President Kravchuk's visit to Washington in March 1994, he and President Clinton agreed to an expanded economic assistance package that would provide up to $700 million to Ukraine.[37] By mid-1994 Ukraine was the fourth largest recipient of U.S. aid. Most recently, by October 1997, about $440 million in Nunn-Lugar assistance had actually been spent in Ukraine. Finally, under strong pressure from the newly elected President Leonid Kuchma, on 16 November 1994, the Parliament agreed to accede to the NPT.

Throughout these discussions about NPT accession, serious defense and military contacts between the United States and Ukraine were taking place. Of the former Soviet republics, Ukraine had developed the most extensive program of defense contacts. Ukrainian units participated in joint exercises with U.S. and NATO troops throughout the 1994–97 period. And by the end of 1997, the U.S. had given its financial and technical support to the creation of a Polish-Ukrainian battalion.

Though all of the nuclear warheads had been removed from Ukraine by June 1996, missiles and launchers remained on Ukrainian territory. By the end of 1997, approximately fifty-four of the SS-19 missiles remained in their silos, with eight of these missiles in storage.[38] All of the SS-24 missiles also remained in Ukraine. Only in May 1997—five years after talks with Ukraine began—did Ukraine finally agree to remove these missiles from their silos for dismantlement. The Cooperative Threat Reduction program (the Nunn-Lugar program) has continued to work with the Ukrainian government to remove the SS-24 missiles from their silos, place them in storage and destroy the silos. This task is likely not to be completed until the year 2001, which is still within the START time frame.

Conclusion

Five years of intensive negotiations on denuclearization between the United States and Ukraine had direct effects on the diplomatic, economic, and security status of Ukraine. The slow process of convincing Ukraine to withdraw its nuclear missiles compelled Washington to deal seriously with Ukraine as an independent state and to recognize the implications of an independent Ukraine for the future of the region as a whole. Ukraine in turn developed a rather sophisticated strategy that centered on the removal of the weapons in exchange for a series of diplomatic and economic demands. The stages of the negotiation process reveal how the weapons became the tools through which Ukraine asserted itself on the world stage.

The history of Ukraine's denuclearization is also significant for the story it does *not* tell about Washington's relationship with Moscow. While the United States viewed the nuclear weapons as an important source of leverage vis-à-vis the shaping of the emerging Ukrainian state, they were rarely viewed as a potentially valuable source of leverage with which to shape and influence the newly emerging Russian state. Indeed, American-Ukrainian "collusion" to use the weapons to influence Moscow was non-existent—an interesting example of possible opportunities missed and a testament to the extraordinary strong status quo bias among the arms control community that dominated the denucleariza-tion process.

Washington consistently argued that Ukraine's security would be enhanced by the removal of the nuclear weapons. Insetad of remaining a nuclear power, Kyiv was encouraged to pursue a stable relationship with Moscow, to focus on the development of bilateral ties with the West, and to strengthen its economy. In retrospect, Ukraine achieved two out of three of these objectives. Unfortu-nately, despite the success of the denuclearization process, Ukraine's troubled economy remains Kyiv's enduring security challenge.

NOTES

1. For more information about the Soviet nuclear legacy in Ukraine see: Harriet Fast Scott, "The Third Largest Nuclear Power," *Air Force Magazine* October 1994; also see *Nuclear Successor States of the Soviet Union* (Washington, DC, May 1994), 10; and "Prospects for Ukrainian Denuclearization after the Moscow Summit Trilateral Statement," Arms Control Association Press Release, Friday 28 January 1994, Washington, DC.

2. For figures on Ukraine's inheritance see "FSU Strategic Nuclear Weapons Outside Russia," *Arms Control Association Press Release* Friday 28 January 1994, Washington, DC. See also Jacob W. Kipp, "The Ukraine's Socio-Economic Crisis," *Military Review* March 1994: 11–12.

3. For a relatively earlier but comprehensive explanation of Ukraine's objectives see Alexander Goncharenko, "Ukraine's National Security and Perspectives of Military Build-Up," Rand-Hoover Symposium on The Role of the Military Sectors in the Economies of the Republics (Washington, DC, RAND, 16–17 November 1992).

4. See Sherman Garnett, *Keystone in the Arch: Ukraine in the Emerging Security Environment,* (Washington, DC, 1997), 113–15. Garnett's study describes three phases, but this paper will make an effort to build and expand upon his categories. He describes the first phase as one of "romanticism and declarations," which lasted until mid-1992. The second was from May 1992–January 1994 and the third began after the Trilateral Statement was signed in January 1994.

5. United Nations, Institute for Disarmament Research, *Ukraine's Non-Nuclear Option* (Research Paper No. 14, 1992), 22 and 23. Ukraine's July, 1990 Declaration of Sovereignty and the "Statement by the Verkhovna Rada of Ukraine on the Non-Nuclear Status of Ukraine" from 24 October 1991 are reprinted here.

6. The term "in the shortest possible time" was a phrase used in the Lisbon Protocol and was repeated very often in conversations with Ukrainian officials. Lee Hocktader, "Ukraine is Clinging to Nuclear Arsenal Despite US Prodding," *The Washington Post* 31 October 1993: A25.

7. James A. Baker, III, *The Politics of Diplomacy* (New York, 1995), 658–68 and 514–39.

8. The White House, Office of the Press Secretary, *Remarks by the President in Address to the Supreme Soviet of the Ukrainian Soviet Socialist Republic* (1 August 1991), 2–4.

9. Baker, 659.

10. Ibid., 658.

11. Information about these meetings was obtained through the author's conversations with key senior level officials in the Bush administration.

12. John Mearsheimer, "The Case for a Ukrainian Nuclear Deterrent," *Foreign Affairs* Summer 1993: 50–66.

13. One example of this assertion of control was Ukraine's unilateral stoppage of the removal of tactical nuclear weapons from Ukraine to Russia in March 1992. The process resumed after a short time and Ukraine's concerns about the safety of the weapons were alleviated.

14. Text of Lisbon Protocol taken from author's copy of the agreement.

15. The author participated in the visit of Ukraine's first defense minister, Konstiantyn Morozov, and witnessed the primary role played by Mr. Hryshchenko regarding arms control and denuclearization issues. Hryshchenko's role remained prominent on these issues for the next three years.

16. This discussion is based on the notes and recollections of the author, who was involved in the U.S. government discussions on how to create an equitable arrangement to resolve the HEU issue.

17. At this time the figure of 16% was often used by Ukraine in its claims to receive a proportion of the USSR's assets.

18. Nuclear missiles are, generally, composed of three main components: warheads, which contain the nuclear material; the ballistic missiles that carry and deliver these warheads; and the silos that house the nuclear tipped missiles. These three components are treated distinctly by the START Treaty and by most of the discussions noted in this paper.

19. Martin J. DeWing, *The Ukrainian Nuclear Arsenal: Problems of Command, Control and Maintenance* (Monterey, CA, October 1993).

20. The reduction of tactical nuclear weapons had begun as part of a 1991 agreement between Presidents Bush and Gorbachev to reduce tactical nuclear weapons. This process managed to continue as Ukraine was consolidating its independence in early 1992. The author's distinct impression at that time was that key members of the new Ukrainian government, like Defense Minister Morozov, were caught off-guard by the speedy removal of the tactical nuclear weapons.

21. Foreign Broadcast Information Service (FBIS)-SOV-92-245, 21 December 1992: 52.

22. See Kravchuk's statement that "no launching may be carried out except on the order of the President of the Russian Federation," FBIS-SOV-92-245, 21 December 1992: 53.

23. It should be noted that not all members of the new Administration were as progressive regarding Ukraine: one official advocated essentially the

slow freezing of Ukraine, by encouraging Russia to cut off energy supplies until Kyiv relinquished the weapons.

24. This example is taken from the author's direct experience in discussions with officials on both sides—frustrated U.S. government officials and U.S. defense contractors as well as Ukrainian representatives.

25. "Deputies Discuss Ratification of START I," FBIS-SOV-93-219, 16 November 1993: 70. Foreign Minister Anatoliy Zlenko at times also used the $2.3 billion figure: "Zlenko: Non-Nuclear Status Requires Massive Aid," FBIS-SOV-93-216, 10 November 1993: 72.

26. "Kravchuk Reiterates Nuclear-Free Concept," FBIS-SOV-92-245, 21 December 1992: 52–53.

27. *The Ukrainian Weekly* 51(21) 23 May 1993: 2.

28. "The United States and Ukraine: Broadening the Relationship," U.S. Department of State, *Dispatch* (Washington, DC: U.S. Department of State, 5 July 1993).

29. Ustina Markus, "Recent Defense Developments in Ukraine," *RFE/RL Research Report* 28 January 1994: 31–32.

30. The author was a participant in these debates, along with her State Department, Defense Department, and National Security Council counterparts and colleagues.

31. Roman Solchanyk, "The Ukrainian-Russian Summit: Problems and Prospects," *RFE/RL Research Report* 2 July 1993: 27–30. See also Marta Kolomayets, "Russia renews pressure, threats regarding Ukraine's nuclear arms," *Ukrainian Weekly* 51(46) 14 November 1993: 1.

32. These principles were confirmed by the Conference on Security and Cooperation in Europe, now called the Organization for Security and Cooperation in Europe.

33. The Statement is reprinted in "Select Documents from the US-Russian Summit," *Arms Control Today* January/February 1994: 21.

34. These low enriched uranium rods could be used as fuel for Ukraine's nuclear energy reactors and thus were a form of much needed energy by Ukraine. See "Annex to Trilateral Statement," *Arms Control Today* January/February 1994: 21–22.

35. The assurances are reprinted in Sherman Garnett, "Ukraine's Decision to Join NPT," *Arms Control Today* January/February 1995: 11.

36. Marta Kolomayets, United Press International, 2 August 1994, "US Vice President Visits Ukraine." Ukraine had agreed to certain NPT provisions, like the agreement not to transfer key missile components to certain states. See also AP, 13 May 1994, "Gore and Ukrainian official sign Nuclear Pact."

37. "Fact Sheet: US Assistance to Ukraine," U.S. Department of State, *Dispatch,* vol. 5 (Washington, DC: U.S. Department of State, 21 November 1994), 776.

38. Conversation with Laura Holgate, Director, U.S. Department of Defense Cooperative Threat Reduction Office, 23 October 1997.

Supporting Documentation

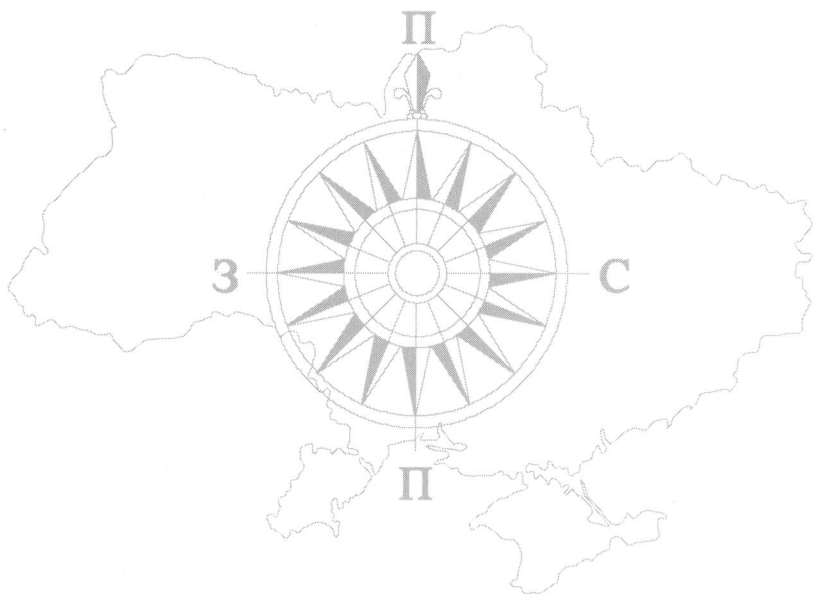

Treaty between the Ukrainian Soviet Socialist Republic and the Russian Soviet Federative Socialist Republic

The Ukrainian Soviet Socialist Republic and the Russian Soviet Federative Socialist Republic, hereinafter referred to as the High Contracting Parties,

on the basis of the Declaration on the state sovereignty of Ukraine of 16 July 1990 and the Declaration on the state sovereignty of the Russian Soviet Federative Socialist Republic of 12 June 1990,

desiring to build democratic states of Ukraine and Russia based on the rule of law,

intending to develop their inter-state relations on the basis of principles of sovereign equality, non-intervention in internal affairs, renunciation of the application of force or of economic methods of pressure, resolution of contested problems through conciliation, as well as other generally recognized principles and norms of international law,

considering that the continued development and strengthening of relations of friendship, good-neighborliness, and mutually beneficial cooperation between them correspond to the essential national interests of the peoples of both states and serve the cause of peace and security,

guided by the desire to develop the friendship of sovereign states,

affirming their dedication to the goals and principles of the United Nations Charter, the Helsinki Final Act, and other documents of the Conference on Security and Cooperation in Europe,

obligating themselves to observe generally recognized international norms on the rights of individuals and peoples, have agreed to the following:

Article 1

The High Contracting Parties recognize each other as sovereign states and obligate themselves to abstain from actions that could harm the state sovereignty of the other Party.

Article 2

The High Contracting Parties guarantee their citizens equal rights and freedoms regardless of their nationality or other differences.

The High Contracting Parties guarantee citizens of the USSR living on the territories of the Ukrainian Soviet Socialist Republic and the Russian Soviet Federative Socialist Republic, after the Parties have adopted laws on citizenship, the right to retain citizenship of the Party on the territory of which they are living.

Questions of obtaining citizenship of one of the Parties by persons living on the territory of the other Party will be resolved by an appropriate Agreement taking into account the legislation of the Parties on citizenship.

Article 3

Each of the High Contracting Parties guarantees citizens of the other Party, and also persons without citizenship who are living on its territory, regardless of their national origins or other differences, civil, political, social, economic, and cultural rights and freedoms in accord with generally recognized international norms of human rights.

Each of the High Contracting Parties protects the rights of its citizens living on the territory of the other Party, and renders them comprehensive assistance and support in accord with generally recognized principles of international law.

Article 4

Desiring to promote the expression, preservation, and development of the ethnic, cultural, linguistic, and religious identities of the national minorities inhabiting their territories, and the established unique ethnocultural regions, the High Contracting Parties take them under their protection.

Article 5

The High Contracting Parties shall develop the cooperation of their peoples and states in the branches of politics, economics, culture, health care, ecology, science, technology, trade, and in the humanitarian and other areas on the basis of equality and mutual benefit, shall promote extensive exchange of information, and shall conscientiously and unwaveringly honor their mutual obligations.

The Parties consider it necessary to conclude appropriate agreements on cooperation.

Article 6

The High Contracting Parties recognize and respect the territorial integrity of the Ukrainian Soviet Socialist Republic and of the Russian Soviet Federative Socialist Republic within their presently existing borders within the USSR.

Article 7

The High Contracting Parties recognize the necessity of a system of collective security, including the collaboration of both states in the area of defense and security, taking into account the desire of both Parties for the further strengthening of peace.

Article 8

The High Contracting Parties recognize that the sphere of their mutual activity, which is carried out on an equal basis through common coordinating institutions of the Parties, includes the following:

—joint action in foreign affairs;
—cooperation in the formation and development of a common economic space, and a common European and Eurasian market, in the area of tariff policy;
—the administration of a system of transportation and communication, including satellite communication and telecommunications;
—cooperation in the area of environmental protection on their territories, including measures to minimize the consequences of the Chornobyl catastrophe, and participation in the creation of an all-encompassing international system of environmental safety;
—the issue of migration policy; and
—the struggle with organized and international crime.

Article 9

The High Contracting Parties recognize that each of them has the right to determine the types and forms of property and to regulate property relations on their territories.

The legal status of state property and property of juridical persons and citizens of one Party that are located on the territory of the other Party is regulated by appropriate agreements.

The High Contracting Parties agree that all questions regarding objects that qualify as all-Union property shall be resolved through separate agreements based on the legislative acts of the Parties on the protection of the economic foundations of sovereignty.

Article 10

The economic relations of the High Contracting parties are regulated by agreements with granting of most favored nation status. The Parties guarantee the development of economic, commercial, and scientific-technical relations on the following levels:

—the organs of state power and administration;
—the banks and the financial system;
—the organs of territorial (municipal) self-administration;
—enterprises, associations, organizations, and institutions;
—joint Ukrainian-Russian and Russian-Ukrainian enterprises and organizations;
—individual entrepreneurs.

The High Contracting Parties have agreed that the concrete mechanisms of inter-economic relations, commercial exchange, all forms of communication and transportation, and also questions of economic and informational coopera- tion shall be regulated by intergovernmental agreements. The Parties shall not unilaterally apply economic measures that destabilize or harm the other Party.

Article 11

The High Contracting Parties shall conclude intergovernmental agreements on mutual supply and services, payments, the prices and circulation of nego- tiable instruments, and also on the dates of conversion to mutual accounting at world prices. This list of agreements is not exhaustive.

The High Contracting Parties obligate themselves to take steps towards coordinating their price policies.

Article 12

The High Contracting Parties guarantee transportation operations for transit through maritime, river, and air ports, railways, the road network, and pipelines located on their territories.

The conditions and procedures for implementation of transportation opera- tions for transit are determined by special agreements of the Parties.

Article 13

The High Contracting Parties reserve the right to conclude additional trea- ties or agreements on cooperation in all other spheres of inter-state relations.

Article 14

The High Contracting Parties consider it expedient to carry out the exchange of plenipotentiary representations.

The procedure for exchange of representations, and their status, shall be regulated by a special agreement.

Article 15

Disputes regarding the interpretation and implementation of the norms of this Treaty are subject to resolution by way of negotiation.

Article 16

This Treaty does not affect the obligations of the High Contracting Parties towards third-party states, nor their right to conclude treaties with third parties concerning their participation in the sphere of joint activity of the Parties determined by this Treaty, and in the sphere of collective security.

Article 17

The High Contracting Parties shall conduct regular bilateral consultations and discussions on issues of the performance of this Treaty.

With the aim of implementing this Treaty, the Parties consider it necessary to also create a permanently functioning interparliamentary commission on cooperation.

Article 18

Each of the High Contracting Parties reserves the right to initiate, in the framework of consultations, discussions on the expediency of prolonging the effect of this Treaty or of separate articles thereof.

The provisions of this Treaty may be supplemented or amended by mutual agreement of the High Contracting Parties.

Article 19

This Treaty is subject to ratification.

The exchange of ratification documents shall take place in the city of Moscow.

This Treaty enters into force on the day of exchange of documents of ratification.

Article 20

This Treaty remains in force for ten years. Its effect shall thereafter be automatically extended for another ten-year period unless either Party announces its intention to denounce it by way of written notification no later than six months before the end of the period of validity of the Treaty.

Concluded in the city of Kyiv on 19 November 1990 in two exemplars, each in the Ukrainian and Russian languages, both texts having equal effect.

For the Ukrainian Soviet
Socialist Republic
President of the Supreme Soviet
of the Ukrainian Soviet
Socialist Republic

For the Russian Soviet
Federative Socialist Republic
President of the Supreme Soviet
of the Russian Soviet
Federative Socialist Republic

L. KRAVCHUK

B. YELTSIN

[Russian and Ukrainian originals. Translated by Andrew D. Sorokowski.]

Agreement on the Creation of the Commonwealth of Independent States

We, the Republic of Belarus, the Russian Federation (RSFSR), and Ukraine, as founding states of the Union of Soviet Socialist Republics, which signed the Treaty of Union of 1922, hereinafter referred to as the High Contracting Parties, hereby state that the Union of Soviet Socialist Republics, as a subject of international law and as a geopolitical reality, ceases to exist.

Based on the historical communality of our peoples and the ties that have developed among them, taking into account the bilateral treaties concluded among the High Contracting Parties,

desiring to build democratic states under the rule of law,

intending to develop our relations on the basis of mutual recognition and respect for state sovereignty, the inalienable right to self-determination, the principles of equal rights and non-interference in internal affairs, the renunciation of the use of force or of economic or any other methods of coercion whatsoever, the resolution of disputes by methods of conciliation, and other generally recognized principles and norms of international law,

considering that the further development and strengthening of relations of friendship, good-neighborliness, and mutually beneficial cooperation among our states correspond to the fundamental national interests of our peoples and serve the cause of peace and security,

reaffirming our loyalty to the aims and principles of the United Nations Charter, the Helsinki Final Act, and other documents of the Conference on Security and Cooperation in Europe,

obligating ourselves to observe generally recognized international norms of the rights of individuals and peoples,

have agreed to the following:

Article 1

The High Contracting Parties hereby create the Commonwealth of Independent States.

Article 2

The High Contracting Parties guarantee their citizens, regardless of their nationality or other distinctions, equal rights and freedoms. Each of the High Contracting Parties guarantees the citizens of the other Parties, as well as persons without citizenship who are living on its territory, regardless of their nationality or other distinctions, civic, political, social, economic, and cultural rights and freedoms in accord with generally recognized international norms of human rights.

Article 3

Desiring to promote the expression, preservation, and development of the ethnic, cultural, linguistic, and religious identity of the national minorities inhabiting their territories, and the unique ethnocultural regions that have developed, the High Contracting Parties take them under their protection.

Article 4

The High Contracting Parties shall develop the cooperation of their peoples and states on a basis of equal rights and mutual benefit in the areas of politics, economics, culture, education, health care, environmental protection, science, commerce, in the humanitarian and other fields; shall promote an extensive exchange of information; and shall conscientiously and unwaveringly honor their mutual obligations.

The Parties consider it essential to conclude agreements on cooperation in these areas.

Article 5

The High Contracting Parties recognize and respect each other's territorial integrity and the inviolability of existing borders within the framework of the Commonwealth.

They guarantee open borders, and the freedom of movement of citizens and exchange of information within the framework of the Commonwealth.

Article 6

The states members of the Commonwealth shall collaborate in safeguarding international peace and security and applying effective measures for the reduction of arms and military spending. They aspire to the elimination of all nuclear arms, and to general and full disarmament under strict international control.

The Parties shall respect each other's aspirations to attain the status of a nuclear-free zone and a neutral state.

The states members of the Commonwealth shall preserve and support a common military-strategic space under joint command, including single control of nuclear arms, the manner of implementation of which is to be determined by a special agreement.

They also jointly guarantee the necessary conditions for the deployment, functioning, and material and social welfare of strategic armed forces. The Parties obligate themselves to conduct a policy by consensus in matters of the social insurance and pension benefits for military personnel and their families.

Article 7

The High Contracting Parties recognize that the following belong to the sphere of their joint activity, which is carried out on the basis of equal rights by joint coordinating institutions of the Commonwealth:

—the coordination of foreign-policy activity;
—cooperation in the formation and development of a common economic space, a pan-European and Eurasian market, in the area of customs policy;
—cooperation in the development of transportation and communications systems;
—cooperation in the sphere of environmental protection and participation in the creation of an all-encompassing international system of environmental safety;
—issues of migration policy; and
—the struggle with organized crime.

Article 8

The Parties are aware of the global nature of the Chornobyl catastrophe and obligate themselves to unite and coordinate their efforts to minimize and overcome its effects.

With this aim, they have agreed to conclude a special Agreement, which will take into account the gravity of the consequences of the catastrophe.

Article 9

Conflicts regarding the interpretation and application of the norms of this Agreement are subject to resolution by way of negotiation among the appropriate organs, and where necessary, on the level of the heads of governments and states.

Article 10

Each of the High Contracting Parties reserves the right to terminate the effect of this Agreement or of individual articles thereof by notifying the parties to the Agreement one year in advance.

The terms of this Agreement can be supplemented or amended by mutual agreement of the High Contracting Parties.

Article 11

From the moment of signing of this Agreement, application of the norms of third-party states, including the former Union of Soviet Socialist Republics, is prohibited on the territories of the states that have signed it.

Article 12

The High Contracting Parties guarantee the performance of international obligations arising for them from the treaties and agreements of the former Union of Soviet Socialist Republics.

Article 13

This Agreement does not affect the obligations of the High Contracting Parties towards third-party states.

This Agreement is open to accession by all states belonging to the former Union of Soviet Socialist Republics, as well as by other states that share the aims and principles of this Agreement.

Article 14

The official place of residence of the coordinating organs of the Commonwealth is the city of Minsk.

The activity of the organs of the former Union of Soviet Socialist Republics on the territories of the states belonging to the Commonwealth is terminated.

Concluded in the city of Minsk on 8 December 1991 in three exemplars, each in the Belarusian, Russian, and Ukrainian languages, all three texts having equal force.

For the Republic of Belarus

S. SHUSHKEVICH
V. KEBICH

For the RSFSR

B. YELTSIN
G. BURBULIS

For Ukraine

L. KRAVCHUK
V. FOKIN

[Translated from the Ukrainian by Andrew D. Sorokowski.]

Reservations of the Supreme Soviet of Ukraine to the Agreement on the Creation of the Commonwealth of Independent States,

signed in the name of Ukraine on 8 December 1991 in Minsk

1) In accord with Article 3, each of the High Contracting Parties, desiring to promote the expression, preservation, and development of the ethnic, cultural, linguistic, and religious identity of the national minorities inhabiting its territory, and the unique ethnocultural regions that have developed, takes them under its protection.

2) in accord with Article 5 of the Treaty, the High Contracting Parties recognize and respect each other's territorial integrity and the inviolability of existing borders existing among them.

They guarantee on a mutual basis the openness of the state borders existing among them to unhindered contacts of their citizens and the transfer of information in the framework of the Commonwealth, and with this aim they shall promptly develop an appropriate legal basis.

3) In accord with Article 6, the States members of the Commonwealth, in reforming the groupings of armed forces of the former Union of Soviet Socialist Republics deployed on their territories and in forming on their basis their own Armed Forces, will cooperate in ensuring international peace and security and in taking effective measures to reduce armaments and military spending. They aspire to the liquidation of all nuclear arms and to general and total disarmament under strict international control.

The Parties will respect the desire of the participants in the Agreement that wish to attain the status of a nuclear-free or neutral state.

Until the total destruction of nuclear arms on their territories, the States members of the Commonwealth shall preserve and maintain under joint command a common military-strategic space and single control of nuclear arms, the procedure for the implementation of which is determined by a special agreement. The effect of this provision terminates with regard to any Party on the territory of which nuclear arms will be destroyed in accordance with an international agreement and under international control.

They also jointly guarantee the necessary conditions for the deployment, functioning, and the material and social security of strategic armed forces.

The Parties obligate themselves to conduct a policy by consensus in matters of social insurance and pension benefits for military personnel and their families.

4) in accord with Article 7 of the Agreement, the High Contracting Parties recognize that the following belong to the sphere of their activity, which is carried out on the basis of equal rights by coordinating institutions of the Commonwealth:

—consultations in the area of foreign policy;

—the development of a common economic space, participation in the pan-European and Eurasian markets, and customs policy;

—the development of their own systems of transportation and communication;

—protection of the environment, and participation in the creation of an all-encompassing international system of environmental safety; and

—the struggle with organized crime.

Coordinating institutions are formed on the basis of parity, and their recommendations are adopted by consensus.

5) in accord with Article 5, disputes with regard to the interpretation and application of the norms of this Agreement are subject to resolution by way of negotiations on the basis of international law.

6) in accord with Article 10, each of the High Contracting Parties reserves the right to suspend or terminate the effect of this Agreement or of individual Articles thereof, by notifying the parties to the Agreement one year in advance.

The terms of this Agreement can be supplemented or amended by mutual agreement of the High Contracting Parties.

7) Article 11 of the Agreement is tautological and is to be excluded.

8) in accord with Article 12, the High Contracting Parties guarantee the performance, in accord with their national legislation, of international obligations arising for them from the treaties of the former Union of Soviet Socialist Republics.

9) this Agreement is subject to ratification and enters into force from the moment of exchange of documents of ratification. The exchange of documents of ratification shall take place in the city of Minsk. The depositary of the Agreement shall be the Government of the Republic of Belarus.

10) to paragraph 1 of the preamble, after the words "Union of Soviet Socialist Republics as" insert the word "state."

11) to paragraph 3 of the preamble, after the word "to build" insert the word "independent."

12) to paragraph 4 of the preamble, after the words "in internal affairs" insert the words "territorial integrity and inviolability of borders."

Head of the Supreme Soviet
of Ukraine

I. PLIUSHCH
city of Kyiv
10 December 1991

Taking into account the importance for the fate of Ukraine of the content of the Agreement signed in Minsk, it is proposed to add to the Reservations which the Supreme Soviet of Ukraine has already adopted one more reservation:

1. To change the name of the Agreement, excluding the work "creation" and writing the word "Commonwealth" with a small initial letter. The title is to read as follows: "Agreement on a commonwealth of independent States."

2. In accord with this, to amend Article 1:
The High Contracting Parties adopt a decision on the commonwealth of independent States.

3. Article 6 is to begin with the words "The High Contracting Parties" instead of "The states members of the Commonwealth."

4. The third paragraph of Article 6 is to begin with the words "The High Contracting Parties" instead of "The states members of the Commonwealth."

Adopted by the Supreme Soviet of Ukraine on 12 December 1991

[Ukrainian original. Translated by Andrew D. Sorokowski.]

Treaty between the Polish Republic and Ukraine on Good-Neighborliness, Friendly Relations, and Cooperation

The Polish Republic and Ukraine, hereinafter referred to as the Parties,

—respecting the aims and principles of the United Nations Charter, the Final Act of the Conference on Security and Cooperation in Europe, the Paris Charter for a New Europe, and other documents of European cooperation;

—reaffirming respect for human rights and fundamental freedoms, and principles of democracy and justice;

—desiring to contribute to the building of a just and peaceful European order, based on general European norms and mechanisms in the area of security;

—appreciating the significance of friendly Polish-Ukrainian relations for the building of European solidarity;

—conscious of their common responsibility for peace, security, understanding, and cooperation on the European continent, including Central Europe;

—convinced that the positive elements of the rich history of Polish-Ukrainian relations will promote increased cooperation between these fraternal peoples;

—taking into account that the Poles and Ukrainians who have lived for centuries on the territories of each Party contribute significantly to the development of both states and to the culture of both peoples, as well as to that of Europe;

—conscious that with the return of full political independence to the Polish state and with the establishment of an independent Ukrainian state, Polish-Ukrainian relations have entered a qualitatively new period;

—expressing satisfaction at the establishment of diplomatic relations between them;

have agreed as follows:

Article 1

In the new political situation, the Parties obligate themselves to develop their relations in the spirit of friendship, cooperation, mutual respect, understanding, trust, and good-neighborliness on the basis of international law, including the principles of sovereign equality, non-application of force or the threat of force, inviolability of borders, territorial integrity, the peaceful settlement of disputes, non-interference in internal affairs, self-determination of nations, respect for human rights and fundamental freedoms, and the good-faith performance of obligations arising from international law.

Article 2

The Parties consider the existing and delineated border between them as inviolable and affirm that they have no territorial claims against each other and shall not advance any such claims in the future.

Article 3

1. With the aim of strengthening security, trust, stability, and cooperation, the Parties shall actively cooperate in the appropriate European mechanisms and structures on the basis of the Final Act of the Conference on Security and Cooperation in Europe, the Paris Charter for a New Europe, the Treaty on Conventional Armed Forces in Europe, the Convention on Nonproliferation of Nuclear Arms, and other international agreements in the area of disarmament.

2. The Parties shall cooperate for the good of security and stability in Europe, with special attention to regional security, and with this aim shall support the process of disarmament in the area of nuclear arms, chemical and other kinds of weapons of mass destruction, as well as conventional arms.

3. With the aim of preventing the proliferation of weapons of mass destruction in the world, and particularly in Europe, the Parties renounce the possession, acquisition, and production of such weapons. The Parties also guarantee full control over the production and maintenance on their territories of materials and substances which serve peaceful purposes but may be utilized for the production of weapons of mass destruction, as well as full control over the export of these materials and substances and of the technologies used to produce them.

Article 4

1. In accord with the principles of the United Nations Charter, the Parties shall resolve disputes that may arise between them exclusively by way of peaceful means and renouncing the use, or threat of use, of force in their mutual relations.

2. Neither of the Parties shall permit any third-party state or states to commit an act of armed aggression from its territory against the other Party.

3. In the event that a third-party state or states should make an armed attack on either of the Parties, the other Party shall not render any military assistance or political support whatsoever to that state or states throughout the entire period of military conflict, and will act on behalf of the resolution of that conflict in accord with the principles and procedures of the United Nations

Charter and the documents of the Conference on Security and Cooperation in Europe.

4. The Parties shall conduct systematic consultations in matters of international security on all levels. Should either of the Parties recognize that a situation or disagreement has arisen that threatens or may threaten the maintenance of international peace and security, or violates them, the Parties shall conduct immediate consultations concerning the methods of settling the disagreement or ending the situation that has arisen.

5. The Parties shall develop mutually beneficial military cooperation on the basis of separate agreements.

Article 5

With the aim of strengthening and further institutionalizing the Conference on Security and Cooperation in Europe and other pan-European structures, the Parties shall act in the interests of political, economic, ecological, cultural, scientific, humanitarian, and legal cooperation, and above all of the joint creation, development, and general adoption of pan-European standards in these areas.

Article 6

1. The Parties shall hold consultations on various levels, including the highest, with the aim of ensuring the harmonious development of mutual relations, as well as cooperation in matters of a multilateral nature that are a subject of interest for both Parties, with particular consideration of international security problems.

2. The Parties shall create favorable conditions for the extensive development of interparliamentary contacts.

3. The Ministers of Foreign Affairs of both Parties shall meet at least annually.

4. The Parties shall develop cooperation between corresponding organs of state authority and administration. Depending on their needs, they shall form mixed commissions on the basis of appropriate agreements.

5. The Parties express their common interest in multilateral regional cooperation.

Article 7

1. The Parties shall favor mutually beneficial economic cooperation, including commercial cooperation, based on market principles, and shall guarantee convenient conditions for such cooperation with consideration for the protection of investments, technology, copyright and patents, and shall enforce the

appropriate international-legal regulations in the areas of capital flow and movement of labor, goods, and services, as well as concluding appropriate agreements in the area of economic cooperation.

2. The Parties shall facilitate the development of cooperation by state and private enterprises as well as by other economic subjects.

3. The Parties shall engage in exchanges of experience and shall assist each other in the process of creating and developing a market economy.

4. The Parties shall promote the development of scientific and technical cooperation.

Article 8

1. The Parties shall collaborate with the aim of perfecting links for transportation between and through their countries, and the infrastructure connected with them in all branches of transportation, including pipeline transport and power lines.

2. The Parties shall take steps to modernize and develop telecommunications links.

3. The Parties shall promote international cooperation in the area of transportation and communication. Their corresponding organs will conclude separate agreements in this area, meeting international standards and norms.

Article 9

1. The Parties shall aspire to assure permanent environmental safety and a significant reduction of existing environmental pollution. In accord with international standards, they shall also aspire to prevent trans-border pollution, among other measures through the application of safe technologies and environmentally clean production, especially in border regions through which the Bug and San [rivers] flow.

2. The Parties shall aim for the total elimination of radiation, chemical, and biological threats, in accord with the standards of the International Atomic Energy Agency and other corresponding international standards. They shall immediately inform each other and create early warning and mutual assistance systems in the event that such threats should arise or threaten to appear.

3. The Parties shall participate in the creation of a coordinated international strategy for environmental protection, and in particular shall assign due importance to the protection of fauna and flora in both states.

4. The appropriate organs of the Parties shall conclude separate agreements concerning environmental safety and cooperation, in accord with international standards.

Article 10

1. The Parties shall promote the establishment and development of direct contacts and cooperation between regions, administrative-territorial units, and towns of the Polish Republic and Ukraine. Special attention shall be devoted to cooperation in border regions. The Parties shall collaborate in the field of long-term development planning for border regions.

2. With the aim of putting these decisions into effect, an Intergovernmental Commission for Affairs of Interregional Cooperation shall be created.

3. The Parties shall increase the number of border crossings and shall rationalize the conduct of customs and border control.

Article 11

1. In accord with generally binding international standards concerning the protection of ethnic minorities, the Parties recognize the right of the Polish minority in Ukraine and of the Ukrainian minority in the Polish Republic, individually or together with other members of the given minority, to the preservation, expression, and development of their ethnic, cultural, linguistic, and religious identity without any discrimination whatsoever and in conditions of full equality before the law. The Parties shall undertake essential actions for the implementation of this right, in particular the right to:

—the study and mastery of their native language and in their native language, free use of it, and access to, and dissemination and exchange of, information in that language;

—the establishment and maintenance of their own educational, cultural, and religious institutions and associations;

—the confession and practice of their own religion;

—the use of given and family names in the versions accepted in their native language;

—the establishment and maintenance of unhindered contacts among themselves within their country of residence, as well as across borders.

2. The Parties confirm that belonging to an ethnic minority is a matter of a person's individual choice, and that no unfavorable consequences may result from it for that person. Each Party shall protect upon its territory the ethnic identity of the minority of the other Party from any activity whatsoever threatening that identity, and shall create the conditions for its strengthening.

3. Each person belonging to the Polish minority in Ukraine and the Ukrainian minority in the Polish Republic is obligated, as is every citizen, to loyalty towards the state of his residence, guided by the legislation of that state.

Article 12

1. The Parties shall undertake and support activities aimed at the preservation and development of positive traditions of the common heritage and overcoming prejudices and negative stereotypes in relations between the two peoples. With these aims, the Parties shall create the conditions for the mutual free dissemination of accurate information on all areas of their social and cultural life.

2. Appreciating the especial significance of cooperation in the humanitarian field, the Parties shall support free contacts between citizens of both states, as well as the cooperation of social organizations, political parties, and scholarly and creative associations.

3. Recognizing the far-reaching role of the younger generation in building new relations between peoples, the Parties shall promote the further development of friendly relations between the youth of both states.

4. The Parties shall provide support for the development of contacts in the areas of sport and tourism.

Article 13

1. Based on the positive values of the centuries-long common cultural heritage of Poland and Ukraine and their contribution to European civilization, the Parties shall promote cooperation in the areas of culture, scholarship, and education, maintaining world and European standards, set out in detail in the UNESCO conventions, the European Cultural Convention of 1953, and the documents of the Conference on Security and Cooperation in Europe, including those of the Cracow Symposium on the Cultural Heritage of the States Participating in the Conference on Security and Cooperation in Europe.

2. With the aim of mutual dissemination of knowledge on the national heritage in the area of culture, learning, and education, and also striving to promote new achievements in this area, each Party, on the basis of separate agreements, shall set up on the territory of the other—with its broad support for this activity—centers of information and culture. The Parties shall also facilitate the dissemination of the press, books, and audio-visual materials of the other Party and shall act jointly in the areas of radio, television, and press agencies.

3. The Parties shall increase cultural exchange in various forms and shall promote cooperation between cultural institutions and associations, including creative groups, as well as direct contacts between creative artists.

4. The Parties shall ensure the necessary legal, material, and other protection for the valuables, monuments, and objects connected with the cultural and historical heritage of the other Party, and shall also act in the interests of their discovery, preservation, restoration, introduction into cultual circulation, in-

cluding the provision of free access to them. Furthermore, in accord with the norms of general international law, with bilateral agreements and other international standards, the Parties shall make efforts toward the discovery and return of cultural and historical goods that have disappeared, have been illegally removed, or in some other illegal manner have come to be on the territory of the other Party.

5. With the aim of resolving these matters, the governments of the Parties shall appoint plenipotentiaries who shall undertake appropriate actions.

Article 14

The Parties shall act in the interests of the development of cooperation between schools, colleges, and scholarly institutions, among other things in the area of exchanges of scholars, lecturers, students, doctoral candidates, and scholarship recipients, and shall promote joint research projects.

Article 15

The Parties shall support educational cooperation, including the teaching of the Polish language in Ukraine and of the Ukrainian language in the Polish Republic in the framework of schools and colleges, as well as beyond them.

Article 16

1. The Parties shall develop, intensify, and improve legal and consular relations, including legal aid in civil, criminal, and administrative matters, taking into account their legal systems as well as bilateral and multilateral agreements, in particular the relevant conventions of the Council of Europe.

2. The Parties shall cooperate in combatting organized crime, terrorism, economic crimes, crime connected with narcotics, illegal trade in works of art, illegal acts constituting a threat to the security of civil aviation and maritime navigation, production and circulation of counterfeit currency, smuggling, and other types of criminality. The terms of such cooperation shall be agreed upon separately.

Article 17

1. The Parties shall develop comprehensive collaboration in the field of health care and public health, in particular in the area of combatting infectious diseases, social diseases, and others caused by environmental conditions, and the prevention of these diseases. The Parties shall implement mutual exchange of information in these areas.

2. The Parties shall collaborate in the area of social security insurance and care.

Article 18

1. The Parties shall preserve and provide legal protection for, as well as maintain in accord with the norms of international law, including humanitarian law, as well as with popular and religious customs, military and civilian graves, cemeteries, and burial places that are currently or in the future will be open on their territories, and which constitute memorial and honorary objects for the citizens of the other Party.

2. The citizens of both Parties shall have access to graves, cemeteries, and burial places of their relatives which are located on the territory of the other Party.

Article 19

The provisions of the present Treaty do not infringe the rights and obligations arising from bilateral and multilateral agreements binding each of the Parties in their relations with other states.

Article 20

The present Treaty shall be registered at the Secretariat of the United Nations Organization in accord with Article 102 of the United Nations Charter.

Article 21

1. The present Treaty is subject to ratification, and shall enter into force on the day of exchange of documents of ratification, which shall take place in Kyiv.

2. The present Treaty shall remain valid for a period of fifteen years. After this period, its binding force is subject to automatic extension for five years at a time, if neither Party denounces it by way of notification one year before the expiration of the given period.

Drawn up in Warsaw on 18 May 1992 in two exemplars, each in the Polish and Ukrainian languages, both texts having equal force.

For the Polish Republic   For Ukraine

[signature; Lech Wałęsa]   [signature; Leonid Kravchuk]

[Polish and Ukrainian originals. Translated by Andrew D. Sorokowski.]

Trilateral Statement by the Presidents of the United States, Russia, Ukraine

Presidents Clinton, Yeltsin, and Kravchuk met in Moscow on January 14. The three Presidents reiterated that they will deal with one another as full and equal partners and that relations among their countries must be conducted on the basis of respect for the independence, sovereignty and territorial integrity of each nation.

The three Presidents agreed on the importance of developing mutually beneficial, comprehensive and cooperative economic relations. In this connection, they welcomed the intention of the United States to provide assistance to Ukraine and Russia to support the creation of effective market economies.

The three Presidents reviewed the progress that has been made in reducing nuclear forces. Deactivation of strategic forces is already well underway in the United States, Russia, and Ukraine. The Presidents welcomed the ongoing deactivation of RS-18s (SS-19s) and RS-22s (SS-24s) on Ukrainian territory by having their warheads removed.

The Presidents look forward to the entry into force of the START-I Treaty, including the Lisbon Protocol and associated documents, and President Kravchuk reiterated his commitment that Ukraine accede to the Nuclear Non-Proliferation Treaty as a non-nuclear-weapon state in the shortest possible time. Presidents Clinton and Yeltsin noted that entry into force of START-I will allow them to seek early ratification of START-II. The Presidents discussed, in this regard, steps their countries would take to resolve certain nuclear weapons questions.

The Presidents emphasized the importance of ensuring the safety and security of nuclear weapons pending their dismantlement.

The Presidents recognized the importance of compensation to Ukraine, Kazakhstan, and Belarus for the value of the highly-enriched uranium in nuclear warheads located on their territories. Arrangements have been worked out to provide fair and timely compensation to Ukraine, Kazakhstan, and Belarus as the nuclear warheads on their territory are transferred to Russia for dismantling.

Presidents Clinton and Yeltsin expressed satisfaction with the completion of the highly-enriched uranium contract which was signed by appropriate authorities of the United States and Russia. By converting weapons-grade uranium into uranium which can be used for peaceful purposes, the highly-enriched uranium agreement is a major step forward in fulfilling the countries' mutual non-proliferation objectives.

The three Presidents decided on simultaneous actions on transfer of nuclear warheads from Ukraine and delivery of compensation to Ukraine in the form of fuel assemblies for nuclear power stations.

Presidents Clinton and Yeltsin informed President Kravchuk that the United States and Russia are prepared to provide security assurances to Ukraine. In particular, once the START-I enters into force and Ukraine becomes a non-nuclear-weapon state party to the Non-Proliferation Treaty (NPT), the United States and Russia will:

—Reaffirm their commitment to Ukraine, in accordance with the principles of the CSCE Final Act, to respect the independence and sovereignty and the existing borders of the CSCE member states and recognize that border changes can be made only by peaceful and consensual means; and reaffirm their obligation to refrain from threat or use of force against the territorial integrity or political independence of any state, and that none of their weapons will ever be used except in self-defense or otherwise in accordance with the Charter of the United Nations;

—Reaffirm their commitment to Ukraine, in accordance with the principles of the CSCE Final Act, to refrain from economic coercion designed to subordinate to their own interest the exercise by another CSCE participating state of rights inherent in its sovereignty and thus to secure advantages of any kind;

—Reaffirm their commitment to seek immediate UN Security Council action to provide assistance to Ukraine, as a non-nuclear-weapon state party to the NPT, if Ukraine should become a victim of an act of aggression in which nuclear weapons are used;

—Reaffirm, in the case of Ukraine, their commitment not to use nuclear weapons against any non-nuclear-weapon state party to the NPT, except in the case of an attack on themselves, their territories or dependent territories, their armed forces, or their allies, by such a state in association or alliance with a nuclear weapon state.

Presidents Clinton and Yeltsin informed President Kravchuk that consultations have been held with the United Kingdom, the third depositary state of the

NPT, and the United Kingdom is prepared to offer the same security assurances to Ukraine once it becomes a non-nuclear-weapon state party to the NPT.

President Clinton reaffirmed the United States commitment to provide technical and financial assistance for the safe and secure dismantling of nuclear forces and storage of fissile materials. The United States has agreed under the Nunn-Lugar program to provide Russia, Ukraine, Kazakhstan, and Belarus with nearly USD 800 million in such assistance, including a minimum USD 175 million to Ukraine. The United States Congress has authorized additional Nunn-Lugar funds for this program, and the United States will work intensively with Russia, Ukraine, Kazakhstan, and Belarus to expand assistance for this purpose. The United States will also work to promote rapid implementation of the assistance agreements that are already in place.

****

Annex to the January 14 Trilateral Statement
by the Presidents of the United States, Russia, and Ukraine.

****

The three Presidents decided that, to begin the process of compensation for Ukraine, Russia will provide to Ukraine within ten months fuel assemblies for nuclear power stations containing 100 tons of low-enriched uranium. By the same date, at least 200 nuclear warheads from RS-18 (SS-19) and RS-22 (SS-24) missiles will be transferred from Ukraine to Russia for dismantling. Ukrainian representatives will monitor the dismantling of these warheads. The United States will provide USD 60 million as an advance payment to Russia, to be deducted from payments due to Russia under the highly-enriched uranium contract. These funds would be available to help cover expenses for the transportation and dismantling of strategic warheads and the production of fuel assemblies.

All nuclear warheads will be transferred from the territory of Ukraine to Russia for the purpose of their subsequent dismantling in the shortest possible time. Russia will provide compensation in the form of supplies of fuel assemblies to Ukraine for the needs of its nuclear power industry within the same time period.

Ukraine will ensure the elimination of all nuclear weapons, including strategic offensive arms, located on its territory in accordance with the relevant agreements and during the seven-year period as provided by the START-I

Treaty and within the context of the Verkhovna Rada Statement on the non-nuclear status of Ukraine. All RS-22s (SS-24s) on the territory of Ukraine will be deactivated within ten months by having their warheads removed.

Pursuant to agreements reached between Russia and Ukraine in 1993, Russia will provide for the servicing and ensure the safety of nuclear warheads and Ukraine will cooperate in providing conditions for Russia to carry out these operations.

Russia and the United States will promote the elaboration and adoption by the IAEA of an agreement placing all nuclear activities of Ukraine under IAEA safeguards, which will allow the unimpeded export of fuel assemblies from Russia to Ukraine for Ukraine's nuclear power industry.

The United States and Russia, as leading exporters of conventional weapons, military equipment and dual-use technologies, are convinced that additional measures are needed on an international basis to increase responsibility, transparency and, where appropriate, restraint in this area. They expressed their willingness to work with other countries in bringing about the early establishment of a new multilateral regime in order to achieve these objectives, which would supplement existing non-proliferation regimes, in particular through arrangements to exchange information for the purpose of meaningful consultations.

For the United States:

[Signature; William J. Clinton]

For the Russian Federation:

[Signature; Boris Yeltsin]

For Ukraine:

[Signature; Leonid Kravchuk]

Moscow
January 14, 1994

Joint Declaration of the Presidents of the Polish Republic and Ukraine on Understanding and Unity

The President of the Polish Republic and the President of Ukraine, conscious of their historical responsibility before the present and future generations of Ukrainians and Poles and the role of Poland and Ukraine in strengthening security and stability in East-Central Europe, and also appreciating the importance of a strategic partnership of both countries, guided by the provisions of the Treaty on Good-Neighborliness, Friendly Relations and Cooperation of 18 May 1992, certain that the future of Polish-Ukrainian relations must be built on truth and justice as well as on a profound and sincere understanding and unity, desiring to jointly overcome the complex heritage of Polish-Ukrainian destinies, lest the shadows of the past should dim today's ties of friendship and partnership between the two countries and peoples, hereby declare:

In the centuries-long history of Polish-Ukrainian interaction as neighbors there are many moving examples of sincere friendship, mutual aid and cooperation between the two peoples. It contains instances of brotherhood in arms, mutual cultural influences enriching both peoples, and neighborly kindness. Nevertheless, one also must not overlook tragic instances, such as the decades of wars in the seventeenth and eighteenth centuries, manifestations of the Polish government's anti-Ukrainian policy in the 1920s and 1930s, and the persecution of the Polish population in Soviet Ukraine during the Stalinist repressions. One must not forget the shedding of blood of Poles in Volhynia, especially in 1942–1943, nor the atrocities of the Ukrainian-Polish conflicts in the first postwar years.

A separate, dramatic page in the history of our relations was Action "Vistula," which struck the Ukrainian community in Poland. Passing over all these facts in silence, or presenting them in a one-sided manner, will not ease the pain of the victims or those close to them, nor will it promote deeper understanding between our peoples. The path to true friendship leads first of all through truth and mutual understanding. Let us recognize that no goal can justify crimes, violence, and the application of collective responsibility. At the same time, let us remember that sometimes the sources of these conflicts lay beyond Ukraine and Poland, that they were conditioned by circumstances independent of Poles and Ukrainians, and through undemocratic political systems imposed on our peoples against their will. Let us honor the innocent victims—the Poles and Ukrainians murdered, killed in battle, or forcibly resettled. Let us condemn those who inflicted their sufferings.

At the same time, let us express our gratitude to all those who during these difficult years worked for the cause of bringing our peoples closer together. Today, Poland and Ukraine are sovereign states, good neighbors and strategic partners. For this reason, too, it is so especially important to overcome the bitterness that has remained in the memories of many Ukrainians and Poles. We are prompted to do this not only out of respect for democratic values, regard for human rights, for the fundamental principles and norms of international law, but also out of a desire to see Ukraine and Poland in a united Europe. The interpretation of our common past, its complex periods, should be the task of specialists who in an atmosphere of openness will carefully examine the facts and prepare their objective evaluation. For a better mutual understanding between the Polish and Ukrainian peoples, a dialogue of opinion-forming communities should be initiated.

Greater advantage should be taken of the possibilities presented by Polish citizens of Ukrainian descent and Ukrainian citizens of Polish descent who through their efforts are making a significant contribution to the cultural and economic development of our states. They should be the initiators of close cooperation between Poland and Ukraine. For their part, both states should see to their welfare, and support the development of the Polish minority in Ukraine and of the Ukrainian minority in Poland. The Polish Republic and Ukraine shall make efforts that the consciousness of young Ukrainians and Poles not be weighed down by the memory of history's tragic pages. May future generations live in a common European home in which there is no room for prejudice and suspicion!

In this conviction we, presidents of the Polish Republic and of Ukraine, resolve to jointly sponsor perpetuation of the idea of Polish-Ukrainian understanding and unity. In ancient times, our ancestors would pour water over their sabers as a sign of peace, alliance, and fraternity. And today we, Poles and Ukrainians, desire to pour feelings of friendship and solidarity into our hearts. On the threshold of the twenty-first century let us remember the past, but let us think of the future!

President of the Polish Republic   President of Ukraine

Aleksander Kwaśniewski   Leonid Kuchma

Kyiv, 21 May 1997

[*Polish and Ukrainian originals. Translated by Andrew D. Sorokowski.*]

Treaty on Friendship, Cooperation, and Partnership between Ukraine and the Russian Federation

Ukraine and the Russian Federation, hereinafter the High Contracting Parties,

based on the close historic ties and the relationship of friendship and cooperation between the peoples of Ukraine and Russia,

noting that the Treaty of 19 November 1990 between the Ukrainian SSR and the RSFSR fostered the development of good neighborly relations between the two states,

reaffirming their obligations which proceed from the terms of the Agreement between Ukraine and the Russian Federation on the further development of inter-state relations, signed at Dagomys on 23 June 1992,

considering that the strengthening of friendly relations, good-neighborliness, and mutually beneficial cooperation corresponds to substantial interests of their peoples and serves the cause of peace and international security,

desiring to endow these relations with a new quality and to strengthen their legal basis,

filled with a determination to ensure the irrevocability and continuation of the democratic processes in both states,

taking into account the agreements reached in the framework of the Commonwealth of Independent States,

reaffirming their support of the norms of international law, first of all of the goals and principles of the United Nations Charter, and honoring the obligations undertaken in the framework of the Organization for Security and Cooperation in Europe,

have agreed as follows:

Article 1

As friendly, equal, and sovereign states, the High Contracting Parties shall base their relations upon mutual respect and trust, strategic partnership and cooperation.

Article 2

In accord with the provisions of the UN Charter and the obligations of the Final Act of the Conference on Security and Cooperation in Europe, the High

Contracting Parties shall respect each other's territorial integrity and reaffirm the inviolability of the borders existing between them.

Article 3

The High Contracting Parties shall build their mutual relations on the basis of the principles of mutual respect for their sovereign equality, territorial integrity, inviolability of borders, peaceful resolution of disputes, non-use of force or the threat of force, including economic and other means of pressure, the right of peoples to freely determine their fate, non-interference in internal affairs, observance of human rights and fundamental freedoms, cooperation among states, the conscientious performance of international obligations undertaken, and other generally recognized norms of international law.

Article 4

The High Contracting Parties proceed from the premise that good neighborliness and cooperation between them are important factors in increasing stability and security in Europe and the world. They shall realize close cooperation with the aim of strengthening international peace and security. They shall use necessary means in order to foster the process of general disarmament, the creation and strengthening of a system of collective security in Europe, as well as the intensification of the UN's peace-making role and the increase of the effectiveness of regional security mechanisms.

The Parties shall make efforts to ensure that the resolution of all contested problems should take place exclusively by peaceful means, and cooperate in the prevention and resolution of conflicts and situations that affect their interests.

Article 5

The High Contracting Parties shall conduct regular consultations with the aim of ensuring further deepening of bilateral relations and exchange of views regarding multilateral problems of mutual interest. Where necessary, they shall coordinate their positions for the realization of agreed-upon actions.

In furtherance of these aims, regular high-level meetings shall be held by agreement of the Parties. The Ministers of Foreign Affairs of the Parties shall meet at least twice a year.

Working meetings between representatives of other ministries and agencies of the Parties shall be held as necessary to discuss issues of mutual interest.

The Parties may create mixed commissions for the resolution of separate issues in various areas on a permanent or temporary basis.

Article 6

Each of the High Contracting Parties shall abstain from participation in, or support of, any actions whatsoever directed against the other High Contracting Party, and obligates itself not to enter into any agreements with third countries directed against the other Party. Neither of the Parties will permit its territory to be used to the detriment of the other Party's security.

Article 7

In the event that a situation should arise which, in the opinion of one of the High Contracting Parties, creates a threat to peace, violates the peace, or affects the interests of its national security, sovereignty and territorial integrity, it may appeal to the other High Contracting Party, proposing to immediately conduct appropriate consultations. The Parties shall exchange appropriate information and, where necessary, take agreed-upon or joint measures in order to resolve such a situation.

Article 8

The High Contracting Parties shall develop their relations in the sphere of military and military-technical cooperation, the ensurance of state security, as well as cooperation in border issues, customs, export and immigration control on the basis of separate agreements.

Article 9

The High Contracting Parties, reaffirming their resolve to continue along the path of reduction of armed forces and armaments, shall foster the process of disarmament and shall cooperate in the matter of unwavering performance of agreements in the area of reducing armed forces and armaments, including nuclear weapons.

Article 10

Each of the High Contracting Parties guarantees rights and freedoms to citizens of the other Party on the same foundations and to the same extent that it does to its own citizens, except for cases established by the national legislation of the Parties or by their international treaties.

Each of the Parties shall protect, in the established manner, the rights of its citizens residing on the territory of the other Party, according to the obligations arising from the documents of the Organization for Security and Cooperation in Europe and from other generally accepted principles and norms of international law and agreements in the framework of the Commonwealth of Independent States, of which they are participants.

Article 11

The High Contracting Parties shall use the necessary means, including the ratification of appropriate legislative acts, on their territories for the prevention and termination of any actions that constitute instigation of violence, or violence, against individuals or groups of citizens that is based on national, racial, ethnic, or religious intolerance.

Article 12

The High Contracting Parties guarantee the ethnic, cultural, linguistic, and religious identity of national minorities on their territories and shall create the conditions for the encouragement of this identity.

Each of the High Contracting Parties guarantees the right of persons belonging to national minorities to freely express, preserve, and develop their ethnic, cultural, linguistic, or religious identity and to support and develop their culture, individually or together with other persons belonging to national minorities, without being subject to any attempts at assimilation against their will.

The High Contracting Parties guarantee the right of persons who belong to national minorities to fully and effectively realize their human rights and fundamental freedoms, and to enjoy them without any discrimination and in conditions of full equality before the law.

The High Contracting Parties shall encourage the creation of equal opportunities and conditions for learning the Ukrainian language in the Russian Federation and the Russian language in Ukraine, for the preparation of teaching personnel to lecture in these languages in educational institutions, and with this aim shall provide equivalent state support.

The High Contracting Parties shall conclude agreements on cooperation in these matters.

Article 13

The High Contracting Parties shall develop economic cooperation on the basis of equal rights and mutual benefit, and shall refrain from actions that might cause economic harm to each other. With this aim, recognizing the necessity of the gradual formation and development of a common economic space by way of creating conditions for the free movement of goods, services, capital, and labor, the Parties shall take effective measures to agree upon a strategy for the implementation of economic reforms, the deepening of economic integration on the basis of mutual benefit, and the harmonization of economic legislation.

The High Contracting Parties shall guarantee the broad exchange of economic information and its accessibility to enterprises, entrepreneurs, and experts of both Parties.

The Parties shall endeavor to coordinate their financial, monetary-credit, budgetary, foreign exchange, investment, price, tax, trade and economic, and tariff policies, to create equal opportunities and guarantees for subjects of economic activity; they shall foster the formation and development of direct economic and trade relations on all levels, and specialization and cooperation by technologically linked manufacturers, enterprises, associations, corporations, banks, and producers and consumers.

The High Contracting Parties shall foster the preservation and development, on a mutually beneficial basis, of production and scientific-technical cooperation between industrial enterprises in the elaboration and production of modern scientifically advanced production, including production for the needs of defense.

Article 14

The High Contracting Parties shall guarantee favorable conditions for direct trade and other economic relations and cooperation on the level of administrative-territorial units in accord with national legislation in force, devoting special attention to the development of economic ties between border regions.

Article 15

The High Contracting Parties guarantee favorable economic, financial, and legal conditions for entrepreneurial and other economic activity by enterprises and organizations of the other Party, including the stimulation and mutual protection of their investments. The Parties shall encourage various forms of cooperation and direct relations between subjects of economic activity of both states regardless of their forms of ownership.

Article 16

The High Contracting Parties shall interact in the UN and other international organizations, including economic and financial ones, and shall support each other in admission to international organizations and in accession to agreements and conventions of which one of the Parties is not a participant.

Article 17

The High Contracting Parties shall broaden their cooperation in the sphere of transport, and shall ensure the freedom of transit of persons, freight, and means of transport across each other's territory in accord with generally recognized norms of international law.

The conveyance of freight and passengers by rail, air, sea, river, and automobile transport between the two Parties, and by transit across their territories, including operations through sea, river, and air ports and rail and automobile networks, as well as operations along communication lines, main pipeline and electrical networks located on the territory of the other Party, are effected in the manner and according to the conditions provided by separate agreements.

Article 18

The High Contracting Parties shall cooperate in conducting searches and disaster rescue actions, and also in the investigation of extraordinary incidents in transport.

Article 19

The High Contracting Parties shall safeguard compliance with legal procedures for state property and property of juridical persons and citizens of one High Contracting Party that is to be found on the territory of the other High Contracting Party, in accord with the legislation of the latter Party, unless otherwise provided by agreement of the Parties.

The Parties postulate that issues of property relations that affect their interests are subject to regulation on the basis of separate agreements.

Article 20

The High Contracting Parties devote special attention to the development of cooperation in ensuring the functioning of national fuel and energy complexes, transportation systems, and systems of communication and information technology, fostering the preservation, rational exploitation, and development of complexes and individual systems that have taken shape in these sectors.

Article 21

On the basis of separate agreements, the High Contracting Parties cooperate in research and utilization of outer space, in joint production and elaboration of aerospace technology on the basis of equality and mutual benefit, and in accord with international law. The High Contracting Parties foster the preservation and development of the cooperative ties that have been formed between enterprises in the aerospace sector.

Article 22

The High Contracting Parties shall mutually foster the remediation of accidents arising as a result of extraordinary situations along communication lines, main pipelines, energy systems, means of communication, and other objects that constitute mutual interests.

The procedure for joint action in carrying out disaster and reconstruction work shall be set out in separate agreements.

Article 23

The High Contracting Parties cooperate in the spheres of education, science, and technology, in the development of research activity, fostering direct contacts between their scientific research organizations and the realization of joint programs and projects, especially in the sphere of advanced technologies. The matter of the application of the results of joint research achieved in the course of collaboration shall be settled in each specific case by way of creating separate agreements.

The Parties shall act jointly in the area of personnel training, and shall encourage the exchange of specialists, scholars, graduate students, interns, and students. They shall recognize the equivalency of each other's educational documents, academic degrees and academic titles, and shall conclude a separate agreement on this matter.

The Parties shall conduct the exchange of scientific-technical information as well as cooperation in matters of the protection of copyright and contiguous rights, and other forms of intellectual property in accord with national legislation and the international obligations of their countries in this area.

Article 24

The High Contracting Parties shall develop cooperation in the area of culture, literature, art, mass media, tourism, and sports.

The Parties shall collaborate in the area of preservation, restoration, and utilization of their historical-cultural heritage.

The Parties shall comprehensively foster the strengthening and broadening of creative exchange and cooperation between collectives, organizations, and associations of persons engaged in literature and art, cinematography, book publishing, their countries' archives, holding traditional days of national culture, arts festivals and exhibitions, tours of artistic collectives and soloists, the exchange of delegations of cultural workers and specialists on the state, regional, and local levels, and the organization of national cultural centers on the territories of their states.

The Parties shall render state support for the elaboration and implementation of joint programs of revival and development of the tourist industry, the development of promising new recreation areas, and the preservation, restoration, and effective utilization of cultural-historical and religious monuments and objects. The strengthening of contacts between sports organizations and clubs and the joint conduct of inter-state sports initiatives shall be broadly encouraged.

The Parties shall jointly develop and implement mutually beneficial programs for the development of the material-technical base of television and radio, including satellite transmission, and shall ensure the organization, on a basis of parity, of television and radio broadcasts in the Russian language in Ukraine and in the Ukrainian language in Russia.

The Parties shall foster the development of contacts between individuals, political parties and citizens' movements, trade unions, religious organizations and associations, health, sports, tourist and other associations and unions.

The entire complex of issues provided for by this article shall be the subject of separate agreements.

Article 25

The High Contracting Parties shall cooperate in the area of the protection and improvement of the state of the environment, the prevention of transborder pollution, rational use and conservation of natural resources, remediation of the effects of extraordinary situations of a natural and artificial character, and foster agreed-upon actions in this sphere on the regional and global levels, aiming at the creation of an all-encompassing system of international environmental safety.

The Parties postulate that the matter of environmental protection and the ensurance of environmental safety, including the matter of the protection and utilization of ecosystems and resources of the Dnipro River and other transborder rivers, and of actions during extraordinary environmental situations, are subject to regulation on the basis of separate agreements.

Article 26

The High Contracting Parties shall collaborate in the remediation of the effects of the accident at the Chornobyl Atomic Energy Station and shall conclude a separate agreement in this matter.

Article 27

The High Contracting Parties shall develop cooperation in the sphere of social protection, including the social security of citizens. They shall form special agreements with the aim of resolving issues of labor relations, employment, social protection, compensation for losses incurred through disability or other harm to health connected with accidents in production, the social security of citizens of one Party who carry out labor activity or have earned seniority on the territory of the other Party, and on other matters in this area which require negotiated resolutions.

The Parties shall ensure the free and prompt transfer of pensions, monetary aid, alimony, payments in compensation of losses caused by disability or other harm to health, and of other socially significant payments to citizens of one Party who permanently reside or temporarily remain on the territory of the other Party.

Article 28

The High Contracting Parties shall collaborate in matters of restoring the rights of deported peoples in accord with the arrangements made in the framework of the CIS on a bilateral and multilateral basis.

Article 29

As Black Sea coastal states, the High Contracting Parties are prepared to further develop comprehensive cooperation in the matter of saving and conserving the natural environment of the Azov-Black Sea basin, of conducting oceanographic and climatological research, utilization of the recreational potential and natural resources of the Azov and Black Seas, and the development of navigation and exploitation of maritime communications, ports and structures.

Article 30

The High Contracting Parties are conscious of the importance of conserving a technologically unified system for Ukraine and the Russian Federation for the gathering, processing, dissemination, and utilization of hydro-meteorological information and data on the state of the environment to safeguard the interests of the population and the national economy, and shall comprehensively foster the development of cooperation in the sphere of hydrometeorology and monitoring of the environment.

Article 31

The High Contracting Parties devote special attention to the development of mutually beneficial joint production in the area of health care and the improvement of the sanitary-epidemiological situation, the production of medicines and medical technology, and the training of highly qualified personnel for the Parties' health care institutions.

Article 32

The High Contracting Parties shall cooperate in the resolution of issues of regulating migratory processes, including measures for warning and prevention of illegal migration from third countries, on which they shall form a separate agreement.

Article 33

The High Contracting Parties shall collaborate in the struggle with crime, first of all with organized crime, with terrorism in all its forms and manifestations, including criminal actions directed against the security of navigation, civil aviation, and other forms of transportation, with illegal circulation of radioactive materials, arms, narcotic paraphernalia and psychotropic substances, and contraband, including the illegal transfer across borders of objects of cultural, historical, and artistic value.

Article 34

The High Contracting Parties shall cooperate in the legal sphere on the basis of separate agreements.

Article 35

The High Contracting Parties shall foster the development of contacts and cooperation between the parliaments and parliamentarians of both states.

Article 36

This Treaty does not affect the rights and obligations of the High Contracting Parties that arise from other international treaties to which they are party.

Article 37

Disputes regarding the interpretation and application of the terms of this Treaty are subject to resolution by way of consultations and negotiations between the High Contracting Parties.

Article 38

The High Contracting Parties shall conclude other mutual agreements necessary for the implementation of the terms of this Treaty, as well as agreements in areas of mutual interest.

Article 39

This Treaty is subject to ratification and enters into force on the day of exchange of instruments of ratification.

From the day of its entry into force, this Treaty terminates the effect of the Treaty between the Ukrainian Soviet Socialist Republic and the Russian Soviet Federative Socialist Republic of 19 November 1990.

Article 40

This Treaty is to remain in effect for ten years. Its effect will thereafter be automatically extended for successive ten-year periods, if neither of the High Contracting Parties declares its wish to terminate its effect to the other High Contracting Party by way of written notification no less than six months before the end of the current ten-year period.

Article 41

This Treaty is subject to registration at the Secretariat of the United Nations Organization in accord with Article 102 of the UN Charter.

Done in the city of Kyiv on 31 May 1997 in two exemplars, each in the Ukrainian and Russian languages, both texts being authentic.

For Ukraine   For the Russian Federation

[signature; L. Kuchma]   [signature; B. Yeltsin]

[Russian and Ukrainian originals. Translated by Andrew D. Sorokowski.]

Treaty on Relations of Good-Neighborliness and Cooperation between Ukraine and Romania

Ukraine and Romania, hereinafter "the Contracting Parties,"

convinced that good-neighborliness, mutual respect and cooperation between two states correspond to the fundamental interests of their peoples,

conscious of their common strategic interest in strengthening the independence, sovereignty, territorial integrity and stability of each of them,

welcoming the positive historical changes in Europe, and inspired by a common aspiration to a united Europe—a continent of peace, security and cooperation,

guided by the aims and principles of the UN Charter and proceeding on the basis of the supremacy of generally recognized norms of international law,

reaffirming their determination to fulfill their obligations under the Helsinki Final Act, the Paris Charter for a new Europe, as well as other documents of the Organization for Security and Cooperation in Europe,

confident that respect for fundamental human rights and freedoms is an important prerequisite for the creation of a new Europe united by common values of democracy, freedom, and the rule of law,

denouncing the unjust acts of totalitarian and military-dictatorial regimes, which in the past have negatively influenced relations between the Ukrainian and Romanian peoples, and convinced that overcoming this painful heritage of the past is possible only by way of developing relations of friendship and cooperation between two peoples who aspire to the creation of a single Europe,

believing that an objective evaluation of the past will foster the strengthening of mutual understanding and trust between these two states and peoples,

convinced of the necessity of implementation by both Contracting Parties of a prospective, active policy of understanding and harmony, good-neighborliness and partnership,

and taking into account the potential of both countries and their possibilities for the development of mutually beneficial bilateral cooperation,

have agreed as follows:

Article 1

1. The Contracting Parties base their relations on mutual trust, respect, cooperation and partnership.

2. In their mutual relations, as in their relations with other states, the Contracting Parties shall respect the principles of the United Nations Charter and the Helsinki Final Act: sovereign equality, non-application of force or the threat of force, inviolability of borders, territorial integrity of states, peaceful regulation of disputes, non-interference in internal affairs, respect for human rights, equal rights and self-determination of nations, cooperation among states, and the conscientious performance of obligations undertaken in accord with international law.

Article 2

1. In accord with the principles and norms of international law and the principles of the Helsinki Final Act, the Contracting Parties confirm as inviolable the existing border between them, and therefore shall refrain, now and in the future, from any claims whatsoever against this border, and also from any demands or actions whatsoever aimed at the seizure and usurpation of part or all of the territory of the other Contracting Party.

2. The Contracting Parties shall form a separate treaty on the border regime between the two states and shall resolve the issue of the delimitation of their continental shelf and of exclusive economic zones in the Black Sea on the basis of principles and procedures negotiated by way of exchange of letters between the ministers of foreign affairs, which shall take place simultaneously with the signing of this Treaty. Understandings reached by way of such exchange of letters shall come into force simultaneously with the coming into force of this Treaty.

Article 3

1. The Contracting Parties confirm that under no circumstances will they resort to the threat of force or to the use of force against the territorial integrity or the political independence of the other Contracting Party, or to any other actions whatsoever that are incompatible with the provisions of the UN Charter and the principles of the Helsinki Final Act. They shall also refrain from support of such actions and shall not permit any third party to use their territories for the realization of such actions against the other Contracting Party.

2. Any problems or disputes between the Contracting Parties shall be resolved exclusively by peaceful means in accord with the norms of international law.

Article 4

1. The Contracting Parties, recognizing the indivisible character of European security, shall cooperate with the aim of building a single Europe com-

posed of peace-loving, democratic, and independent states. In accord with their international obligations, they shall promote a policy of cooperation and good-neighborliness, and strengthening of stability, peace, and security in their region and on the continent.

2. The Contracting Parties shall cooperate with the aim of strengthening confidence-building measures among states, and the prevention and peaceful resolution of regional conflicts.

Article 5

The Contracting Parties shall strengthen and expand cooperation in the framework of international organizations, including regional and subregional ones. They shall support each other in their efforts directed towards integration into European and Euro-Atlantic structures.

Article 6

1. Should a situation arise which, in the opinion of one of the Contracting Parties, could create a threat to peace or international security, the Contracting Parties shall conduct consultations regarding measures that will promote detente and elimination of the situation.

2. The Contracting Parties shall conduct regular consultations on various levels on issues of security and disarmament that are of mutual interest, and shall inform each other about the discharge of obligations assumed in accord with international documents in this area signed by both Contracting Parties.

3. The Contracting Parties shall realize cooperation in the military sphere between the corresponding state organs on the basis of separate agreements.

Article 7

1. The Contracting Parties shall actively promote the process of disarmament in Europe and the further reduction of armed forces and armaments to the appropriate levels of defense sufficiency on a bilateral and multilateral basis.

2. The Contracting Parties shall act jointly for the support and strengthening of the regime of nonproliferation of nuclear arms, for its consistent observance, and also for the prohibition of the production, accumulation and/or utilization of weapons of mass destruction.

Article 8

In accord with the terms of the European Framework Convention on transborder cooperation between territorial communities or authorities, the Contracting Parties shall encourage and support direct contacts and mutually beneficial cooperation between administrative-territorial units of Ukraine and Romania, especially in border regions. They shall also promote cooperation between administrative-territorial units of both states in the framework of existing Euroregions as well as of the recently formed "Upper Prut" and "Lower Danube" regions, in which administrative-territorial units of other interested states can be invited to participate. The Contracting Parties shall act towards the inclusion of this cooperation in the framework of the corresponding activity of European institutions.

Article 9

The Contracting Parties shall expand cooperation between themselves as well as with other Danubian and Black Sea states in all spheres of mutual interest.

Article 10

1. In order to ensure the development and deepening of bilateral relations, as well as the mutual exchange of ideas on international issues, the Contracting Parties shall promote regular contacts between their central and local offices. With this aim, each year meetings at the level of heads of state or government, or meetings of the ministers of foreign affairs, shall be held, during which the implementation of this Treaty will also be discussed.

2. The Contracting Parties shall encourage the further development of interparliamentary contacts.

Article 11

The Contracting Parties shall support the expansion of direct contacts between their citizens as well as between nongovernmental organizations and civic associations of both countries.

Article 12

1. The Contracting Parties shall collaborate with each other and within the framework of international organizations and conferences with the aim of development and implementation of international standards regarding the promotion and defense of human rights and fundamental freedoms for all, including the rights of persons who belong to national minorities.

2. When necessary, the Contracting Parties shall consult with each other for the purpose of improving and reconciling their national legislation in this area, the development of contacts between individuals, and the resolution of problems of a humanitarian nature that are of mutual interest.

Article 13

1. With the aim of the defense of the ethnic, cultural, linguistic, and religious identity of the Ukrainian minority in Romania and the Romanian minority in Ukraine, the Contracting Parties shall apply international norms and standards that determine the rights of persons belonging to national minorities, namely, the norms and standards that are to be found in the Framework Convention of the Council of Europe on the protection of national minorities, as well as in the document of the Session of the Copenhagen conference on the human dimension of the Organization for Security and Cooperation in Europe of 29 June 1990, the Declaration of the UN General Assembly on the rights of individuals belonging to national or ethnic, religious, and linguistic minorities (Resolution 47/135) of 18 December 1992, and Recommendation 1201 (1993) of the Parliamentary Assembly of the Council of Europe regarding the supplementary Protocol to the European Convention on Human Rights regarding the rights of national minorities, with the understanding that this Recommendation does not apply to collective rights and does not obligate the Contracting Parties to give appropriate persons the right to the special status of territorial autonomy based on ethnic criteria.

2. The Ukrainian minority in Romania includes citizens of Romania regardless of the regions in which they reside, who belong to this minority by their free choice, with regard to their ethnic origin, language, culture or religion.

The Romanian minority in Ukraine includes citizens of Ukraine regardless of the regions in which they reside, who belong to this minority by their free choice, with regard to their ethnic origin, language, culture or religion.

3. The Contracting Parties obligate themselves, when necessary, to use appropriate means with the aim of developing in all spheres of economic, social, political, and cultural life the full and genuine equality of individuals belonging to a national minority with individuals belonging to the majority of the population. In this regard, they shall take into account the actual status of persons who belong to national minorities.

4. The Contracting Parties reaffirm that persons to whom this article applies have, in particular, the right, individually or together with other members of their group, to freely express, preserve, and develop their ethnic, cultural, linguistic, and religious identity, the right to preserve and develop their culture, and the right to defense against any attempt whatsoever at assimilation against their will. They have the right to fully and effectively realize human rights and fundamental freedoms without any discrimination and in conditions of full equality before the law. Persons belonging to these minorities have the right to effective participation in public affairs, including participation through representatives elected according to law, and also in cultural, social, and economic life.

5. The Contracting Parties shall create equal conditions for learning their native language for persons belonging to the Ukrainian minority in Romania and the Romanian minority in Ukraine. The Contracting Parties confirm that the above-mentioned persons have the right to be educated in their native language in the necessary number of schools and educational state and specialized training institutes distributed according to the geographical distribution of the corresponding minorities.

They also have the right to use their native language in their relations with state organs in accord with national legislation and the international obligations of the Contracting Parties.

6. The Contracting Parties recognize that in exercising the right of association, persons who belong to these national minorities, in accord with internal legislation, may found and support their own organizations, societies, and also educational, cultural, and religious establishments and organizations.

7. The Contracting Parties shall respect the right of persons who belong to national minorities to have access to information and to the mass media in their native language, as well as to freely exchange and disseminate information. They shall not interfere with the creation and use by these persons of their own mass media, in accord with internal legislation of each of the Parties. Individuals to whom this article applies have the right to maintain contacts among themselves and with citizens of other states and to participate in the activities of nongovernmental organizations on both the national and the international levels.

8. The Contracting Parties shall refrain from taking measures that would change the proportional make-up of the population in localities where persons belonging to national minorities reside, intended to limit the rights and freedoms of these persons, which are based on the international norms and standards mentioned in paragraph 1 of this article.

9. Any person who belongs to a national minority and who believes that his rights safeguarded by this article have been violated has the right to petition the appropriate state organs by the procedure established by law.

10. The Contracting Parties recognize the obligation of persons to whom this article applies to be loyal to the state of which they are citizens, to obey its national legislation, and also to respect the rights of other persons, especially of those who belong to the majority of the population or to other national minorities.

11. None of the provisions of this article is to be interpreted as limiting or denying the human rights recognized according to the laws of the Contracting Parties or to agreements made between them.

12. None of the provisions of this article is to be interpreted as granting the right to engage in any activity or to act contrary to the aims and principles of the UN Charter or of other obligations established by international law or by

the provisions of the Helsinki Final Act and the Paris Charter for a New Europe, including the principle of the territorial integrity of the state.

13. For the purpose of cooperation in the monitoring of the performance of the obligations provided for in this article, the Contracting Parties shall create a mixed intergovernmental commission which shall meet at least annually.

Article 14

1. The Contracting Parties shall create favorable conditions for the development of mutually beneficial bilateral commercial-economic relations and shall perfect their mechanism in accord with the norms and practice of world trade. They shall grant to each other most favored nation status in economic relations under the conditions provided in a bilateral agreement.

2. In accord with its internal legislation and international law, each of the Contracting Parties shall create on its territory favorable conditions for the economic activity of physical and juridical persons of the other Contracting Party, including mutual encouragement and protection of investments.

Article 15

The Contracting Parties shall create the necessary conditions for effective cooperation in the field of fundamental scientific and applied research, and for the development and application of advanced technologies. They shall foster the expansion of direct contacts between scientists, research, design, and production associations, and other institutions in these areas.

Article 16

1. Taking into account their possibilities, the Contracting Parties shall develop cooperation in the area of the protection and improvement of the state of the environment, and remediation of the effects of industrial accidents and natural calamities. They shall collaborate in the area of rational use of natural resources, the increase of ecologically clean production, and the implementation of effective methods of nature conservation and renewal with the aim of improving the environmental safety of both countries.

2. The Contracting Parties shall activate cooperation between themselves and with other countries and international organizations with the aim of controlling, preventing, and reducing pollution of the waters of the Danube and the Black Sea.

3. The Contracting Parties shall immediately inform each other of incidents of environmental catastrophes and industrial accidents that may have transborder consequences, and on the measures that they use to remedy these consequences.

4. The Contracting Parties shall conclude a separate agreement on bilateral cooperation on issues of environmental protection.

Article 17

The Contracting Parties shall expand cooperation in the area of transport, in particular guaranteeing the freedom of transport of persons and freight across their territories in accord with national legislation and international norms and practice. Toward this aim they shall conclude appropriate treaties.

Article 18

The Contracting Parties shall cooperate with the aim of harmonizing policies and programs of development of national infrastructures, including energy systems, as well as transportation and telecommunication networks.

Article 19

1. The Contracting Parties shall develop cooperation in the areas of culture, scholarship, and education.

2. The Contracting Parties shall foster the mutual familiarization of their citizens with the cultural achievements of both countries, and shall support state, citizens', and individual initiatives aimed at this goal, and shall also encourage the expansion of exchanges between creative unions, associations, and institutions of culture, scholarship and education.

3. The Contracting Parties shall develop cooperation, especially on the basis of direct agreements between universities and other educational institutions, scientific-research and scholarly centers of both countries, and also will support mutual exchanges of pupils, students, lecturers, and scholars.

4. In accord with their internal regulations, the Contracting Parties shall encourage cooperation and direct exchanges between archives, libraries, and museums, and shall guarantee access to documentary sources existing in them for scholars and other citizens of the other Contracting Party.

5. The Contracting Parties shall encourage the study of the Ukrainian language in Romania and of the Romanian language in Ukraine, and with this aim they shall create the appropriate conditions and opportunities, especially by promoting the training of lecturers and the organization of teaching.

6. The Contracting Parties shall conclude appropriate agreements on the mutual recognition of educational documents and diplomas of secondary and higher education, as well as on scholarly titles and academic degrees.

7. With the aim of putting the provisions of this article into effect, the Contracting Parties shall form agreements and appropriate programs.

Article 20

The Contracting Parties shall collaborate with the aim of the preservation and restoration of Ukrainian historical and cultural monuments and memorial sites in Romania and, conversely, of Romanian ones in Ukraine, and the guarantee of access to them in accord with the legislation of each Contracting Party.

Article 21

The Contracting Parties shall encourage cooperation in the area of the mass media. They shall promote efforts directed toward the mutual and objective information of the citizens of both countries, and with this aim they shall encourage the free exchange and dissemination of information about social, political, economic, cultural, and scientific life in their countries in accord with internal regulations and their international obligations.

Article 22

The Contracting Parties shall develop cooperation in the area of health care, medical research, tourism, and sport. They shall see to the social security of their citizens who are to be found on the territory of the other Contracting Party, and with this aim they shall conclude appropriate agreements.

Article 23

The Contracting Parties shall cooperate in the struggle with crime, especially with organized crime, terrorism, aircraft hijacking and piracy on the seas, illegal financial operations, illegal circulation of narcotic and psychotropic substances, arms, explosive and poisonous substances, nuclear and radioactive materials, as well as with contraband, including cultural treasures. With this aim they shall conclude appropriate agreements, and shall take joint measures within the framework of international cooperation in this field.

Article 24

1. The Contracting Parties shall develop consular relations, and also cooperation in the area of legal aid in civil, family, and criminal cases.
2. With the aim of creating the necessary conditions for the movement of passengers and goods across the Ukrainian-Romanian state border, the Contracting Parties shall cooperate in perfecting procedures for border crossing and customs control, and also shall take measures to open new entry points and to

develop existing ones. They shall conclude appropriate agreements for this purpose.

Article 25

On the basis of this Treaty, the Contracting Parties shall conclude separate agreements in areas of mutual interest.

Article 26

This Treaty is not directed against any third-party state and does not affect the rights and responsibilities of the Contracting Parties established by bilateral and multilateral treaties that each of them has concluded with other states and international organizations.

Article 27

This Treaty remains in effect for ten years. Its effect shall automatically be extended for a new five-year period unless either of the Contracting Parties, not less than one year before the end of the given period of its effectiveness, notifies the other Contracting Party in writing of its intention to denounce this Treaty.

Article 28

This Treaty is subject to ratification in accord with the procedures provided for by the legislation of each of the Contracting Parties, and comes into force on the day of exchange of documents of ratification.

Article 29

This Treaty shall be registered at the UN Secretariat in accord with Article 102 of the United Nations Charter.

Done at Constanţa on 2 June 1997 in two original exemplars, each in the Ukrainian and Romanian languages, both texts being equally authentic.

For Ukraine   For Romania

[signature; Leonid Kuchma]   [signature; Emil Constantinescu]

[Romanian and Ukrainian originals. Translated by Andrew D. Sorokowski.]

Charter on a Distinctive Partnership between the North Atlantic Treaty Organization and Ukraine

Madrid, 9 July 1997

I. Building an Enhanced NATO-Ukraine Relationship

The North Atlantic Treaty Organization (NATO) and its member States and Ukraine, hereinafter referred to as NATO and Ukraine,

—building on a political commitment at the highest level;

—recognizing the fundamental changes in the security environment in Europe which have inseparably linked the security of every state to that of all the others;

—determined to strengthen mutual trust and cooperation in order to enhance security and stability, and to cooperate in building a stable, peaceful and undivided Europe;

—stressing the profound transformation undertaken by NATO since the end of the Cold War and its continued adaptation to meet the changing circumstances of Euro-Atlantic security, including its support, on a case-by-case basis, of new missions of peacekeeping operations carried out under the authority of the United Nations Security Council or the responsibility of the OSCE [Organization for Security and Cooperation in Europe];

—welcoming the progress achieved by Ukraine and looking forward to further steps to develop its democratic institutions, to implement radical economic reforms, and to deepen the process of integration with the full range of European and Euro-Atlantic structures;

—noting NATO's positive role in maintaining peace and stability in Europe and in promoting greater confidence and transparency in the Euro-Atlantic area, and its openness for cooperation with the new democracies of Central and Eastern Europe, an inseparable part of which is Ukraine;

—convinced that an independent, democratic and stable Ukraine is one of the key factors for ensuring stability in Central and Eastern Europe, and the continent as a whole;

—mindful of the importance of a strong and enduring relationship between NATO and Ukraine and recognizing the solid progress made, across a broad range of activities, to develop an enhanced and strengthened relationship between NATO and Ukraine on the foundations created by the Joint Press Statement of 14 September 1995;

—determined to further expand and intensify their cooperation in the framework of the Euro-Atlantic Partnership Council, including the enhanced Partnership for Peace [PfP] program;

—welcoming their practical cooperation within IFOR/SFOR and other peacekeeping operations on the territory of the former Yugoslavia;

—sharing the view that the opening of the Alliance to new members, in accordance with Article 10 of the Washington Treaty, is directed at enhancing the stability of Europe, and the security of all countries in Europe without recreating dividing lines;

are committed, on the basis of this Charter, to further broaden and strengthen their cooperation and to develop a distinctive and effective partnership, which will promote further stability and common democratic values in Central and Eastern Europe.

II. Principles for the Development of NATO-Ukraine Relations

NATO and Ukraine will base their relationship on the principles, obligations and commitments under international law and international instruments, including the United Nations Charter, the Helsinki Final Act and subsequent OSCE documents. Accordingly, NATO and Ukraine reaffirm their commitment to:

—the recognition that security of all states in the OSCE area is indivisible, that no state should pursue its security at the expense of that of another state, and that no state can regard any part of the OSCE region as its sphere of influence;

—refrain from the threat or use of force against any state in any manner inconsistent with the United Nations Charter or Helsinki Final Act principles guiding participating States;

—the inherent right of all states to choose and to implement freely their own security arrangements, and to be free to choose or change their security arrangements, including treaties of alliance, as they evolve;

—respect for the sovereignty, territorial integrity and political independence of all other states, for the inviolability of frontiers, and the development of good-neighborly relations;

—the rule of law, the fostering of democracy, political pluralism and a market economy;

—human rights and the rights of persons belonging to national minorities;

—the prevention of conflicts and settlement of disputes by peaceful means in accordance with UN and OSCE principles.

Ukraine reaffirms its determination to carry forward its defense reforms, to strengthen democratic and civilian control of the armed forces, and to increase their interoperability with the forces of NATO and Partner countries. NATO reaffirms its support for Ukraine's efforts in these areas. Ukraine welcomes NATO's continuing and active adaptation to meet the changing circumstances of Euro-Atlantic security, and its role, in cooperation with other international organizations such as the OSCE, the European Union, the Council of Europe and the Western European Union in promoting Euro-Atlantic security and fostering a general climate of trust and confidence in Europe.

III. Areas for Consultation and/or Cooperation between NATO and Ukraine

Reaffirming the common goal of implementation of a broad range of issues for consultation and cooperation, NATO and Ukraine commit themselves to develop and strengthen their consultation and/or cooperation in the areas described below. In this regard, NATO and Ukraine reaffirm their commitment to the full development of the EAPC and the enhanced PfP. This includes Ukrainian participation in operations, including peacekeeping operations, on a case-by-case basis, under the authority of the UN Security Council, or the responsibility of the OSCE, and, if CJTF [Combined Joint Task Forces] are used in such cases, Ukrainian participation in them at an early stage on a case-by-case basis, subject to decisions by the North Atlantic Council on specific operations.

Consultations between NATO and Ukraine will cover issues of common concern, such as:

—political and security related subjects, in particular the development of Euro-Atlantic security and stability, including the security of Ukraine;

—conflict prevention, crisis management, peace support, conflict resolution and humanitarian operations, taking into account the roles of the United Nations and the OSCE in this field;

—the political and defense aspects of nuclear, biological and chemical non-proliferation;

—disarmament and arms control issues, including those related to the Treaty on Conventional Armed Forces in Europe (CFE Treaty), the Open Skies Treaty and confidence and security building measures in the 1994 Vienna Document;

—arms exports and related technology transfers;

—combating drug-trafficking and terrorism.

Areas for consultation and cooperation, in particular through joint seminars, joint working groups, and other cooperative programs, will cover a broad range of topics, such as:

—civil emergency planning, and disaster preparedness;

—civil-military relations, democratic control of the armed forces, and Ukrainian defense reform;

—defense planning, budgeting, policy, strategy and national security concepts;

—defense conversion;

—NATO-Ukraine military cooperation and interoperability;

—economic aspects of security;

—science and technology issues;

—environmental security issues, including nuclear safety;

—aerospace research and development, through AGARD [Advisory Group for Aerospace Research and Development];

—civil-military coordination of air traffic management and control.

In addition, NATO and Ukraine will explore to the broadest possible degree the following areas for cooperation:

—armaments cooperation (beyond the existing CNAD [Conference of National Armaments Directors] dialogue);

—military training, including PfP exercises on Ukrainian territory and NATO support for the Polish-Ukrainian peacekeeping battalion;

—promotion of defense cooperation between Ukraine and its neighbors.

Other areas for consultation and cooperation may be added, by mutual agreement, on the basis of experience gained.

Given the importance of information activities to improve reciprocal knowledge and understanding, NATO has established an Information and Documentation Centre in Kyiv. The Ukrainian side will provide its full support to the operation of the Centre in accordance with the Memorandum of Understanding between NATO and the Government of Ukraine signed at Kyiv on 7 May 1997.

IV. Practical Arrangements for Consultation and Cooperation between NATO and Ukraine

Consultation and cooperation as set out in this Charter will be implemented through:

—NATO-Ukraine meetings at the level of the North Atlantic Council at intervals to be mutually agreed;

—NATO-Ukraine meetings with appropriate NATO Committees as mutually agreed;

—reciprocal high-level visits;

—mechanisms for military cooperation, including periodic meetings with NATO Chiefs of Defense and activities within the framework of the enhanced Partnership for Peace programme;

—a military liaison mission of Ukraine will be established as part of a Ukrainian mission to NATO in Brussels. NATO retains the right reciprocally to establish a NATO military liaison mission in Kyiv.

Meetings will normally take place at NATO Headquarters in Brussels. Under exceptional circumstances, they may be convened elsewhere, including in Ukraine, as mutually agreed. Meetings, as a rule, will take place on the basis of an agreed calendar.

NATO and Ukraine consider their relationship as an evolving, dynamic process. To ensure that they are developing their relationship and implementing the provisions of this Charter to the fullest extent possible, the North Atlantic Council will periodically meet with Ukraine as the NATO-Ukraine Commission, as a rule not less than twice a year. The NATO-Ukraine Commission will not duplicate the functions of other mechanisms described in this Charter, but instead would meet to assess broadly the implementation of the relationship, survey planning for the future, and suggest ways to improve or further develop cooperation between NATO and Ukraine.

NATO and Ukraine will encourage expanded dialogue and cooperation between the North Atlantic Assembly and the Verkhovna Rada.

V. Cooperation for a More Secure Europe

NATO Allies will continue to support Ukrainian sovereignty and independence, territorial integrity, democratic development, economic prosperity and its status as a non-nuclear weapon state, and the principle of inviolability of frontiers, as key factors of stability and security in Central and Eastern Europe and in the continent as a whole. NATO and Ukraine will develop a crisis consultative mechanism to consult together whenever Ukraine perceives a direct threat to its territorial integrity, political independence, or security.

NATO welcomes and supports the fact that Ukraine received security assurances from all five nuclear-weapon states parties to the Treaty on the Non-Proliferation of Nuclear Weapons (NPT) as a non-nuclear weapon state party to the NPT, and recalls the commitments undertaken by the United States and the United Kingdom, together with Russia, and by France unilaterally, which took the historic decision in Budapest in 1994 to provide Ukraine with security assurances as a non-nuclear weapon state party to the NPT. Ukraine's landmark decision to renounce nuclear weapons and to accede to the NPT as a non-nuclear weapon state greatly contributed to the strengthening of security and stability in Europe and has earned Ukraine special stature in the world community. NATO welcomes Ukraine's decision to support the indefinite extension of the NPT and its contribution to the withdrawal and dismantlement of nuclear weapons which were based on its territory. Ukraine's strengthened cooperation with NATO will enhance and deepen the political dialogue between Ukraine and the members of the Alliance on a broad range of security matters, including on nuclear issues. This will contribute to the improvement of the overall security environment in Europe. NATO and Ukraine note the entry into force of the CFE Flank Document on 15 May 1997. NATO and Ukraine will continue to cooperate on issues of mutual interest such as CFE adaptation. NATO and Ukraine intend to improve the operation of the CFE treaty in a changing environment and, through that, the security of each state party, irrespective of whether it belongs to a political-military alliance. They share the view that the presence of foreign troops on the territory of a participating state must be in conformity with international law, the freely expressed consent of the host state or a relevant decision of the United Nations Security Council. Ukraine welcomes the statement by NATO members that "enlarging the Alliance will not require a change in NATO's current nuclear posture and, therefore, NATO countries have no intention, no plan and no reason to deploy nuclear weapons on the territory of new members nor any need to change any aspect of NATO's nuclear posture or nuclear policy—and do not foresee any future need to do so."

NATO member States and Ukraine will continue fully to implement all agreements on disarmament, non-proliferation and arms control and confidence-building measures they are part of.

The present Charter takes effect upon its signature.

The present Charter is established in two originals in the English, French, and Ukrainian languages, all three texts having equal validity.

[signatures, see next page]

Підписано в Мадриді, 9 липня 1997 р.
SIGNED IN MADRID ON 9 JULY 1997
SIGNÉ A MADRID, LE 9 JUILLET 1997

За Україну
For Ukraine
Pour l'Ukraine

Президент України
THE PRESIDENT OF UKRAINE
LE PRÉSIDENT DE L'UKRAINE

За Організацію Північно-Атлантичного Договору
For the North Atlantic Treaty Organization
Pour l'Organisation du Traité de l'Atlantique Nord

Генеральний секретар НАТО
THE NATO SECRETARY GENERAL
LE SECRÉTAIRE GÉNÉRAL DE L'OTAN

Королівство Бельгія
the Kingdom of Belgium
le Royaume de Belgique

Канада
Canada
le Canada

Королівство Данія
the Kingdom of Denmark
le Royaume du Danemark

Французька Республіка
the French Republic
la République française

Федеративна Республіка Німеччина
the Federal Republic of Germany
la République fédérale d'Allemagne

Грецька Республіка
the Hellenic Republic
la République hellénique

Республіка Ісландія
the Republic of Iceland
la République d'Islande

Італійська Республіка
the Italian Republic
la République italienne

Велике Герцогство Люксембург
the Grand Duchy of Luxembourg
le Grand-Duché du Luxembourg

Королівство Нідерланди
the Kingdom of the Netherlands
le Royaume des Pays-Bas

Королівство Норвегія
the Kingdom of Norway
le Royaume de Norvège

Португальська Республіка
the Portuguese Republic
la République portugaise

Королівство Іспанія
the Kingdom of Spain
le Royaume d'Espagne

Турецька Республіка
the Republic of Turkey
la République turque

Сполучене Королівство
Великої Британії і Північної Ірландії
the United Kingdom of Great Britain and Northern Ireland
le Royaume-Uni de Grande-Bretagne et d'Irlande du Nord

Сполучені Штати Америки
the United States of America
les Etats-Unis d'Amérique

INDEX

Abkhazia 13, 33, 81–82. *See also* Georgia

Aksiuchits, Viktor 23

Albright, Madeleine 257

Alexandrova, Olga 60

Aliyev, Heidar 200

Ambartsumov, Yevgenii 29

American-Ukrainian Advisory Committee 8

Antall, Jószef 9, 12, 47, 48, 62, 75n64

Armenia 81
conflict in Nagorno-Karabakh 13, 83

Asia
elite attitudes and perceptions of Ukrainian independence and statehood 192–93, 202

Aslund, Anders 156

Aspin, Les 110, 276, 277, 278

Astrakhan, Khanate of 80

Axworthy, Lloyd 128, 131, 135

Azerbaijan 33, 81, 172
conflict in Nagorno-Karabakh 13, 33, 82, 83, 88
oil and gas resources 83, 181

Azov Sea 254

Baburin, Sergei 35, 36

Baker, James 272, 273

Balladur, Edouard 13

Baltic states 33, 45. *See also* Estonia, Latvia, Lithuania

Belarus (*formerly* Belorussian SSR) 23, 32, 52, 60, 266
diplomatic relations with Ukraine 73n29

Belavezha meeting (8 December 1991). *See* CIS (formation of)

Berehovo Raion 64, 65

Bessarabia, southern 12, 65–66, 67, 68, 263

Black Sea (region) 79–86, 176
ecology 85
stability 95–96

Black Sea Economic Cooperation project (BSEC) 83, 84–85, 89, 95, 216
Turkish leadership and initiative within 89, 98n13

Black Sea Fleet 19–20, 34–39, 46, 82, 86, 104, 107, 109, 116, 119, 124n16, 131, 148, 161, 200, 226, 233, 236, 251, 252, 253, 254, 267n11

Bovin, Aleksandr 22

Brazauskas, Algirdas 57

Britain. *See* United Kingdom

Brzezinski, Zbigniew 105, 249

Bug Euroregion 72n13

Bukovina, northern 12, 65, 67, 68, 263

Bulgaria 60, 81, 83

Bush, George 126, 272, 273, 274, 285n20
"Chicken Kiev" speech 104, 106, 146, 193, 273
presidential administration of 127

Canada 125–37
and the Baltic states 126
Canadian International Development Agency (CIDA) 136

Harvard Ukrainian Research Institute
PUBLICATIONS OFFICE

The Strategic Role of Ukraine. Diplomatic Addresses and Essays (1994–1997). Yuri Shcherbak. Harvard Papers in Ukrainian Studies. Softcover, ISBN 0-916458-85-7.

Political Communities and Gendered Ideologies in Contemporary Ukraine (The Petryshyn Memorial Lecture, Harvard University, 26 April 1994). Martha Bohachevsky-Chomiak. Harvard Papers in Ukrainian Studies. Softcover, ISBN 0-916458-72-5.

The Great Soviet Peasant War. Bolsheviks and Peasants, 1917–1933. Andrea Graziosi. Harvard Papers in Ukrainian Studies. Softcover, ISBN 0-916458-83-0.

Carpatho-Ukraine in the Twentieth Century: A Political and Legal History. Vincent Shandor. URI Publications. Clothbound, ISBN 0-916458-86-5.

The Military Tradition in Ukrainian History: Its Role in the Construction of Ukraine's Armed Forces. Kostiantyn P. Morozov, et al. Harvard Papers in Ukrainian Studies. Softcover, ISBN 0-916458-73-3.

Kistiakovsky: The Struggle for National and Constitutional Rights in the Last Years of Tsarism. Susan Heuman. Harvard Series in Ukrainian Studies. Clothbound, ISBN 0-916458-61-X.

To receive a free catalogue of all Ukrainian Research Institute publications (including the journal Harvard Ukrainian Studies) please write, fax, or call to:

HURI Publications
1583 Massachusetts Avenue
Cambridge, MA 02138
USA
tel. 617-495-3692 fax. 617-495-8097

e-mail:
huri@fas.harvard.edu
on-line catalog:
http://www.sabre.org/huri (follow the publications path)